Studies of Shang Archaeology

Contributors

Chin-huai An, Institute of Archaeology of Honan, Cheng-chou, Honan

Noel Barnard, Department of Far Eastern History, Australian National University, Canberra

Cheng-lang Chang, Institute of History, Chinese Academy of Social Sciences, Peking

Kwang-chih Chang, Department of Anthropology, Harvard University, Cambridge, Massachusetts

Ping-ch'üan Chang, Institute of History and Philology, Academia Sinica, Taipei, Taiwan

Chen-hsiang Cheng, Institute of Archaeology, Chinese Academy of Social Sciences, Peking

[†] *Nai Hsia*, Chinese Academy of Social Sciences, Peking

Chih-hsi Kao, Hunan Provincial Museum, Ch'ang-sha, Hunan

Yün Lin, Department of History, Chi-lin University, Ch'ang-ch'un, Chi-lin

Hsi-chang Yang, Institute of Archaeology, Chinese Academy of Social Sciences, Peking

Wei-chang Yin, Institute of Archaeology, Chinese Academy of Social Sciences, Peking

---

[†] The editor regrets to have to note the death on June 19, 1985, of Dr. Hsia Nai, the preeminent archaeologist of China for the past three decades.

STUDIES OF
SHANG ARCHAEOLOGY

Selected Papers from
the International Conference
on Shang Civilization

EDITED BY K. C. CHANG

Yale University Press • New Haven and London

Copyright © 1986 by Yale University. All rights reserved. This book may not be reproduced, in whole or in part, in any form (beyond that copying permitted by Sections 107 and 108 of the U.S. Copyright Law and except by reviewers for the public press), without written permission from the publishers.

Designed by Nancy Ovedovitz and set in Monophoto Apollo type by Asco Trade Typesetting Ltd., Hong Kong. Printed in the United States of America by Vail-Ballou Press, Binghamton, New York.

Library of Congress Cataloging in Publication Data
International Conference on Shang Civilization (1982: East-West Center)
   Studies of Shang archaeology.
   Bibliography: p.
   Includes index.
   1. China—History—Shang dynasty, 1766–1122 B.C.—Congresses. 2. China—Antiquities—Congresses. I. Chang, Kwang-chih. II. Title.
DS744.157   1982   931   85–10044
ISBN 0-300-03578-0

The paper in this book meets the guidelines for permanence and durability of the Committee on Production Guidelines for Book Longevity of the Council on Library Resources.

10 9 8 7 6 5 4 3 2 1

NOTICE: The views expressed in this publication are those of the editor and individual authors and are in no way the official views of the Committee on Scholarly Communication with the People's Republic of China or its sponsoring organizations—the American Council of Learned Societies, the National Academy of Sciences, and the Social Science Research Council.

The International Conference on Shang Civilization was supported by grants from the National Endowment for the Humanities, the Wenner-Gren Foundation for Anthropological Research, and the East-West Center, Honolulu, Hawaii. The conference was part of the exchange program between the Committee on Scholarly Communication with the People's Republic of China and the Chinese Academy of Social Sciences in Peking. The Committee was founded in 1966 by the American Council of Learned Societies, the National Academy of Sciences, and the Social Science Research Council. Sources of funding for the Committee include the National Endowment for the Humanities, the U.S. Information Agency, the National Science Foundation, the Ford Foundation, the Starr Foundation, and the MacArthur Foundation.

The Committee represents American scholars in the natural sciences and engineering, social sciences, and humanities. It has developed exchange programs with the Chinese Academy of Social Sciences, the Chinese Academy of Sciences, the Chinese State Scientific and Technological Commission, the China Association of Science and Technology, and the Ministry of Education. In addition to conferences and delegation visits, the Committee administers a short-term exchange program for American and Chinese scholars and a National Program for Advanced Study and Research in China. Members of the Committee on Scholarly Communication with the People's Republic of China represent a broad range of fields, including China studies.

Administrative offices of the Committee are located in the National Academy of Sciences, Washington, D.C., 20418

Contents

Foreword
K. C. Chang   vii

1 A Reexamination of Erh-li-t'ou Culture
Yin Wei-chang   1

2 The Shang City at Cheng-chou and Related Problems
An Chin-huai   15

3 The Shang Dynasty Cemetery System
Yang Hsi-chang   49

4 Yin-hsü Tomb Number Five and the Question of the P'an Keng/Hsiao Hsin/Hsiao Yi Period in Yin-hsü Archaeology
K. C. Chang   65

5 A Study of the Bronzes with the "Ssu T'u Mu" Inscriptions Excavated from the Fu Hao Tomb
Cheng Chen-hsiang   81

6 A Brief Discussion of Fu Tzu
Chang Cheng-lang   103

7 A Brief Description of the Fu Hao Oracle Bone Inscriptions
Chang Ping-ch'üan   121

8 A New Approach to the Study of Clan-sign Inscriptions of Shang
Noel Barnard   141

	Appendixes to Chapter 8	184
9	The Classification, Nomenclature, and Usage of Shang Dynasty Jades *Hsia Nai*	207
10	A Reexamination of the Relationship between Bronzes of the Shang Culture and of the Northern Zone *Lin Yün*	237
11	An Introduction to Shang and Chou Bronze *Nao* Excavated in South China *Kao Chih-hsi*	275
	References Cited	301
	Index	319

Foreword

Shang civilization of ancient China, dating approximately from the eighteenth to the eleventh century B.C., is the first Chinese civilization that can be studied on the basis of both archaeological and textual evidence. To know how Shang began is to know how civilization, textual history, urbanism, and state society began in China. To know how the people of Shang lived is to know how people lived at the beginning of civilized society in at least one area of the world. The Shang scholarship is thus of tremendous interest and import to China scholars, world historians, and social scientists alike.

But data left from Shang are scarce, diverse, and fragmentary. Traditional texts, as synthesized by Ssu-ma Ch'ien in *Shih Chi* (c. 100 B.C.), give a bare outline of Shang history, mostly pertaining to the lives of Shang kings. Bronze vessels and weapons, many inscribed, have long been known from Shang dynasty, but they have been seen to bear primarily on art and technology. In 1899, the world of scholars became aware of a new kind of data on Shang history, namely, inscriptions on the oracle bones found at Yin-hsü, the ruins of the last Shang dynasty capital city. From then on, we witness the birth and the vigorous growth of a new discipline, dealing exclusively with these inscriptions. Beginning in 1928, scientific archaeology has been brought to bear on Shang studies, first at Yin-hsü itself, later at many other sites—among them Cheng-chou, found in 1950, and Erh-li-t'ou in Yen-shih, found in 1959, both in the province of Honan also. Dozens of sites are now known, some have been excavated, and Shang civilization is now seen occurring in much of the middle and the lower Yellow River valley and in the middle Yangtze River valley of China.

Confronted with Shang history data brought to light from these diverse sources, Shang scholars have experienced both exhilaration and frustration. They are overwhelmed by the richness of the new data and excited at the same time by the potential for major discoveries inherent in such young sciences as the Shang studies. But each new find brings to home the certainty of still newer and possibly more important discoveries to come. Moreover, archaeologists and epigraphers have their respective issues and problems, and a holistic study of the Shang remains an ideal that is hard to realize. In short, at this time and for the immediate future, the field of Shang studies is in a state of flux and, thus, in a period of great opportunities.

Despite its youth—or possibly because of it—and because of the opportunities it offers, the science of Shang studies boasts many hundreds of practitioners throughout the world and is truly international in scope. The Chinese mainland is, of course, the source of all the new discoveries, and the archaeologists and epigraphers there are, not surprisingly, the leaders of this discipline. The Academia Sinica in Taiwan is the custodian of the Yin-hsü treasures uncovered during the period 1928–37, and many scholars there have made significant contributions in studying them as well as reporting them. Outside China, Shang studies, especially the study of the oracle bone inscriptions and of the bronzes, have engaged the research interests of many scholars in Hong Kong, Japan, the United States, Canada, and many other countries. These scholars do read each other's works when they can and correspond among themselves if they can. But the flow of information and of ideas has been slow and difficult in many cases. There are no specialized journals or newsletters. There have been no international gatherings exclusively for Shang studies. Mainland and Taiwan scholars cannot communicate with each other at all.

The International Conference on Shang Civilization, held September 7–11, 1982, at the East-West Center in Honolulu, Hawaii, was a historic occasion, at least in the eyes of Shang scholars. Sponsored by the Committee on Scholarly Communication with the People's Republic of China, which is in turn sponsored jointly by the American Council of Learned Societies, the National Academy of Sciences, and the Social Science Research Council, the conference brought together forty-eight scholars from China (both mainland and Taiwan), the United States, Canada,

FOREWORD

Australia, West Germany, Japan, and Hong Kong. Thirty-five papers on various aspects of Shang civilization were presented. (A list of the titles of the papers together with their abstracts, plus a descriptive report of the conference, is being published in *Early China*, vol. 9, 1985.) A number of observers and graduate students from many universities also participated in the conference. All this would not have been possible without the financial assistance of the National Endowment for the Humanities, the Wenner-Gren Foundation for Anthropological Research, and the East-West Center, Honolulu.

The papers collected here all pertain to Shang archaeology and directly related issues. The papers by Yin, Yang, Cheng, Chang Cheng-lang, Chang Ping-ch'üan, Hsia and Kao have since been published in Chinese, but the rest appear here for the first time. The papers by K. C. Chang and by Barnard were submitted in English; the rest have been translated from Chinese originals by a group of advanced graduate students at Harvard and Yale: Robert Murowchick, who translated the paper by Yin Wei-chang; Lothar von Falkenhausen, who translated the papers by An Chin-huai and Chang Cheng-lang; Laurence Scott Davis, who translated the paper by Yang Hsi-chang; Susan Weld, who translated the papers by Cheng Chen-hsiang and Chang Ping-ch'üan; Jeffrey Kao, who translated the papers by Hsia Nai and Kao Chih-hsi; and David Goodrich, who translated the paper by Lin Yün.

This is a very important collection of Shang archaeological studies. As a first book in any language on various important aspects of Shang archaeology, written by a group of specialists at the forefront of new researches, it serves to define the field in essential and systematic ways both for other specialists and for those who look at the Shang from the outside. This may become clearer as we briefly comment on each of the essays that constitute the book.

The first paper, "A reexamination of Erh-li-t'ou culture," by Yin Wei-chang, confronts a topic that is hotly debated among Chinese archaeologists and ancient historians, namely, the archaeological identification of the Hsia dynasty and Hsia civilization in the traditional history based on texts and legends. Ever since the discovery of the Erh-li-t'ou culture in the 1950s there have been contrary views pertaining to the identification of this culture—with its geographic center in northwestern Honan and southern Shansi, the territory traditionally attributed to Hsia—in historical terms. Many archaeologists, including Yin Wei-chang, see a significant disconformity between the earlier and the later strata at the

Erh-li-t'ou site, and they interpret this in terms of a dynastic break, thereby attributing the later, and culturally more prosperous, half of the site's history to a new, conqueror's dynasty, Shang. A corollary of this view is to locate here the early Shang royal capital city, Western Po. The contrary view, advocated by an equally forceful group of authors, sees the whole Erh-li-t'ou culture as culture of the Hsia and interprets the same disconformity as the result of intrusion of Shang elements brought here by the conquest. The difference of opinion may appear largely one of definition and emphasis, but it is at the heart of the question of the beginning of Chinese history, and its resolution will have to depend on new data that do not as yet exist, namely, Erh-li-t'ou inscriptions. It is, thus, fitting that the Yin Wei-chang essay begins this book on "Shang" archaeology.

By the stage of Shang history characterized by the city at Cheng-chou, there is no longer any question about the culture's identity. By this time Shang civilization had acquired all the hallmarks of an urban and literate civilization so well known from its final phase at An-yang with flourishing bronze art and oracle bone inscription. The essay entitled "The Shang city at Cheng-chou and related problems," by An Chin-huai, the major archaeologist who has excavated and studied the Shang city at Cheng-chou since its discovery in the 1950s, summarizes what is currently known about this city, one of the earliest in the history of China. The stage of Shang history that this city represents depends on one's view of the Erh-li-t'ou culture. Some archaeologists (for example, Yin Wei-chang) would place the later strata at Erh-li-t'ou at Early Shang and Cheng-chou at Middle Shang. Others (for example, Tsou Heng of Beijing University, who unfortunately was not able to attend this conference) call the whole Erh-li-t'ou culture Hsia and see Cheng-chou as Early Shang. Still others, including this editor, adhere to the traditional view of deriving the Shang mainly from the east and see Cheng-chou as Middle Shang, to be preceded by an Early Shang, with a center in eastern Honan and southwestern Shantung, that has yet to be brought to light.

The seven essays that follow discuss various aspects of the stage of Shang civilization represented by the major Shang site in An-yang, Honan. An-yang was identified as the last Shang capital, Yin, in 1896. Excavation of this site, which began in 1928, has provided perhaps 90 percent of all the basic data, archaeological and textual, on Shang civilization, and the researches of these data account for perhaps 99 percent of all scholarly publications on Shang civilization. Could there be more

FOREWORD

to write about at An-yang? Indeed, there is, as shown by the papers selected to appear in this volume, which deal with important new issues.

Most Shang scholars are agreed that Yin was the capital city under the last twelve kings of the Shang dynasty:

P'an Keng
Hsiao Hsin
Hsiao Yi
Wu Ting
Tsu Keng
Tsu Chia
Lin Hsin
K'ang Ting
Wu Yi
Wen Wu Ting
Ti Yi
Ti Hsin

Oracle bone inscriptions found at the site are generally attributable to the reigns of the nine kings from Wu Ting to Ti Hsin. Other remains of the dynastic period may coincide with these reigns or they may be dated beyond them. During this period one detects some change in the typology and style of artifacts.

In 1976, a Shang tomb was found at Hsiao-t'un, one of An-yang's main archaeological loci, and it has proved to be perhaps the single most important tomb ever found here, for two reasons. One, it had not been plundered prior to excavation and so its yield of furnishings is the richest of all Shang tombs found so far, even though many other Shang graves were much larger and were presumably much more richly furnished originally. Altogether more than 440 bronzes, more than 590 jades, over 560 bone objects, and about 7,000 cowrie shells were found in the tomb. The other reason for the tomb's importance is that its occupant can be identified as a Fu Hao, a royal consort, whose clan name was Hao (or Tzu, alternate pronunciation of the same character), a person of some importance as recorded in the oracle bone inscriptions. Thus, this is the earliest archaeological find in Chinese history that can be identified with a historical figure.

However, the dating of the tomb is by no means without controversy. The name Fu Hao appears in the oracle bone inscriptions of the reigns of both Wu Ting and Wu Yi/Wen Wu Ting, and her tomb, the one found in 1976, has thus been variously assigned to the earlier Wu Ting period or to the later Wu Yi or Wen Wu Ting period. In his paper for the conference, "A brief discussion of Fu Tzu," Chang Cheng-land contends that the name often pronounced as Fu Hao must really be pronounced Fu Tzu, Tzu being the clan name of the Shang, to make explicit the fact, which is often implicitly assumed, that the name was used by all of the endogamous partners of the kings of succeeding generations. Chang Cheng-lang believes that the objects found in the tomb are heterogeneous stylistically and may span a long period of time. Therefore, even though many of the objects bear the name Fu Hao, the name alone does not necessarily indicate that they belonged to a single person. Thus, in Chang Cheng-lang's view, the objects may have belonged to several different persons, all named Fu Tzu, but these objects were then buried in the tomb of the Fu Tzu of a later period, presumably the reign of Wu Yi or Wen Wu Ting.

Chang Cheng-lang's theory represents a minority opinion at our conference, however. In his paper, "A brief description of the Fu Hao oracle bone inscriptions," Chang Ping-ch'üan goes to the other extreme and insists that only one Fu Hao is recorded in all the Shang inscriptions and that this Fu Hao was a consort of Wu Ting. The pros and cons of Chang vs. Chang are technical to the extreme but do not, in my opinion, conclusively settle the issue. These papers, however, provide all the essential data and arguments for interested readers.

In the same tomb were found bronzes inscribed with the name Ssu T'u Mu. Chang Ping-ch'üan, among others, points to the possibility that this was an alternate name of Fu Hao. In her essay, "A study of the bronzes with the 'Ssu T'u Mu' inscriptions excavated from the Fu Hao tomb," Cheng Chen-hsiang argues for the hypothesis that Ssu T'u Mu was the name of another of King Wu Ting's many consorts, who was known in later ritual schedules as Pi Kuei. From these schedules we have learned of the names of three "official" royal consorts, Pi Hsin, Pi Kuei, and Pi Wu. Fu Hao herself is generally believed to be Pi Hsin, a posthumous name also found among the tomb's many inscriptions. The name Pi Wu appears on a bronze tetrapod excavated before the war. If Cheng is correct then all three royal consorts of King Wu Ting are accounted for in bronze inscriptions, although Cheng does not explain why Pi Kuei's bronzes were interred in Pi Hsin's grave.

The Fu Hao question is by no means as merely technical and arcane as it may appear, for the dating of the Fu Hao tomb in essential ways

FOREWORD

determines our understanding of the whole cultural development of Shang during the An-yang period. The Fu Hao objects display the whole range of artistic achievements seen at An-yang; if these achievements had already been attained at the time of Wu Ting, which is practically at the beginning of An-yang's capital status, then the developmental history of Shang is to be looked at as more accelerated than we used to think. My own essay addresses the question of looking for the remains of the first theee kings' reigns who are widely believed to have moved to An-yang also.

The three essays by Yang Hsi-chang, on "The Shang dynasty cemetery system," by Noel Barnard, on "A new approach to the study of clan-sign inscriptions of Shang," and by Hsia Nai, on "The classification, nomenclature, and usage of Shang dynasty jades," discuss broader issues than the Fu Hao tomb, although these issues have been redefined by the tomb's discovery. The tomb was found at Hsiao-t'un, a locus heretofore believed to be one of palaces and temples, and the whole question of the "royal" cemetery, always believed to be confined to Hsi-pei-kang, northwest of Hsiao-t'un, has to be reassessed. Yang Hsi-chang's paper addresses the question of the cemetery system of the Shang dynasty from the new perspective. The new data on the clan-sign inscriptions from the Fu Hao tomb and also from the western sector of the Yin-hsü site, reported in 1979, provide new and invaluable material for the study of Shang clans and lineages by Noel Barnard. Both essays give new insights on Shang society.

The paper by Hsia Nai, a new, definitive study of Shang dynasty jades, is, again, based in large part on the new finds of jades from Fu Hao tomb.

The two final papers, by Lin Yün, on "A reexamination of the relationship between bronzes of the Shang culture and the northern zone," and by Kao Chih-hsi, on "An introduction to Shang and Chou bronze *nao* excavated in South China," look at the northern and the southern frontiers of Shang civilization. One can assume and always has assumed on general principles that Shang civilization had significant interactions in all directions with its alien (or not so alien) neighbors, but lack of data in the neighboring areas and an isolating perspective had hindered our understanding of the specifics of those interactions. Lin Yün's detailed comparisons of selected artifact types bring the northern zone to our attention. Instead of a "frontier" acting as a barrier we see that it was actually a zone of sustained activities. On the other side, Kao Chih-hsi uses a single artifact type, the *nao*-bell, to present a southern manifestation of Shang civilization. These papers show us that the study of Shang outside the Yellow River valley is only just beginning.

These essays selected from the Shang Conference represent some of the cutting edges of a very lively field of scholarly research. The editor and the authors are grateful to Yale University Press, which published my *Shang Civilization* in 1980, for enabling the world of scholars to have access to some of the major new studies since the late 1970s. We are particularly grateful to Lawrence Kenney of Yale University Press for his meticulous editorial pen, which greatly improved the quality of the book, and to Sally Cobb Serafim for her help with characters and spellings. The translation and the preparation of the manuscript for publication have been aided by grants from the Committee on Scholarly Communication with the People's Republic of China and from the Joint Committee on Chinese Studies of the American Council of Learned Societies. Lisa Anderson helped with the illustration.

—K. C. Chang

BIBLIOGRAPHIC NOTE

Citations are given in the footnotes in abbreviated form (the author, the year of publication, and the page or illustration number), and full bibliographic information is available in the References Cited. There are several exceptions to this general rule:

1. Some common traditional Chinese texts are cited in full in the text or in the footnotes as is the common practice in the sinological literature.

2. A few items from *K'ao-ku*, *K'ao-ku-hsüeh-pao*, and *Wen-wu* referred to only once in Hsia Nai's article are given in full in the footnotes of his paper.

3. A few commonly adopted abbreviations of oracle bone inscription catalogues are used in Chang Cheng-lang's and Chang Ping-ch'üan's papers without appearing again in the References Cited. Full bibliographic information on these abbreviations can be found in Keightley 1978a: Bibliography A.

Studies of Shang Archaeology

1

A Reexamination of Erh-li-t'ou Culture

Yin Wei-chang

The discovery of the Erh-li-t'ou culture and subsequent research into it together represent one of the great achievements of Chinese archaeology during the past twenty years. The major sites for this culture occur throughout western Honan and southern Shansi provinces. About one hundred sites have been discovered. The Erh-li-t'ou culture exhibits certain distinct characteristics. On the basis of stratified deposits at Erh-li-t'ou sites (fig. 1), the cultural remains have been divided into four periods.[1] Radiocarbon dating of the stratigraphy[2] has shown that the Erh-li-t'ou culture predates the Erh-li-kang period of Shang culture of Cheng-chou. Thus, its discovery has great significance in the study of ancient Chinese history.

Chinese academic circles are currently debating whether or not the Erh-li-t'ou culture was, in fact, that of the Hsia dynasty. This discussion centers around two differing opinions. One side maintains that Erh-li-t'ou I–IV constitute the Hsia dynasty culture.[3] The other opinion holds that although a certain element of continuity is evident in the development of the four periods, a change of epoch-making significance appeared between Erh-li-t'ou II and III. It is possible that the period represented by Erh-li-t'ou III and IV extends into the Shang dynasty.[4] Obviously, these opposing opinions not only reflect a differing under-

1. K'ao-ku 1965; K'ao-ku 1974.
2. K'ao-ku 1961b: 82; Hsia 1977: 222.
3. Tsou 1979; Tsou 1980, section III.
4. Yin 1978.

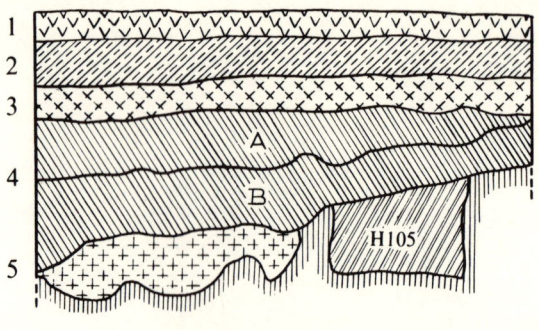

       ▨ Cultivated soil
       ▨ Reddish-brown soil
       ▨ Light gray soil
       ▨ Yellow-gray soil
       ▨ Reddish-yellow soil
       ▨ Black-gray soil
       ▨ Uninhabited soil

Fig. 1. Stratigraphic profile of the south wall of Y.L. II. T102: (1) surface soil; (2) Han dynasty layer; (3) Erh-li-t'ou III; (4) Erh-li-t'ou II; (5) Erh-li-t'ou I, including H105.

standing of the nature of the Hsia and Shang cultures, but also illustrate the divergent interpretations of the content and character of Erh-li-t'ou culture. Consequently, if we are able in both theory and practice to integrate our conceptions of Erh-li-t'ou culture, this in itself will have great significance, regardless of whether we are searching for the Hsia culture or investigating the Shang. In this chapter, I wish to reanalyze the content of Erh-li-t'ou culture, emphasizing the cultural composition of the remains of Erh-li-t'ou III and IV.

    The correct way to attain knowledge is always to look from the known to the unknown. In a certain sense, every scientific advance implies making progress in both the depth and breadth of people's understanding of the world around them. Our understanding of the Shang culture can be traced back to the start of excavations at Yin-hsü, An-yang, in 1928. The substantive results obtained from this series of excavations at An-yang not only eliminated the doubts and suspicions of historians who were skeptical of the antiquity of ancient Chinese civilization, but also provided conclusive evidence with which to define accurately the material culture of the Shang dynasty. When similar cultural remains predating those of Yin-hsü, An-yang, were found during the 1950s at Erh-li-kang in Cheng-chou, it was relatively easy to recognize them as cultural remains of the Shang, despite a lack of strong textual evidence at that time.[5] Although researchers do not agree upon whether the Shang town at Cheng-chou was the capital city of Ao 隞 of King Chung Ting 仲丁[6] or the capital Po 亳 and King T'ang, 湯,[7] there is no disagreement that the Erh-li-kang period remains at Cheng-chou do indeed belong to the Shang dynasty. This being the case, analytical research carried out on the vast amount of archaeological materials obtained from Shang sites such as An-yang and Cheng-chou makes possible a relatively clear understanding of the content, characteristics, and periodization of Shang dynasty material culture. At the same time, we are, with the aid of this material, able to identify and differentiate Shang culture from non-Shang cultures of the Central China Plain. Thus, when we examine the content of Erh-li-t'ou culture by means of analyzing the characteristics of each period, we can determine whether or not Shang cultural elements exist among Periods III and IV.

For the past several years I have analyzed the constituent elements of the Erh-li-t'ou culture, the results of which I published in an article entitled "An Examination of the Erh-li-t'ou Culture[8] (hereafter referred to as "Examination"). That article argued not only that the Erh-li-t'ou culture had both specific characteristics and a certain style, but also that differences exist between the cultural traits of Erh-li-t'ou III and IV and those of I and II. The article further pointed out that among the remains of Period III there appeared a new class of pottery vessel types in addition to those commonly seen in Periods I and II. Among these were the *ting* 鼎, deep-bellied *kuan* 罐 with a folded rim, round-bellied *kuan* with flaring mouth, *p'an* 盤, deep-bellied *p'en* 盆, flat-bottomed *p'en* 盆, *tou* 豆, filtering and squeezing vessels, and the wide-mouthed *kang* 缸 (fig. 2). The new category of ceramic vessels included the *li* 鬲, *chia* 斝, round-bottomed *p'en* with an everted rim, wide-mouthed *tsun* 尊, and the *weng* 甕 with a small mouth and tall neck. The quantity of vessels in this latter group increased during Erh-li-t'ou IV, indicating a tendency both to replace and absorb previous vessel types. The excavation of and research into the Shang site at Cheng-chou have clarified the fact that

5. Hsia 1951: 724; C. M. An 1952.
6. C. H. An 1961.
7. Tsou 1978; Tsou 1981.
8. Yin 1978.

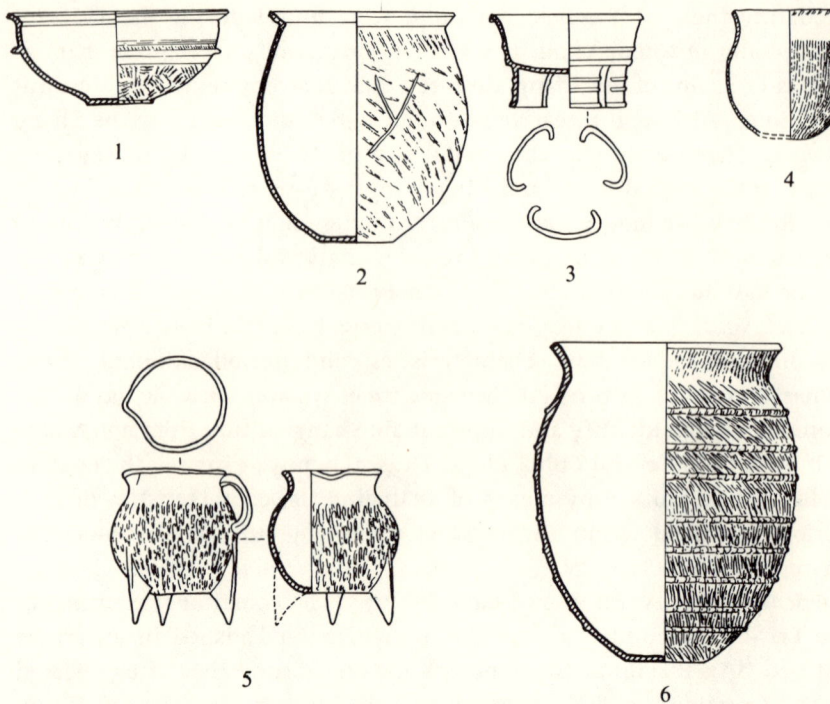

Fig. 2. Erh-li-t'ou I and II pottery types: (1) deep basin; (2) deep pot with beveled rim; (3) *p'an*-basin on tripod; (4) round pot with flaring mouth; (5) *ting*-tripod; (6) big-mouth jar.

this new group of ceramic types is characteristic of the Erh-li-kang period of Shang culture. Consequently, the appearance of this group of cultural elements could be taken to be indicative of Shang culture.

Recently published material has substantiated this argument. A close resemblance in shape exists between this group of cultural elements, which appeared during Erh-li-t'ou III, and comparable vessels from Erh-li-kang period remains of the Shang dynasty. The following examples may be cited:

Very few *Li* 鬲 tripods are found among Erh-li-t'ou III remains, and these include many different shapes. Some are thick, with a low crotch and relatively shallow, pouched legs, while others resemble the *kuan* 罐 with a round belly and flared mouth, standing atop three pouched legs, the rim retaining the decorated rim pattern characteristic of the flared-mouth *kuan* (fig. 3:3). However, during Period IV there is an obvious increase in the quantity of pottery *li*-tripods, the shape being relatively

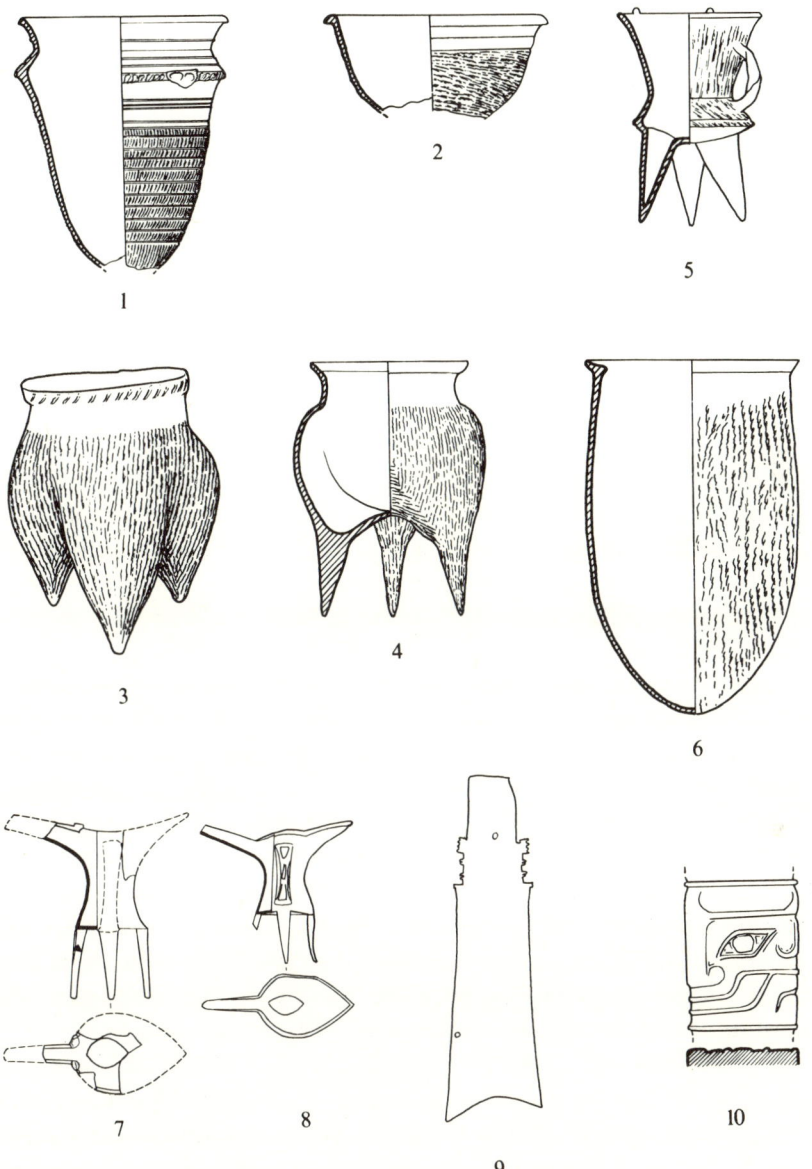

Fig. 3. Periods III and IV artifacts from Erh-li-t'ou: (1) big-mouth jar; (2) basin with outcurled rim; (3, 4) *li*-tripods; (5) *chia*-tripod; (6) deep pot; (7, 8) bronze *chüeh*-tripods; (9) jade *chang*; (10) animal mask design on jade handle (partial).

stabilized. Some of these *li*-tripods had already developed into a type with a deep crotch, an everted rim, and somewhat thin belly, standing on tall, conical legs. The forms are very close to those found in the lower levels of Erh-li-kang.

The large-mouthed *tsun* so characteristic of Erh-li-kang period Shang culture had already appeared by Erh-li-t'ou III, conspicuous in the manner of an index fossil. The large-mouthed *tsun* of Period III developed into one with a flared mouth, narrow neck, and an angled shoulder to which was added an appliquéd decoration, while the zone below the shoulder was decorated with a cord-marked pattern. The average diameter of the mouth is smaller than that of the shoulder (fig,. 3:1). The large-mouthed *tsun* of Period IV has a mouth diameter roughly equal to that of the shoulder, identical to that type found in the lower levels of Erh-li-kang.

The pottery *chia* 斝 is a type of vessel shape commonly seen in the Erh-li-kang period of Shang. Although not numerous among the excavated remains of Erh-li-t'ou III and IV, the pottery *chia* of Period III has a flaring mouth, narrow neck, and a side handle, with three bulbous legs added underneath. This type also exhibits two short posts added on top of the rim (fig. 3:5), a distinctive feature. These characteristics are identical to those on comparable vessel types of the Erh-li-kang period. The bronze *chia* of the late Shang period generally retain the above mentioned characteristics and can be regarded as a representative vessel shape of the Shang culture. This special form is obviously very significant.

The round-bottomed *p'en* 盆 with everted rim and the narrow-mouthed *weng* 甕 with tall neck are rather numerous among the excavated remains of Erh-li-t'ou III and IV. Their shapes and the fact that their bellies are covered with crisscrossed cord-marked pattern, while their inner wall often carries impressed dots (fig. 3:2), make them identical to comparable vessel types of the Erh-li-kang period. Thus, a relationship between these two periods is not difficult to establish.

In addition to these, one can find identical or similar characteristics among other comparable ceramic types of the Erh-li-kang period of Shang and Erh-li-t'ou III and IV. These vessel types include the basin-shaped *ting* 鼎, thin-stemmed *tou* 豆, *tseng* 甑, flat-bottomed *p'en*, and vessel lids.

As for bronze vessels, containers are represented only by the *chüeh* 爵 among the excavated remains of Erh-li-t'ou III and IV. The shape of the *chüeh* includes a narrow spout and tapered tail atop a narrow-waisted body with a flat bottom. The vessel sits on three prismatic, pointed legs (fig. 3:8). The bronze *chüeh* excavated from the lower levels of Erh-li-kang are identical to the above vessels with respect tho their spout, tail, bottom, and legs, but were formed with a straight-sided waist. Moreover, a new convention appeared: short posts added at the base of the spout. Certain differences exist between these two *chüeh* vessel shapes from Erh-li-t'ou and Erh-li-kang. Nevertheless, the pottery *chüeh* of Erh-li-t'ou IV exhibited the technique of attaching a clay disk at the joint of the spout and the mouth, and short posts also appear on one bronze *chüeh* collected on the surface at Erh-li-t'ou (fig. 3:7). From these features, one can see the direction of change through time. One can also find vessel shape characteristics common to excavated bronze vessels of the Erh-li-kang period (such as the rectangular *ting* 鼎, *li*, *chia*, *ho* 盉, and *ku* 觚) and to comparable pottery vessel types of Erh-li-t'ou III and IV. In terms of decoration, designs such as the animal mask pattern and the "cloud and thunder" pattern, which are commonly seen on bronze vessels of the Shang dynasty, can also be found among the decorative motifs of Erh-li-t'ou III and IV. For example, the style of the animal head pattern on handle-shaped jades (fig. 3:10) found from period III burials at Erh-li-t'ou is identical to the basic pattern on bronze vessels of the Shang dynasty. The shape of weapons such as the *ko* 戈 and arrowhead; tools such as the *tao* 刀, *pen* 錛, *fu* 斧, and *tsao* 鑿; and bronze bells from Erh-li-t'ou III and IV are identical to comparable objects from the Erh-li-kang period.

Regarding archaeological features and other material relics, my essay "Examination" pointed out that the ashy pits, pottery kilns, crucibles used in bronze casting, oracle bones, and other remains of Erh-li-t'ou III and IV are identical to comparable remains of the Erh-li-kang period. In addition, rammed earth platform foundations and other types of building construction technology, the appearance of regular dented patterns resulting from *hang-t'u* construction, and methods of platform pole insertion discovered at Erh-li-t'ou sites are all identical to comparable remains from sites such as Cheng-chou and An-yang.

Still other archaeological elements in Erh-li-t'ou III and IV are the same as those from Shang sites such as Cheng-chou and An-yang. These include musical instruments such as the clay *hsün* 塤 and the stone *ch'ing* 磬; ritual objects like the *chang* 璋, *tsung* 琮, *ko* 戈, and *yüeh* 鉞; and ornamental pieces such as handle-shaped jades. For example, the jade *chang* excavated at Erh-li-t'ou (fig. 3:9) is identical to a piece taken from Erh-li-kang.[9] The other types of jade ritual objects mentioned above have been frequently excavated from later Shang dynasty tombs.[10]

To be sure, in comparing some objects from Erh-li-t'ou III and IV with Erh-li-kang remains from Cheng-chou, we can also note differences. For example, the distinctive "false-waisted" *tou* of the Erh-li-kang period is not seen in Erh-li-t'ou III and IV. Also, the form of the *kuei* 簋 is not the same in both periods. The quantity of *li*, *chia*, *yen* 甗, and other pouch-legged vessels is also rather small in Erh-li-t'ou IV, while the *ting*, *kuan*, and other types of pottery cooking vessels are relatively numerous. However, these differences are of secondary importance when compared to the characteristics that are identical. Just as pottery vessels commonly seen in Erh-li-kang remains, such as the large-mouthed *tsun*, *chia*, *yen*, and "false-waisted" *tou*, are rarely or never seen among the late Shang pottery vessels from An-yang Yin-hsü, Erh-li-kang pottery vessels such as the *li*, *kuei*, and *kuan* are not necessarily identical to comparable vessels from the Hsiao-t'un 小屯 period of Shang.

It is a normal phenomenon for the later of two archaeological cultures to retain certain elements of the earlier culture. Such retention is determined by the nature of the continuity of the cultures. The development of a culture cannot be arrested, so that the culture of earlier periods—or of a previous dynasty—is inevitably inherited or assimilated by later cultures. Instances of culture assimilation are not rare throughout history. Consequently, not only Erh-li-t'ou III and IV, but also the Shang culture of the Erh-li-kang period continues to use certain commonly seen vessel forms from Erh-li-t'ou I and II. For example, the *ku* 觚 and *chüeh*, two vessel froms often seen in Shang contexts, had already appeared by Erh-li-t'ou II. This phenomenon is understandable. The problem confronting us today is this: during Erh-li-t'ou III and IV there appears a group of implement and vessel types that is close to those forms characteristic of Erh-li-kang period Shang culture. Moreover, the quantity of objects in this group becomes more and more numerous over time and shows a tendency to replace those utensils inherent in this culture. In the final analysis, what does this phenomenon reflect? This is the question that researchers must answer.

---

9. Chao 1966: 58.
10. The famous Yin-hsü tomb of Fu Hao contained thirty-three jade pieces; see Chung-kuo-she-hui-k'o-hsüeh-yüan K'ao-ku-yen-chiu-so 1980a, pp. 178–81.

My essay "Examination" also pointed out that among the remains of Erh-li-t'ou IV, there is an obvious increase in vessel types that had made their appearance during Period III. These vessels include the *li*, wide-mouthed *tsun*, and the round-bottom *p'en* with everted rim. On the other hand, the characteristic three-footed *p'an* is no longer seen among Period IV vessels, and there is a distinct decrease in the flared-mouth *kuan* with decorative border. The occurrence of decorative patterns such as cord-marking and thick cord-marking as well as of impressed dots on the vessel interior was widespread. Finally, the basketry patterns, fine cord-marking, and decorated rim on the flared-mouth *kuan* declined or disappeared. Several pottery vessel shapes still reflect the blending of elements from two cultures. Although vessels such as the deep-bellied *p'en*, *tseng*, and flared-mouth *kuan* retain their original shape (most still have cockscomb-shaped single "ears" [*pan* 鋬]), they develop everted rims and rounded bottoms; the surface cord-marks came to be paddle-impressed in crisscross fashion, and the inner vessel surface of *p'en* and *kang* is decorated with designs such as impressed dots. As a matter of fact, some of the features of the pottery *li* of Erh-li-t'ou III—for example, the shape of three pouched legs added to the flared-mouth *kuan* and the traditional technique of appliqué decoration below the rim—are retained as before. Such continuation can also be taken as an example of the blending of elements from two cultures. Moreover, vestiges of this type of blending are even more obvious in Erh-li-t'ou IV. Vessel forms not seen in Erh-li-t'ou I and II, such as the pouch-legged *li* and *chia* and round-bottomed vessels, increase in quantity in Erh-li-t'ou IV. This type is in sharp contrast to the more numerous flat-bottomed vessel types with solid feet (*ting* category) of Erh-li-t'ou I and II. Although the number of cultural elements represented by this new group of vessel forms was not as large as at Erh-li-kang, the number had nevertheless increased, indicating that the earlier cultural elements were tending to be replaced and absorbed. This phenomenon apparently can be taken as the general direction of cultural development. Even though implements and vessels that are characteristic of the two earlier periods continue to be used —to the point that some types can even be seen among the Erh-li-kang remains—they have been blended with or replaced by new types.

Although some scholars acknowledge that differences and changes exist between the remains from Erh-li-t'ou II and those from Erh-li-t'ou III, they nevertheless believe that these two periods cannot be readily separated. They delineate a temporal dividing line between the two subsequent periods, Erh-li-t'ou IV and Erh-li-kang.

What is the most reasonable interpretation for the changes that occur between Erh-li-t'ou II and III and for the new cultural elements that appear in III and IV? We must look for the answer in the circumstances resulting in analogous situations as reflected in archaeological materials from other periods.

The primary objective of our research is to study the remaining material culture created by the social production and everyday practices of ancient people. Every type of artifact and other remains with which we come into contact are alike in that they are produced according to people's needs, but the activities of human production and daily life all have a purpose. Therefore, one should look at the social elements of that time to seek the reasons behind the changes. In other words, when new changes appear in cultural features, one proper investigative route is to interpret them in relation to changes occurring in society at that time. Changes that take place in a society—for example, those that occur during a dynastic succession—are indeed reflected in its cultural features. For example, the dynastic succession from Shang to Chou that resulted from King Wu's 武 expedition against King Chòu 紂 produced among the early Chou remains from the Central China Plain not only several vessel shapes with Chou cultural elements, but also vessels and implements in the Shang style. For example, vessels such as the late Shang-style *li* exist uninterrupted as before, but the small crotched *li* (or Chou-style *li*) is rarely seen. Because of the existence of this kind of situation archaeologists have encountered many difficulties in trying to determine whether cultural remains are late Shang or early Chou.

Here I would like to cite an analogous situation that can be seen over a vast region following the Ch'in unification of the Six Kingdoms. Ch'in-shih-huang used his administrative powers to carry out the process of unification. But, except in those aspects where material objects testify to his success in unifying the kingdoms, such as his systems of coinage and of weights and measures, his unified government did not lead to overall uniformity, judging from the material culture from various areas. For a fairly long period of time the cultural features of every region retain numerous elements of their former cultures. In some areas, objects in the style of Ch'in culture are scarce. Western Hupei is an excellent example. This area was relatively near the Ch'in state, and in 278 B.C. it became part of the Ch'in kingdom when Pai Ch'i 白起 sent an expedition against the capital city Ying 郢. However, although the Ch'in tombs discovered in this area contain a few objects which are obviously Ch'in, they also retain relatively numerous articles characteristic of the Ch'u culture. For example, bronzes such as the *ting* and *p'an* found among the late Warring States period tombs at Ch'ien-p'ing 前坪, near Yi-ch'ang 宜昌, have clear Ch'u characteristics, identical to comparable vessels excavated from the tomb of the Ch'u king near Shou-hsien Chu-chia-chi 壽縣朱家集. However, according to the inscriptions on bronze seals found in the tomb, they should be considered Ch'in tombs rather than Ch'u tombs.[11] The burial goods and their association as found in the Ch'in-Han tombs at Feng-huang-shan 鳳凰山, near Chiang-ling 江陵, are not very similar to the Ch'u tombs, but some tombs still have the combined set of *ting*, *ho*, and *hu* 壺, with Ch'u characteristics noticeable in their forms. The very distinctive Ch'u vessel type *tui* 敦 continues even into the Western Han period.[12] These examples make clear the fact that even though a society and government change, the cultural features of that society do not necessarily change with equal rapidity. This fully bears out the fact that political developments cannot cause the sudden interruption of a culture's continuity. On the contrary, the changing of material culture characteristics as a reflection of political events is a very slow, gradual process.

These examples help us interpret the data gathered from Erh-li-t'ou III and IV, where some cultural elements are blended with earlier forms while others are replaced by new ones. In particular, the tombs of Erh-li-t'ou III and IV show not only some burial goods commonly seen in Erh-li-t'ou I and II, such as the *ting*, flared-mouth *kuan*, three-footed *p'an*, *ku*, *chüeh* and *ho* (with some changes in form, of course), but also new forms highly characteristic of the Shang, such as the round-bottomed *p'en* with everted rim and the small-mouthed *weng* with tall neck.[13] Thus, in my essay "Examination" I suggested that the differences and changes that occur between Erh-li-t'ou II and III were caused by political changes. Because the circumstances examined here are similar to those pertaining at the time of the Shang–Chou succession and to those of the Chou-Ch'in

---

11. Hupei Province Museum 1976.
12. T. W. Kuo 1982: 175–76.
13. K'ao-ku 1983.

transition, it is reasonable to relate these changes to the Shang overthrow of Hsia, when King T'ang 湯 replaced King Chieh 桀.

What needs to be considered in this: the discovery of large-scale palace ruins and other Erh-li-t'ou III remains makes it clear that this was at one time an important city of ancient China. Some people consider it to be the location of the Hsia capital of Chen-hsün 斟鄩[14] or Yang-ch'eng 陽城.[15] According to ancient documents, ever since Pan Ku's commentary in the "Ti-li-chih" chapter of the *Han Shu* 漢書地理志 under the heading Yen-shih hsien 偃師縣 ("Shih-hsiang, Yin T'ang's capital" 尸鄉, 殷湯所都), most historians have considered Yen-shih 偃師 to be T'ang's capital city of Hsi Po 西亳. Some have even attempted to identify its exact location. At present, the location of the Yen-shih Erh-li-t'ou ruins seems fairly consistent with the recorded location of Hsi Po. Looking at cultural characteristics, we find the appearance in Erh-li-t'ou III of a group of vessels and implements identical to those with features typical of Erh-li-kang period Shang culture, the two groups providing mutual evidence. This shows that Erh-li-t'ou III and IV at Yen-shih are remains from the early Shang period, and the upper levels of the Erh-li-t'ou ruins are the remains of T'ang's capital, Hsi Po.

In view of the above analysis, a clear distinction may be made between the cultures represented by Erh-li-t'ou III and IV and by Erh-li-t'ou I and II. According to customary archaeological practice, the remains of the later two periods ought to be placed in the category of Shang culture. At present, most people refer to all four periods together as the Erh-li-t'ou culture or interpret them as Erh-li-t'ou culture in the broadest sense of the word.

The extensive palace foundation, workshops, and other important ruins discovered in the Erh-li-t'ou III stratum at Yen-shih reveal the general layout of the major early Chinese cities. Material that has been discovered shows that, compared to earlier times, economic production level of the society of this period had undergone several changes. The division of labor became more elaborate and an urban/rural division appeared; the early stages of a slave society had already been established. Bronze vessels are excavated again and again from sites of this period, showing that the culture had already entered the Bronze Age. All of this indicates that the social development of the Shang people at the

14. Tsou 1980: 229; S. L. Huang 1978: 37–38; Sun 1980.
15. Sun 1980.

time of King T'ang possibly reached an important turning point. From the time King T'ang founded the Shang dynasty, there appeared on the Central China Plain a slave society at the level of civilization development. These circumstances give us a deeper understanding of historial civilization and its development from the Shang period through the Bronze Age.

2

The Shang City at Cheng-chou
and Related Problems

An Chin-huai

INTRODUCTION

The Shang city of Cheng-chou is located on the east side of the modern metropolitan district of Cheng-chou, now the provincial capital of Honan; within the old walled city lay the governmental seat of the former Cheng Hsien. Following the excavations at Yin-hsü near An-yang by the Institute of History and Philology of the Academia Sinica in the 1920s and 1930s, this important site was discovered by Chinese archaeologists in the 1950s, after the founding of the New China. Like An-yang, Cheng-chou is situated on the middle lower course of the Yellow River, in the heart of the territory that was once dominated by the Shang dynasty. The area of the site is large and its cultural strata are deep and thick; they contain plentiful remains of every kind. Chronologically, it is the type site for the early period of Middle Shang, for the most part predating Yin-hsü, An-yang. Even more important, the nucleus of the site is a walled enclosure constructed in pounded earth, dating to the early period of the Middle Shang; this is the earliest and largest Shang city wall discovered to date in China. In order to preserve the historically important and valuable Shang remains at Cheng-chou, the State Council of the People's Republic of China included them in its initial register of national monuments in 1961 and has ordered them to be maintained.

In the last thirty-odd years, following the initial work, the Honan Archaeological Research Institute (formerly the Archaeological Team of

Fig. 4. Lower Erh-li-kang pottery types (excavated from Erh-li-kang).

the Honan Provincial Cultural Bureau) has conducted long-term, systematic, and relatively extensive archaeological testing, survey, and excavation work at the Shang sites of Cheng-chou. The long-term task was undertaken in conjunction with the basic modern constructions of the newly prosperous city of Cheng-chou. The work has yielded much information and has opened up new perspectives for the study of Shang political, economic, and cultural history—particularly for that of the early and middle periods of Shang.

THE SHANG CULTURAL SEQUENCE AT CHENG-CHOU

Shang remains were first discovered in Cheng-chou in the autumn of 1950 at Nan-kuan-wai and Erh-li-kang. In 1952, following a preliminary survey of the Shang sites of Cheng-chou, scientific excavation began on a larger scale, focusing on the vicinity of Erh-li-kang. After the determination of the principal cultural contents of the Shang dynasty site at Erh-li-kang, the early Middle Shang remains newly discovered here were designated as the Erh-li-kang period of Shang. Erh-li-kang was further subdivided into Lower and Upper on account of stratigraphic relationships, intersecting pits of early and late dates, and ceramic seriation (figs. 4, 5).[1] Later, cultural remains and tombs of the Erh-li-kang period were

---

1. Honan Province Bureau of Culture 1959.

THE SHANG CITY AT CHENG-CHOU

also successively discovered and excavated at localities inside as well as in the neighborhood outside the old walled city of Cheng-chou, namely Pei-kuan-wai, Pai-chia-chuang, Tze-ching-shan North, Jen-min Kung-yüan, Te-hua-chieh, and Ming-kung-lu. Shang sites are thus clustered in an area of some twenty-five square kilometers around Cheng-chou.

Fig. 5. Upper Erh-li-kang pottery types (excavated from Erh-li-kang).

In the spring of 1954, during the course of excavations within the People's Park (Jen-min Kung-yüan) of Cheng-chou, besides stratigraphically superimposed Lower and Upper Erh-li-kang layers, a Late Shang stratum corresponding to those of Yin-hsü, An-yang, was found overlying the Upper Erh-li-kang deposits. At that time, the Late Shang cultural remains of Jen-min Kung-yüan were defined as the Jen-min Kung-yüan period of Shang.[2] This discovery provided stratigraphic support for the notion that Erh-li-kang was earlier than Yin-hsü. Since then the term *Erh-li-kang* has become the representative designation for the stage of Shang culture preceding Yin-hsü, and it is widely used by the archaeological community. Throughout the country, whenever archaeological survey and excavation yield early Middle Shang remains similar to those of Erh-li-kang at Cheng-chou, they are referred to as belonging to the Erh-li-kang period of Shang culture.

In the spring of 1955, during excavations at a locality outside the southern gate of the old city of Cheng-chou (Nan-kuan-wai), besides stratigraphically superimposed Lower and Upper Erh-li-kang layers, an earlier stratum was found underneath the Lower Erh-li-kang deposits. At that time, it was designated as the Nan-kuan-wai period of Shang.[3]

In the summer of 1956, another Early Shang site predating Lower Erh-li-kang was discovered near the village of Lo-ta-miao in the west of the Cheng-chou metropolitan area. As it was somewhat different from Nan-kuan-wai, its cultural remains were at that time designated as the Lo-ta-miao period of Shang.[4] Later, deposits and pits pertaining to the Lo-ta-miao period were also discovered underneath Lower Erh-li-kang layers at Tung-chai in the west of the Cheng-chou metropolitan area and within the northeastern part of the walled enclosure of the Shang city as well as underneath a section of the eastern wall of the Shang city. This was a further step in establishing scientific proof that, based on stratigraphic relationships, Lo-ta-miao preceded Lower Erh-li-kang.[5]

In 1958, Early Shang cultural remains of the same kind as those of Lo-ta-miao were discovered at Erh-li-t'ou in Yen-shih, Honan, namely, in the late phase of the Erh-li-t'ou culture (Periods III and IV of the original

2. Wen-wu 1954.
3. K'ao-ku-hsüeh-pao 1973a.
4. Wen-wu 1957.
5. Honan Province Institute of Archaeology ms-a; Wen-wu 1983d; Wen-wu-tzu-liao-ts'ung-k'an 1977a.

report).[6] Since that phase contains richer cultural deposits and artifactual remains than the Lo-ta-miao sites at Cheng-chou and is even more representative as a type site of Early Shang culture, the terms *Late Erh-li-t'ou culture, Erh-li-t'ou III*, or *Erh-li-t'ou IV* have become more frequently used as a designation of Early Shang culture whenever sites or remains corresponding to the Lo-ta-miao period at Cheng-chou have been encountered. The overall sequence of development documented by the Shang sites at Cheng-chou is as shown in the accompanying chart.

Early Shang	Early Period of Middle Shang	Late Shang
Lo-ta-miao Period Nan-kuan-wai Period	Erh-li-kang Period	Jen-min Kung-yüan Period
(=Late Erh-li-t'ou Culture)		(=Yin-hsü Period at An-yang)

The ceramic shapes and ornaments from each period at the Cheng-chou Shang sites—from Lo-ta-miao through Lower and Upper Erh-li-kang into the Jen-min Kung-yüan period—display a high degree of homogeneity; they should be seen as a single local cultural type developing in an unbroken continuum. Some of the common characteristics seen throughout the sequence include ceramic types: cooking vessels such as *li, yen*, sand-tempered *kuan*, and *tseng*; drinking vessels such as *chia, chüeh*, and *ku*; eating vessels such as *tou, kuei*, and *po*; storage vessels such as *weng, p'en*, wide-mouthed *tsun, tsun*, and *kang*; and, in addition, covers and pottery strainers. The main mode of ornamentation is cord-marking, but applied, stamped, string-marked, and incised decoration is also encountered throughout. Most of the pottery is gray. The period markers are merely factors in a process of development and change in the ceramic shapes and ornaments. Change is most conspicuous in the following traits:

- In *li* vessels, the bent-over rim develops into an everted rim, and the height of the crotch between its three hollow legs decreases over time; in *yen* vessels, such developments of rim and crotch more or less correspond to those in the *li*.
- In *chia* vessels, a wide mouth develops into a constricted mouth.

6. K'ao-ku 1965; K'ao-ku 1974.

- The *chüeh* retain a slender body with attached handle bar throughout; but the earliest examples have a spout and a tail, an oval mouth, a flat bottom, and three solid feet; over time, the tail is lost, the mouth becomes round, the bottom becomes rounded, and the legs become breastlike.
- Whereas the bowl of the *tou* remains shallow, the high stem of the earliest type develops into a high ring-foot, which gradually becomes lower.
- From shallow-bellied, flat-bottomed vessels whose diameter at the mouth is smaller than that at the shoulder, the wide-mouthed *tsun* pass through a stage at which both diameters are the same and then develop into deep-bellied, round-bottomed *tsun* with the huge "trumpet" mouth and no shoulder.
- The ceramic *kuei* at first has a slightly constricted mouth with a ring-foot, then develops a straight mouth and a deep ring-foot, and later a flaring mouth and a ring-foot with tapering walls.

The cord-marking on the exterior of the vessels on the whole develops from relatively deeply incised traces of fine cords into relatively shallow traces of rough cords.

Even though the Nan-kuan-wai period, too, predates the cultural remains of Lower Erh-li-kang, its ceramic characteristics display clear differences from those of Lo-ta-miao. The predominant color of the pottery is dark brown, and the Nan-kuan-wai *li, yen, chia, chüeh*, sand-tempered *kuan*, and *weng* are quite different from the corresponding Lo-ta-miao types. For instance:

- *Li* vessels have a bent-over rim, a cylindrical belly, and flat, hollow feet which end in high points.
- *Yen* have a bent-over rim, a slender, elongated belly as well as high, hollow feet; but they lack pointed feet.
- *Chia* vessels have a wide-open mouth, a long neck, a slender waist, flat, hollow legs, and high foot-points, and some have a pair of vertical *chu* on the rim.
- *Chüeh* have a spout but no tail, a rounded bottom, and three columnar, solid feet.
- Sand-tempered *kuan* have a slender and elongated waist and a flat bottom.
- *Weng* have a small mouth, a bent-over rim, a rounded, bulging belly, and a flat bottom.

The cord-marking on the exterior of the vessels is relatively fine but often quite eroded.[7] From these traits we deduce that the ceramic shapes and colors of Lower Erh-li-kang are not directly derived from Nan-kuan-wai. At the same time, Nan-kuan-wai sites constitute only a small proportion of the Shang remains at Cheng-chou: so far, the only two known are an area of about 1,000–2,000 square meters at the locality of Nan-kuan-wai and a pit by the Shang city's south wall. These both show that Lo-ta-miao and Nan-kuan-wai cannot belong to one and the same local culture of Early Shang.

Considering the archaeological evidence obtained through survey and excavation of Shang cultural remains all over Honan province, we find that Lo-ta-miao is encountered as a local manifestation of Early Shang culture mainly in the central and western parts of the province, whereas Nan-kuan-wai is the Early Shang local culture of southeastern Honan. As to their relationship at Cheng-chou, our preliminary opinion is that while the Early Shang Lo-ta-miao local culture was developing at Cheng-chou, the Nan-kuan-wai local culture extended for a brief period to the point where the gate in the south wall of the Cheng-chou was built later; there, it left to posterity the not-very-extensive Nan-kuan-wai sites. Erh-li-kang developed locally at Cheng-chou, evolving directly and continuously out of Lo-ta-miao (that is, late Erh-li-t'ou), but with regard to certain individual pottery shapes it apparently was also influenced by Nan-kuan-wai.

Even though the cultural record of the Shang sites at Cheng-chou pertains primarily to the early period of Middle Shang—Lower and Upper Erh-li-kang—it also incorporates some remains of the Early Shang Lo-ta-miao and Nan-kuan-wai and of the Late Shang Jen-min Kung-yüan periods. This fact indicates that there was continuous human settlement in the area of the Shang city at Cheng-chou throughout the Early, Middle, and Late Shang, early Middle Shang Erh-li-kang being the period of greatest florescence.

The site of the Shang city at Cheng-chou has thus yielded important scientific evidence for the study of the successive stages of development of Shang material culture and their stratigraphic relationships. In the 1940s Chinese and foreign scholars concerned with the study of Shang dynasty material culture could base themselves only on the Late Shang remains from An-yang. Not until the discovery and excavation of Erh-li-

---

7. See note 3.

kang and Lo-ta-miao in the fifties was the gap of Early and early Middle Shang in the cultural history of China filled in. The Shang sites of Cheng-chou are among the important archaeological discoveries in China during the last thirty years.

THE HANG-T'U CITY WALLS

The single most important discovery at the Shang site of Cheng-chou is a *hang-t'u* enclosure of immense size dating to the Erh-li-kang period. Located at the center of the site, it fills the area of the old walled city of Cheng-chou and extends beyond its northern gate. The enclosure is approximately rectangular, slightly longer north and south. The east wall is approximately 1,700 meters long, the west wall 1,870, the south wall 1,700, and the north wall 1,790, totaling almost seven kilometers.

After the Shang enclosure had been abandoned, the walls were successively reused and altered from the Chou and Han periods onward, until the Ming and Ch'ing dynasties, for the construction of walled cities known from historical records by such names as Kuan Ch'eng, Kuan Ch'eng Hsien, Cheng-chou Ch'eng, and Cheng Hsien Ch'eng. Moreover, the walls have been damaged by local people digging for earth and by erosion. The parts of the Shang *hang-t'u* city walls that are aboveground have been seriously destroyed; what has been preserved is mainly buried underground. Only a part of the east and south walls and fragments of the north and west walls are now visible (fig. 6). At its highest point the remaining wall is 9 meters, whereas at its lowest portion it is about 1 meter high; the greatest width at the base is 22.4 meters, the narrowest 4.8 meters; in some of the corners, the walls are preserved to a thickness of approximately 30 meters. The entire plan of the Shang *hang-t'u* enclosure is clear and can be followed along the base of the wall. The structure is a relatively well preserved example of an early Middle Shang city wall.

According to the evidence of the test trenches excavated into the *hang-t'u* walls, two principal methods of construction were employed. One consisted of first leveling the ground a bit and then pounding the earth layers of the so-called main wall directly on the ground. In the other method, after the ground had been leveled, a flat-bottomed foundation trough somewhat wider at the top than at the bottom was first excavated following the outline of the wall to be built, but closer to its inner face. Then *hang-t'u* layers were piled up beginning from the bot-

Fig. 6. Shang city wall remains at Cheng-chou.

tom of the foundation trough. When ground level was reached, the construction of the main wall was started at the full width of the wall.

This second method was observed in two interconnected test trenches in the south wall, CST 3 and 4. Here, a foundation trough 10.8 meters long, 2.50 meters wide at the top, 2.30 meters wide at the bottom, and 0.55 meters deep had been excavated along the base of the wall. This trough had been filled with successive layers of *hang-t'u*. After the *hang-t'u* layers emerged at ground level, construction of the main wall began at a width of 10.6 meters.

Once the work reached the surface, wooden boards were used to delimit the edges of the wall under construction, forming, so to speak, an aboveground foundation trough. A further detail of construction method was observed during the excavation of east wall trench CET 7: the main wall was constructed in horizontal sections. Wooden planks were erected on both sides so as to delimit the interior and exterior faces of the wall under construction as well as the side where the wall was as yet unfinished. In these moldlike troughs boarded on three sides, the *hang-t'u* layers of the main wall were piled up one by one. When two or three

Fig. 7. Impressions of wooden boardings on the walls of the Shang city at Cheng-chou.

layers of *hang-t'u* had thus been laid within the board troughs, the wooden facings were moved up on all three sides and more layers accumulated therein. In this way the height of the wall steadily grew. When the height reached that of the previously completed section of wall, the next section was commenced according to the same procedure. Each of these sections was about 3.8 meters long. Thanks to this boarding method, the inner and outer faces of the finished main wall were nearly dead straight. At excavation, on both faces of the main wall and at the end points of every section, relatively clear traces of horizontally laid wooden boards could still be observed (fig. 7). Judging from the relatively well preserved traces of these construction boards in CST 3 and 4, each one was about three meters long and 0.16–0.19 meters wide. The fragmentary traces of such boards are now preserved to a height of around 1.50 meters.

Moreover, along the base of the wall, adjacent to the boarded inner and outer faces of the main wall, sloping *hang-t'u* layers were discovered; they were highest where they joined the wall, gradually lowering toward the outside. These sloping chunks of *hang-t'u* were perhaps con-

THE SHANG CITY AT CHENG-CHOU

Fig. 8. Pestle impressions on layers of stamped earth inside the Shang city wall at Cheng-chou.

structed at the same time as the main wall, to support the boards on its two sides. At the same time, they also served the function of a so-called protective wall that protected the bases of the main wall. On the outer face, this protective wall was 4 meters wide, on the inner face 7.25 meters. Furthermore, on the top surface of the sloping protective wall, by the bases of the inner and outer sides of the main wall, an incompletely preserved layer with many pieces of broken "ginger-rock" was found. They had been placed here at the time of construction, apparently with the intention of protecting the *hang-t'u* layers at the bases of the wall from erosion by rainwater.

The entire Shang city wall was built layer by layer, by first putting the earth in place and then pounding it solid. Each layer of *hang-t'u* is 8–10 centimeters thick, but sometimes unusually thick or thin layers occur. On each layer of *hang-t'u* the round and either pointed or rounded impressions of the pestles used for pounding are preserved (fig. 8). The usual diameter of the impressions is 2–4 centimeters, their depth 1–2 centimeters. Occasionally, however, a small number of rectangular or triangular impressions have been observed. Judging from the forms and distributions of these pounding-pestle impressions, we have concluded that the principal tools used in *hang-t'u* construction were perhaps tied-up bundles of wooden sticks.

Since the *hang-t'u* layers are thin and the pounding impressions are tightly spaced, and moreover since the earth used in the construction of the city wall consists of sticky red loam mixed with sand—both obtainable in the immediate vicinity of the building site—the earthen layers of the city walls are extremely hard. The method of constructing earthen walls of pounded earth with the help of wooden boards was an important technological invention of the Chinese people of antiquity. This technique of engineering has been continuously employed for several millennia in earthen architecture and is widely used even to this day for building the walls of earthen houses in the Honan area.

When was the enclosure of the Cheng-chou Shang city built and used? The stratigraphic evidence obtained from twenty-two test trenches sectioning all four sides of the enclosure suggests that its construction and use began in the Erh-li-kang period of earlier Shang. There are three main reasons for supposing this:

1. In many trenches along the interior face of the walls, upon the sloping protective wall at the bottom of the wall, Lower and Upper Erh-li-kang cultural deposits, small house foundations, pits, and tombs were found. In the tombs, Lower and Upper Erh-li-kang artifacts were found, including ceramics, lithic, bone, and shell tools, and small quantities of primitive porcelain and stamped hard pottery. It can be inferred that after the construction of the enclosure, the people then living near the city walls allowed their old ashes and pieces of broken ceramics, bone, stone, shell, primitive porcelain, and stamped hard pottery to accumulate like garbage at the bottom of the city wall's interior face, thereby creating sloping midden deposits of clear stratification and varying thicknesses. In addition, the bottoms of some storage pits, houses, and graves rested upon the sloping *hang-t'u* layers on the interior face of the enclosure, and in some cases they have intruded into the *hang-t'u* layers of the protective wall. Such phenomena have been observed so far only on the interior, never on the exterior of the Shang city walls. These stratigraphic conditions prove that the erection and use of the Shang walled enclosure at Cheng-chou cannot have begun any later than the Erh-li-kang period.

2. Beneath the Shang dynasty *hang-t'u* layers in several of the

trenches, some Lung-shan cultural remains were found. Besides, CET 7, beneath the Shang *hang-t'u* of the eastern wall, yielded cultural strata pertaining to Lo-ta-miao, and in CST 4, repairs of the lower *hang-t'u* layers on the inside of the southern wall had partially destroyed a Nan-kuan-wai storage pit. These stratigraphic relationships prove that the time of construction of the Shang walls at Cheng-chou cannot have been any earlier than Lo-ta-miao and Nan-kuan-wai, that is, the period corresponding to Late Erh-li-t'ou.

3. In every one of the twenty-two test trenches dug into the Shang city walls, the *hang-t'u* layers of the walls have yielded a number of different ceramic sherds and other objects. It has been ascertained that those of Lo-ta-miao (that is, Erh-li-t'ou) date are most numerous; there are, moreover, smaller numbers of Nan-kuan-wai and Lower Erh-li-kang sherds. On the other hand, no potsherds or other objects later than Upper Erh-li-kang have been found. One may infer that when the *hang-t'u* enclosure was built with earth excavated from the surrounding area, Lo-ta-miao cultural layers or refuse pits as well as a small number of Nan-kuan-wai layers and pits were dug up in the vicinity of the walls, and as a result many Lo-ta-miao and a few Nan-kuan-wai potsherds and other objects became mixed into the *hang-t'u* layers of the Shang city wall. Moreover, since the Shang city wall was constructed during the Lower Erh-li-kang period, broken fragments of pottery and other objects used by the people who participated in its construction also inevitably came to be pounded into the *hang-t'u* layers. This is why a few Lower Erh-li-kang potsherds and other objects were found there as well. Afterward, when the wall was repaired during the Upper Erh-li-kang period, the Shang city wall's *hang-t'u* layers quite naturally came to contain some Upper Erh-li-kang sherds in addition to an even greater number of Lower Erh-li-kang sherds and other objects. This proves even more convincingly that the walled enclosure of the Cheng-chou Shang city cannot have been constructed at any time later than the Lower Erh-li-kang period.

According to these proofs, construction and use of the Shang dynasty *hang-t'u* enclosure at Cheng-chou started during the early Middle Shang Lower Erh-li-kang period, but during Upper Erh-li-kang the walls were partially repaired and continued to be used. At the same time, a wood charcoal sample obtained from the *hang-t'u* layers of the eastern wall at CET 7 has yielded a radiocarbon date of 3235 ± 90 B.P. (that is, 1285 ± 90

B.C.). The tree-ring calibration date is 3570±135 B.P. (that is, ca. 1620 B.C.). These dates fall exactly within the period recorded as the early Middle Shang.[8]

The discovery and excavation of the early Middle Shang *hang-t'u* enclosure at Cheng-chou has not only disproven the old theory, which alleged that there was as yet no city wall in Shang, but also advanced our understanding of the origins of the Chinese city and made possible the formulation of new questions for research. In 1974, another early Middle Shang walled city site dating to Upper Erh-li-kang was excavated in P'an-lung-ch'eng of Huang-p'i, Hupei.[9] And in 1977 two *hang-t'u* walled city sites dating to Middle and Late Lung-shan (corresponding to Hsia and proto-Shang) were separately excavated at two localities in Honan: Wang-ch'eng-kang near Kao-ch'eng-chen of Teng-feng, and P'ing-liang-t'ai of Huai-yang-hsien.[10] They predate the Shang dynasty walled settlements by several centuries and provide new information pertinent to the study of the origins and development of ancient Chinese cities.

Why are the 3,500-year-old Shang enclosure walls so well preserved? Primarily because after the early Middle Shang enclosure was destroyed and abandoned, the enclosure was continuously overbuilt and reused from the Warring States period of Eastern Chou until the Ming, Ch'ing, and Republican periods. From the Han period onward, only a reduced area comprising the southern two-thirds of the Shang enclosure was used, whereas the northern third was abandoned and suffered dilapidation and erosion caused by rain. But since the Cheng-chou sites are near the Yellow River, aeolian deposits rapidly covered the remaining fragmentary portions of the Shang enclosures with accumulating sands and preserved the remains of the ancient *hang-t'u* city wall.

THE DEVELOPMENT OF *HANG-T'U* TECHNOLOGY IN ANCIENT CHINA

According to archaeological evidence of *hang-t'u* construction from the available sites in China, it is now known that during the transition period from primitive society to slaveholding society the inhabitants of dispersed settlements all over the Shantung peninsula, the Great Plain of eastern Honan and the area of western Honan were already using

---

8. Wen-wu-tzu-liao-ts'ung-k'an 1977a.
9. Wen-wu 1983a.
10. Wen-wu 1983b.

the *hang-t'u* technique in constructing the floors of their houses and the foundations of walls as well as walled enclosures. The preserved ancient textual records, which say that "Kun began the pounding of city walls," perhaps refer to this stage of the history of constructing *hang-t'u* city walls.

In recent years two *hang-t'u* enclosures dating back more than 4,000 years have been excavated: one in west Honan around Sung Shan within the area of political control of the slaveholding Hsia state, the other in east Honan which was the area of activity of the former chiefs of the Shang tribe at the time of the Hsia dynasty. These two sites are the earliest *hang-t'u* enclosures in China.

The first site is on top of the Wang-ch'eng-kang ridge, which is located about 0.5 kilometers west of Kao-ch'eng-chen in Teng-feng, at the confluence of the Ying and Wutu rivers. The site consists of two adjoining *hang-t'u* enclosures dating to the middle to late period of the western Honan Lung-shan culture. Much of the eastern enclosure has been washed away by the Wutu River; only its southwestern corner is preserved. Perhaps it was because the eastern enclosure had been washed away by the river that the western enclosure was built, incorporating the west wall of the former as its east wall. Since both the eastern and the western enclosure have undergone significant destruction throughout the dynasties, the greatest preserved portion is the foundation troughs and the *hang-t'u* layers in these troughs.

As far as we can tell from the state of preservation of the western enclosure, its west wall was 94.8 meters long and its southern wall 97.6 meters long; the fragmentary remains of the north and east walls measure approximately 30 meters and 65 meters, respectively; the latter is also the west wall of the eastern enclosure, whose south wall is preserved to a length of 40 meters. During the process of excavation of profile trenches into the walls on each side, cultural deposits and refuse pits characteristic of the Western Honan Lung-shan were discovered stratigraphically superimposed upon or intruding into their foundation troughs and the *hang-t'u* layers therein. This discovery proves that the *hang-t'u* enclosure cannot have been constructed any later than the Late Western Honan Lung-shan culture. At the same time, the *hang-t'u* layers in the foundation troughs of the settlement walls were found to contain a small amount of cultural remains, including potsherds and animal bones. The majority of the potsherds belong to the middle period of the Western Honan Lung-shan, and so far no potsherds later than the middle or late period have been discovered there. This, then, proves that the construction of this walled settlement cannot have taken place any earlier than the middle period of Western Honan Lung-shan. We therefore believe that the Wang-ch'eng-kang settlement is a site of the middle to late period of the Western Honan Lung-shan culture. Moreover, inside the walled area, remains of some contemporary *hang-t'u* architectural foundations as well as refuse pits have been discovered. From a carbon sample collected from a refuse pit located within the enclosure and contemporary with its wall, a radiocarbon date of 4010 ± 85 B.P. has been obtained, which becomes 4415 ± 140 B.P. after the application of tree-ring calibration. This falls approximately within the period recorded as the Early Hsia dynasty.

The construction method of these two Middle to Late Lung-shan enclosures was as follows: a trapezoidal foundation trough with sloping walls, wider at the top than at the bottom, was dug along the outline of the wall to be constructed. The foundation trough excavated in a test trench (GWT 23) in the middle portion of the west wall was about 4.4 meters wide at the top, 2.54 meters wide at the bottom, and 2.04 meters deep. Within it, *hang-t'u* was laid in the bottom of the trough and stamped solid layer by layer. The stamped layers are mostly from 10 to 15 centimeters thick, but there are also instances of layers that are only 6 to 8 centimeters thick. On the face of each *hang-t'u* layer, a layer of fine sand about 1 centimeter thick was laid, perhaps to prevent the loam of the *hang-t'u* layers from sticking to the stamping tools during the stamping process. In many cases traces of the pounding pestles are preserved on top of each of these fine sand layers. The size and depth of the pestle impressions vary. They can be classified into (a) round impressions with rounded bottom, (b) oval impressions with rounded bottom, and (c) irregularly shaped impressions. The diameter of the pounding pestles is mostly from 4 to 10 centimeters, and their impressions were 1 to 2.5 centimeters deep. Judging from the shape of the impressions, we surmise that locally collected river pebbles were used as pounding tools. In fact, during excavation of GWT 23, some river pebbles of 8 to 18 centimeters diameter—possibly remains of the stamping tools of that time—were found placed on top of some *hang-t'u* layers. To judge from the pattern in which the *hang-t'u* layers of the settlement wall at Wang-ch'eng-kang are superimposed upon one another, a relatively primitive method of pounding seems to have been used.[11]

11. See note 9.

As to the problem of the identity of this locality, the Old Text version of the *Bamboo Annals* says: "Among the descendants of Hsia 夏, Yü 禹 resided in Yang-ch'eng 陽城." *Shih-pen* says: "The capital of Yü of Hsia was at Yang-ch'eng." The first section of the Wan-chang chapter in *Mencius* says: "Yü yielded to the son of Shun 舜 of Yang-ch'eng." In the *Hsia Pen-chi* of *Shih Chi*, it is said that "Yü declined in favor of Shang Chün the son of Shun, and lived in Yang-ch'eng." These quotations show not only that there was a place by the name of Yang-ch'eng in the Hsia dynasty, but also that whenever it is mentioned it is linked to the name of Yü of Hsia.

Yü was the first king to reign after the Hsia dynasty had established its slaveholding state. This fact suggests that the Yang-ch'eng of the Hsia dynasty is the site of an early capital or at least of a site where King Yü lived. Concerning the location of Yang-ch'eng, the first section of *Chou Yü* in *Kuo Yü* says: "In former times, the cradle of Hsia was at the foot of Ch'ung Shan 崇山." The commentary by Wei Chao (third century A.D.) says: "Ch'ung Shan is a high mountain; the Hsia dwelt at Yang-ch'eng, which is a place near Ch'ung Shan." Ch'ung Shan is identical with Sung Shan 嵩山, which is located within the confines of Teng-feng Hsien in Honan. Also, according to *Shui Ching Chu*, chapter 22: "The Ying River 潁水 originates as Ying Stream 潁川 at Shao-shih Shan 少室山 northwest of Yang-ch'eng Hsien. Further to the southeast, it flows through the southern part of the hsien." The commentary by Li Tao-yuan relates: "To the east of the Ying River, the Wutu 五渡 River flows in, ... which to the southeast flows by the west side of Yang-ch'eng, ... and further to the southeast joins the Ying River. The Ying River flows by the south of the old city, the place where anciently when Shun handed down his throne Yü yielded to Shang Chün and lived here. Here, also Po Yi yielded to Chi, and Chou Kung erected the earthen (platform) and used the Kuei tablet in order to make calendrical observations of the sun." According to *K'uo Ti Chih*, "Yang-ch'eng is 13 *li* to the north of Chi Shan." The locations indicated for Yang-ch'eng in *Shui Ching Chu* and *K'uo Ti Chih* correspond exactly to the area around Kao-ch'eng in present-day Teng-feng-hsien.

In recent years, through archaeological survey and excavation of the environs of Kao-ch'eng, the sites of the Yang-ch'eng of the Spring and Autumn, Warring States, and Han periods have been found. Reliable confirming evidence has been found in the form of numerous Warring States pottery fragments, into which inscriptions like "Yang-ch'eng

陽城" and "Inventory of the Yang-ch'eng storehouse 陽城倉記" were incised. And then, on the Wang-ch'eng-kang ridge—separated only by the Wutu River to the west of the Yang-ch'eng of Spring and Autumn and Warring States times—a walled settlement from the period corresponding to Early Hsia has been excavated! This is certainly no accident. The settlement of Spring and Autumn and Warring States times was probably named Yang-ch'eng for the simple fact that the Yang-ch'eng of the Hsia dynasty was located here. Therefore, the Middle to Late Lung-shan site of Wang-ch'eng-kang is perhaps indeed the site of Early Hsia Yang-ch'eng.

The other site of an early *hang-t'u* enclosure was excavated at P'ing-liang-t'ai of Huai-yang-hsien, Honan. It dates from the pre-Shang Eastern Honan Lung-shan culture. From test excavations and probing we have learned that the walled area is approximately square. Each face of the city wall is a little more than 180 meters long, and the perimeter is approximately 720 meters. The city wall as well as some house foundations excavated within the enclosure were all constructed of *hang-t'u*. The dates are approximately identical to those of the Wang-ch'eng-kang settlement site in Teng-feng.[12]

The remains of Middle to Late Lung-shan *hang-t'u* walled enclosures and house foundation platforms at Wang-ch'eng-kang of Teng-feng and P'ing-liang-t'ai of Huai-yang prove that over two thousand years before Christ Chinese people had created the technology of pounded earth and were using it not only to construct the foundations of their houses, but also to build town walls.

Succeeding the Early to Middle Lung-shan walled settlement site of Wang-ch'eng-kang at Teng-feng in time are the *hang-t'u* foundation platforms of palaces excavated in the late strata of the Erh-li-t'ou site in Yen-shih, Honan. One of them is 108 meters long and 100 meters wide, and its height, counting only what is above the water table, is 3.1 meters. On the surface of this *hang-t'u* platform, fragments of the bases of the palace walls and its surrounding open corridors are still preserved, with rows of regularly spaced postholes and pillar support stones. This platform consists of separate layers of reddish-brown sticky loam and streaky soil. Each *hang-t'u* layer is ordinarily 8–9 centimeters thick, but there are thicker and thinner ones. On top of the face of each *hang-t'u* layer are densely dispersed concave, round, and round-bottomed impressions of

12. See note 10.

pounding pestles. The diameter of the pestles is usually 3–5 centimeters, and the impressions are 1–2 centimeters deep. Since the impressions are dense and numerous, the *hang-t'u* was apparently pounded very hard. Around the perimeter near the bottom of the *hang-t'u* platform, gently sloping *hang-t'u* layers, pounded at a slight angle toward the outside, have also been discovered, and a hard surface of broken pieces of "ginger rock" had been laid on top of them. This served as a protective wall to prevent the bottom of the *hang-t'u* platform from being washed away by rainwater.

In the Late Erh-li-t'ou building method at Erh-li-t'ou of Yen-shih, the *hang-t'u* layers are more equal in thickness than those of the *hang-t'u* enclosure at Wang-ch'eng-kang of Teng-feng. The pounding impressions are of a more regular form, and the *hang-t'u* is more solid; apparently, tied-up bundles of wooden sticks were used as pounding tools. On the whole, the impressions demonstrate that the *hang-t'u* techniques of Late Erh-li-t'ou, even though they developed directly from those of Middle and Late Lung-shan, typified by Wang-ch'eng-kang, had progressed to a higher level.

Concerning the date of the *hang-t'u* platforms of the great palace at Erh-li-t'ou of Yen-shih, the preliminary report (Erh-li-t'ou Team, Archaeological Institute, Academia Sinica, 1974) states:

> The refuse pits sunk into the floor of the *hang-t'u* platform and those that are contemporary with them number over fifty. Their shapes are not uniform, and they can be classified into round, square, long oval, oval, and irregular. The walls of the round pits are neat and straight and their bottoms relatively level, whereas those of other types of pits are for the most part not regular. They all date from Erh-li-t'ou IV.... There are altogether eight refuse pits that are either located below the *hang-t'u* platform or are contemporary with those that are. H 75 is located beneath the northern part of the platform; this refuse pit's southern half was dug away when the platform was being constructed, so that only the northern half is preserved. The most common type of ceramic ornament is basketry impression, which is found on about 50 percent of the excavated sherds; this dates to Erh-li-t'ou I (namely, Early Erh-li-t'ou). H 110 was found beneath the southern part of the platform, by which it had been covered entirely. It dates to Erh-li-t'ou II... On top of the platform, there are refuse pits and tombs from Erh-li-t'ou IV, and underneath there are refuse pits from Erh-li-t'ou II. The stratigraphic relationship shows clearly that the palace construction must have occurred within Erh-li-t'ou III. ... As to absolute chronology of Erh-li-t'ou III, a radiocarbon date of

3195±90 B.P. (1245±90 B.C.), calibrated to 1300–1590 B.C., has been obtained by the laboratory of our Institute. This time frame corresponds to Early Shang. The general appearance of the culture of this period also displays Shang characteristics. Most recently, we have discovered an Erh-li-t'ou IV culture, which closely links Erh-li-t'ou III and Erh-li-kang. It has also been stratigraphically ascertained that Erh-li-t'ou III is earlier than Erh-li-kang. Thus, we have determined that this palace site is indeed Early Shang.

Shu Hsü 書序 says: "T'ang 湯 began living in Po 亳, following the abode of the former kings." The commentary by Cheng K'ang adds: "Now Yen-shih, Honan." See also *K'uo Ti Chih*: "The ancient walls of the town of Po 亳 are located seventeen *li* west of Yen-shih-hsien of Lo-chou [=Lo-yang]. It was at first the abode of Ti K'u 帝嚳; then, it was the capital of T'ang of Shang." Combining this textual evidence with the fact that at the Early Shang site at Erh-li-t'ou of Yen-shih archaeological excavations have brought to light the *hang-t'u* foundations of great palaces as well as bronze, pottery, and bone manufacturing sites and a great number of refuse pits and graves with bronze funerary goods, we believe that the area of Erh-li-t'ou of Yen-shih was perhaps the site of the capital of Po, the Hsi Po 西亳 of Ch'eng T'ang.[13]

The early Middle Shang Erh-li-kang culture developed in direct progression from the Early Shang Erh-li-t'ou culture. Therefore, the Erh-li-kang technique of *hang-t'u* architecture also developed in a process of continuous improvement directly from that of Late Erh-li-t'ou. The pounding marks on many *hang-t'u* platforms located in the northeastern part of the walled enclosure of the Cheng-chou Shang city clearly lie in a continuum of development with those at Erh-li-t'ou. But the Erh-li-kang period itself witnessed improvements upon the techniques of former periods. The most prominent example is the boarding method employed during the pounding construction. The shape of the pounding pestles evolved toward a pointed or round-pointed tip and the diameters of the impressions became smaller than they had been in Late Erh-li-t'ou. Consequently the impressions had to be both more numerous and more tightly spaced than they had been in Late Erh-li-t'ou. As a result, the *hang-t'u* walls became harder and more solid. The accumulation of sloping *hang-t'u* surfaces at the bottom of the wall, inside as well as outside, and the placement of a layer of broken pieces of "ginger rock" on top of them must also have developed directly from Late Erh-li-t'ou.[14]

13. K'ao-ku 1974.
14. Wen-wu 1983d.

The site of another Middle Shang *hang-t'u* enclosure, Upper Erh-li-kang in date and less extensive than that of Cheng-chou, was discovered in the winter of 1974 at P'an-lung-ch'eng of Huang-p'i, Hupei. Inside the enclosure, the *hang-t'u* foundations of contemporary great palaces were excavated. On top of the foundation platforms transverse and longitudinal rows of regularly spaced postholes with stone pillar bases had been preserved.[15] The presence of this site indicates that the process of improvement and development of the *hang-t'u* technique continued uninterrupted in the post-Erh-li-kang period; the construction of the new enclosure was certainly not fortuitous but consistent with the process of development of *hang-t'u* technology in China.

Comparing the *hang-t'u* technology of Late Shang with Erh-li-kang, we note an even more widespread use and considerable progress toward perfecting the technique. For instance, during the archaeological excavations of the Late Shang capital at the "Waste of Yin" (Yin-hsü) of Anyang, many large and small *hang-t'u* platforms were excavated in the area of Hsiao-t'un alone. Their shapes are rectangular, U-shaped, and elongated. The more extensive ones are over 40 meters long and more than 10 meters wide; the smaller ones measure about 5 by 3 meters. In some, the north–south axis is longer, in others, the east–west axis. Two building procedures were used: in one, the pounding of the platform proceeded after the area to be overbuilt had been leveled or after earlier pits had been filled. In the other, a foundation pit was built first, within which the pounding of earth then proceeded upwards. The height (or thickness) of a *hang-t'u* platform was usually 1–4 meters, and the thickness of the individual *hang-t'u* layers was 10–11 centimeters. In all cases the boarding method was used. The surface of each *hang-t'u* layer was densely covered with impressions of round and round-bottomed pounding pestles, whose diameter was 3 to 5 centimeters and whose depth was about 2.5 centimeters. After the construction of the *hang-t'u* platform, postholes were sunk in accordance with the plan of the superstructure. Into these, stone bases were laid, and wooden pillars were erected on top of them. Most of the pillar bases are natural-shaped boulders, but bronze bases were also found. Occasionally one side of a *hang-t'u* platform was stamped particularly solidly, so that pillars could be erected directly on the surface of the *hang-t'u*. This method was used especially on some large *hang-t'u* foundation platforms as well as near the gates. Furthermore, skeletons of adults and children were found, apparently remnants

15. *Wen-wu* 1976.

of a custom of sacrificial interment of slaves in the course of the building process.

From the methods of construction as well as the shape of the pounding pestles found in the foundations at Yin-hsü, An-yang, one can clearly perceive that the Late Shang *hang-t'u* construction method came into being as a result of continuous development from Erh-li-kang.[16]

All of the evidence cited above proves that architectural construction with pounded earth has a long history in China. This important invention was made by peoples of primitive clan societies in the process of house and wall construction. As the society developed, the *hang-t'u* technique—originally used for laying floors and erecting the walls of houses and the walls surrounding house compounds—did also: the extent of the surrounding walls was enlarged, and *hang-t'u* walls came into being.

The appearance of city walls in the historical record is closely linked to the germination and development of class society. Walls are a product of irresolvable conflict between two opposing classes. Only when forced to ward off the rebellious struggle of the ruled class and the havoc wreaked by invading powers from the outside did the ruling class of that time make use of the already mastered *hang-t'u* technology to erect fortified enclosures. They did so by enlarging and heightening the *hang-t'u* walls surrounding the elite living precincts. In this way, *hang-t'u* technology became an instrument of defense in the service of the ruling class.

The size of the city walls at Wang-ch'eng-kang of Teng-feng and P'ing-liang-t'ai of Huai-yang is not large; yet in both cases there is strong evidence that they belong to city wall architecture of the beginning stage of slaveholding society. Later, as a consequence of the advanced development of the Shang slaveholding society and the continual improvement of the earth-pounding technique, not only did the great *hang-t'u* palace foundation platforms attain unprecedented scale and height, but the number of walled enclosures constructed of *hang-t'u* increased; some individual walled enclosures became larger and larger. The early Middle Shang city wall at Cheng-chou was constructed after the Shang slaveholding society had reached an advanced stage of development.

The later development of *hang-t'u* city wall construction also proceeded along the lines of social evolution and therefore demonstrates a

---

16. Shih 1933; H. H. Hu 1955.

step-by-step increase in the scale and number of walled cities; the walled enclosures of capital city sites especially were enlarged by comparison with earlier periods. For this, the many large city sites of the Spring and Autumn and Warring States periods, still preserved to this day throughout China, provide a reliable proof.

But the evidence so far excavated on ancient *hang-t'u* enclosures comes from two Hsia/Proto-Shang sites, the early Middle Shang sites of Cheng-chou and P'an-lung-ch'eng, and moreover, the walled cities of the Spring and Autumn and Warring States periods. Why, then, have no Early Shang and Late Shang *hang-t'u* enclosures been discovered? For instance, the Early Shang *hang-t'u* palace platforms at Erh-li-t'ou are constructed on an impressive scale (it may be argued even that this was the site of "T'ang's capital Hsi Po"); and it has long been proven that Yin-hsü is the site of the Late Shang capital. According to the principles of development of city-building in ancient China, not only should Erh-li-t'ou of Yen-shih and Yin-hsü of An-yang both contain remains of *hang-t'u* walled enclosures, but such walls should have been of relatively large scale. But so far no remains of *hang-t'u* walls have been found at either site. There are two possible reasons for this: either the *hang-t'u* wall remains at these two places have been so pillaged and destroyed by people of ancient times digging for earth that no traces remain or the extent of the walls is so large that it has not yet been discovered by our surveys.

To say that there were no *hang-t'u* walled enclosures in Early and Late Shang contradicts our notion of the principles of development of the *hang-t'u* wall architecture in accordance with social development. In the course of future excavation at Shang sites in all areas, Early and Late Shang *hang-t'u* will possibly be found; moreover, additional *hang-t'u* enclosure sites dating to early Middle Shang as well as to Middle to Late Lung-shan (= Hsia) will probably be discovered and excavated at many places.

OTHER SITES IN AND AROUND THE SHANG CITY OF CHENG-CHOU AND THEIR SIGNIFICANCE

The geographic disposition of the Shang walled enclosure at Cheng-chou and the layout of the various sites inside and outside the walls fundamentally correspond with the laws governing the distribution of sites in China's Hsia, Shang, and Chou dynasties.

In virtually all cases relatively high places near rivers were chosen as sites of ancient Chinese cities and particularly of capitals, preferably wedges of land at the confluence of two rivers. For instance, the Middle to Late Lung-shan walled settlement at Wang-ch'eng-kang of Teng-feng is located on an elevated platform located above the confluence of the Ying and Wutu rivers. The palace precinct at Erh-li-t'ou of Yen-shih is located on a high area at the confluence of the Yi and Lo rivers. The Upper Erh-li-kang city of P'an-lung-ch'eng of Huang-p'i is located on a high platform surrounded on three sides by water. Yin-hsü of An-yang is located on high ground above a bend of the Huan River. This principle for the choice of city sites was adhered to even more strictly from the Chou period onward. The reasons for choosing high elevations near rivers were that the cities had to be close to a river but in a location not endangered by inundation; furthermore, high elevations were easily defended against attacks.

The geographic location chosen for the Shang city site of Cheng-chou follows the pattern of siting of other ancient cities in China. It is an elevated promontory extending from the hill chains west of Cheng-chou; east of the city is the vast East Honan Great Plain. The Chin-shui River, which originally ran outside the northwest side of the Shang walls, was diverted by engineers in the 1940s and now flows through the northern part of the city about 0.25 kilometer from the north wall. On the southeast side, the city overlooks the Hsiung-erh River; it is thus on a high area between two rivers. From the present physiographic conditions of the area inside and outside the walls, it appears that the inside and the outside of the city are virtually on the same level, but archaeological excavations have proved that the layers of alluvium deposited by the river to the north of the Shang city are very thick, and that the area within the walls was originally a great deal higher than its surroundings. Furthermore, while the east, south, and west walls of the Shang *hang-t'u* enclosure were oriented to the points of the compass, the construction of the eastern portion of the north wall followed the natural outlines of the terrain at the time, and its direction is from southeast to northwest.

The layout of sites and features both inside and outside the Shang city walls of Cheng-chou seems to be the result of careful planning (fig. 9). The northeastern part of the walled area is relatively high with respect to the entire landform of the area. Initial probing and excavation have shown that a great number of *hang-t'u* foundation platforms of different sizes are distributed over an area of more than 300,000 square

THE SHANG CITY AT CHENG-CHOU

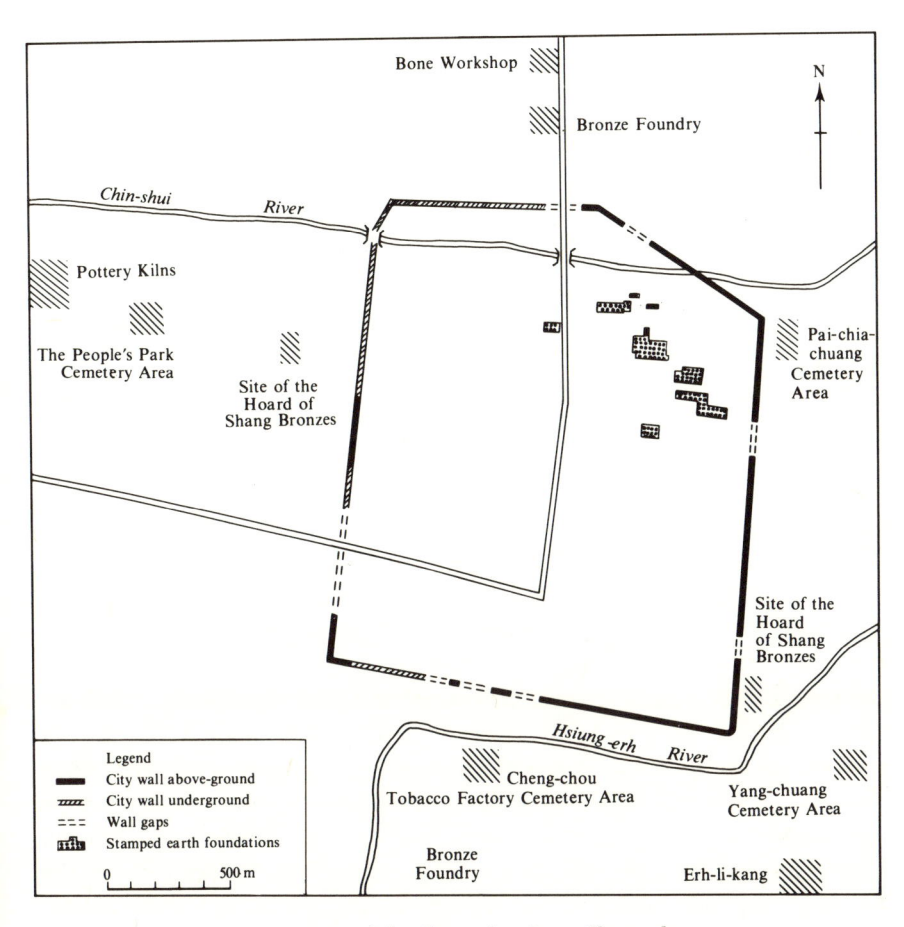

Fig. 9. Layout of the Shang city site at Cheng-chou.

meters within the northeastern part of the enclosure, with which they are contemporary. The largest of these surviving *hang-t'u* platforms measures nearly 1,000 square meters, and the smallest has an area of tens of square meters. The height of the preserved *hang-t'u* foundation platforms, according to the information obtained through excavation, is up to 2.5 meters for the high ones and about 1 meter for lower ones.

The methods employed in constructing the platforms, the thickness of the *hang-t'u* layers, and the shape of the pounding pestle marks all correspond exactly with those of the Shang *hang-t'u* city walls. This shows that when the Shang *hang-t'u* enclosure was built, many *hang-t'u* platforms of different sizes were constructed in the northeastern section at the same time. On the surface of some of the *hang-t'u* platforms are preserved laid floors of white ashy surface and floors of fine clay, as well as such architectural remains as postholes, stone pillar bases, and "ginger-rock"-lined hollows for the placement of stones, all arranged in neat rows running transversely and longitudinally.

Of the three relatively extensive *hang-t'u* foundation platforms that have been excavated, one runs more than 60 meters east and west (the eastern end has not yet been uncovered) and 13 meters north and south. Along the southern and northern edges of the top of the platform there are two rows of rectangular pillar pits. The pits are quite regularly spaced and neatly excavated according to cardinal directions. In the pits, the rotten wood of the pillars, which were 30–40 centimeters in diameter, as well as their base stones have been found. The distance between the center points of the wooden pillars in the postholes of each row is usually about 2 meters. The discovery of such a large architectural site was unprecedented in the Cheng-chou Shang city.

The second of the large *hang-t'u* foundation platforms uncovered has suffered serious damage; even so, one can perceive some details of the superstructure plan in the southwest corner, fragments of which are preserved. Three regular rows of round postholes can be made out on the surface of the platform, leading around its corner. In them, too, traces of the rotten wood of pillars 30–40 centimeters in diameter are frequently preserved, as are their stone bases. As in the first example, the transverse and longitudinal distances between the centers of the traces of wood preserved in the pits are usually about 2 meters. Judging from the spacing and distribution of the wooden pillars at this architectural site, we surmise that it was a large building with an open corridor running around it.

The third large *hang-t'u* architectural foundation site has yielded two north–south rows of regularly spaced hollows lined with fragments of "ginger rock." These hollows were for the erection of pillars. Apparently this building had undergone functional changes several times, as on the surface of the *hang-t'u* platform several layers of ashy earth stamped solid are stratigraphically superimposed, as is a floor of white ashy rock which had been polished several times. What is worth noting are the finds unearthed from the Erh-li-kang cultural strata and the finds in the fill of the ashy pits; in addition to a great quantity of ceramic, lithic, bone, and shell artifacts as well as oracle bones and small amounts of proto-porcelain and stamped hard pottery sherds, there were many objects such as jade hairpins, bronze hairpins, and fragments of jade. Jade and bronze hairpins are generally not encountered at sites outside the enclosure of the Shang city. We believe that this is so because such objects were used exclusively by the great slaveowners, who resided in the northeastern portion of the walled area. The density and the scope of these remains—as well as the fact that tombs of slaveowners and sacrificial pits in conjunction with high-status goods were unearthed in this area—suggest that the *hang-t'u* foundation platforms in the northeastern part of the Shang walled enclosure are the site of the palace where the slaveholding aristocrats resided.[17]

Test excavations have located an Erh-li-kang ditch several times 10 meters long from east to west and about 5 to 6 meters wide (the ends have not yet been found). The ditch runs inside the Shang city walls, along the northern edge of the area where *hang-t'u* foundations are clustered. Our preliminary opinion is that this ditch was perhaps the moat around the northern portion of the palace precinct, but whether or not it constitutes a defense installation is not yet clear owing to the limited amount of information obtained from the excavations.

Between the outside of the northeast part of the *hang-t'u* foundation platforms cluster and the eastern section of the northern portion of the Shang city wall, on elevated land, some middle to small slaveowners' tombs have been excavated. They contained such bronze ritual vessels as *chüeh, ting, li, chia, ku,* and *p'an,* as well as jade artifacts, as funerary offerings.[18] In the northeastern part of the cluster of *hang-t'u* foundation platforms eight sacrificial dog burials, arranged in a neat row, were found. In each of these were inhumed at least five and up to twenty-three dogs. In one of the pits, besides six dog skeletons, two human skeletons were discovered. These dog pits probably have some relation with the ritual sacrifices performed by the Shang slaveowners.[19] Moreover, in the central part of the cluster of *hang-t'u* foundation platforms another ditch yielded many human skulls that had been sawed open. This seems to indicate that the slaveowning class sawed off human skullcaps for use as vessels.[20]

In the other areas of the Shang city, the dense overbuilding in the old

---

17. See note 14.
18. Wen-wu 1955b.
19. C. H. An 1961.
20. Wen-wu 1974.

walled city of Cheng-chou has hindered archaeological probing and excavation. But from some preliminary soundings made in empty spots in the inner part of the city, we have learned that distributed beneath this area of the city are Erh-li-kang cultural strata and such sites as a few small *hang-t'u* platforms and storage pits. It appears that the area within the Shang enclosure was mainly a residential area inhabited by slave-owning aristocrats.

No reliable information has been gathered on the city gates of the Cheng-chou Shang city. During the archaeological testing of the Shang dynasty enclosure, eleven gaps of varying widths have been discovered in the walls on all four sides. Some were seemingly made after the abandonment of the Shang city by people digging for earth. The three openings that are most likely the sites of the Shang gates are located, respectively, in the center of the north wall and of the south wall and somewhat to the south of the center of the west wall. This conjecture may be supported by the following three arguments:

1. Following its abandonment, the Shang enclosure of Cheng-chou was occupied by the Warring States city of Kuan-ch'eng. The method used to restore the *hang-t'u* walls of Shang times was to add another Warring States *hang-t'u* wall abutting the outside of the original four outer faces. Now, in this Warring States outer enclosure there were openings in the center of the south wall and of the north wall and one somewhat to the south of the center of the west wall. The three openings were exactly in line with the gaps in the Shang city walls. Moreover, two of them coincide exactly with the south and west gates of the Kuan-hsien and Cheng Hsien cities from the Han till the Ming and Ch'ing dynasties, and the northern openings are in an axial relationship with the later north gate. It is unlikely that when the Warring States and later periods reused the Shang walls they altered the locations of the city gates, given the unchanging location of the walls. By analogy, when the walls of the Yüan capital of Ta-tu were reused in Ming dynasty Peking and when the T'ang city of Lo-yang inherited the foundations of the city of the Sui dynasty the location of the city gates basically did not shift. Numerous similar examples lead one to infer that the gates of the old city of Cheng Hsien and Kuan Ch'eng were situated at the exact same places as those of the Shang city of Cheng-chou.

2. Outside the walled area, along the axes going through these three wall openings or in locations close by, several important Erh-li-kang sites have been discovered. For instance, outside the gap in the center of the

north side of the Shang city wall and located in its axis there were manufacturing sites such as a bronze-casting workshop and a bone-working site; outside the southern opening, there was a Shang pottery workshop and another Shang slaveowners' cemetery with bronze funerary offerings; the site of Tu-ling Chang-chai Nan-chieh, where, in 1974, two large square *ting* from Erh-li-kang times were unearthed, is also located outside the Shang city, near the center of the west wall. These manufacturing workshops and graveyards, as well as the axes of traffic within the walled enclosure, were interlinked, and there should have been gates in the city wall relating to these important sites. Therefore, it is probable that these openings in the city walls were indeed the locations of the gates of the Shang city.

3. No *hang-t'u* foundation remains have been found in a 30-meter-wide stretch of land along the extended axis of the north gate of the city within the cluster of *hang-t'u* foundation platforms in the northeastern part of the Shang city that may have been the former palace precinct. And the remains of Shang dynasty *hang-t'u* architectural foundations of different sizes are aligned with some regularity along the eastern and western flanks of this stretch of land. This stretch of land was likely a section of the main road that traversed the city from north to south and led through the palace precinct. Such evidence may prove that the gap in the central part of the Shang north wall was the location of a city gate in the Shang dynasty enclosure.[21]

The four workshop sites excavated in the Cheng-chou Shang city were all situated outside but near the walled enclosure. This arrangement, we believe, corresponds to the social conditions of the early slaveholding society. For the walled enclosure was a defense installation in a class society. Many of those working in the shops were slaves, whereas the enclosure served as the place of residence mainly of the slaveholding aristocratic class. In the highly developed slaveholding society in Early Shang, the conflicts between the slaveholding aristocratic class and the slaves became rather acute. In order to ward off a rebellion by the slaves the slaveholding aristocratic class deliberately scattered the locations of the manufacturing sites in the environs outside the enclosure.

Two bronze-casting workshops have been excavated. One of them is located approximately 500 meters outside the south wall, the other 130 meters outside the north wall. At both sites, excavated finds include

21. See note 5.

house foundations, soil surfaces with corroded bronze (that is, bronze-casting sites), pottery crucibles, bronze-smelting slags, decayed charcoal, fragmentary pieces of bronze, and a large number of ceramic molds for the casting of bronze artifacts. Among these molds there were those of production tools such as picks, adzes, knives, daggers (*ko*), and arrowheads, and of bronze vessels such as *li, ting, chia, chüeh,* and *ku*.[22]

A pottery workshop was excavated in a location about 1,300 meters outside the west wall; here, a relatively dense cluster of eleven pottery kilns as well as house foundations and pottery-making areas were excavated. Furthermore, pottery-making implements such as pottery stamps, pottery paddles, and pottery anvils were found as well as a great number of finished pieces of clay-tempered gray ware (such as *p'en, kuei,* wide-mouthed *tsun, tseng,* and *weng* vessels), fragments of misfired or cracked pottery vessels, and a few unfired raw ceramics (of *p'en* and *tseng* types). However, the types of sand-tempered ceramics that abound at the Shang city site (such as *li, yen,* and *kuan*) have been rarely found. One may infer that this is the site of a workshop specializing mainly in the production of clay-textured gray ware, and there probably was another workshop specializing in the production of the sand-tempered gray ware. Thus a division of labor existed at the time between firing clay-textured and firing sand-tempered pottery.[23]

A bone-working shop was found about 300 meters outside the north wall. A large amount of animal bone was excavated here—long bones and ribs of cattle, pig, and deer as well as deer antler. Much of the bone material had already been sawed open and showed traces of sawing and cutting. Finished and half-finished bone implements and rough as well as fine sandy whetstones used for polishing them were also found. Among the finished and half-finished bone implements found, hairpins, arrowheads, and spatulas were most plentiful. Especially among the bone material that already showed traces of sawing, there were also quite a few human long bones. At this workshop, bone implements were thus made not only from animal, but also from human bones, apparently those of slaves.[24]

On the basis of this manufacturing evidence, one can prove that there was a clear-cut division of labor not only between different professions

22. Liao 1957; Honan Province Institute of Archaeology ms-b.
23. Wen-wu 1955a.
24. See note 5.

at that time, but also within the pottery-making industry. It entailed specialization in the fabrication of different types of products.

The distribution of these workshops outside the walls of the Shang city, the scale on which they operated, and the division of labor within individual industries reflect the fact that the objects produced by these workshops did not serve only the particular needs of their producers; the main use of the manufactured items was as trade items to be sold and exchanged. Apparently, the walled enclosure of the Shang city of Cheng-chou was not merely a royal city where the slaveholding aristocracy resided, but also the center of Erh-li-kang industry and commerce, where industrial and agricultural products were bought, sold, and exchanged. In the sense of the Chinese word for *city*, a binom containing the words for "walled city" (*ch'eng*) and "market" (*shih*), Shang dynasty Cheng-chou would have been a true city (*ch'eng-shih*).

Four Erh-li-kang cemeteries have been discovered: Pai-chia-chuang and Yang-chuang outside the eastern wall, one in the courtyard of the Cheng-chou tobacco factory (Cheng-chou Yen-ch'ang) outside the southern wall, and one around Tu-ling outside the western wall. The physiographic location of each of these four cemeteries is relatively elevated. Grave goods in many medium and small graves include ritual bronze vessels such as *chia, chueh, ku, yu, tsun,* and *lei*, pottery vessels such as *li, p'en,* and *tou*, as well as jade objects such as sword-shaped *huang* ornaments. Two somewhat extraordinary finds were the discovery of two large bronze square *ting* and one bronze *li* underneath Chang-chai Nan-chieh,[25] and a cache outside the southeast corner of the city wall from which thirteen ritual bronze vessels were unearthed. This cache included the following types: large square *ting*, large round *ting*, round *ting* with flat feet and shallow body, *ku, yu, lei, tsun,* and *yü*.[26] This find was unprecedented at Cheng-chou for the great number, magnificent manufacture, and large size of the bronzes found. The biggest of the four large square *ting* is 100 centimeters high and weights 86.4 kilograms; the smallest is 87 centimeters high and weighs 64.25 kilograms. The large round *ting* is 77.3 centimeters high and weighs 33 kilograms. These square and round *ting* are the largest earlier Shang bronze ritual vessels so far known. In all likelihood these bronze ritual vessels were not made

25. Wen-wu 1975a.
26. Wen-wu 1983c.

Fig. 10. Bronze vessels from Upper Erh-li-kang stratum in Cheng-chou.

for use by ordinary slaveowners; they were probably used by nobles of the royal house of the earlier Shang dynasty (fig. 10).

In other Erh-li-kang cultural strata, which are spread over a wide area both inside and outside the Shang city walls, a great number of storage pits (caches), wells, refuse pits, ditches, and small house foundations have been excavated. Storage pits and wells are most numerous; storage pits are for the most part rectangular and straight-walled (well-shaped), but there are also a minority of oval straight-walled, round straight-walled, and irregular ones. On the walls of some storage pits and wells, steps leading alongside the walls have been uncovered. Considerable numbers of ceramic, lithic, bone, and shell artifacts as well as oracle bones were found buried in the fill of many of the excavated storage pits, wells, and ditches. Somewhat more extraordinarily, in the fill of a small number of storage pits and wells were found buried entire cattle and pig skeletons. Moreover, some complete human skeletons and human skulls were mixed into some of these storage pits and wells; in some cases the skull had become separated from the body.[27] These dead humans, disposed of and buried together with animal remains, are apparently evidence of the cruel conditions that pertained for the slaves in this slaveholding society.

Various factors indicate that the Shang city at Cheng-chou was by no means an ordinary city: the scale and the solidity of construction of the city; the fact that a palace precinct, various kinds of manufacturing sites,

27. See note 1.

and slaveowners' cemeteries were distributed inside and outside the enclosure; and especially the fabrication of large bronze vessels for the exclusive use of noble members of the royal house. Cheng-chou was most likely the site of a capital city of the earlier part of the Shang dynasty.

THE QUESTION OF IDENTITY OF THE SHANG CITY AT CHENG-CHOU

We have arrived at the point where it is proper to ask: which earlier Shang capital was the Cheng-chou Shang city? On the basis of the record in *Shih Chi: Yin Pen-chi*, the Shang dynasty from its founding by Ch'eng T'ang 成湯 to the last ruler King Chòu 紂 comprised seventeen generations and thirty-one kings. During this time, the capital was located in six places: "T'ang initially resided at Po," "Ti Chung Ting 帝仲丁 moved to Ao 隞 (also written as 囂)," "Ho T'an Chia 河亶甲 moved to Hsiang 相," "Tsu Yi 祖乙 moved to Hsing 邢" (also written as Keng 耿), "Nan Keng 南庚 moved to Yen 奄," and "P'an Keng 盤庚 moved to Yin 殷." We believe that these records are trustworthy. But the location of these six capital sites is unknown, with the exception of the P'an Keng's capital of Yin, which ample archaeological evidence has proved to have been the site of Yin-hsü at An-yang. Even though some textual references and traditions pertain to the locations of the five others, they have not yet been substantiated by archaeological evidence. To which earlier Shang capital site, then, does the walled enclosure of Cheng-chou belong? There are two current hypotheses. According to one, it is the site of Chung Ting's new capital of Ao;[28] the other says that it is the site of T'ang's initial capital of Po.[29] Earlier researchers have all come to the conclusion that the site of Ao was within present-day Cheng-chou city. The *Shu Hsu* 書序 says: "Chung Ting moved to Hsiao 囂." Ao 隞 and Hsiao 囂 have the same sound, and Li Tao-yüan in his notes on the *Chi Shui* chapter of *Shui Ching* says: "The Chi 濟 River, flowing east, passes north of the mountain to Ao Shan 敖山.... On this mountain, there is a walled city, namely the place to which Ti Chung Ting of the Yin dynasty moved." *K'uo Ti Chih* says: "The ancient city of Hsing-yang 滎陽 is seventeen *li* southwest of Hsing-tse-hsien near Cheng-chou; it is the place of the Ao of Yin dynasty." In Sui and T'ang times, the "Ao Granary 敖倉" was constructed within the confines of present-day Cheng-chou

---

28. See note 19.
29. Tsou 1980.

city. This indicates that Ao was named after the mountain Ao Shan. And Ao Shan should have been within the confines of present-day Cheng-chou city. As to the location of Chung Ting's new capital site of Ao, according to available archaeological information from the present-day metropolitan district of Cheng-chou, since the Cheng-chou Shang city is the largest site, and at its center there is located a *hang-t'u* walled enclosure dating to earlier Shang times and containing both inside and out a large number of remains of all kinds, the preconditions for the location of a capital city have been met and have been perfectly substantiated by hard archaeological evidence. And Chung Ting's move to Ao also happened exactly in the early Middle Shang period! On the principle that one should combine archaeological and textual evidence, we believe it is highly likely that the Cheng-chou Shang city is the site of Ao. We also believe that future discoveries at the Cheng-chou Shang city site will confirm that it was indeed the site of the early Middle Shang capital of Ao. Such discoveries will surely provide even more evidence that will elucidate some of the important problems of early Middle Shang history.

3

The Shang Dynasty Cemetery System

Yang Hsi-chang

A cemetery system is the rules by which each kind of burial is interred within a specified area of land. Life below ground reflects life above ground. Having thoroughly understood an ancient burial, one may figure out the status, position, and wealth of the deceased; moreover, having thoroughly understood a cemetery system, one can figure out the society, the relations of property, of descent, and of kinship of the people of the time.

Archaeologists have verified that Shang was the first monarchical slave state in Chinese history. Over the past several decades, Shang architectural remains and burial sites have been discovered in many places; of these, some were burial groups, such as those at Liu-li-ko in Hui Hsien, Hou-li at Lo-shan, Kao-ch'eng's T'ai-hsi, and Yin-hsü at An-yang. Yin-hsü at An-yang was the area directly under the Shang king's control; T'ai-hsi and Hou-li, among others, were places controlled by local nobles.

Having begun in 1928, excavation at the site of Yin-hsü has now been under way for more than fifty years. During the ten years from 1928 to 1937, more than ten large tombs and more than one thousand sacrificial pits were excavated at the royal burial grounds at Hsi-pei-kang. At places like Hsiao-t'un, Ta-ssu-k'ung-ts'un, and Hou-kang, many Shang dynasty tombs were excavated. In the last thirty years at Hsiao-t'un, Hsi-pei-kang, Ta-ssu-k'ung-ts'un, Hou-kang, and Miao-p'u, as well as in the western sectors of Yin-hsü (west of Hsiao-min-t'un and Pai-chia-chuang, south of Pei-hsin-chuang and north of Mei-yüan-chuang), Shang burials totaling approximately 2,500 tombs have been excavated. T'ai-hsi and Hou-li are cemetery grounds that have been discovered in recent years; compared with Yin-hsü, there is less material forthcoming from these sites.

The cemetery areas at Yin-hsü can be divided into the royal tomb district, lineage burial grounds, and slave burial sites. In other locations, only lineage burial grounds and aristocratic lineage burial grounds have been discovered to date.

THE ROYAL CEMETERY AT HSI-PEI-KANG

Located on the north bank of the Huan River, on slightly elevated terrain, Hsi-pei-kang of Yin-hsü is the site of the Shang dynasty royal tombs. Facing the palace grounds of Hsiao-t'un across the river, it occupies an area about 450 meters long from east to west and about 250 meters wide from north to south and divides into two sections, one on the east and one of the west.[1] In the western section are seven large tombs with four tomb ramps each and one unfinished tomb; in the east are one large tomb with four tomb ramps, three large tombs with two tomb ramps, and one large tomb with one tomb ramp.[2] In the vicinity of the large tombs in the eastern sector there are also a great number of sacrificial pits. Based on work of the past few years, no additional large-scale tombs such as the twelve mentioned above (see fig. 11) have been found, only a large number of sacrificial pits.

The eight tombs with four tomb ramps were all rather large in scale. The shape of their funerary chambers was either cross-shaped (like the character *ya* 亞) or rectangular-shaped earth pits (M 1400, M 1001, and M 1217 had cross-shaped ones, while the rest were rectangular). On each of the four sides of the funerary chambers there extended a sloping ramp (in the case of six of these tombs, all four ramps were sloping; only M 1002 and M 1217 had sloping ramps to the south, while their other three ramps to the east, west, and north were in the form of stairways). In the largest of the tombs, M 1217, the area of the entire funerary chamber was 330 square meters;[3] this amounts to more than 160 times the size of the commonly encountered Shang rectangular, vertical-shaft type tomb, which generally had an area of only about two square meters.

1. C. Li 1977: 74–94; H. H. Hu 1955: 74–97.
2. Yang and Yang 1977: 13–14.
3. Liang and Kao 1968.

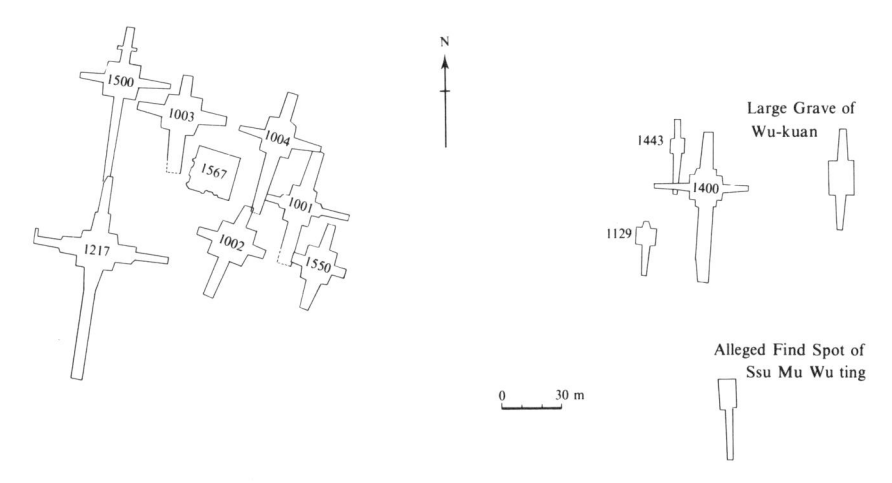

Fig. 11. Layout of large graves of Hsi-pei-kang.

The large tombs of Hsi-pei-kang have been opened and plundered more than once. Only a few articles of overlooked loot remain: the huge Cow and Deer square *ting* caldrons, the exquisite marble sculptures, numerous white pottery vessels, the sets of bronze helmets, and the bundles of *ko* halberds and *mao* lances. Other burial sites at Yin-hsü have yielded nothing that can compare with these artifacts.

The large tombs of Hsi-pei-kang do not necessarily all belong to kings; perhaps only those eight large tombs which have four tomb ramps are of sufficient scale and format to be called royal tombs. The other four, having only one or two ramps and being of smaller scale, are perhaps those belonging to the spouses of the kings or to some other noble personage.

We have previously divided Yin-hsü culture into four periods, based on the typology of excavated artifacts and on relationships of stratigraphic correlation. The first period corresponds approximately to the early part of King Wu Ting's reign and even earlier; the second period is approximately equivalent to the latter part of Wu Ting's reign and to the reigns of Tsu Keng and Tsu Chia. The third period is around the time of Lin Hsin, K'ang Ting, Wu Yi, and Wen Ting; the fourth covers approximately the reigns of Ti Yi and Ti Hsin. Based on formal criteria which can be applied to the funerary articles from the eight large tombs with four ramps each in Hsi-pei-kang, three of the tombs are datable to Period II (M 1001, M 1550, and M 1400), four correspond to Period III (M 1002,

M 1004, M 1217, and M 1500), and one to Period IV (M 1003). There are no Period I tombs.[4]

In the distribution of royal tombs in Hsi-pei-kang there is a definite layout. The large tombs are in the western sector, while the sacrificial pits are in the eastern sector. Among the eight large tombs in the western sector there is no stratigraphic overlapping of the funerary chambers at the base, except where tomb ramps are disturbed by overlying ramps. The eight tombs can be divided into four groups, with each group having two members, a northern and a southern tomb. The tombs to the south are later than those to the north. M 1001 is north of M 1550; the western tomb ramps of M 1550 overlies the southern ramp of M 1001. M 1004 is north of M 1002; the northern ramp of M 1002 overlies the southern ramp of M 1004. M 1500 is north of M 1217; the northern ramp of M 1217 has disturbed the southern ramp of M 1500. To the south of M 1300 is M 1567. The latter is a tomb whose construction was not completed; following the example of the first three groups, M 1567 should be later than M 1003. M 1003 is of the fourth Yin-hsü period, and M 1567 should also belong to Period IV, being later than M 1003. Corresponding to Period IV are the reigns of Ti Yi and Ti Hsin. In this way, we can infer that M 1567 was to be the tomb of Ti Hsin. The tombs of Shang kings were probably constructed while their owners were living; before his tomb was completed, Ti Hsin had already perished in the overthrow of his regime, so he was not buried in this tomb.

To the eight tombs of the western section should be added M 1400 of the eastern sector to make a total of nine tombs. From Wu Ting to Ti Hsin there were exactly nine kings.

The eastern sector was the ceremonial area where Shang kings made sacrifices to their ancestors. It can be divided into northern and southern portions. The southern portion is completely made up of sacrificial pits. The northern part can be divided into three zones. The easternmost zone is the large tomb section, which includes M 1400 and the large grave of Wu-kuan. The central zone is a section of sacrificial pits, and the western zone is an empty sector. According to criteria such as distances between graves and pits, the size of the pit opening, and the burial situation inside the pits, these pits can be differentiated into a large number of groups; some groups consist of one row of pits, some consist of several rows. The sacrificial pits of a single group probably belong to the same

4. H. C. Yang 1981.

occasion of ceremonial activity. The overwhelming majority of the sacrificial pits are laid out with their axis running north and south; they are arranged neatly and do not disturb any other pits. Sacrificial pits with east-west axis are rare, and they disturb the pits which run north and south; therefore we can infer that pits that are oriented east-west are later than the ones oriented north-south in this particular burial sequence. The small graves of Hsi-pei-kang are not necessarily all sacrificial pits. Some may be auxiliary graves.

Although none of the large tombs at Hsi-pei-kang is from the first period, some of the smaller graves, such as Wu-kuan 59M1, are.[5] As has been explained, Period I corresponds to the early part of Wu Ting's reign and even earlier. Among the funerary pottery vessels in Wu-kuan 59M1, the pottery *kuei* is a classic example of a Period I vessel, but the pottery *li* already approaches the style of Period II. For this reason, this tomb ought to be dated to the late phases of Period I; it probably corresponds to the early part of Wu Ting's reign. No grave earlier than Wu-kuan 59M1 has yet been found at Hsi-pei-kang. Thus we infer that the sacrificial pits at Hsi-pei-kang began to be used in the early part of Wu Ting's reign.

In the Yin-hsü area, besides the royal tomb area of Hsi-pei-kang, there are numerous sacrificial pits in the palatial area of Hsiao-t'un. The palatial area of locus north at Hsiao-t'un can be divided into three groups: north, central, and south. In the vicinity of foundation B7 of the central group, more than one hundred sacrificial pits have been investigated. The contents and layout arrangements of these pits closely resemble those of Hsi-pei-kang. The excavators believe that these sacrificial pits are related to the religious rituals carried out in the course of construction (packing the base, laying the foundation, settling the doors, and "dedicating" *lo-ch'eng* 落成) of the buildings of foundation B7.[6] However, to judge from the articles buried in them, these sacrificial pits do not belong to the same period at all; moreover, in the vicinity of other architectural remains in locus north of Hsiao-t'un, such a large number of sacrificial pits are rarely found. For these reasons, we infer that foundation B7 was perhaps a kind of temple building.[7] These sacrificial pits are the traces of ceremonies in which human sacrifices were made to

---

5. K'ao-ku 1979c.
6. Shih 1947: 30–39.
7. K. C. Chang 1980: 95.

ancestors. They are of the same kind as the sacrificial pits at the royal tombs at Hsi-pei-kang. This indicates that only Shang kings were able to employ this kind of ritual of sacrificial pits to sacrifice to their ancestors.

The large tombs and vast numbers of sacrificial pits of Hsi-pei-kang manifest the ultimate heights of status and power reached by the Shang king, acting as "I, the unique man."

THE TOMBS OF ROYAL SPOUSES

Concerning the burial grounds of royal spouses, we are at present still in an exploratory phase.

In the eastern section of Hsi-pei-kang, there are three tombs with two tomb ramps and one with one ramp, the latter being the tomb from which the large Ssu Mu Wu *ting* caldron came. As for the dating of the Ssu Mu Wu *ting* caldron, in the past it was thought that Wen Ting had had it made for the spouse of his father, Wu Yi; however, after the tomb of Fu Hao 婦好 was discovered, and the Ssu Mu Hsin square *ting* caldron from the Fu Hao tomb was compared with it, the two *ting* caldrons were seen to be similar. Therefore, we can move up the proposed dating of the Ssu Mu Wu *ting* caldron to Period II of the Yin-hsü culture.[8] In the cyclical sacrificial calendar—which lists various rituals performed on various days to various ancestors—among the spouses of Wu Ting is one named Pi Wu 妣戊; Tsu Chia 祖甲 also had a spouse by the name of Pi Wu. For this reason, we infer that the Ssu Mu Wu *ting* caldron was perhaps made for the spouse of Wu Ting or of Tsu Chia. And since the eastern sector of Hsi-pei-kang has one tomb which belongs to a royal spouse, we infer that among the other tombs perhaps there still exist tombs of royal spouses.

The large tomb of Wu-kuan and M 1443 are both from Yin-hsü cultural Period II; the dating of M 1129 is unclear, but because the several large tombs of the eastern section are all of the second period, it is estimated that it also is of the second period. Since these tombs have all been plundered, at present we cannot draw on any excavated artifacts to determine the tomb's owners.

Although controversy still surrounds the issue of the dating and ownership of M 5, excavated in 1976 in the northwest part of Hsiao-t'un,

---

8. Tu 1980: 63–64.

THE SHANG DYNASTY CEMETERY SYSTEM

researchers believe that its owner was a royal spouse. This is at present the only tomb of a royal spouse which can be identified with certainty. In the area surrounding M 5, nine rectangular, vertical-shaft type graves of a slightly smaller scale than M 5 have been found; of these, M 17 and M 18 have been excavated.[9] The area of the funerary chamber of M 18 is comparatively large—about ten square meters plus—and features a coffin and an outer coffin chamber, with five human sacrificial victims. There are more than ninety burial articles, including twenty-four bronze vessels (five bronze *ku* 觚 and five bronze *chüeh* 爵), thirteen of which have inscriptions. On one bronze *chia* 斝 and one *tsun* 尊 are found "Tzu Yü 子漁." A bronze *hsien* 甗 carries the character 品, while another bronze, a *kuei* 殷, has the inscription "Lord 品" 品侯. Tzu Yü is one of the people whose names are commonly seen in the oracle inscriptions from the reign of Wu Ting; empowered to make offerings at the altar of the major lineage, he was a critically important member of the king's descent group. Lord 品 was one of the high-ranking officials belonging to the Shang king and often received orders from the king. Thus the owner of M 18 ought also to be a high-ranking aristocrat. Osteological reports on the human skeletal remains indicate that the owner may have been female. Based on this, we cannot eliminate the possibility that the owner of M 18 was a royal spouse. Therefore, we infer that this area was perhaps a burial ground for Shang royal spouses.

In the late period of Yin-hsü, with the expansion of the palace area, the ground for the burial site at M 5 had already become a residential sector. In the vicinity of M 5, there are quite a few architectural remains. The chamber atop M 5 suffered damage and destruction. It appears as though the people of the Shang had already forgotten that this place had been the burial area of the spouse of the former kings.

Judging from the material excavated, we surmise that the royal spouses, unlike the kings, did not have any specific burial area.

THE LINEAGE (*tsu* 族) CEMETERIES

The many tomb groups in the Yin-hsü area are lineage burial grounds. Among these, more work has been done on those in Ta-ssu-k'ung-ts'un, Hou-kang, Miao-p'u-pei-ti, and the western section of Yin-hsü.[10] The

---

9. K'ao-ku-hsüeh-pao 1981.
10. K'ao-ku-hsüeh-pao 1979.

overwhelming majority of the tombs in these cemetery sectors are rectangular, with vertical shafts, while only a small number have one or two tomb ramps.

Approximately 1,500 graves from the western area of Yin-hsü have been excavated since 1969. They can be divided into eight burial sectors; between each pair of burial sectors lies an empty area. The assemblages of pottery grave goods from each burial sector differ; bronze vessels buried in many of the graves carry lineage emblems, these being identical within a single burial sector but different from those of other burial sectors. Within a single burial area, various subsectors can be isolated, each containing within it clusters of anywhere from ten to thirty or forty tombs. As for the ritual articles placed in these tombs, less than 10 percent of the burial goods consist of bronze vessels such as *ku* and *chüeh*; of the rest, most are pottery artifacts. A small portion of the tombs are comparatively poor: some have no funerary articles except one or two cowrie shells. About one-sixth of the graves have bronze weapons interred in them; these are scattered among the various subsectors of the burial areas. Osteological findings show that the skeletal remains of the tomb owners where there are weapons buried are all male. Each burial sector represents a lineage, and each lineage has its own lineage emblem. The subsectors within a cemetery area are the burial grounds for family branches of a lineage. Within the same lineage burial ground, there are those lineage members of high position—the aristocracy—whose funerary chamber is larger and whose burial articles include more bronze vessels than the ordinary tombs. The graves of lineage members of lower position—the ordinary people, who comprise 90 percent of the occupants of the cemetery—contain no bronze goods and are small, rectangular, vertical shafts. Although the aristocracy and the ordinary people were interred in the same cemetery, they in fact belonged to different classes. The aristocracy were the rulers, while the ordinary people were exploited and enslaved.

According to ancient documents, the Yin people had lineages with various degrees or levels of organization. From *Tso Chuan*, the fourth year of Duke Ting's reign:

> Previously, when King Wu defeated the Shang, and King Ch'eng settled them, they separated a portion for the Duke of Lu, with ... six lineages of Yin people; the clan-polity (shih 氏) of T'iao, the clan-polity of Hsü, that of Hsiao, that of Su, that of Ch'ang Shao, and that of Wei Shao. [The Chou] had them lead their major masses, even to the most distantly related of them.... [The Chou] separated a portion for K'ang Shu [of Wei] with ... seven lineages of

THE SHANG DYNASTY CEMETERY SYSTEM 57

the Yin people: the clan-polity of T'ao, the clan-polity of Shih, that of Fan, that of Ch'i, that of P'an, the clan-polity of Chi, and the clan-polity of Chung K'uei.

The lineage burial grounds of Yin-hsü reflect the principle of the Yin people of amassing by lineages and residing together while living and of putting lineages together in burial after death. However, at present it is difficult for us to ascertain from the eight burial groups in the western sector of Yin-hsü which degree or level of the Yin people's lineage organization corresponds to which rank at the lineage burial grounds.

From the lineage emblems, we know that there were some lineages whose original clan name (*hsing* 姓) differed from the Shang king's, while others possessed the same clan name. For example, the lineage emblem in the seventh sector is ейн. In Wu Ting's time, there was a Lady 員 (婦 員), with a different clan name from the Shang king. This is a clan and lineage with a different clan name. In the first burial sector, a lineage emblem on a bronze vessel is Tzu Wei 子韋, and in the eighth burial sector there is a Tzu 狀 (子狀). Tzu Wei and Tzu 狀 are seen in the oracle bone inscriptions of the Wu Ting period; they are both agnatic relations of the Shang king and are among the many Tzu lineages. In the twelfth year of Duke Hsiang in the *Tso Chuan*, we read:

> [Members of] the same clan 同姓 gather at the temple of the distant ancestor 宗廟; [members of] the major line [the corporate unit of investiture] 同宗 gather at the temple of the founding ancestor 祖廟; [members of] the same lineage 同族 gather at the temple of the fathers 禰廟.

"Clan" (*hsing*), "major line" (*tsung*), and "lineage" (*tsu*) express differences in kin distance. Based on this, Tzu Wei and Tzu 狀 are in the same clan as the Shang king; so among each of the small graves in a burial sector there ought to be a relationship of identity of lineage (*t'ung tsu* 同族).

The lineage burial grounds of Yin-hsü reflect not only the descent relations and kinship organization of the Yin people, but also their socioeconomic and rank system. In the burial grounds, the following factors can reflect the circumstances of status, rank, and wealth of the tomb owner in life: the form of burial, the size of the funerary chamber, the existence or lack of a coffin and coffin chamber, the types and amount of grave goods, and the existence or lack of human sacrificial burials. The nearly 1,000 graves discovered from 1969 to 1977 at the lineage burial ground in the western sector of Yin-hsü can be roughly divided into five types: (1) 5 tombs with one tomb ramp each, thus forming a shape like the character *chia* 甲. All have been plundered; all contain coffins and other chambers and numerous human sacrificial victims, chariot-and-horse fittings, and bronze vessels; (2) approximately 20 rectangular, vertical-shaft tombs with funerary chambers of an area of five to ten square meters. They have coffins and outer chambers and bronze ritual vessels; most have human sacrificial victims; (3) approximately 50 to 60 rectangular, vertical-shaft type tombs with funerary chambers of an area around three square meters. The grave goods number relatively few bronze ritual vessels; only a few of these tombs have outer coffin chambers or human sacrificial victims; (4) about 750 of the graves are rectangular, vertical-shaft type with funerary chambers of an area about two square meters. They contain coffins but no outer coffin chambers and have only pottery vessels, no bronze ritual vessels or human sacrificial victims; (5) about one-tenth of the graves are small, with no grave goods; some of these are not even outfitted with a coffin.

Although the lineage cemeteries at Yin-hsü were based on kinship relations, and people of differing statuses and wealth were buried in the same grounds, the aristocracy nevertheless had burial grounds for their family branches. Some of the larger tombs are clustered together, separated from the other groups of small tombs by some distance. For example, in the western sector of Yin-hsü, four graves with one tomb ramp each in the third burial sector are arranged side by side (M 698, M 699, M 700, and M 701). In the tomb ramp of M 698 are a chariot and a horse. In the seventh burial sector, tomb M 93 has one tomb ramp; to its west there are one rectangular, vertical-shaft type tomb whose funerary chamber has an area of ten square meters as well as two burial pits for chariots and horses and one burial pit for a horse. Some researchers have called the Hou-kang burial sector excavated in 1971 an aristocratic burial area; actually, it is a lineage burial ground.[11] Here, there are three groups of burials arranged parallel to each other from east to west; among the burials in the western group are four tombs with two tomb ramps each, one tomb with one tomb ramp, and many rectangular, vertical-shaft tombs whose areas are rather large. Of these burials, about one-half have human sacrificial victims. The human sacrificial victims here constituted 90 percent of the number for the entire area. This was a burial ground for an aristocratic family branch (*chia tsu* 家族). The tombs of the middle

11. K'ao-ku 1972a.

and eastern groups were all rectangular, vertical-shaft type graves, with a smaller area for their funerary chambers. Only three tombs had any sacrificial victims, and there were few grave goods. These are probably burials belonging to commoners. The evidence provided by these burial areas reflects the fact that a difference in wealth and nobility existed between family branches within the same lineage.

It is not only the case that the burial areas of each family segment within the same cemetery exhibit differences of status between them; quite noticeable differences exist also between individual lineage burial areas. The status of some lineages was high, of others, low. For example, as explained above, the cemetery at Hou-kang has four large tombs with two tomb ramps each, one with one tomb ramp, and many rectangular, vertical-shaft type graves with human sacrificial victims. In comparison, the burial area at Miao-p'u-pei-ti appears impoverished. Among more than one hundred graves excavated from 1962 to 1964 none had tomb ramps, all are rectangular, vertical-shaft graves, only two had bronze vessels among the grave goods, and none had human sacrificial victims. In most of the graves there are only a few pottery vessels and a few cowrie shells.

There are many differing explanations for the social identity of the "masses" *chung* 衆 or "people of the masses" *chung jen* 衆人, words found in oracle bone script. I agree with the argument that says that "masses" or "people of the masses" were members of village communities (*ts'un she* 村社). They had a lineage form of social organization, were broken down into units of one hundred families, and were under the leadership of a lineage head. Massed together for the king, they would clear wilderness, plant millet, go to war, hunt, and carry out labor corvée; they would also participate in religious activities internal to their lineages. They were at once the essential producers for the society of the Shang dynasty and the essential martial force behind the military activities carried out by the Shang king. They were not slaves.[12]

If the situation of the commoners—the owners of the large numbers of rectangular, vertical-shaft graves without bronze burial goods—is compared with the situation of the "masses" or "people of the masses" in the oracle bone records, their background social identities are equivalent. For this reason, we infer that the owners of this type of tomb are the "masses" or "people of the masses" of the oracle bone writings.

12. C. L. Chang 1973; F. H. Chu 1981.

SLAVE CEMETERIES

In general, when slaves in the Yin dynasty are discussed, they are usually connected with the sacrificial victims in the graves. There certainly were slaves among the human sacrificial victims in the tombs; however, they were not all slaves. The human sacrifices in the large tombs of Hsi-pei-kang sometimes were of a rather high aristocratic background. Conversely, burial sites for slaves were not always in or near the tombs of aristocrats or slave masters; those slaves who had not been used to accompany others' burials or for human sacrifice had their own places for burial.

In the layers of dirt and in the ash pits in the sites of the western part of Hsiao-t'un, of Ta-ssu-k'ung-ts'un, and Miao-p'u-pei-ti, we often discover human skeletons without any grave pit. The overwhelming majority of these human skeletons have no burial accessories; only exceptionally are there traces of wooden frames, of mat, and of hemp cloth. Mostly their burial posture is fully extended, either face up or face down; a minority are flexed. A small number of the skeletons are missing an upper arm or have had a lower leg severed. Judging from the burial posture, one gathers that most are regular burials rather than forced deaths. The overwhelming majority of the skeletons have no grave goods by their side; only exceptionally will there be a pottery *li* vessel, a stone sickle, one or two sea cowries, or even an ornament like a jade tube.

We infer that these skeletons without burial pits were slaves, some of whom worked in field production and some of whom were favored domestic servants who waited on their masters. They had lost the means of production; while living they had nothing, and after death, having no burial pit, no burial accessories, and no grave goods, they were casually covered over with dirt or with ash in ash pits.

Such types of graves are found only in the middle of dwelling sites; they have never been discovered in the lineage cemeteries of the western section of Yin-hsü. Becoming slaves, these people lost all connections with their own clans and lineages, so they could not be buried in their lineage cemeteries. This kind of situation has been recorded in ethnographic documents. The Maori of New Zealand believe that once a person becomes a slave, he no longer receives the protection of the community spirits; the residents of his former tribal settlement no longer recognize him as the same kind of being as them. He has lost all right to membership in his clan and lineage.[13] Among the Indians of Alaska, a slave after death has no rights to enjoy the burial ceremonies of a free man, so his corpse is thrown into the ocean.[14]

SHANG BURIALS OUTSIDE YIN-HSÜ

Based on the nature of the burial grounds, the Shang dynasty burial groups which have been found in regions outside the capital city of Yin-hsü can be divided into two types: the lineage cemetery and the aristocratic burial grounds.

The burial ground at T'ai-hsi 台西, in Kao-ch'eng 藁城, Hopei, about 250 kilometers north of An-yang, is a lineage cemetery.[15] Here, more than 110 graves were cleared, some of them arranged rather densely, clustered together. The great majority were small-scale, rectangular, vertical-shaft graves about two meters long and more or less a meter wide; only a small number of pottery vessels or ornaments were placed as grave goods in each grave. Other than these, there were five slightly larger tombs which contained not only human sacrificial victims, but also bronze vessels such as *chia*, *ku*, and *chüeh*. The date of this burial ground corresponds approximately to the early period on Yin-hsü. The densely arranged areas within the burial grounds were places for the interment of members of family branches, both ordinary people and aristocrats. However, judging from the format of burial and the bronze vessels serving as grave goods, one supposes that the position of the aristocrats really was not very high. The characteristics of this burial area are similar to those of the lineage burial grounds at Yin-hsü.

The cemetery at Hou-li 後李 in Lo-shan 羅山, Honan, about 475 kilometers south of An-yang, is an aristocratic burial ground.[16] Within a space of one hundred meters long by about thirty meters wide, seventeen Shang burials were excavated. The funerary chambers in these were comparatively large; sixteen were rectangular, vertical-shaft graves, while one had a tomb ramp. Each tomb had bronze vessels as grave goods, from as few as two to as many as seventeen. There was also a great quantity of bronze weapons, tools, and jade ornaments. In M 8 there

13. Lowie 1920.
14. Averkieva 1961.
15. Hopei Province Museum 1977: 14–27.
16. K'ao-ku 1981a; Chung-yüan-wen-wu 1981.

were human sacrificial victims, two in the fill and two atop the outer coffin shell. Twenty-three bronze vessels from seven tombs bore identical lineage emblems. No small-scale, rectangular, vertical-shaft graves were discovered in this burial ground. The dating of this cemetery, which was the burial ground for a family branch of local feudal lords, corresponds to cultural Periods II–IV of Yin-hsü. This sort of burial area has not been discovered at Yin-hsü.

THE SHANG BURIALS AND SHANG SOCIETY

The slave system of the Shang dynasty was founded upon the level of production of the Bronze Age. In accordance with the essential economic division of the Bronze Age, agricultural production has as implements stone, wooden, bone, and shell tools, etc. Such forces of production could contribute very much surplus labor only through massed teamwork under the coercive supervision of slave masters. The contemporary forces of production still did not have the means of fulfilling all the conditions for using slave labor on a massive scale, so great numbers of war prisoners could be killed off as sacrificial victims in ceremonies. The essential producers in the society were still the common members of village communities. Given the conditions of production in the Bronze Age, the slave system could only be one that is widely found among agricultural communes.

Despotism was made possible through the widespread existence of agricultural communes. The rulers of the Shang dynasty used the indigenous village community organization, reorganized it by lineage forms, and made it over into a small, enslaved group subjected to exploitation. The supposedly free members of village communities became the disguised slaves of a dictatorship.

Although agricultural communes already are a form of territorial government organization, descent relationships were tenaciously conserved. The branching lineage system was developed out of such kinds of descent relationships. The rulers of the Shang dynasty transformed these into a political organization which would maintain their own rule; political and lineage authority were synthesized into one. The Shang monarchy thus resembled a suprasegmental lineage: many aristocrats from many centers and localities, whether bearing the same clan name or a different clan name, all served as subjects to the Shang king; thus the king was like the lineage head of a large lineage. In the same way, local feudal lords were the lineage heads of all the aristocratic slave masters within their territorial spheres of authority. Within every feudally invested lineage, there were strictly demarcated rank relations; the lineage head was thus the master of the lineage as well as the ruler in terms of political authority, and the ordinary people and the slaves were the ruled ones.

The cemeteries of the Shang dynasty reflect the classes, ranks, descent, and kinship categories of this kind of slave system and branching lineage society. The Shang kings were the highest rulers, towering over everything and the possessors of all; in the land which they directly controlled, there existed for them alone a burial ground, a special way of burial, and special funeral rituals. Other people within the network of a branching system of descent were buried in lineage cemeteries, without discriminating differences of rank and wealth in choice of site. However, within a lineage cemetery, aristocratic slave masters had their own plots for their family branches, along with a way of burial, presence of grave goods, and funerary ceremonial, all of which corresponded to their personal position and indicated that their special status was higher than that of other members of the lineage. As for the local feudal lords, within their territorial spheres of authority they were like kings of small monarchies, occupying the highest position of the aristocracy; therefore, their lineage branch had its own burial grounds, and the other lineages, irrespective of their position and rank, were all buried in a lineage cemetery. Having lost all rights, the slaves were buried in layers of dirt or in ash pits in the vicinity of residential foundations, without any grave pit and with few burial accessories or grave goods.

4

Yin-hsü Tomb Number Five
and the Question of
the P'an Keng/Hsiao Hsin/Hsiao Yi
Period in Yin-hsü Archaeology

K. C. Chang

If Tomb Number Five at Yin-hsü is that of Fu Hao, royal consort of King Wu Ting, as most students of the matter believe it is,[1] then its abundant artifactual remains (including bronzes, jades, and pottery) may serve as chronological markers for the period of King Wu Ting and the kings who immediately preceded and followed him in the archaeology of Yin-hsü. Having these markers, we are in a position to study the history of change of the Shang civilization during its 273 years at Yin-hsü according to typology, stratigraphy, and data on absolute chronology. This, in my opinion, is the main significance of the excavation and study of Yin-hsü Tomb Number Five.

On the basis of the excavated materials from Tomb Five and Tombs 17 and 18,[2] as well as a comparison of the artifacts taken from them with those from the "royal tombs" at Hsi-pei-kang excavated before the war,[3] we have learned that at the time of the Shang's arrival at Yin-hsü to establish their royal capital there their material culture was characterized by the following features:

1. Divination by bones and by turtle shells and inscriptions on them. By King Wu Ting's period—Period I of Tung Tso-pin[4]—all the essential

---

1. K'ao-ku 1977b; Chung-kuo-she-hui-k'o-hsüeh-yüan K'ao-ku-yen-chiu-so 1980a: 224–28.
2. K'ao-ku-hsüeh-pao 1981.
3. Liang and Kao 1962–76.
4. Tung 1933.

characteristics of the oracle bone inscriptions of the Yin-hsü had been developed. Even though no inscribed oracle bones were found in Tomb Five, the inscriptions on the bronzes found in the tomb contain the name of Fu Hao (Hou Hsin), whose activities are seen frequently in Period I inscriptions. The same is true for the name Tzu Yü in the inscriptions on bronzes found in Tomb 18.

2. The decorative designs on the bronze vessels were fully developed and often cover a major part of the vessels; the animals and birds in the designs had been clearly separated from the background spirals. In the classificatory scheme of Max Loehr,[5] these designs are classifiable as Styles IV and V.

3. Bronzes were increasingly inscribed, but the inscriptions are largely limited to societal emblems and ancestral "dedications." The latter were sometimes considered to be a late Yin-hsü feature,[6] but the ancestral name found in Tomb Five (Hou Hsin) indicates that their use can be pushed back at least to King Wu Ting's period. Longer, narrative inscriptions, however, still appear to be confined to the late Yin-hsü period.

4. According to the four-stage classification of Yin-hsü ceramics widely adopted in recent years,[7] the period of Shang cultures represented by Tomb Five corresponds to Period II. Few ceramic remains came to light in Tomb Five itself, but a pottery *chüeh*-tripod found there "has the typical characteristics of Period II culture of Yin-hsü."[8] "The pottery buried" in Tombs 17 and 18 also "belongs to Period II in the four-period scheme."[9] Period II pottery has the following characteristics:

> There are two kinds of *li*-tripods: one somewhat rectangular in body shape, deep, with shorter legs than previously, and the other smallish, more straight-walled, decorated with attached rings. The second kind is fewer. The body of the *kuei* is more constricted than previously, with small and slightly flared ring-foot, string designs on the surface, flat inside surface of the rim, and a ring of incised line along the rim. Most *tou* are of two kinds: one, derived from the previous period, has deeper basin, obscure angle at the rim, and smaller ring-foot, and the other, seen more frequently, has shallow basin, flat rim, and small and tall ring-foot. *Ku* and *chüeh* tripods are seen mostly in burials. The body of the *ku* is bigger and more massive in general, and the

5. Loehr 1953.
6. Kane 1973.
7. Tsou 1964; Chung-kuo-she-hui-k'o-hsüeh-yüan K'ao-ku-yen-chiu-so 1980a: 221–24.
8. Chung-kuo-she-hui-k'o-hsüeh-yüan K'ao-ku-yen-chiu-so 1980a: 219, 225.
9. K'ao-ku-hsüeh-pao 1981.

chüeh has a big and roundish body, broad and short spout. The spout was apparently formed by stretching the rim, and a clay dot is placed on the spout at each side.[10]

5. The opening at the top of Tomb Five was covered by a rammed earth foundation, possibly the base of a sacrificial altar. The association of rammed earth foundation with this tomb is consistent with its dating from the period of Yin-hsü history characterized by the rammed earth house foundations in ground-house architecture. Shih Chang-ju's judgment according to stratigraphy and location of inscribed oracle bones of the various periods is that the Northern Group of house foundations at Hsiao-t'un was the first to be built here, probably around the time of King Wu Ting. In fact, in his view, rammed earth house foundations began to be built at Yin-hsü only after the Shang had established their royal capital here. Before that, even though there were Shang people at Hsiao-t'un, they built only semisubterranean houses.[11]

6. Even though Tomb Five is located at Hsiao-t'un, the artifacts it has yielded are fundamentally identical with the artifacts excavated from the earlier of the "royal tombs" at Hsi-pei-kang (such as Tomb 1001), and we can state with confidence that the period of Tomb Five is a period during which "large tombs" were built. The so-called large tombs are those of large scale in construction and furnishing, with two or four ramps leading from the ground to the floor of the tomb. Tomb Five had no ramp; its scale—looked at from the perspective of construction, sacrificial humans, and buried objects—is large enough, but the type of tomb it represents—pit graves lined with wooden chambers—was quite common at Hsiao-t'un before the Tomb Five period; large tombs with ramps, however, were new.

The Shang civilization complete with the above features appeared for the first time in ancient China in the period of Tomb Five. Inasmuch as Tomb Five marks the level of Shang civilization reached around the time of King Wu Ting, the hypothesis that the Tomb Five period represents the beginning of the period when the Shang capital was located at Yin-hsü would be consistent with the actual conditions of Chinese archaeology in general. On this point ancient China scholars do not disagree. What I wish to bring up for discussion has to do with the nature of Yin-hsü prior to the period represented by Tomb Five. As far as the neolithic

---

10. Cheng and Ch'en 1981: 513–14.
11. Shih 1969; Shih 1955; C. Li 1977: 103–04.

and later periods are concerned, the ancient cultures in the An-yang area prior to the Tomb Five period can be grouped into three stages: (1) Yang-shao culture (Hou-kang phase, Ta-ssu-k'ung-ts'un phase); (2) Lung-shan culture (Ta-han phase); and (3) Shang culture prior to the Tomb Five period. The existence and interrelationship of these cultures have been established ever since the 1931 excavation at Hou-kang.[12] There may be a number of controversial issues pertaining to many chronological segments, but I would like to concentrate on the third of the above cultures, namely, the Shang culture before the Tomb Five period.

The bulk of the material that has been brought to light by archaeologists at Yin-hsü in the last five plus decades is dated to the period of Tomb Five and the periods subsequent to it, namely, the period of time represented by the five periods of the oracle bone inscriptions. On the other hand, Shang cultural data at Yin-hsü earlier than the Tomb Five period are scarce and scattered. A Yin-hsü-wide, detailed cultural stratigraphy is still difficult to formulate because the material excavated before the war has yet to be reported in full, but new material discovered since the war is also confined to a very few individual loci. From what I have knowledge of from published data, the major sites where pre-Tomb Five period Shang material is available include the following:

1. Architectural Remains at Hsiao-t'un before the Rammed Earth House Foundations

In the history of the settlement at Hsiao-t'un, intermediate between the semisubterranean pits of the Lung-shan culture and the rammed earth house foundations of the Tomb Five and the subsequent periods, there was a phase of Shang civilization characterized by subterranean or semisubterranean houses and pits and by a system of water ditches. Because the remains of the underground pits at Hsiao-t'un have not yet been fully described in publications, we have no detailed information about these early houses. According to a recent statement by Shih Chang-ju, "the water ditches (at Hsiao-t'un) are the remains of a drainage system during the period of the pit houses and storage pits."[13] If this was the case it stands to reason that the area of the ditches should largely coincide with the area of the Hsiao-t'un settlement prior to the building

---

12. Liang 1933.
13. Shih 1969: 141.

of the rammed earth house foundations. The area of the water ditches is known: about 170 meters long N–S and 90 meters wide E–W.[14] The remains of the pit houses are said to be strewn along both sides of the water ditches,[15] forming a village of considerable size. The houses may cluster into discrete groups, perhaps accommodating lineage groups, similar to the clusters of burials in a cemetery of later date in the western part of Yin-hsü.[16] "To give an example: the area in Hsiao-t'un most densely packed with pit houses was the southwestern portion of area C: a section of water ditch and forty-seven pits of various sizes are found in an area 20 meters long N–S and 18 meters wide E–W. These pits cluster in four or five groups, each consisting of a large pit house and several smaller pits."[17] Taking this area as an example of the whole, the Hsiao-t'un village at the time could have had some two hundred pit houses. "These pit houses are for the most part large and shallow, with fairly straight walls ... and ramps or stairs leading up to the ground. Comparing the diameters with the depths of these pits we find that in most cases the diameter and the depth are equal. Only rarely is the depth greater than the diameter. According to the shape of the pit and the position of the stairs, six types are recognized: round, with stairs along the side; round, with a stair in the middle; oval, with stairs on one side; oval, with stairs on two sides; oval, with stairs in the middle; square, with stairs on the side.... These pits were probably covered with a roof."[18]

In Li Chi's *Illustrated Corpus of Yin-hsü Pottery* we find nine whole pottery vessels illustrated which bear field numbers that indicate provenance in the above-described cluster of forty-seven pits in area C of Hsiao-t'un, including a *li*-tripod from YH 190, a *kuei*-vessel from YH 302, a *yü*-vessel from YH 285, and a flat-base pot from YH 272.[19] Measured by the four-period classification mentioned above, all of these vessels evidently belong to Period I. Period I pottery remains were brought to light also in 1973 from ash pits at Hsiao-t'un Locus South,[20] suggesting that the Shang occupation of that period in Hsiao-t'un had extended further

14. Shih 1959: 203.
15. Ibid., 268.
16. K'ao-ku-hsüeh-pao 1979: 113–17.
17. Shih 1955: 167.
18. Ibid., 131–36.
19. C. Li 1956.
20. K'ao-ku 1975.

to the south. In short, stratigraphically speaking, there is considerable correlative relationship between the Hsiao-t'un before the rammed earth house foundations and Period I pottery.

2. Earlier Shang Tombs in Hsiao-t'un (M 188, 232, 333, 388)

Shih Chang-ju theorizes that all the Hsiao-t'un tombs excavated before the war were functionally related to the house foundations and that their dating must be correlated with the latter also. He believes that the Northern Group of house foundations was the earliest, the Middle Group next in time, and the Southern Group the latest. Consequently, all the tombs within the Middle Group he sees as Middle Yin-hsü period in date, and all the tombs within the Southern Group he sees as late Yin-hsü in date.[21] However, some of the tombs in both Middle and Southern Groups were quite unattached to any of the house foundations and were spatially independent. Some of them have yielded bronze vessels in their remains, which in both form and decorative style resemble more the bronze vessels of Middle Shang found in Cheng-chou and Hui-hsien than the common Yin-hsü types. For these reasons some students of Yin-hsü history have proposed to take these tombs out of the complex of house foundations, believing that instead they contain remains from an earlier period at Hsiao-t'un.[22] Detailed reports of all of the tombs have been made available during the last three decades,[23] furnishing us with important new information. On the basis of these reports, one is confident of the early dating of four of these tombs: M 188 and M 232 in the Middle Group and M 333 and M 388 of the Southern Group.

The four tombs all belong to the common Chinese Bronze Age type in construction with vertical pit and wooden chamber. None had ramps, but all had sacrificial humans and dogs. In these respects they are not unlike Tomb Five, but in the artifacts they have yielded they differ. Among the bronze vessels found in these tombs, the most common types include the *tsun*-beaker of medium mouth and wide shoulders, *p'ou*-urn, *ku*-cup with large flare mouth, *chia*-tripod with flat or roundish base, and *ting*-tripod with deep body, round bottom, and conical legs. Compared with those of Tomb Five, their decorative designs are characterized by much less clear separation of animal and background spirals. This

21. Shih 1959.
22. Tsou 1964; Kane 1975.
23. Shih 1970–80.

indefinite separation places them in Loehr's Styles I, II, III, which separates them from Tomb Five but groups them closer to the Middle Shang bronzes from Pai-chia-chuang of Cheng-chou, Liu-li-ko of Hui-hsien, and P'an-lung-ch'eng of Huang-p'i. Very few pottery vessels were found in these tombs. For dating purposes the most useful are the two pottery *tou* from M 388, which have shallow dish and rim beveled outward, characteristic modes of Period 1.[24] Both *tou* have on the inside of the ring-foot an incised character, *yüeh* ("ax").

3. An Earlier Shang Tomb at Wu-kuan-ts'un Locus North

This tomb was excavated in 1959 in the eastern sector of the Hsi-pei-kang Royal Cemetery but was not reported until 1979.[25] Again the tomb is of vertical pit and wooden chamber construction, and it has sacrificial humans and dogs and a "waist pit." Among the artifacts found in the grave are sixteen bronzes and eight pottery vessels. Including such types as *p'ou*, *li*, *ting*, *chüeh*, and *ko*-halberd, the bronzes resemble those of the earlier tombs of Hsiao-t'un in both form and decoration but differ markedly from Tomb Five. Of the pottery, "its *li* and *kuei* are of typical Period I types, similar to those found in the storage pits of Early Hsiao-t'un Locus South (H 13) and stratum 1 of Ta-ssu-k'ung-ts'un (H 17). The bronze *p'ou*, *ku*, and *ko*-halberd with musical-stone-shaped inserting blade ... in essence resemble those from M 232. M 232 appears, however, slightly earlier according to the form of its *ting*-tripod. ... The bronze vessels from this grave as an assemblage are in some ways similar to those from M 333 of Hsiao-t'un and are probably dated to the same general period."[26] The unique importance of this grave is in its yielding significant numbers of both bronzes and pottery, thereby more firmly than ever tying together the bronze forms and decorations of Yin-hsü before the Tomb Five period with Period I pottery.

Period I pottery and associated artifacts have been found at a few other localities in addition to the above, including stratum 1 of Ta-ssu-k'ung-ts'un,[27] stratum 1 of Hsiao-t'un Locus South,[28] and stratum 1 of Miao-p'u Locus North.[29] From these it appears that the Shang relics

24. Shih 1980: 244–48.
25. K'ao-ku 1979c.
26. Ibid., 226.
27. K'ao-ku 1961a; K'ao-ku 1964.
28. K'ao-ku 1975: 32–34.
29. Exhibits at the An-yang Station, Institute of Archaeology, 1977.

characterized by Period I pottery and by the bronze types in the earlier tombs named above are found in an area about two kilometers N–S and E–W on both banks of the Huan River, from Wu-kuan-ts'un North and Ta-ssu-k'ung-ts'un in the north to Hsiao-t'un South and Miao-p'u North in the south. If this area can be seen as the cultural center or focus of Period I in Yin-hsü history, then very conspicuous cultural changes took place from Period I (prior to the Tomb Five period) to Period II (Tomb Five period), including:

1. The occupational area of Yin-hsü expanded, from an earlier area one kilometer long both north and south of the Huan River to a much larger area about six kilometers E–W and four kilometers N–S. In other words, the earlier Yin-hsü was a small village group, whereas the Yin-hsü of the Tomb Five period was turned into a larger urban society.

2. The expanded Yin-hsü of the Tomb Five and subsequent periods was characterized by three important new features: oracle bone inscriptions, rammed earth house foundations, and the large tombs. All of these were evidently new elements having to do with the Shang royal house.

3. At the Yin-hsü before the Tomb Five period there were semisubterranean houses, drainage ditches, and nobility burials with rich furnishings and sacrificial humans and dogs. But the pottery at this time was Period I, and the bronze vessels resemble those of the Erh-li-kang phase at Cheng-chou, especially those of late Erh-li-kang at the site of T'ai-hsi-ts'un in Kao-ch'eng. On entering the Tomb Five period, on the other hand, Period I pottery came to an end and Period II pottery became predominant, and in bronze decorative styles Loehr's styles IV and V came to replace I–III. Inscriptions became numerous on bronzes.

4. Thus it is clear that significant and marked changes took place in the history of Yin-hsü from before the Tomb Five period to the Tomb Five period. What is the nature of these changes? What is the place of Yin-hsü in the history of the Shang prior to the Tomb Five period? At least on the surface, the various aspects of culture involved in these changes all appear to have had much to do with the new status of Yin-hsü as a royal capital. In other words, the simplest and most logical interpretation of the changes is that the Yin-hsü prior to the Tomb Five period was the Yin settlement before King P'an Keng's capital was moved to it, and that the whole series of changes that occurred with the onset of the Tomb Five period resulted from the momentous event of King P'an Keng's move of his capital to this site. Under this interpretation, the

period of kings P'an Keng, Hsiao Hsin, and Hsiao Yi must be an initial subperiod of the Tomb Five period. When Tung Tso-pin formulated the Period I of his five-period classification of oracle bone inscriptions he indeed included in it the reigns of King Wu Ting and King Wu Ting's "Three Fathers" (P'an Keng, Hsiao Hsin, and Hsiao Yi). Unfortunately, no one has been able so far to identify precisely and without doubt the inscriptions of the P'an Keng/Hsiao Yi period in the existing corpus of inscriptions.[30]

A hypothesis gaining popularity in recent years identifies the period of Yin-hsü history prior to the Tomb Five period with the period of the reigns of kings P'an Keng, Hsiao Hsin, and Hsiao Yi and attributes the new developments of the Tomb Five period to institutional changes implemented under the reign of King Wu Ting. This new interpretation appears to have begun in 1964 with Tsou Heng's attempt to construct a Yin-hsü-wide cultural stratigraphy.[31] In 1973 at the excavation of Hsiao-t'un Locus South evidence was reportedly found to link Period I potsherds with oracle bone inscriptions of the Shih group of inquirers. This linkage, according to the excavators, not only shows that this inquirers' group is dated to King Wu Ting's reign rather than to the reigns of King Wu Yi and King Wen Wu Ting, but also proves that Period I pottery could continue into the King Wu Ting period.[32] If so, the new view that links Period I pottery with the period of the reigns of P'an Keng, Hsiao Hsin, and Hsiao Yi appears to have some factual support. In a recent essay, Yang Hsi-chang summarizes his "chronological division of the history of Yin-hsü culture" as follows:

Period 1: P'an Keng, Hsiao Hsin, Hsiao Yi, and early years of Wu Ting
Period 2: Later years of Wu Ting, Tsu Keng, and Tsu Chia
Period 3: Lin Hsin, K'ang Ting, Wu Yi, and Wen Wu Ting
Period 4: Ti Yi and Ti Hsin

A necessary corollary of a scheme such as this is that there was no Shang occupation at Yin-hsü prior to P'an Keng's removal of his capital there. In his discussion of the royal cemetery at Hsi-pei-kang, Yang speculated that perhaps only the large tombs with four ramps were truly "tombs of kings." Since there are only eight large tombs at Hsi-pei-kang with four

---

30. Ch'en 1956a: 139; Keightley 1978: 97-98; Yen 1978: 1115-22.
31. Tsou 1964.
32. K'ao-ku 1975.

ramps and, further, since none of them dates from before Period II, he further suggested that the royal cemetery was initiated with Wu Ting's burial rather than P'an Keng's. If, furthermore, both the oracle bone inscriptions of Hsiao-t'un and the royal burials at Hsi-pei-kang began with Wu Ting, Yang argued, then "the capital site or sites of kings P'an Keng, Hsiao Hsin, and Hsiao Yi were perhaps not located at Yin-hsü in An-yang at all."[33] The question is not explained, however, as to why, then, Period I relics were dated precisely to the period of the three kings' reigns.

The question of the three kings' reigns and the question of the emergence of a new cultural phase at the beginning of the Tomb Five period are one, I believe. The nature of the cultural transformation that led to the Tomb Five period is consistent with the change Yin-hsü underwent to capital status but appears surely more cataclysmic than any reform movement in government. According to the "Annals of Yin" in *Shih Chi*, King Wu Ting employed Fu Yüeh and "improved on his governance and carried out virtuous policies. The whole world was pleased and the Yin's way once more prevailed." The poem "Dark Bird" of *Shih Ching* describes King Wu Ting's reign thus: "Even their inner domain was a thousand leagues / In them the people found sure support / They opened up new lands as far as the four seas / Men from the four seas came in homage." The document "Absence of Ease" in *Shu Ching* claims that Wu Ting "enjoyed ruling the country for fifty-nine years." These examples point to a textual tradition crediting Wu Ting with major achievements. The oracle bone inscriptions dating to the Wu Ting period also paint the king as one who attended to all state business personally, was diligent in performing rituals and hunts, engaged in conquests, and received tributes—in short, one whose scale of activities conforms with the textual image. Nevertheless, cultural and social changes that could have resulted from this kind of regal attention and diligence must still be quantitative changes viewed from within the history of the Shang capital, whereas the changes that resulted in the Tomb Five period were qualitative changes, those that came about from the transformation of an ordinary town inhabited by nobility to a royal capital. In other words, it is reasonable to attribute such changes to King P'an Keng's move of his capital. It would be unconvincing to characterize them as the result of a Wu Ting revival.

33. H. C. Yang 1981: 52.

In the perspective of the larger context, one readily recognizes the fact that both of the proofs offered to support the identification of the Yin-hsü prior to the Tomb Five period with the reigns of kings P'an Keng, Hsiao Hsin, and Hsiao Yi are suspect. The first has to do with the question of the number of kings' tombs at Hsi-pei-kang. The assertion that only the four-ramp tombs are those of kings is speculative and unsupported. Under this view one takes on the burden of explaining the occurrence of one such tomb in the eastern sector and seven of them in the western sector. The second proof in question concerns the association of the inscriptions of the Shih group of inquirers with Period I pottery. In fact, there is no compelling reason for the pre-Tomb Five period at Yin-hsü not to yield oracle bone inscriptions. Among the relics found in the first stratum at Ta-ssu-k'ung-ts'un was an inscribed piece bearing the message, "[On day] hsin, made the inquiry, at Yi(Yin)." This is commonly dated to the Wu Ting period, but there is no reason that it cannot be an oracle performed by mere nobility at Yin-hsü before P'an Keng's arrival. As far as the reported association of oracle bone inscriptions with Period I potsherds at Hsiao-t'un Locus South, the archaeological facts remain to be examined in detail, but in any event it suggests at most that Period I pottery could continue into the Wu Ting period but cannot be used as chronological proof for the whole Period I, which "could be earlier than Wu Ting."[34] Indeed, the pottery chronology and the division of Yin-hsü history should be clearly separated, the former being one of the many criteria of the latter. In other words, the above discussion has made it clear that Yin-hsü before the Tomb Five period had Period I pottery, but that Period I pottery could continue into the Tomb Five period.

Assuming as we are that the beginning of the Tomb Five period coincided with King P'an Keng's move to Yin-hsü, one must also assume that the period of the three kings from P'an Keng to Hsiao Yi must be found within the period of Tomb Five. According to the *Bamboo Annals* (*chin-pen*), P'an Keng moved his capital to Yin in the fourteenth year of his reign, and he "did Yin over" in his fifteenth year. King P'an Keng is generally believed to have died in the twenty-eighth year of his reign, or the thirteenth year at Yin, but in one source (*Shih Chi*, as quoted in

---

34. K'ao-ku-hsüeh-pao 1981: 514. According to Chung-kuo-she-hui-k'o-hsüeh-yüan K'ao-ku-yen-chiu-so 1980a, p. 222, the associated pottery may actually belong to Period II rather than Period I as originally assessed.

volume 83 of *Yü-lan*) he is said to have died in the eighteenth year of his reign, or his third year at Yin. The length of the reign of the next king, Hsiao Hsin, P'an Keng's brother, is given as three years in *chin-pen* but as twenty-one years in other sources (*Huang-chi Ching-shih* and *T'ung-chien Wai-chi*). The next king, Hsiao Yi, another brother, reigned ten (*chin-pen*) or twenty (*Shih Chi*, as quoted in volume 83 of *Yü-lan*) years. The next king, Wu Ting, son of Hsiao Yi, reigned fifty-nine years and left an enormous number of identifiable relics. The place of Wu Ting in Yin-hsü archaeology is clear and firm, but his "three fathers" could have reigned only sixteen years, if we took the shortest figures among the textual variations. Not only could the remains left behind by the Shang during this short interval not possibly account for all of the pre-Tomb Five period deposits at Yin-hsü, but also it is possible that they number so few as to be as yet unrecognizable.

The most reliable way to recognize the material from the reigns of the three kings in the archaeological remains of Yin-hsü is to identify the oracle bone inscriptions dating from before King Wu Ting among the inscriptions loosely placed in Period I. These inscriptions may already be available but remain unrecognized. In accordance with the idea that a dualism existed in the royal house of the Shang dynasty,[35] if the oracular institutions under kings P'an Keng, Hsiao Hsin, and Hsiao Yi were in any way different from those under Wu Ting, their customs would be more like those of Tung Tso-pin's "New School." Kings of the New School engaged in oracular activities more efficiently but less frequently, and they may have left fewer records. In a recent paper Liu Yüan-lin selected six pieces of oracle bones from the vast collection of the Academia Sinica resulting from excavations before the war and pronounced them to be "early An-yang," that is, "before Wu Ting," because of the primitive nature of the techniques used to prepare the bones for divination. Their numbers and texts are as follows:

1. Field number 5.2.66: "[Day] Ting-wei: XX"
2. *Chia*-2342: "[Day] Ping-wu, divined: To conquer Hua?"
3. *Chia*-2815: "[Day] Hsin-, [inquired]: Perform *sui*-ritual to -? On the following Hsin day perform *sui* to Father? Phoenix." [translation highly tentative]
4. *Chia*-2344: "[Day] Yi-ssu, divined: X"

---

35. K. C. Chang 1967.

5. *Yi*-9105 (from Hou-kang): "[Day] Ping-ch'en: Receive harvest? XXX"

6. Field Number 3.2.139: "X"

While these pieces are classified as "pre–Wu Ting" on the basis of preparatory technology, they were unearthed in pits associated with inscriptions of later dates. Liu compares these pits to "modern libraries ... wherein one finds books printed in Ch'ing, Ming, Yüan, or even Sung Dynasties," in other words, archives in which earlier documents were filed with later documents.[36] If Liu's speculation proves to be valid, these inscriptions could be dated to the period at Yin-hsü before P'an Keng's arrival, or to the three kings' reign from P'an Keng to Hsiao Yi. But phases such as "to conquer Hua" and "receive harvest" appear to suggest royal activities and, therefore, the latter alternative. Liu's suggestion is certainly noteworthy but cannot be convincing without corroborative evidence.[37]

The question of the number of kings' tombs at Hsi-pei-kang, discussed earlier, assumes additional significance in this context. According to the *Bamboo Annals* (*ku-pen*), the Shang's royal capital was located at Yin for 273 years until the end of the dynasty. Accordingly, most students of Shang history believe that Yin-hsü was the capital city under twelve Shang kings: P'an Keng, Hsiao Hsin, Hsiao Yi, Wu Ting, Tsu Keng, Tsu Chia, Lin Hsin, K'ang Ting, Wu Yi, Wen Wu Ting, Ti Yi, and Ti Hsin. Ti Hsin, the last monarch, is described in historical texts as having committed suicide, and he is believed to have been beheaded by the Chou invaders ("Shih-fu-chieh" in *Chou Shu*). Excluding him, we assume that eleven kings were buried at Yin-hsü. At Hsi-pei-kang there happened to be eleven large tombs. The division of these tombs into an eastern sector of four and a western sector of seven coincides with the dualistic division of the eleven kings according to the principle of alternate generations (seven—P'an Keng, Hsiao Hsin, Hsiao Yi, Tsu Chia, Lin Hsin, Wu Yi, and Ti Yi—in the west and four—Wu Ting, Tsu Keng, K'ang Ting, and Wen Wu Ting—in the east). Some scholars[38] believe that the earliest tomb in the western sector is M 1001; if this is so, then it could be the tomb of P'an Keng! But this interpretation of the cemetery layout at Hsi-pei-kang is not universally accepted. Yang Hsi-chang, for

36. Y. L. Liu 1974: 127.
37. Cf. Keightley 1978a: 98.
38. E.g., C. Li 1959.

example, gave three reasons for his unwillingness to accept this view:

> (1) There are actually twelve large tombs at Hsi-pei-kang, the twelfth being the one whence the Ssu Mu Wu *ting* is alleged to have been discovered. (2) If the Ssu Mu Wu *ting* tomb is that of a royal consort (rather than a king), then some of the other large tombs could also be consorts' tombs rather than kings'. (3) According to our classification none of these tombs belonged to Period I of the Yin-hsü, namely, the period of P'an Keng, Hsiao Hsin, and Hsiao Yi.[39]

From the point of view of archaeology, the third of the above reasons ought to be the most important, but it obviously cannot stand. As discussed earlier, there can be no equation mark between the so-called Period I of Yin-hsü culture and the period of the three kings P'an Keng, Hsiao Hsin, and Hsiao Yi. The tomb where the Ssu Mu Wu *ting* was allegedly found has never been excavated; its position is some distance apart from the other four tombs of the eastern sector, and the shape of its opening—according to drillings—differs from that of the other eleven large tombs of Hsi-pei-kang. It may not even be within the royal cemetery confines.

Alexander Soper has also speculated about the identity of some of the masters of the large tombs. Since tombs 1001, 1550, 1002, and 1004 in the western sector appear to cluster together, with 1001 at the center and the other three seemingly appended on the outside, he suggests that 1001 was the tomb of Wu Ting and that the other three were the tombs of his three sons, Tsu Chi, Tsu Keng, and Tsu Chia. Soper, however, does not regard 1001 as the earliest royal tomb in Yin-hsü. He assigns 1443, 1129, and the large tomb at Hou-kang to the three kings before Wu Ting because they are the three smallest, built at Yin-hsü before Wu Ting, his conquests, and his accumulated wealth.[40] Soper's view is no less speculative than mine or Yang Hsi-chang's, but before detailed data and precise dates become available practically all we can do with regard to the Hsi-pei-kang layout is speculate.

Fifty-four years have passed since the first excavations at Yin-hsü. Largely because of the disturbances created by wars, the archaeologists who had excavated Yin-hsü before the war and those who have been working there since the war have not had any opportunity to exchange

---

39. H. C. Yang 1981: 50.
40. Soper 1966: 26–27.

information and views. Consequently, many major questions pertaining to the archaeology of Yin-hsü remain unanswered, and the topic discussed here is but one of them. My objective is primarily to clarify the issue conceptually so that we are clear of our footing in reexamining old data or in acquiring new ones. To summarize my conclusions: the period represented by Tomb Five represents the initial period from the time of the removal of the Shang royal capital to Yin, and Yin-hsü prior to the Tomb Five period was probably a late Middle Shang town or village network ruled over by nobility. Among the archaeological data brought to light at Yin-hsü, the earlierst king we can identify is Wu Ting. Our next important task is to identify the remains left during the reigns of P'an Keng, Hsiao Hsin, and Hsiao Yi. In my view, this can be accomplished only by examining the remains of the Tomb Five period. It would be futile to attempt to identify P'an Keng, Hsiao Hsin, and Hsiao Yi among the Yin-hsü remains that are earlier than the Tomb Five period.

5

A Study of the Bronzes with the "Ssu T'u Mu" Inscriptions Excavated from the Fu Hao Tomb

Cheng Chen-hsiang

The discovery in 1976 of the Fu Hao tomb at Yin-hsü in An-yang provided numerous important materials for the investigation of the history and archaeology of the Yin dynasty. In the report entitled *Yin-hsü Fu Hao Mu*,[1] I have already presented a relatively detailed account, but the problems which this tomb involves are both numerous and complex, so there are certain questions that still await further research by specialists and scholars. This essay is intended to further investigate the bronzes with the "Ssu T'u Mu 司㺇母" inscriptions.

Altogether, 210 bronze ceremonial vessels were unearthed from the Fu Hao tomb, including 190 bearing cast inscriptions of nine different kinds. Among the inscriptions, there are some which still await critical study, so, for convenience in printing, we will temporarily use similar modern characters in place of inscribed characters which have not yet been transcribed in print or are at present still undeciphered. The nine types of inscriptions are: Fu Hao (婦好) or Hao (好); Ssu Mu Hsin (司母辛); Ssu T'u Mu (司㺇母) or Ssu (Hou) T'u Mu K'ui (司 [后] 㺇母癸); Ya Kung (亞弓); Ya Ch'i (亞其); Ya-Ch'i (亞啓); Tzu Su Ch'üan (子束泉) or Su Ch'üan (束泉); ?* (威); and ? (宜㝱). Among these, the "Fu Hao"

---

1. Chung-kuo-she-hui-k'o-hsüeh-yüan K'ao-ku-yen-chiu-so 1980a.

*A question mark will be inserted in the text when the correct reading of any character is unknown (translator's note).

inscriptions altogether number 109 pieces, making up about half of the total number of ceremonial vessels. They comprise a rather complete variety of vessel types, including cooking vessels, food vessels, wine vessels, and water vessels, and contain a proportionately high number of large- and medium-sized bronzes, many of which form pairs or sets and which make up an important part of the entire group of bronzes from this grave. In addition to appearing on these vessels this type of inscription occurs on two large bronze *yüeh* (鉞) axes. The inscription "Fu Hao" must be the name used by the person who had these objects made, and it would follow that the occupant of the grave is Fu Hao. Based on the stratigraphy of this tomb and the investigation of some of the burial goods found inside, the tomb must belong to the second of the four periods into which the Yin-hsü culture has been divided (that is, Ta-ssu-k'ung-ts'un 大司空村 second period)[2] and must date approximately from late Wu Ting (武丁) to Tsu Chia (祖甲).[3] Putting records relating to Fu Hao from divination inscriptions of the Wu Ting period together with Kuo Mo-jo's research on the phrase "Fu (帚 (婦)) X,"[4] we believe that "Fu Hao" must have been a consort of Wu Ting. Among the inscriptions there are also examples using the single word "Hao," which must be an abbreviation for "Fu Hao," Fu being the title and Hao the name.

Highly pertinent to the occupant of the tomb are five inscribed vessels bearing the inscription "Ssu Mu Hsin": a pair each of large *fang ting* and four-footed *kuang* and a rectangular vessel with tall ring-foot. The large *fang ting* are of imposing dimensions and weight, surpassed in size only by the large Ssu Mu Wu *ting*; the four-footed *kuang* are fashioned in a curious, refined style seldom seen among the objects from Yin-hsü. Apart from these, there is one exquisitely sculpted stone ox bearing the inscription "Ssu Hsin (司辛)." This series of inscription has been variously read as "Ssu Mu Hsin (司母辛)," "Hou Mu Hsin (后母辛)," and "Hou Hsin (姤辛)."[5] Because, among the more than thirty inscriptions reading "Ssu Mu Hsin" or "Ssu Tu Mu," there are no clear-cut examples where "nü (女)" and "hou (后)" are written together, it seems more appropriate to explain the inscription in question as three rather than two characters. As to whether the first character should be read "Ssu

2. K'ao-ku 1964: 380–81.
3. Cheng and Ch'en 1981: 511.
4. M. J. Kuo 1934: 6–7.
5. K'ao-ku 1977b.

(司)" or "Hou (后)," both readings make sense here; we read it as "Ssu Mu Hsin (司母辛)" simply because by far the great majority of examples of "Ssu (司)" among all the inscriptions discovered are written the right way around. According to the Yi-Hsin cyclical sacrificial calendar, Wu Ting had three legally recognized consorts: "Pi Wu (妣戊)," "Pi Hsin (妣辛)," and "Pi Kuei (妣癸)." One of these consorts has the ritual name "hsin (辛)," which precisely corresponds to the appellation "Ssu Mu Hsin" in the inscriptions and to "Mu Hsin (母辛)" in ancestral sacrifices (recorded on oracle bones) of the Tsu Keng and Tsu Chia periods. For these reasons, we believe "Mu Hsin" and "Fu Hao" were one and the same person. "Fu Hao" was her name when alive, "Hsin" her ritual name, and "Mu Hsin" the posthumous name used for her by the generation of Wu Ting's sons.

Except for the bronze vessels bearing the inscription "Fu Hao," bronzes bearing the inscription "Ssu T'u Mu" are the most numerous, comprising altogether twenty-six pieces, including a pair each of square *hu*, round *chia*, and round *tsun*, eleven *ku*, and nine *chüeh*. The inscriptions are all written in the normal configuration (rather than reversed), but in arrangement may be divided into two types: in one, the three characters are written one above the other in a vertical line, whereas in the other the two characters "Ssu T'u (司䍃)" are written one above the other, with the character "Mu (母)" to their right. The first kind of arrangement accounts for the majority of the inscriptions, while the second appears only on the *ku* vessels. In addition, a pair of large square *tsun* bear on the inside bottom inscriptions of four characters in two columns, one column consisting of the three characters "Ssu T'u Mu," all written backwards, and, to the right, one "kuei (癸)" character. Adding these two, we have twenty-eight pieces altogether, all wine vessels, among which eight large- and medium-sized ceremonial vessels were placed inside the outer coffin (*kuo*) along the east and west sides of the inner coffin (*kuan*), together with other large- and medium-sized inscribed wine vessels.

The appearance in the Fu Hao tomb of this group of bronzes inscribed "Ssu T'u Mu" is worthy of note, for in form and decorative design they are close to vessels of similar types which bear the inscription "Fu Hao." The two groups are basically from the same period. This kind of assemblage of roughly contemporary Yin dynasty ritual vessels with the same inscription is seldom encountered; in particular, large- and medium-sized paired ritual bronzes are even rarer. Further study of these inscribed bronzes, in the light of previously discovered materials, will be instructive.

GENERAL DESCRIPTION OF THE "SSU T'U MU" INSCRIBED BRONZES

The "Ssu T'u Mu" Inscribed Bronzes Unearthed in the Fu Hao Tomb

The "Ssu T'u Mu" inscribed bronzes unearthed in the Fu Hao tomb all made up pairs or sets. Following I will briefly describe each kind of vessel and then compare it with vessels of the same kind bearing the inscription "Fu Hao."

1. Square *hu* (方壺). Two vessels, making up a pair. One (No. 807, fig. 12, left), has a rectangular mouth, a constricted neck and narrow

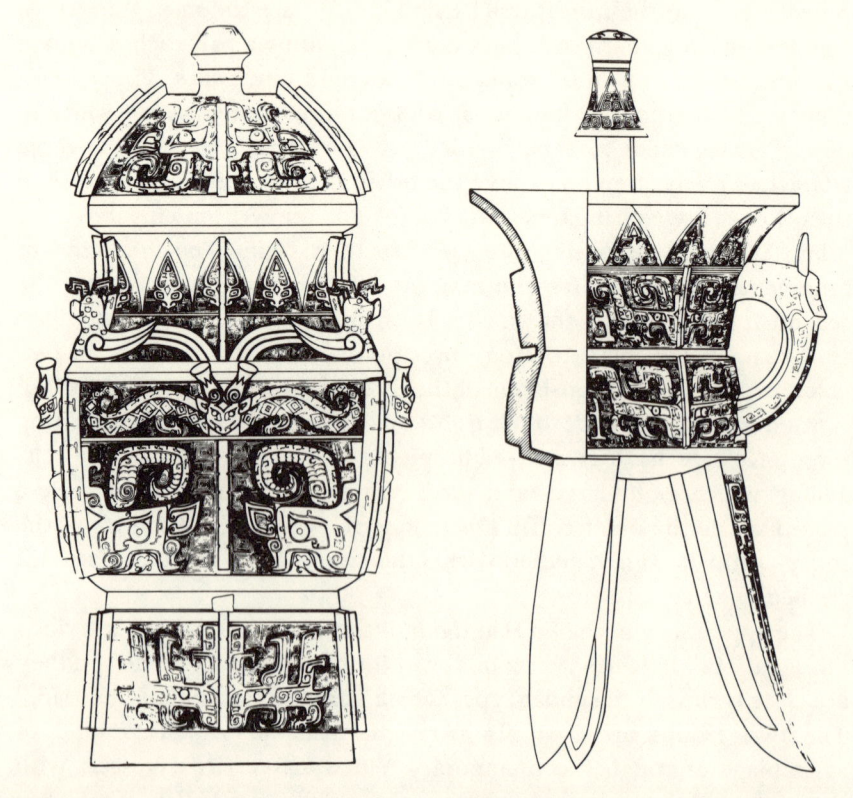

Fig. 12. Bronze square *hu* and *chia* from Tomb Number Five at Yin-hsü: (*left*) square *hu*, #807; (*right*) *chia*, #857.

shoulder, a relatively straight-sided body, a flat bottom, a tall, rectangular ring-foot, and a rectangular hole in each of the sides of the foot. It has flanges down the middle of all four sides and at the four corners. Beneath the rim it is incised with cicada-shaped decorations; from the four corners of the shoulders protrude mythical birds; each of the four sides of the upper body bears a dragon with one head and two bodies; the four corners of the body are decorated with large *t'ao-t'ieh*; and the four sides of the base are also decorated with *t'ao-t'ieh* designs. Inside the vessel, in the center of the bottom, are inscribed the three characters "Ssu T'u Mu" (fig. 14:1). The cover is formed of four sloping sides and a flat top, with a knob in the center; the four sloping sides have *t'ao-t'ieh* decorations; and the cover also has flanges aligning with those on the body of the vessel. Overall height, 64 centimeters; length of mouth, 23.5 centimeters; width, 19.5 centimeters; weight, 31 kilograms. Its companion piece (No. 794) is comparatively well preserved, but its designs are not very clear. Inside on the bottom it has the three-character inscription "Ssu T'u Mu" (fig. 14:2). Overall height, 64.4 centimeters; width across the mouth, 23.4 centimeters; width, 19.8 centimeters; weight, 35 kilograms.

2. Round *chia* (圓斝). Two vessels, making up a pair. One (No. 857, fig. 12, right) has a pillar with an umbrella-shaped cap on each side at the rim, a body divided into two sections, upper and lower, an almost flat bottom and three prismatic, pointed feet. Beneath the rim are twelve triangular decorative elements. The upper and lower sections of the body are each adorned with three groups of *t'ao-t'ieh* designs, differing only in minor details. On the inside wall beneath the rim it has the inscription "Ssu T'u Mu" (fig. 14:3). Overall height, 65.7 centimeters; diameter at the lip, 30.7 centimeters; approximate weight, 20 kilograms. The composition of the bronze alloy (in mean figures, as below) is as follows: copper, 78.10 percent; tin, 14.99 percent; lead, 5.32 percent; zinc, 0.07 percent; total (metallic content), 98.49 percent. On the companion piece (No. 860), part of the decorative designs are relatively badly corroded. It also has the inscription "Ssu T'u Mu" on the inside wall just beneath the lip. Overall height, 66.5 centimeters; diameter at the rim, 30.7 centimeters; approximate weight, 20.5 kilograms. The composition of the bronze is: copper, 81.03 percent; tin, 13.79 percent; lead, 4.19 percent; zinc, 0.14 percent; total, 99.15 percent.

3. Round *tsun* (圓尊). Two vessels, making up a pair. One (No. 793) has a flaring mouth, narrow shoulders, a tall ring-foot, and around the

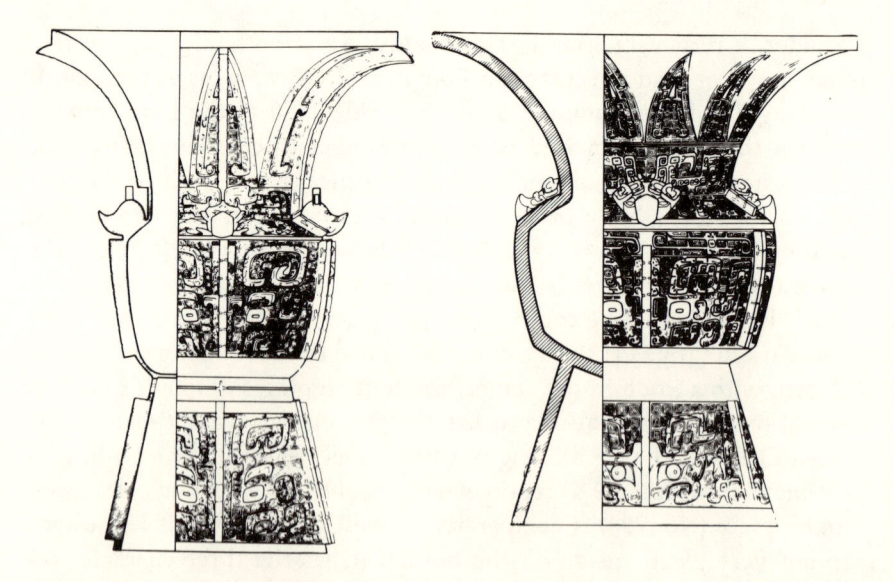

Fig. 13. Bronze square and Round *tsun* from Tomb Number Five at Yin-hsü: (*left*) square *tsun*, #806; (*right*) round *tsun*, #867.

foot three small cross-shaped holes. Beneath the rim are palm-leaf designs; under those are designs of *k'uei* animals; on the shoulder are alternating beasts' heads and short flanges, three each; and the body and the foot are each decorated with three groups of *t'ao-t'ieh* designs. On the inside wall beneath the lip is the three-character inscription "Ssu T'u Mu" (fig. 14:7). Overall height, 47 centimeters; diameter at the lip, 41 centimeters; weight, 23 kilograms. On the companion piece (No. 867, fig. 13, right), one side of the decorations on the body is relatively clear, but the ring-foot is incomplete and had to be restored. On the inside wall beneath the lip is the three-character inscription "Ssu T'u Mu" (fig. 14:8). Overall height, 46.7 centimeters; diameter at the lip, 41.6 centimeters; approximate weight, 23.5 kilograms.

4. Large square *tsun* (大方尊). Two vessels making up a pair. One (No. 806, fig. 13, left) has an almost square mouth, with a flaring lip, a narrow shoulder, a relatively shallow body, and a tall ring-foot. Each of the four sides of the foot has a cross-shaped hole, and there is a flange in the middle of each of the four sides of the body and at each of the four corners. Beneath the lip are palm-leaf decorations, and the bottom of the neck is decorated with paired *k'uei* monster designs. To each of the four sides of the shoulder has been added a mythical beast with one head and

BRONZES WITH THE "SSU T'U MU" INSCRIPTIONS 87

Fig. 14. Some inscriptions on bronze vessels from Tomb Number Five at Yin-hsü: (1, 2) square *hu*, #807, #794; (3, 4) round *chia*, #857, #860; (5, 6) square *tsun*, #868, #806; (7, 8) round *tsun*, #793, #867.

two bodies: the beast's head protrudes, and the bodies and tails resemble those of a dragon. The four sides of the body and foot are decorated with *t'ao-t'ieh* designs. On the inside, in the middle of the bottom is a four-character inscription, one column consisting of the three characters "Ssu T'u Mu," with the character "kuei" to the right (fig. 14:6). Overall height, 55.6 centimeters; width across the lip, 37.5 centimeters; width, 37 centimeters; height of the ring-foot, 19.9 centimeters; approximate weight, 31 kilograms. The composition of the bronze is: copper, 82.53

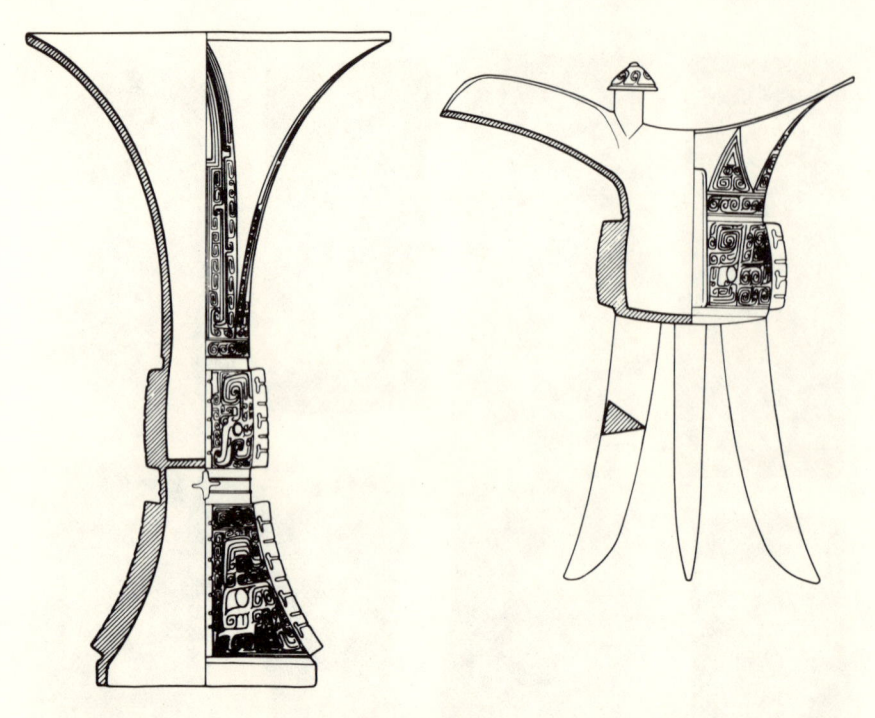

Fig. 15. Bronze *ku* and *chüeh* from Tomb Number Five at Yin-hsü: (*left*) *ku*, #625; (*right*) *chüeh*, #661.

percent; tin, 14.45 percent; lead, 0.60 percent; zinc, 0.08 percent; total, 97.66 percent. On the companion piece (No. 868), the beasts' heads were missing horns, and these had to be restored. On one side of the body is preserved a fragment of the original silk wrapping. On the inside, in the middle of the bottom, is the four-character inscription "Ssu T'u Mu kuei" (fig. 14:5). Overall height, 56 centimeters; width across the lip, 37.5 centimeters; width, 36.9 centimeters; weight, 32 kilograms. The composition of the bronze is: copper, 79.17 percent; tin, 17.11 percent; lead, 0.66 percent; zinc, 0.14 percent; total, 97.08 percent.

5. *Ku* (觚). Eleven pieces, forming a set. Each of these has a trumpet-shaped mouth, a relatively thick body, and cross-shaped holes on two sides at the upper end of the ring-foot. There are four flanges on both the body and the foot. Most of the inscriptions are well preserved, although some of the characters are incomplete (fig. 16). The height of most is greater than 28 centimeters, and the weight, approximately 1.5 kilograms. On one example (No. 625, fig. 15, left), there are palm-leaf designs

BRONZES WITH THE "SSU T'U MU" INSCRIPTIONS 89

Fig. 16. Inscriptions on bronze *ku* vessels from Tomb Number Five at Yin-hsü: (1) #625; (2) #606; (3) #612; (4) #615; (5) #628; (6) #617; (7) #649; (8) #631.

under the lip; the body is decorated with two upside-down *k'uei* monster designs; and the foot with *t'ao-t'ieh* designs. On the inside wall of the foot is the three-character inscription "Ssu T'u Mu" (fig. 16:1). Height, 28.3 centimeters; diameter at the lip, 16.3 centimeters; weight, 1.7 kilograms. The composition of the bronze is: copper, 77.94 percent; tin, 20.30 percent; lead, 1.31 percent; zinc, 0.15 percent; total, 99.70 percent. In another sample *ku* (No. 631), the composition of the alloy is: copper, 82.28 percent; tin, 15.13 percent; lead, 0.82 percent; zinc, 0.11 percent; total, 98.34 percent.

6. *Chüeh* (爵). Nine vessels, together forming a set. Each of these has a narrow spout, a pointed tail (lip opposite the spout), pillars with mushroom-shaped caps on top, a flat bottom, a semicircular belt-shaped handle, and three flanges on the body. Inside the handle, all these vessels have the inscription "Ssu T'u Mu" (fig. 17). Their height is approxi-

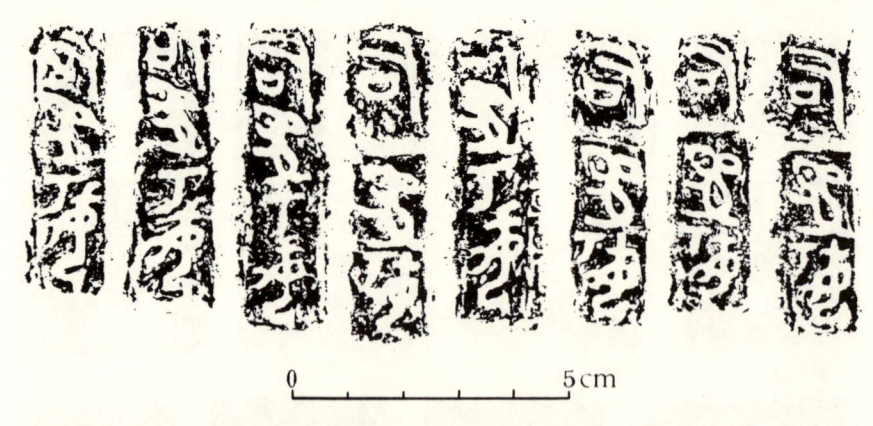

Fig. 17. Inscription on bronze *chüeh* from Tomb Number Five at Yin-hsü: (*left to right*) # 681, 678, 658, 654, 672, 677, 661, 689.

mately 22 centimeters and their weight roughly 1 kilogram. No. 661 (fig. 15, right), an example of this set, is intact, is decorated with round whorl designs on the pillar caps, has leaf-shaped designs on the spout, and triangular designs on the tail. Beneath the rim are small triangular designs; the body is decorated with a *t'ao-t'ieh*, whose body and tail are formed of *lei-wen* designs that are not easy to distinguish from the background pattern. Inside the handle is the inscription "Ssu T'u Mu" (fig. 17, second from right). Overall height, 22.3 centimeters; weight, 1.1 kilograms.

In the pairs and sets of vessels described above, the overall body of decoration is basically the same, but there are always slight differences of detail in the decor and the background designs. The forms of the characters in the inscriptions on the paired vessels are similar, as if written by one person, but the differences in this respect are still more evident than the differences in decoration. The question of why the decorative designs manifest differences still requires further investigation. In the pair of round *chia*, the composition of the alloy is similar, both containing relatively high proportions of lead, whereas in the pair of large square *tsun*, the composition, although close, did show some differences. The composition of the alloys in the two *ku* which have been chemically tested show relatively greater differences. The paired vessels were probably made at basically the same time, but it is possible that some were cast from bronze ingots smelted in different furnaces.

In the following paragraphs I will compare the "Ssu T'u Mu" inscribed vessels with the "Fu Hao" inscribed vessels of the same kind. One round *chia* inscribed with "Fu Hao" (No. 751) resembles the "Ssu T'u Mu" inscribed round *chia* in form, but its decor is different. The "Fu Hao" vessel's overall height is 64 centimeters, about 2 centimeters taller than its "Fu Hao" counterpart. The pillar caps on the "Ssu T'u Mu" vessel lack flanges, while those on the "Fu Hao" vessel have four small flanges, quite fine and delicate. The composition of the bronze in the "Fu Hao" vessel is: copper, 79.45 percent; tin, 18.70 percent; lead, 0.66 percent; zinc, 0.14 percent; total, 97.08 percent; its tin content is thus about 3.7 percent higher than that of the "Ssu M'u Tu" vessel, and its lead content is less than 1 percent.

The form of the square *tsun* inscribed with "Ssu T'u Mu Kuei" differs in some respects from the form of the similar vessel inscribed with "Fu Hao" (792). The body of the "Fu Hao" vessel is deeper and its ring-foot shorter; its overall height is 43 centimeters. The "Ssu T'u Mu" vessel is 55.6 centimeters high, about 12 centimeters higher than the "Fu Hao" vessel. However, the "Fu Hao" piece is more elegant and refined: it has not only a protruding beast's head cast into the middle of each of the four sides, but also a standing, mythical bird at each of the four corners on its shoulder, making a very beautiful effect.

As for the "Ssu T'u Mu" round *tsun* and square *hu*, there are no corresponding types of vessels in the "Fu Hao" group. The casting technique of the *hu* is quite advanced. Its shoulder bears standing mythical birds, quite similar to the birds cast onto the four corners of the "Fu Hao" square *tsun*; in both cases, the technique of separate casting was used. To summarize, the type, materials, decor, and casting methods of the medium- and large-sized "Ssu T'u Mu" bronzes are very close to those of some of the medium-sized "Fu Hao" vessels, but in certain details the former never quite match the refined elegance of the "Fu Hao" examples and are slightly inferior in quality.

The same holds true for the *ku* and *chüeh* vessels. There are two kinds of *chüeh* with the "Fu Hao", inscription. One is the large, round-bottomed *chüeh*, of which there is one pair, about 38 centimeters in height. The other kind is represented by a set of ten flat-bottomed *chüeh*, average height greater than 26 centimeters, with umbrella-shaped pillar caps, three flanges around the body and a flange on the spout and the tail. The "Ssu T'u Mu" flat-bottomed *chüeh* have only the three flanges on the body and mushroom-shaped pillar caps, their pillars and knobs are shorter, and their overall height is approximately 22 centimeters. Of the two, the "Fu Hao" vessels make a much more impressive appearance.

On the "Ssu T'u Mu" *ku*, only the body and the ring-foot have four flanges. The twenty-two corresponding "Fu Hao" vessels (this includes three pieces with the inscription "Fu nü [婦女]") can be divided into three types. One is rather small, with open fretwork on the ring-foot. The other two types are quite tall. On one, the flanges are divided into three sections, from the ring-foot and the body up to the rim. On the other kind, only the body and the ring-foot have flanges; this kind is basically the same in form as the "Ssu T'u Mu" *ku* vessels; only the decoration is different. The technique of dividing up the piece-molds in the two former kinds of "Fu Hao" *ku* is relatively complex.

The similarity of the two groups of "Ssu T'u Mu" and "Fu Hao" vessels reflects the owners' comparability in status. If one considers in addition the *tsun* and *chia* inscribed with "Tzu Yü (子漁)" found in grave number 18 at Hsiao-t'un (M 18),[6] this is even more evident, for the "Tzu-Yü" pieces are only 36.7 centimeters in height and 12.8 kilograms in weight. Thus the "Ssu T'u Mu" round *tsun* is more than 10 centimeters taller than the "Tzu Yü" vessel. Of course, "Tzu-Yü" may have owned larger *tsun*, but the "Tzu Yü" *tsun* cannot be considered unusually small, in light of the round *tsun* bearing the inscription "Tzu Su ch'üan (子束泉)" (about 33.2 centimeters in height) which was excavated from the Fu Hao tomb. Therefore, from this investigation of the "Ssu T'u Mu" ritual vessels discovered, it appears that their owner's social position was higher than that of "Tzu Yü" and quite close to that of Fu Hao.

Compilation of Other Bronzes Bearing the Inscription "Ssu T'u Mu"

Bronzes bearing the inscription "Ssu T'u Mu" were recorded in the Sung dynasty; others were discovered before liberation in the Yin dynasty graves excavated at Hsiao-t'un. The following is a summary description of the other "Ssu T'u Mu" bronzes that I have seen.

1. The *Wang Fu Chai Chung Ting K'uan-shih* (王復齋鐘鼎款識) by Wang Hou-chih (王厚之) of the Sung dynasty lists a bronze *hsien* (甗)[7] which is recorded as having two inscriptions above and below. One of the inscriptions is "Ssu T'u Mu"; the other is the so-called "*hsi* (兕) shape drawn inside of a *ya* cartouche" (fig. 18:4, 5). However, only the

---

6. K'ao-ku-hsüeh-pao 1981: 497–98.
7. H. C. Wang 1802: 20.

BRONZES WITH THE "SSU T'U MU" INSCRIPTIONS 93

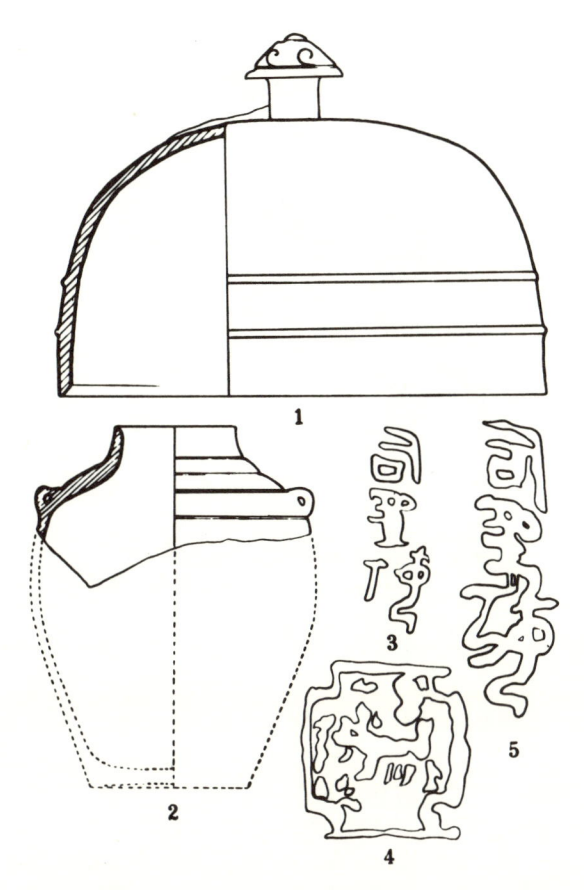

Fig. 18. Bronze lid with inscription excavated at Hsiao-t'un: (1) Bronze vessel lid excavated from M 066 at Hsiao-t'un; (2) pottery *lei* excavated from M 066 at Hsiao-t'un; (3) inscription on bronze lid; (4, 5) bronze *hsien* inscriptions in traditional catalogues.

inscriptions are recorded; there is no sketch of the vessel and the description is very brief. It does not explain whether the *hsien* is in two separate pieces or joined. If it is in two separate pieces, there is reason to doubt that the top and bottom belong to a single set. Of the two sets of divided *hsien* dug up in the Fu Hao grave, one set only has the inscription "Fu Hao" on the top portion; the other set has the single character "Hao (好)" on both top and bottom. However, the piece described above has different inscriptions on top and bottom; moreover, the so-called *hsi* character is written inside of the *ya* cartouche, which also differs from the way that the emblems from the Fu Hao grave such as "Ya kung" and

Fig. 19. Inscription on bronze *yüeh*-ax in traditional catalogue.

"Ya Ch'i" are written vertically one above the other. According to our excavated materials, the practice of writing the "ya" as a frame outside of another character first appeared in Period III[8] (Lin Hsin to Wen Ting). It is still unclear whether or not it could have been current as early as the Wu Ting era. From the difference between the inscriptions on the top and bottom portions of this *hsien*, it seems not to have belonged to a set. However, there is no doubt that the inscription "Ssu T'u Mu" had already appeared by the Sung dynasty.

2. Volume 1 of *Shodō Zenshū*, (*Chūgoku ichi: In, Shū, Shin*),[9] edited by Akatsuka Kiyoshi, Umehara Sueji et al., lists a bronze ax bearing the inscription "Ssu T'u Mu," recording only its inner surface and the inscription upon it (fig. 19) rather than the whole piece. This ax, its stem about 6.8 centimeters long and 6.2 centimeters wide, is relatively small.

3. A vessel lid inscribed "Ssu T'u Mu" was unearthed in a Yin grave (numbered M 066 in the original report) which was excavated before the war in the area north of Hsiao-t'un.[10] The lid resembled that of a *lei*, and

8. See the bronze inscriptions from tomb 62 M 172 at Miao-p'u-pei-ti and material in the collection at the An-yang Archaeological Station.
9. Akatsuka et al. 1965, plate 22, upper right corner.
10. Shih 1976: 9–12.

the outer surface was decorated with two rings of raised thread patterns. Overall height, 9.1 centimeters; diameter at the lip, 13 centimeters; (fig. 18:1, 3). The inscription was transcribed by Shih as the three characters "Ssu Ma Nü (司馬女). According to the report's introduction, this grave was roughly three-fourths obliterated by H 45, an intrusive pit dating after the Sui and T'ang dynasties; its length from east to west was unclear, and its width, 1.1 meters. The grave chamber was largely destroyed but at the bottom of the southern wall were two tibia and fibula bones with the feet extended pointing west, a human burial in face-down position. (Note: The position of the skeleton seems to indicate that it was not that of the chief occupant of the grave.) The above-mentioned vessel lid was unearthed at the middle of the western end of the grave, together with a broken pottery *kuan* pitcher, which is similar to a *lei* in form (fig. 18:2). This *lei* resembles a pottery *lei* unearthed in grave 17 (M 17) at Hsiao-t'un.[11] Hsiao-t'un M 17 belongs to Yin-hsü Period II. M 066 and Hsiao-t'un M 17 are close in date and generally contemporary with the Fu Hao grave.

DISCUSSION OF THE BRONZES WITH "SSU T'U MU" INSCRIPTIONS

When the bronze grave goods from the Fu Hao grave were excavated, many were broken or incomplete, corrosion was quite severe, and most required piecing together and restoration. However, one round *tsun* and one square *hu* bearing "Ssu T'u Mu" inscriptions were basically complete when excavated; their inscriptions were relatively legible, so that they came to light in the first stages of the process of putting the bronzes in order. Other inscriptions, such as "Fu Hao," "Ssu Mu Hsin," and "Ya Kung," were also discovered at that time. Since the square *hu* and round *tsun* with the "Ssu T'u Mu" inscriptions were both paired vessels of medium size, they attracted much attention. However, after all the bronze ritual vessels had been examined and put in order, it was discovered that the "Fu Hao" vessels were by far the most numerous and also represented a complete range of vessel types, while the "Ssu T'u Mu" bronzes included only wine-serving vessels. Therefore it was decided that Fu Hao must have been the chief occupant of the tomb. Most scholars agreed with us that the "Ssu Mu Hsin" bronzes must have been sacrificial vessels made for "Fu Hao." But all still wondered whom the

---

11. K'ao-ku-hsüeh-pao 1981: 510–11.

female appellation "Ssu T'u Mu" referred to and why it appeared in the tomb of Fu Hao. At the time only the inscriptions on the round *tsun*, the square *hu*, the round *chia*, and some of the *ku* and *chüeh* had been discovered, while the inscriptions on the square *tsun* had not come to light. In view of the fact that the size and materials of the above-described vessels were comparable to those of certain of the Fu Hao vessels, such as the round *chia*, flat round *hu*, and square *lei*, people speculated that the status of the person to whom the inscription referred was relatively high. As a result, people began to feel that the theory suggested by Wang Kuo-wei in the essay "On Female *Tzu* Names" ("Nü-tzu shuo" [女字説]) was correct. He believed that the phrase "x *mu* (某母, or Mother X)" in the Chou bronze inscriptions referred to a woman's *tzu* (字), or style-name, that whenever a maternal clan had a bronze cast for a daughter upon her marriage, she was referred to on it as "X *mu*," and that when she herself had a bronze cast, or cast one for someone else, she also referred to herself as "X *mu*." He said, "A woman's *tzu* name was written as 'X *mu*,' just as a man's *tzu* name was written 'X *fu* (某父, or Father X)'.... No honorific for men could surpass the title Father, and no honorific for women could be better than the title Mother."[12] In his article "Investigation of the Ts'ai Ta-shih Ting" Kuo Mo-jo wrote: "In antiquity, both married and unmarried women were called X mu, ... X *mu* must be a woman's name; in some instances, the character *mu* (母) is omitted."[13] These analyses clarify the investigation of the relationship between "Ssu T'u Mu" and "Fu Hao." The character "Ssu (司)" has sometimes been interpreted as "Hou (后)"; here, both would make sense and, whether interpreted as "Ssu" or "Hou," would not affect the personal name, which must be "T'u Mu," with the *mu* omitted in some cases. This name does not appear in the oracle bone inscriptions. Since it appears in the Fu Hao tomb on precisely those bronzes which lack the inscription "Fu Hao," we can speculate that it must be Fu Hao's *tzu* name, and that "T'u Mu" and "Fu Hao" are one and the same person. A number of scholars have come to this conclusion independently. One colleague has, moreover, done a study of the character "t'u (兔)." He believes that this character "is made up of the elements 'ch'üeh (兔)' and 'k'ao (丂),' with *k'ao* functioning as the phonetic.... '兔母' is Fu Hao's *tzu* name and '兔' should be pronounced like the character 'ch'iao (巧).' 'Ch'iao' and 'Hao'

---

12. K. W. Wang 1959, vol. 3, p. 164.
13. M. J. Kuo 1957a, vol. 8, p. 178.

anciently belonged to the same rhyming groups, and their meanings are close."[14] In 1977, when T'ang Lan came to the Institute of Archaeology for a visit, we consulted with him about the view that the words "T'u Mu" from the "Ssu T'u Mu" inscriptions might be Fu Hao's *tzu* name. T'ang expressed support for this view, so we provisionally decided that "T'u Mu" was Fu Hao's *tzu* name.

The two large square *tsun* bearing the inscription "Ssu T'u Mu Kuei (司㞷母癸)" were quite badly damaged, and it was not until September 1978 that they were restored in An-yang and their inscriptions discovered. The discovery of these inscriptions led us to further consider the problem, for the three characters "Ssu T'u Mu" inscribed on these two *tsun* were all written backward, unlike the other twenty-six examples, in which they were written the right way. The character "Ssu (司)" written backward becomes "Hou (后)," which makes the inscription "Hou T'u Mu Kuei (后㞷母癸)," in which "Hou T'u Mu" would be the name of a living person and "Kuei" a deceased person's ritual name. Following this line of reasoning, one could explain the bronzes in question as sacrificial vessels which were cast by "Hou T'u Mu" for someone whose ritual calendar day was "Kuei" and which, for some reason, were not presented to the deceased but buried in Fu Hao's own grave after her death. The excavation report, *Yin-hsü Fu Hao Mu*, adopts this interpretation of the inscriptions in question. But we felt then that this was just one possibility and that the inscriptions still required further research.

For the reasons outlined above, we do not now completely deny the possibility that "T'u Mu" is "Fu Hao"'s *tzu* name. However, one can derive another possible explanation from the inscription "Ssu T'u Mu Kuei," that is, that all three characters "Ssu T'u Mu" are reversed and that "Ssu T'u Mu Kuei" should be read together as a single phrase. This way, the inscription could be interpreted as concerning "T'u Mu," whose ritual calendar name was "Kuei," and "Ssu" could be read as "Tz'u (祠)," meaning to perform a sacrifice. The grammatical structure would then resemble that of phrases like "Ssu Mu Wu (司母戊)" or "Ssu Mu Hsin (司母辛)," except for the addition of the personal name "T'u." Ch'en Meng-chia once pointed out that in the oracle bone inscriptions "among the female ancestors there are those which follow the temple name with her personal name."[15] As Li Hsüeh-ch'in (李學勤) has noted,

14. H. C. Li 1977: 34.
15. Ch'en 1956a: 491.

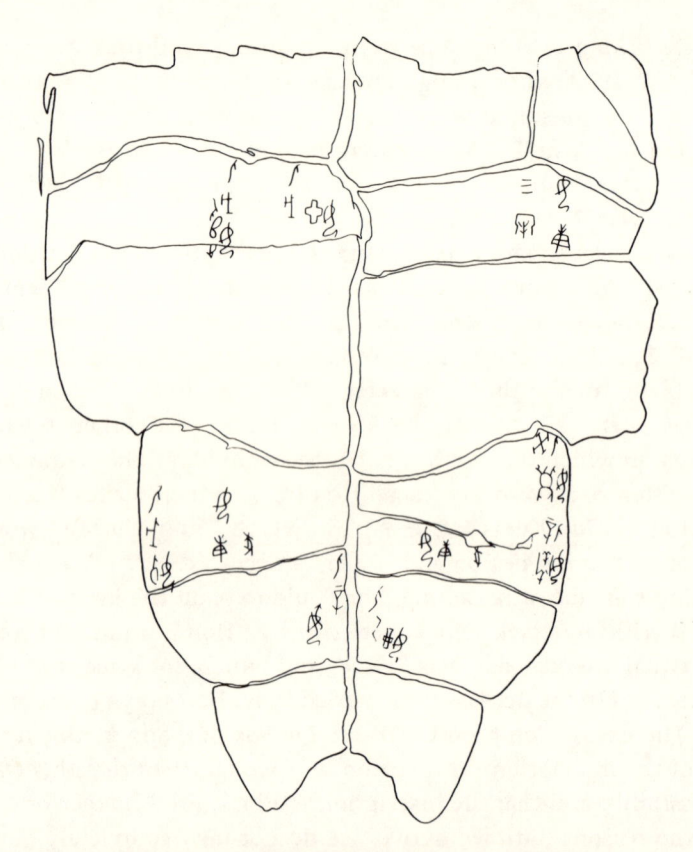

Fig. 20. Oracular plastron inscription: (yi-4677).

"When *pi* (妣) or *mu* (母) occurs in the oracle bone inscriptions, a personal name is sometimes also recorded."[16] One oracle bone inscription reads, "Ch'i pi kuei ta mu, pi chia kung mu Hui (其秉妣癸吴母, 妣甲龚母, 宙)."[17] One plastron used for divination[18] bears the following inscriptions: Pi Wu? (妣戊嬛), Pi Wu Ya (妣戊婭), Pi Wu? (妣戊姐), Pi Hsin T'a (妣辛妥), Pi Hsin? (妣辛姗), Pi Kuei Min (妣癸蠅), Pi Yi Ya (妣乙婭) (fig. 20). On the same shell, the phrase "Mu Keng (母庚)" also appears three times: twice written separately in a vertical column and once written horizontally and joined together. The character "mu (母)" is written in a way closely resembling the form of "nü (女)" when used

16. H. C. Li 1977: 34.
17. Chalfant and Britton 1935: 1456, 1716.
18. Tung 1948–53: pl. 4677.

as a radical. Because the characters "mu (母) and "nü (女)" are not distinguished in the oracle bone inscriptions, Ch'en Meng-chia once suggested that characters like "Ya (婭)"[19] and "T'a (妏)" on the above-described shell should be read as "Ya Mu (亞母)" and "T'a Mu (它母)" and so forth, and that all the instances of X Mu (某母)" in the inscriptions on this shell were run together. No matter whether one reads these inscriptions as one word with a *nü* (女) radical, as in "Ya (婭)," "T'a (妏)," and "Min(媲)," or as two separate words, as in "Ya Mu (亞母)," "T'a Mu (它母)," and "Min Mu (黽母)," they all must refer to the personal or *tzu* names of female ancestors and in this respect resemble the "Ssu T'u Mu Kuei" bronze inscriptions. However, the examples in the oracle bone inscriptions all put the ritual name first and the personal name last; this naming order is quite clear-cut. In contrast, the inscriptions on the two *tsun* have the three characters "Ssu T'u Mu" run together in a vertical column and the character "Kuei" at the right side, as if putting "Kuei" at the end. This configuration can be explained either as "T'u Mu, whose ritual name is Kuei" or as "Mu Kuei, whose *tzu* names is T'u." Based on a comparison with the inscription Ssu Hsin (司辛) on the stone ox, one could also read these inscriptions as "Ssu Kuei T'u Mu." According to the last two readings, the person referred to must be of the same generation as Fu Hao, while the appellation used in the first reading is not very clear; but no matter which reading is chosen, it is unlikely that the person referred to is one and the same as Fu Hao. The view that "Ssu T'u" and "Fu Hao" are not the same person was once espoused by a colleague in 1977 but did not attract attention at that time. After the discovery of the two large square *tsun*, we felt that the question of whether or not "Ssu T'u" and "Fu Hao" were the same person required further investigation.

In interpreting the "Ssu T'u Mu Kuei" inscriptions, we are inclined to explain them as meaning "Mu Kuei," whose *tzu* or personal name is "T'u." Among the three legally recognized consorts of Wu Ting was one with the ritual name "Kuei," and the oracle bone inscriptions of the Keng and Chia periods also contain records of sacrifices to "Mu Kuei." For example:

Divination on the day *jen-ch'en*.
Chu asked:

19. Ch'en 1956a: 491.

On next day *kuei-ssu*, should we sacrifice
three sheep, five Ch'iang ... to Mu Kuei?[20] ... On
day ... -ssu, Yi asked: ... *to yin*
to Mu Kuei liao?[21]

From the likelihood that "T'u Mu" was close in status to Fu Hao, and that her ritual name was "Kuei," it is possible that she is the "Mu Kuei" sacrificed to in the "Ch'u (出) group of oracle texts" from the Keng and Chia periods. The two square *tsun* must be sacrificial vessels made for her by a member of the generation of Wu Ting's sons. Ch'en Meng-chia once said, "Of the so-called Ch'u (出) group of diviners, Hsiung (兄) and Ch'u probably performed divinations in the early part of the reign of Tsu Keng." He noted further that "Hsiung and Ch'u should be dated to the Tsu Keng period or as early as the last part of the Wu Ting era."[22] Both diviners Hsiung and Ch'u performed divinations about sacrifices to "Mu Hsin (母辛)," and the diviner Ch'u once divined about a sacrifice to "Mu Kuei." These two consorts probably both died quite early. But from the analysis of the large square *tsun* from the Fu Hao grave, the woman whose ritual name was Kuei probably died even earlier than Fu Hao. Materials recording sacrifices to "Mu Kuei" among the oracle bone records of the Keng and Chia era by diviners of the Ch'u group are not numerous, and the sacrifices in no way match the magnificence of those made to "Mu Hsin." According to the most complete part of the above inscription, the sacrifice to "Mu Kuei" required three sheep and five Ch'iang, while the sacrifice to "Mu Hsin" used "Three oxen and ten Ch'iang."[23] There is also an incomplete divinatory text which records that "Ch'u divined for the king ... [about sacrificing] 100 sheep and ... blood to Mu Hsin."[24] This evidence is consistent with the conclusion reached above as to the appearance of the ritual vessels unearthed in the tomb.

The "Ssu T'u Mu" inscribed vessels from the Fu Hao tomb are all wine vessels; the vessel lid excavated before the war from tomb M 066 at Hsiao-t'un probably is a wine vessel also. We speculate that M 066 cannot be "Ssu T'u Mu"'s own tomb; it must be that her belongings

20. H. H. Hu 1954: #3309.
21. Shang 1933: 110.
22. Ch'en 1956a: 190–92.
23. Chalfant and Britton 1939: 674.
24. M. J. Kuo 1937: 384.

have been discovered scattered in other people's tombs. From the materials described above—such as the *hsien* listed in the Sung dynasty work and the *yüeh* ax recorded in the *Shodō zenshū* (書道全集),—and in addition from the fact that there is a patterned association of specific ritual vessels, wine vessels, food vessels, and cooking vessels excavated from Yin dynasty tombs, one can ascertain that "Ssu T'u Mu" inscribed vessels should include wine vessels, food vessels, cooking vessels, and weapons. Up to the present, very few have been found; perhaps they were destroyed early or perhaps have simply not been unearthed yet. The bronzes with the "Ssu T'u Mu" inscription from the Fu Hao grave must have belonged to a single person; their dates of casting may have differed somewhat, but the length of time between castings cannot have been too long. Among them, the latest are probably the two large square *tsun*.

Other inscribed vessels, apart from those inscribed with "Fu Hao," are largely wine vessels: these are sets of *ku* and *chüeh* and pairs of *tsun* and *chia*. As tradition has it, "the Yin people loved wine," so that gift exchanges of wine vessels between individuals were relatively numerous. The appearance of vessels with another person's name in Fu Hao's tomb probably was related to the ceremonial system of that era. Among these vessels, some whose types are missing among those with the inscription "Fu Hao" (such as the "Ya Kung [亞弜]" large round *ting* and the five *nao*-bells in a set [編鐃] and the "Ssu T'u Mu" round *tsun* and square *hu*), had the function of filling gaps in the group of Fu Hao vessels, thus causing the entire group of vessels in the grave to more nearly approach a perfect set.

CONCLUSION

The "Ssu T'u Mu" inscribed bronzes from the Fu Hao tomb are an important group of Yin dynasty bronzes bearing a single inscription; their date is relatively clear; and they form a valuable set of materials for the study of bronzes of the late Wu Ting period. From an analysis of the inscriptions "Ssu T'u Mu Kuei" on the two large square *tsun*, the "T'u Mu" in the inscription could be either Fu Hao's *tzu* name or another person whose social position was close to that of Fu Hao. She could have been another consort of Wu Ting, or perhaps the "Mu Kuei" sacrificed to in oracle bone inscriptions of the Keng (庚) and Chia (甲) period, in which case she would be the legally recognized consort of Wu Ting "Pi

Kuei (妣癸)" from the Yi and Hsin period cyclical ritual calendar: if the latter hypothesis is correct, then bronzes belonging to Pi Hsin (妣辛) and Pi Kuei (妣癸), two of Wu Ting's legally recognized consorts, have already been discovered. Since the excavation of the Fu Hao group, researchers have suggested that the "Mu Wu (母戊)" from the inscription on the "Ssu Mu Wu (司母戊)" large *ting* may be Wu Tings Consort "Pi Wu (妣戊)." T'ang Lan supports this view; and also suspects that "Pi Wu" may be the "Fu Ching (婦妌)" frequently seen in the oracle bone inscriptions.[25] If this theory stands up, bronzes belonging to all three of Wu Ting's consorts have seen the light of day, a fact which would have important implications for the study of the Yin dynasty ritual system and Yin dynasty ritual bronzes. If proven, it would be an event worthy of celebration in the work of Yin-hsü archaeology.

25. See K'ao-ku 1977b for T'ang Lan's statement.

6

A Brief Discussion of Fu Tzu*

Chang Cheng-lang

Of the more than four hundred bronze vessels unearthed from Tomb Number Five at Yin-hsü between sixty and seventy bear inscriptions relating to Fu Tzu 帚好. There are records about Fu Tzu on some one or two hundred divinatory inscriptions from Yin-hsü, the vast majority of which date to Period I (that is, the reign of Wu Ting 武丁, which may be exemplified by inscriptions No. 2606–2721 in *Ho-chi*); a small number date to Period IV (that is, the reigns of Wu Yi 武乙 and Wen Wu Ting 文武丁; for example, *Ho-chi* No. 32755–32762). Between these two groups of inscriptions are the reigns of Tsu Keng 祖庚, Tsu Chia 祖甲, Lin Hsin 廩辛, and K'ang Ting 康丁—four kings belonging to two generations—a time span of several decades, perhaps as much as a century. How are these conditions to be explained? Was Fu Tzu one or two persons? To which reign does the Fu Tzu in the bronze inscriptions belong? All these are questions of concern to the archaeological community.

The character *fu* 帚 in the oracle inscriptions is equivalent to *fu* 婦, as Kuo Mo-jo and T'ang Lan[1] have already explained. The character *Tzu* 好 consists of the female radical 女 and the phonetic *tzu* 子. It should not be pronounced *hao* as in *hao* for "good." Several dozen divinatory inscrip-

---

*[The name 婦好 has customarily been translated as "Fu Hao," even though it has long been recognized that the name "Hao" was probably derived from "Tzu," name of the Shang clan. Since "Hao" is the modern pronunciation of the character, pronouncing the character as "Hao" does not in any way deny the word's origin from "Tzu." For that reason, the name has been rendered as "Fu Hao" throughout the book. However, in this paper, Chang specifically stated that the word should be pronounced "Tzu," not "Hao." Thus, the name appears as "Fu Tzu" in this chapter only.—ED]

1. M. J. Kuo 1934; T'ang 1934: 24–27.

tions refer to a "Fu X," with the character prefixed by *fu* frequently containing the female radical. Actually, even extremely common names would be attached a *nü* radical; for instance, Fu Ching 帚井 is written as 帚姘, Fu Liang 帚良 as 帚娘. There are too many such cases to be listed here. To quote from the inscriptions:

> Crack-making on day *Kuei-ssu*, present *hui*, *wu*, and *yü* 御 sacrifices to Fu Tzu (written as 帚子)? (*Hsü-ts'un* No. 407)
>
> Inquiring: Not presenting the *yu* sacrifice to Fu Tzu (written as 帚子) in ... ? (*Ho-chi* No. 2833)

The Fu Tzu written as 帚子 in the above records is identical with 帚好. From this we know that the character 好 should be read *tzu*.

Fu Tzu is the form of address to a woman; since it occurs separately in Period I and Period IV, it cannot refer to the same person. The occurrence of the same name in different periods testifies to a common phenomenon in the society of that time; we shall be able to better understand the case of Fu Tzu by relating it to other persons mentioned in the divinatory record:

Name of person	Ho-chi Period I	Ho-chi Period II	Ho-chi Period IV
㫃 (Wu?)	4003–4035		32829–32838
Ch'üeh 雀	4108–4173		32839–32843
卓 (?)	4036–4103		32844–32871 (exc. 32870)
甼 (?)	4104–4107		32872–32874
Ch'a 出	4174–4209		32884–32885
Ping 並	4386–4405		32886–32891
Wang Ch'eng 望乘	3994–4002		32895–32899
Shih Pan 自般	4213–4238		32900–32901
Ch'üan Chih 犬征	4630–4639		32903–32904
Fu Tzu 帚好	2606–2721		32756–32762 (exc. 32758)
Fu Ching 帚井	2756–2772		32763–32764
Tzu Kung (?) 子弓	3073–3086	23531–23533	
Tzu Yü 子斐	3030–3060	23529–23530	32770–32774 (exc. 32772)
Tzu Ching (?) 子橐	3137–3144		32776
Tzu Yû 子漁	2973–3005		32780–32781
Tzu Hsiao 子效	3090–3095		32782

For reasons of convenience, we have selected only a few pieces from *Ho-chi* as examples in this table; in fact, there are many more instances in which the same name occurs in different periods. Some scholars are inclined to identify the Fu Tzu of Period I with the Fu Tzu of Period IV, which at first sight seems not to be difficult, the content of the Period IV material being simple. But it seems impossible to so identify the individuals in all the cases listed in the table above. In a previous article I used the Ch'üan-Chih 犬㣁 clan (tsu 族) and 㠯 as examples; the information about them is clearest, as the following inscriptions may show:

> Crack-making on day Ping-hsü, inquiring: ordering Ch'üan-chih to manage the fields in Ching 京? (P'u-ts'e No. 417) Period I
>
> Crack-making on day Wu-tzu, Pin 賓 inquired: ordering the Ch'üan-chih clan to reclaim the agricultural land (p'o-t'ien 㠯田) in Yü 虞? (Jinbun No. 281) Period I
>
> Crack-making on day X-mou, Ch'u 出 inquired: Ch'üan-chih … ? (Wen-lu No. 152) Period II
>
> Crack-making on day X-yin: ordering Ch'üan-chih to manage the fields in Ching? (Hsü-ts'un No. 1852) Period IV

From this one can see that Ch'üan-chih was the name of a clan which existed continuously from the first through the fourth period. Within this clan, not only rank and emolument but even the same official position were transmitted from generation to generation.

> Crack-making on day Kuei-mou, Pin inquired: [ordering] 㠯 to reclaim the agricultural land in Ching? (P'u-ts'e No. 417) Period I
>
> On day X-mou, inquiring: Shall the King order 㠯 to reclaim the agricultural land in Ching? (Yi-ts'un No. 250) Period IV

Like Ch'üan-chih, 㠯 is a clan whose name and official position were transmitted from generation to generation.[2] Since the day designations are approximately the same and the persons and places mentioned in the above two groups of inscriptions are identical, may we not consider them as one and the same thing? I do not think so. The periodization of oracle bone inscriptions is based on many factors. Although it is artificial, it has its rules and principles. If the results have not been satisfying so far, this is due to the insufficiency of material. In order to analyze a phenomenon, one must consider it in conjunction with other related phenomena. Let us therefore look at the names of diviners recorded in the divinatory inscriptions, where there are also quite a number of instances of the same name occurring in different periods. For example:

---

2. C. L. Chang 1973: 109–10.

Crack-making on day Ping-wu, Yung 永 enquired: 射 shooting at Ch'a 㞢, successful? (*Ching-hua* No. 7) Period I

Crack-making on day Kuei-wei, Yung enquired: will the king in the coming ten-day period not have misfortune? In the first month. On day Chia-shen, presenting the *chi* 祭 sacrifice to Tzu Chia and the 劦 (hsieh) sacrifice to Hsiang Chia? (*Ch'ien-pien* No. 1.19.5) Period V

The diviner Yung is thus seen in Periods I and V.

Crack-making on day Kuei-wei, Chih 㲋 enquired: no misfortune in the coming ten-day period? Shall Fu Ching 帚井 present the offerings? (*Wen-lu* No. 82) Period I

Crack-making on day Ting-mou, Chih enquired: will the king on his way to Jen 及 not encounter rain? (*Kikkō* No. 1.30.14) Period III

The diviner Chih is seen in Periods I and III.

Crack-making on day Ting-mou, K'ou 口 enquired: performing the *yi* 易 sacrifice to the sun on the next keng day? (*P'u-ts'e* No. 692) Period I

Crack-making on day Ping-tzu, K'ou enquired: will the king on his way to T'ien 田 not be harmed? In the twelfth month. (*Wen-lu* No. 726) Period II

Crack-making on day Chia-wu, K'ou enquired: ordering Ko 戈 to take command? In the twelfth month. (*Chia-pien* No. 3399) Period III

K'ou is seen in Periods I, II, and III.

Crack-making on day Ping-wu, Ta 大. (*Ho-chi* No. 19875) Period I, Shih 自 group of diviners.

Crack-making on day Kuei-ch'ou, Ta enquired: on day Tzu, offering five ch'iang 羌 to 引? (*Yi-chu* No. 1055) Period I

Crack-making on day Hsin-mou, Ta enquired: will Huan 洹 not flow by the town of Kao 辜? The seventh month. (*Yi-chu* No. 395) Period II

Crack-making on day Ting-hai, Ta, ... perhaps casting yellow metal (???) ... effectuating generalized good luck and grace ... ? (*Chia-pien* No. 1647) Period III

Ta is seen in the Shih group (generally regarded as the earliest body of divinatory inscriptions), and in Periods I, II, and III.

Crack-making on day Kuei-ssu, Huang 黃 enquired: in the coming ten-day period, no misfortune? (*Kikkō* 1.5.13) Period II

Crack-making on day Kuei-wei, Huang enquired: will the king in the coming ten-day period not have misfortune? Will the king come and attack Jen Fang? (*Chia-pien* No. 3355) Period V

Huang is seen in Periods II and V. On the basis of these records, one can perceive that Yung, Chih, K'ou, Ta, and Huang were all families who specialized in divining from turtle plastrons and who over many generations hereditarily took care of the divinatory business in the service of the Yin royal house. This is of course not a matter by chance but is determined by historical circumstance. However, we have to explain one more point, namely, why, if the individuals whose activities were recorded in oracle bone inscriptions were specialized clans, the record about them is spread so unevenly, so that there is sometimes much, sometimes little material about them, and sometimes nothing whatever. There are many reasons for this: archaeological materials have always contained some degree of chance, and the oracular plastrons and bones now to be seen are by no means the entire record. Therefore, in the study of ancient history, the written record being so fragmentary, we can prove only that something existed but not that something was not there. In the Spring and Autumn period, in the state of Ch'i 齊 there were two *ch'ing* families, Kuo 國 and Kao 高, and in the state of Wei 衛, the Ning 寧 lineage held the rank of *ch'ing* over nine generations, yet how often do they actually appear in *Tso Chuan* and *Kuo Yü*? The *Chou Li* records that the Grand Diviner (Ta Pu 大卜) "determines the Eight Commands of the tortoise shell on behalf of government matters." In Yin times, however, there was no such limitation on the activity of the diviners. The oracular inscriptions of each period are not uniform, as what was divined upon depended upon the wish of the king. For instance, the production of Yin society at the time was mainly agricultural, the king himself depended for his living on grain, and grains were also made into wine to be drunk; yet in the divinatory inscriptions, records on agricultural production activities are confined to Periods I and IV, whereas there are none for the other periods; even so we believe that during these years for which there is no written testimony agriculture continued to develop rather than being at a standstill.

In the compendia on oracle bones used in our above citations, there is, furthermore, much information about individuals of the designation Tzu 子 X. "Tzu" was a term of address for kinsmen, apparently involving some question of generational seniority, but the character "Tzu" did not change when the name prefixed by it appeared throughout several different periods. By the end of the Yin period, Tzu had probably become an honorific—or even aristocratic—form of address for males. An analogy to this may be found in *Chiu T'ang Shu*: the term *t'e-ch'in* 特勤 no longer had the connotation of "son."

If we further examine the phenomenon of identical names appearing in different periods, we find that these names were associated with lineage members and products; they are indeed "the symbols of the polity and the land." These continued through many generations, and some are still preserved in the Western Chou bronze inscriptions. In the following, we shall briefly examine how scholars of antiquity explained these phenomena.

> *Shih Chi, Wu-ti Pen-chi*: "Huang Ti 黃帝 was the son of Shao Tien 少典". [The *So Yin* commentary adds the following gloss]: Shao Tien is the appellation of a state of a lord (*kuo*), and not a personal name. *Vide Kuo Yü*, which says: "Shao Tien married a woman of the Yu Ch'iao Shih 有蟜氏, who gave birth to Huang Ti and Yen Ti 炎帝." Thus Yen Ti was also the son of Shao Tien. Even though the two emperors Huang Ti and Yen Ti were in the same line of succession, there were in between them, according to *Ti-Wang Shih-chi*, eight emperors whose lengths of reign totaled over 500 years. If Shao Tien was the name of their father, how could Yen Ti have succeeded Huang Ti on the throne only after 500 years had elapsed? How long his lifespan would have had to be! See, furthermore, the *Ch'in Pen-chi*, which states: "The descendant of Chuan Hsü 顓頊 was named Nü Hsiu 女脩. After swallowing a dark bird's egg, she gave birth to Ta Ye 大業. Ta Ye married a Shao Tien Shih woman who gave birth to Po Yi 柏翳." From this it is clear that Shao Tien is the appellation of a state, not a personal name.

Ssu-ma Ch'ien's insight is correct. What he calls "appellation of a state" (*kuo-hao* 國號), we call tribes and clans (*shih-tsu* 氏族). The ancient texts repeatedly describe a system of hereditary offices, as, for instance, in the following quotes:

> *Kuo Yü*: *Chou Yü*: Anciently, our former kings' ancestors served as ministers of agriculture (*Hou-chi* 后稷) under Yü and Hsia.
>
> *Shih-chi*, *T'ai-shih-kung Tzu-hsü*: The Ch'ung 重 and Li 黎 shih hereditarily kept in order Heaven and Earth. ... The Ssu-ma 司馬 shih hereditarily supervised the compilation of the History of Chou.

In *Chou Li*, many times given families hold given official positions, for example, the Feng Hsiang 馮相 shih, the Yi Ch'i 伊耆 shih, etc., totaling about forty examples.

Shih-pen, Shih-hsing-pien: The P'eng-tsu 彭祖 shih was the offspring of Ta P'eng 大彭, deriving their shih name from his appellation. They were the guardian officials of the royal storehouses (*Ts'ang-li* 藏吏) under the Shang and *Chu-hsia* 柱下 officials under the Chou; their term of service was over eight hundred years.

Here, eight hundred is a round number; in some books it is specified that "it was 767 years counting backwards to the late Yin period." Thus, not only the clan name was inherited from generation to generation, but also lifespans were added together. In the oracle bones, a Ta Fang 大方 is often seen. It was one of the important exterior dominions of the time. According to Yang Shu-ta, this was the Ta P'eng Shih, P'eng Tsu Shih perhaps being one of its branch descendants, who were hereditarily the recordkeepers of the Shang and the Chou dynasty: "a transmitter but not a maker, believing in and loving the ancients," as *Lun Yü* lauds one of them. From these phenomena we infer that royal offices were hereditarily bestowed on the many clans during the Yin dynasty. Such was the case with female offices also. Knowing this, we are in a better position to explain Fu Tzu, as we will try to do below.

A divinatory inscription of Period I states:

Enquiring on day Ping-wu: will the many *fu* 多帚 not become ill? Enquiring on day Ping-wu: will the many *ch'en* 多臣 not become ill? (*Yi-pien* Bi, 8816)

Such an oracle was cast perhaps because at that time epidemic diseases were rampant. The parallel enquiries about *fu* and *ch'en* indicate that the two were beings of a similar order who were equally close to the Yin king's heart. Compare the following inscription from Period III:

Dedicate *hui* ritual to the many *mu* 多母 with offering? Dedicate *hui* ritual to the favorite *ch'en* with offering? (*Ho-chi* No. 101)

Mu ("Mothers") is an honorific term for women of advanced age, and the "favorite *ch'en*" are none other than courtesans in the entourage of the king. The parallel enquires about the "many *mu*" and the "favorite *ch'en*" are, just as in the previous inscription, counterparts perceived as mutually equivalent. From this we infer that in the entourage of the king of Yin there were some female functionaries. The Yin era belongs to early class society; the historical mission of its rulers was to destroy or sublate the customs and traditions of the clan society. The members of the clans were constrained by custom and tradition and could not easily engage themselves in the new mission; as a result, many newly developing tasks were assigned to the slaves to perform. In this way, primitive slaves (*ch'en* 臣) evolved into incipient officials (*ch'en* 臣). The "many *fu*" and the "many *ch'en*" both fall in between primitive slaves and primitive officials. Under directions from the rulers, they performed public functions, and they also took care of the rulers' personal service. *Kuo Yu: Wu Yü* relates how after Wu 吳 had defeated Yüeh 越,

> Kou Chien 句踐 [of Yüeh] requested an alliance. He ordered the female attendants (*Ti-nü* 嫡女) to take dustpans and brushes to prepare the royal palace (for a festivity); moreover, he made the male attendants (*Ti-nan* 嫡男) take *p'an* 盤 and *yi* 匜 vessels and carry them after the various captains [of Wu]. ... This was strictly according to the code of behavior (*li* 禮) among the feudal lords.

Where did the king of Yin's "many *fu*" come from? I suggest that some of them were sent to court, hereditarily from generation to generation, by conquered or submissive vassals.

There is textual information on the hereditary female attendants (*shih-fu* 世婦) of Yin and Chou. See *Li Chi, Ch'ü Li*, section II:

> The son of Heaven has his queen (*hou* 后), his helpmates (*fu-jen* 夫人), his women of family (*shih-fu* 世婦 [here translated as "hereditary female attendants"]), and his ladies of honor (*pin* 嬪). [These] constitute his wife and concubines. The son of Heaven appoints the officers of Heaven's institution (*T'ien Kuan* 天官), the precedence among them belonging to the six grandees:—the Grand-governor (*Ta Tsai* 大宰), the Grand-minister of the Ancestral temple (*Ta Tsung* 大宗), the Grand-historiographer (*Ta Shih* 大史), the Grand-minister of prayers (*Ta Chu* 大祝), the Grand-minister of justice (*Ta Shih* 大士), and the Grand-diviner (*Ta Pu* 大卜). These are the guardians and superintendents of the six departments of the statutes.

Cheng Hsüan (second century A.D.) annotates: "This is probably the system of Yin." K'ung Ying-ta's subcommentary (eighth century) adds: "This passage comprehensively discusses the matter of establishing the male and female officials, ... the recorder's statements cannot only be derived from the Rites of Chou, but he had perhaps a few scattered notes on those of Hsia and Yin and stated them." *Li Chi, Ch'ü Li* states, moreover:

> The ruler of a state (*kuo-chün* 國君) should not call by their names the highest ministers (*ch'ing-lao* 卿老), nor the [hereditary] ladies (*shih-fu* 世婦). A great officer (*tai-fu* 大夫) should not call in that way a hereditary officer, nor the niece and younger sister of his wife (*chih-ti* 姪娣). [Another] officer (*shih* 士)

should not call by name the steward of his family, nor his principal concubine (*chang-ch'ieh* 長妾).

The term *kuo-chün* refers to the feudal lords (*chu-hou* 諸侯), whose hereditary female attendants were equal in rank to a grand official's *chih-ti* and to an ordinary official's chief concubines. "Not calling by their names" is an expression of reverence. The character *shih* 世 appears twice in this quote; it has two meanings in the ancient texts, "great" and "generation." Anciently, the address *Shih Tzu* 世子 meant the same as *Ta Tzu* 大子, and *Shih Fu* 世父 and *Shih Mu* 世母 meant the same as *Ta Fu* 大父 and *Ta Mu* 大母 (Great Father/Great Mother). But in the case of the *shih-fu*, such an interpretation will not do, as both *shih-fu* and *shih-ch'en* 世臣 were very numerous and their rank was not very high. Nothing warrants their being called "great." In *Mencius; Liang Hui Wang*, Section II, there is the following passage:

> When men speak of "an ancient kingdom," it is not meant thereby that it has lofty trees in it, but that it has ministers (sprung from families which have been in it) for generations (*shih-ch'en* 世臣).

The commentary by Chao Ch'i notes that *shih-ch'en* means "officials who have cultivated virtue over many successive generations." This is consistent with Mencius's discussion of hereditary emoluments (*shih-lu* 世祿) and hereditary official posts (*shih-kuan* 世官). The connotation of *shih-fu* is analogous with that of *shih-ch'en*, namely, "female attendants who have been around over many successive generations." While the hereditary female attendants managed the inner affairs at the court, the high ministers had power over the external matters of government. Both inherited their offices from generation to generation.

In *Chou Li*, a first reference to an unspecified number of *shih-fu* may be found in the section on the Ministry of Heaven (*Tien Kuan* 天官):

> The *shih-fu* are in charge of the sacrifices, the reception of guests, and funerary ceremonies. They direct the women of the palace in washing, cleaning, and preparing the sacrificial grains. When the day of sacrifice has come, they inspect and arrange the ceremonial paraphernalia which the palace women have prepared and generally all that constitutes the delicate viands of the inner court. They are in charge of going to console and attend the funerary services of ministers (*ch'ing* 卿) and grand officials (*tai-fu*).

Another instance is in the section of the Ministry of Spring (*Ch'un Kuan* 春官): "In each palace hall, (there shall be assigned) two *ch'ing*, four *tai-fu* of lower rank and eight *shih* of medium rank." The accompanying text explains:

> The *shih-fu* are charged with supervising the fasting and the sacrifices in the harem, and to arrange in order the ritual paraphernalia. They indicate the ceremonial functions of the empress; they direct the women of the six palaces in preparing the grains and the offerings. They see to the ceremonial functions of the ranked ladies of the interior and of the exterior (*nei tsung* 內宗 and *wai tsung* 外宗). At great entertainments in honor of guests, they do likewise. At great funerary rites, they arrange the wailing that is performed by appointed ladies from the exterior as well as from the interior. If some of these women are not respectful, they reprimand and punish them. Whenever the empress pays homage to another lady (*fu-jen* 婦人), they instruct and direct her. Generally, the *shih-fu* are occupied with all the interior affairs of the court, which have to be communicated to the officials on the outside.

In both texts the *shih-fu*'s functions are described as being basically the same; we can see that they are female officials, living in the palace, attending to the sacrifices, to the entertainment of guests, and to mourning rites. From the text of *Chou Li* itself, it appears that the foremost among them were the *shih-fu* of the Ministry of Spring. They were of different ranks, their organization was very detailed, and their tasks assigned in a very minutely regulated manner. The number of the *shih-fu* who were under the Ministry of Heaven, is not known, and their organizational conditions are not specified. Jointly with the nine *pin* 嬪 [translated by Legge as "ladies of honour"] and the *yü* 御 consorts, they had already entered the ranks of Son of Heaven's closest associates. I presume that the *shih-fu* in Chou times were at first official staff members, and after working in the palace became the Son of Heaven's *pin* and *yü* consorts. This sort of affair is also known from later times: in *Chin-ku Ch'i-kuan* there is a piece called "Shan-fu-lang Ch'üan-chou Chia-ou 單符郎全州佳偶," which describes how a Sung dynasty gentry family had their assigned quotas of female servants, such as "kitchen maid" and "needle-and-thread person," and how they later one by one became their master's mistresses. In a patriarchal system, when the master exerts full control, this cannot be avoided. In *Chou Li, Ch'un Kuan*, directly after the *shih-fu* follow the

> ranked ladies of the interior (*nei tsung* 內宗): all the women of the interior who have an official appointment. Ranked ladies of the exterior (*wai tsung* 外宗): all the women of the exterior who have an official appointment.

The "inner ladies" are those of the same clan (*hsing* 姓) as the king, whereas the "outer ladies" are those of different *hsing*. The origin of the *shih-fu* is none other than that. They were probably all born into certain lineages (*tsung-tsu* 宗族). *Tso Chuan, Chao Kung* records Tzu Ch'an 子產 as saying: "The ladies of the harem should not be of the same surname as the master of it." But Duke P'ing of Chin 晉平公, to whom Tzu Ch'an is remonstrating, "has in his harem four Chi 姬" ladies. "Hsieh 契 was of the Tzu 子 clan." The Fu Tzu 帚好 of Yin thus were possibly "inner ladies." The hereditary female attendants were close to the king; when their age or appearance or some other conditions were not up to standard, the king would not fall in love with them, and they would not be made consorts. Therefore, *Chou Li* assigns them to two different ministries (*kung* 宮).

The one or two hundred divinatory inscriptions about Fu Tzu have time and again been used since the discovery of the Fu Tzu bronzes. Many of these inscriptions are about sacrifices, which corresponds to what *Chou Li* says about the function of the *shih-fu*. The inscriptions that concern Fu Tzu's giving birth to a child attest to a particularly careful divination procedure. They invariably enquire about the day of childbirth, whether it would be a boy or a girl, and whether or not it was auspicious. The inscriptions about Fu Tzu's illnesses also show deep concern, even about such a minor ailment as a toothache. From these minute and trifling details we surmise that Wu Ting and Fu Tzu were husband and wife; she could not have been his daughter-in-law, and it seems even less likely that she was in an ordinary master-servant relationship with Wu Ting. Since the *shih-fu* dwelt in the royal palace, they tend to evolve gradually into family members of the Son of Heaven. The following inscription from Period I is thus not surprising:

> Enquiring: ordering Fu Tzu to muster the many *fu* 多帚 in 彶 (a place name)? (*Ho-chi* No. 2658)

Originally Fu Tzu was probably one of the "many *fu*" and came to be appreciated by Wu Ting and elevated above the others. That she had great military power is not consistent with what *Chou Li* says about the hereditary female attendants' occupations; this must be a result of her having attained Wu Ting's special favors. The fact that at the same time there were many other *fu* besides her indicates that not every *fu* was in such a position; and the fact that there were two different Fu Tzu in successive periods shows that not every Fu Tzu was, either.

Some oracle inscriptions from Period I read:

Enquiring: will perhaps T'ang 唐 take Fu Tzu? Enquiring: will perhaps Ta Chia 大甲? Will perhaps Tsu Yi 祖乙? Enquiring: will perhaps T'ang take Fu Tzu? Enquiring: will Fu Tzu be taken from – – – –? Enquiring: will perhaps Ta Chia take a *fu*? Enquiring: will Fu Tzu be taken or not? Enquiring: will Tzu Yi take a *fu*? (*Ho-chi* No. 2636 *recto*)

Crack-maming on day Chi-mou, Pin 賓 (officiating); the king on inspecting the cracks said: the one from on high (who will take Fu Tzu) will perhaps be (Shang) Chia. (the same bone, *verso*)

Enquiring: will Fu Tzu be taken from on high? Will perhaps Ta Chia take a *fu*? Enquiring: will Fu Yi be taken or not?

Enquiring: will perhaps Tzu Yi take a *fu*? Will perhaps Fu Yi 父乙? (*Ku-fang* No. 1020, *recto*)

Crack-making on day Chi-mou, Pin (officiating); the king on inspecting the cracks said: the one from on high (see above) will perhaps be (Shang) Chia. (the same bone, *verso*)

Crack-making on day Chi-mou, Pin enquired: will perhaps the god (*Ti* 帝) take Fu Tzu? (*Ho-chi* No. 2637)

These three oracular bones all record a Chi-mou date with Pin as the officiating enquirer; moreover, their contents are identical. They may thus be presumed to be contemporary. The last piece contains the character *Ti*. *Li Chi*, *Ch'ü Li*, Section II, states:

> When his place is given to him [namely, the Son of Heaven's] in the ancestral temple, and his spirit-table is set up, he is styled on it "the god (*Ti* 帝)."

Ti is the address for the most recently deceased king, here identical with Fu Yi mentioned on *K'u-fang* No. 1020, referring to Hsiao Yi, father of Wu Ting. Yao Hsiao-sui[3] has said that "taking (ch'ü 取)" is indeed "taking in marriage." A former king "taking" a *fu* in this way means that the marriage ritual was enacted with her on his behalf. We should further note that T'ang is the Founding Ancestor (*kao-tsu* 高祖) of the dynastic Shang; Ta Chia is Wu Ting's Great Ancestor (*ta tsung* 大宗), Tzu Yi is his Middle Ancestor (*chung-tsung* 中宗), and Fu Yi or *Ti* is his deceased father (*ni* 禰). How can all three of these persons have become the marriage partners of one single Fu Tzu? And if this oracle was performed and handled by Wu Ting personally, how could the em-

---

3. Yao 1963: 79–82.

barrassment be avoided? The ancients emphasized the proper orders in human relationships; if the assignment of tasks to *Fu Tzu* was indeed as bizarre as this, there is no way to explain it. Therefore I have arrived at the following points:

1. The term *fu* does not imply that the *fu* were as a rule in a husband-and-wife relationship with the Yin kings. Only when the king and his *fu* engaged in sexual intercourse can they be said to have been husband and wife.

2. Fu Tzu belonged to a group of hereditary female attendants (*shih-fu*); there could have been Fu Tzu under every king and there was not just the one in the reign of Wu Ting.

3. The "many *fu*" were female officials in charge of sacrifices at the temples of the founding ancestor, the Great Ancestor, the Middle Ancestor, and the deceased father. Fu Tzu, too, was one of them.

About the time of the death of the Wu Ting period Fu Tzu, we can read in the divinatory inscriptions of Period I:

> Crack-making on day X-yin, Wei 韋 enquired: performing the *pin* 㱃 rite to Fu Tzu? Enquiring: perhaps not performing the *pin* rite to Fu Tzu? (*Ho-chi* No. 2638)
>
> Performing the *ssu* 司 rite to Fu Tzu? (*Ho-chi* No. 2672)

These inscriptions ask whether to sacrifice to Fu Tzu; on the basis of this sort of material, one can infer that she had already died during the Wu Ting period. Judging from the shapes and ornaments of the bronzes unearthed from tomb Five at Yin-hsü, one surmises that there are early and late ones; the characters in their inscriptions, too, lack uniformity. The stylistic development visible here may exceed that which was possible within one generation. Was the owner of all these Fu Tzu bronzes, then, the Fu Tzu of the Wu Ting period? If one accepts the proposition that "Fu Tzu" were hereditary female attendants who succeeded one another through many successive generations, perhaps this question may be easier to answer.

SUPPLEMENT

Nan-ti No. 917 reads:

> Crack-making on day Yi-yu; performing the *yü* 御 sacrifice on behalf of Fu Hsüan 箙旋 to Fu Tzu, (offering) ten dogs?

This newly discovered information on Fu Tzu has received wide scholarly attention. The character shapes, according to the criteria of the Old School, should date to Wu Yi's reign; according to the New School, it would belong to the Li group of diviners and should date from the time of kings Wu Ting and Tsu Keng. Yi-yu is the day of crack-making; *yü* is a verb denoting a sacrifice performed in order to request protection. Fu Hsüan is the name of a person. "*Yü* Fu Hsüan" means to perform the *yü* sacrifice in order to obtain protection for Fu Hsüan. "To Fu Tzu" explicates the addressee of the sacrifice.

In the divinatory inscriptions from Period I we read:

> Crack-making on day Ting-hai, K'o 殼 enquired: Last Yi-yu day, Fu Hsüan performed the *yü* sacrifice to [from T'ang 自唐], Ta Ting 大丁, Ta Chia 大甲, and Tsu Yi 祖乙 (offering 100 *ch'ang* 鬯 measures [of wine], 100 *ch'iang* 羌, and *mou* 卯 300 sacrificial cattle....?

In *Hou-pien* I No. 28.4 combined with *Yi-ts'un* No. 543, some text is missing behind the character *yü*, but in Period I there is one inscription that reads:

> Enquiring: performing the *yü* sacrifice to from T'ang, Ta Chia, Ta Ting, and Tsu Yi, (offering) 100 *ch'iang* and 100 sacrificial cattle. (*Yi-ts'un* No. 873 and *Chia-pien* No. 1094).

On this basis, we can reconstruct the text of the previous inscription by adding "tzu T'ang." There is absolutely no doubt that K'o was an inquirer of Wu Ting's time. "Last Yi-yu day, Fu Hsuan performed the *yü* sacrifice" and the passage on the first-mentioned inscription, "Crack-making on day Yi-yu; performing the *yü* sacrifice on behalf of Fu Hsüan", are identical in textual meaning. Scholars have taken this as a proof that the two inscriptions are contemporaneous, and this has been used as evidence to support the placement of the Li group of diviners in Period I. However, upon reexamining the matter, I am left with many doubts, as I shall presently explain.

"Last Yi-yu day" denotes the day of sacrifice, the word *hsi* 昔 implying that it refers to a date in the past. The date of divining in this inscription is Ting-hai, and Yi-yu is two days before that. Why should one have chosen Yi-yu as the day of sacrifice? From a great number of sources we can perceive that it was probably on account of some connection with T'ang, who indeed was Ta-yi 大乙, that the sacrifice was performed on day Yi-yu. The following examples show that T'ang was frequently sacrificed to on that date.

A BRIEF DISCUSSION OF FU TZU

Crack-making on day Yi-yu: presenting the 㞢 (*yu*) sacrifice to Ch'eng 成? (*Pa-li* No. 9)

Next Yi-yu day, presenting the *yu* 㞢 and *fa* 伐 sacrifices to from Ch'eng 自成? Next Yi-yu, presenting the *yu* 㞢 and *fa* 伐 sacrifices to the Five Ancestors: Shang Chia, Ch'eng, Ta Yi, Ta Chia, and Tsu Yi? (*Ping-pien* No. 38)

Crack-making on day Chia-shen, K'o enquired: next Yi-yu ... Yi-yu, offering wine to T'ang, indeed ... ? (*Ch'ien-pien* No. 7.35.1)

Enquiring: next Yi-yu offering wine to T'ang, correct? (*Ho-chi* No. 1300, recto)

Crack-making on day [Hsin]-ssu, enquiring: next Yi-yu perhaps offering wine to T'ang?, performing the *yi* 易 sacrifice to the sun? (*Ho-chi* No. 1304)

Crack-making on day Chia-shen: shall the king use four sacrificial cattle to offer to Ta Yi, using them next Yi-yu? (*Ho-chi* No. 19816)

Crack-making on day Chia-shen, X enquiring: next Yi-[yu] presenting the *hsieh* 叠 sacrifice to Ta Yi, no [calamity] in ... ? (*Ho-chi* No. 22734)

[Crack-making on day] X X, Yin 尹 [enquired: next] Yi-yu presenting the *hsieh* 叠 sacrifice to Ta Yi, no calamity? In the eighth month. (*Yi-chu* No. 369)

[Yi]-yu, will the king perhaps present the *yu* 又 sacrifice to Ta Yi? Shall the king receive favor? (*Ho-chi* No. 27089)

Perhaps presenting the *yu* and 彳 sacrifice to Ta Yi? Perhaps on the following day, Yi-yu, offering wine? (*Ho-chi* No. 27100)

Enquiring on day Yi-yu: presenting the *yu* and *liao* 尞 sacrifices to Shang Chia, Ta Yi, Ta Ting, Ta Chia, ... ? (*Ho-chi* No. 23287)

Crack-making on day Yi-yu, enquiring; will the king perform the *pin* 宀 rite to Ta Yi on the following day? Will there be no harm? (*Ho-chi* No. 35490)

These twelve inscriptions contain examples from all five periods. Ch'eng, T'ang, and Ta Yi all refer to the same person, T'ang 湯. The Yi-yu day was used as the day of sacrifice to T'ang uninterruptedly for two to three centuries. It was probably determined by the ritual system of that time. Why did the *yu* sacrifice to Fu Tzu referred to on *Nan-ti* No. 917 also have to be enquired about by crack-making on day Yi-yu? There are two possibilities: (1) there was no special meaning intended. Since some inscriptions about Fu Tzu do not have a Yi-yu date, this one could be entirely fortuitous; but because both sacrifices were offered by Fu Hsuan, this explanation is not satisfactory; (2) some special meaning was intended, namely, that the decision on when to perform the sacrifice was in some way influenced by T'ang. This again could be a reflection of "T'ang 'taking' Fu Tzu" in a ritual marriage, as we have seen above.

In *Ho-chi* No. 2636 *recto*, it is divined about whether T'ang and others will in this way "take" a *fu*. If we compare the persons mentioned in that inscription to the above-mentioned addressees of Fu Hsüan's *yu* sacrifice in the inscription by K'o, we find that T'ang, Ta Chia, and Tsu Yi occur on both, only Ta Ting's place being unfilled on *Ho-chi* No. 2636 *recto*. The character *ch'ü* 取 ("take") is frequently encountered in the oracular inscriptions, where it has a connotation of "picking out, choosing," as in the following examples:

> Crack-making on day Kuei-hai, enquiring: calling upon the many *she* 射 and *wei* 衛 officials? (*Kikkō* No. 2.320.2)

> Crack-making on day Ting-wei, K'o enquired: shall Ch'üeh 雀 choose the *she* officials? Shall perhaps 𧊒 order to choose the *she* officials? (*Ch'ien-pien* No. 7.10.3)

She is the name of a group of officials, similar to the *she-jen* 射人 mentioned in *Chou Li*. Their number was very large, and when the king ordered Ch'üeh and 𧊒 to *ch'ü she* 取射, he meant that some should be picked out.

> Crack-making on day Jen-hsü, K'o enquired: calling upon the many *ch'üan* officials to catch deer with nets in Nung 農? The eighth month. Crack-making on day Jen-hsü, K'o enquired: choosing *ch'üan* officials to catch deer with nets in Nung? (*Yi-p'ien* No. 5329)

Ch'üan is the name of a group of officials, similar to the *ch'üan-jen* in *Chou Li*. The "chosen *ch'üan*" are here placed against the "many *ch'üan*." *Fu* is an official name in the oracular inscriptions, similar to the *shih-fu* in *Chou Li*. *Ch'ü Fu Tzu* means to choose one *Fu Tzu* from among the "many *fu*." T'ang, Tsu Chia, and Tsu Yi all have their ancestral temples. The "chosen *fu*" would watch over their temples and present the appropriate sacrifices. In Yin times, each king had many *fu*, and all had *fu* of the Tzu clan among them. Such a divination as "will T'ang choose Fu Tzu?" would have been mere routine; they could have been performed at any time. It is impossible that such an event would have occurred only once. As the "chosen Fu Tzu" were mainly responsible for managing the sacrifices, they were bound to the temples of the former kings in death as in life. For this reason, when one sacrificed to one of the former kings, one would also perform a rite in honor of his deceased *fu* Tzu. Some scholars believe that there was but one Fu Tzu in the Yin period, namely, Wu Ting's mate, but this is incompatible with much of the evidence.

A BRIEF DISCUSSION OF FU TZU 119

Such a locus as "will T'ang choose Fu Tzu?" would no longer be explainable. The diviner K'o was a central figure in the Pin group of diviners of Period I and left a great number of divinatory records. Among the over 17,000 Wu Ting period oracle bones excavated from Cache Deposit 127 at Yin-hsü, those of K'o constitute the greatest part, outnumbering even those of the diviner Pin. In this cache, no Li 歷 group inscriptions were found. I believe the diviner K'o's dates to be relatively early, antedating the Ch'u 出 and Li groups, with which for that reason they were never mingled. *Nan-ti* Nos. 910 and 911 are the *recto* and *verso* of the same bone; on the verso there are the four characters "Jen-tzu (day), K'o officiated." They were among the carved narratives of Period I and they are similar to the characters carved on the bridges of the turtle plastrons and those of the glenoid cavities of the bovine scapulas. On the *recto* of the bone there are three rows of Li group inscriptions, and the narrative carvings of the Li group of inscriptions (see *Ho-chi* 35166—35218) are quite dissimilar indeed from that of "Jen-tzu (day), K'o officiating." We may infer that this is a bone that entered the stocks in Period I, to be used only by the diviners of the Li group at the end of the period. It is not a product of cooperation between the Pin and the Li groups.

Finally, a short conclusion on *Nan-ti* No. 917. This inscription is not contemporaneous with those of the diviner K'o; it must be much later. Fu Hsüan is the name of a lineage (possibly a family of hereditary officials), which could appear as the same name in several periods. Fu Tzu was a hereditary female attendant, as they existed throughout all the reigns of the Yin dynasty; the one who was Wu Ting's mate was but one of them. The day of the oracle, Yi-yu, was determined by ritual custom; it was used in this way throughout the generations, and the Fu Tzu who was thus sacrificed to was one whom "T'ang had chosen as his *fu* Tzu," not Wu Ting's mate. *Nan-ti* No. 917 cannot be dated earlier than the middle of Wu Ting's reign because the *Kan-chih* dates (Yi-yu) and the performer of the *yu* sacrifice (Fu Hsüan) are identical to those in the oracular texts of the Pin group of diviners (K'o).

7

A Brief Description of the Fu Hao Oracle Bone Inscriptions

Chang Ping-ch'üan

In the spring of 1976, on elevated land north of Hsiao-t'un village at the southwest edge of the palace and temple remains of Yin-hsü, a grave that had never been plundered was discovered: Yin-hsü Tomb Number Five. The objects excavated there were both numerous and magnificent. Among them were inscribed ritual bronzes, of which dozens bore the two characters "Fu Hao (婦好)" cast on them.[1] For this reason, the grave was called the Fu Hao tomb. Of course, the oracle bone inscriptions are the most valuable tool for dating this tomb, and the divination inscriptions in which the name Fu Hao appears naturally offer the most effective supporting evidence. For this reason, the Fu Hao divination inscriptions have attracted universal attention, particular interest, and heated debate.

The Japanese scholar Shima Kunio was the first to undertake the work of assembling the Fu Hao inscriptions. His *Inkyo Bokuji Sōrui* was not written especially for the purpose of gathering the Fu Hao inscriptions; however, his compilation and listing of entries, as well as their grouping and categorization, are quite comprehensive. He collected all the oracle bone materials that he could find, and line by line and word by word copied out as entries the divination inscriptions on each one, according to the original form of the characters on the bone and shell. He then arranged them in categories and compiled them into a book. The advan-

---

1. K'ao-ku-hsüeh-pao 1977a: 62.

tage of this book is that one can see the characters as they are in the original rubbings and thereby avoid much repetitive and laborious checking as well as following all sorts of different kinds of transcriptions and the consequent misunderstandings and misinterpretations. The difficulty with the book is that those who do not know the oracle bone script cannot use it; also, some of the fragments included in it are accidentally mixed up, and the supplemented characters are not always correct, so that, on the whole, it is not convenient for the beginning scholar. The Fu Hao inscriptions collected in the *Sōrui* include 203 entries; of these, 41 were repeated occurrences, all of which have been individually annotated. In addition to these, there are 59 fragmentary inscriptions in which only the characters "Fu Hao" or "Hao" are preserved; for these, only the location of the fragment is recorded, to facilitate research.[2] Altogether, there are 262 entries. This compilation can be said to be complete; it lacks only those materials discovered or pieced-together after publication.

The Fu Hao appearing in oracle bone inscriptions from Period I, the era of Wu Ting, has been a familiar figure for some time. Since a number of articles specifically discuss or describe her,[3] I do not plan to add further discussion here. I wish merely to present a few ideas about the so-called Period IV Fu Hao inscriptions. Perhaps I will be able to make a contribution to the investigation of this side of the problem. In another work, *Inkyo bokuji kenkyū*, Shima said of the Period IV Fu Hao inscriptions: "Fu Hao appears frequently in Period I. As will be noted below, she also is often found on Period IV oracle shells and bones."[4] The "oracle shells and bones" "noted below" are a reproduction of his copies of seven oracle bone inscriptions, which I now transcribe in modern script as follows:*

戊辰貞 帚好亡囗 (*Ning* [寧] 1.491).
Divination on day *Wu-ch'en*: Will Fu Hao not suffer a disaster?

丙戌貞 帚好亡囗 (*To* [掇] 1.444).
Divination on day *Ping-hsü*: Will Fu Hao not suffer a disaster?

2. Shima 1967: 139–41.
3. Articles that focus on the problem of Fu Hao include Wang, Chang, and Yang 1977, Yen 1981.
4. Shima 1958: 457. (Page numbers are those of Chinese translation).

*Oracle bone inscriptions quoted herein will be presented first as transcribed by the author in modern script, then (if possible) translated into English using conventions outlined in Keightley, 1978. For citations to collections of oracle bone inscriptions, the abbreviations listed in Keightley, 1978, are used. [Translator's note]

婦好龍？(To 1.444).
Will Fu Hao [ ] dragon?

己亥卜，辛丑歆婦好祀？(Chia Pien [甲編] 668).
Crack-making on day Chi-hai. On day hsin-ch'ou, offer Fu Hao a li sacrifice?

□口卜，既☒婦好？(Yi [佚] 649).
Crack-making on day ... Already ... Fu Hao?

丙戌貞：婦好亡囚？(Ye [鄴] 3.458).
Divination on day Ping-hsü: Will Fu Hao not suffer a disaster?

甲申卜：貞：婦好母？八月 (Hsu Ts'un [續存] 1443).
Crack-making on day Chia-shen: Divined: Will Fu Hao give birth? Eight month.

This is probably the first time that an oracle bone scholar has pointed out that some of the Fu Hao inscriptions belong to Period IV. It is likely that all the Period IV Fu Hao inscriptions cited by various scholars afterward are included in the above list. However, Shima Kunio's purpose in citing these inscriptions was not to prove that there was also a Fu Hao in Period IV. He wished merely to use this example to explain his views on the chracter *fu* (婦) in the oracle bone inscriptions, that is, that the oracle bone *fu* was not *Fu* (婦), as in *fu-nü* (婦女), or "women," but instead the name for one kind of high official. Thus, Fu Hao would be neither an individual's name nor a king's consort. The general tenor of his argument went as follows:

> There are some "Fu X" who are addressed [in the inscriptions] in two periods, just as is true in the case of *hou* (侯) and *tzu* (子). Therefore these kinds of appellations are not individuals' names but instead hereditary titles.[5]
>
> *Fu x* is not a person's name, so it is of course not sound to understand the phrase as meaning the king's consort.[6]
>
> A *Fu* can therefore be enfeoffed with lands, is concerned with military campaigns and field cultivation, and in position compares to the *chiang-shuai* (將帥) and the members of the same lineages.[7]
>
> In essence, the pronunciation of the word *fu* is like *mu* (母), *wu* (巫) and *wu* (舞). [This officer] corresponds to the *fu* (服) of the "Chiu-kao" (酒誥)[8] and the *mu-shih* (牧師) of the *Chu-shu Chi-nien*;[9] his position was equal to that of

5. Ibid., 452.
6. Ibid., 454.
7. Ibid.
8. See Karlgren 1950: 44, 46.
9. Fang and Wang 1981: 35.

the *chiang-shuai* (將帥) and *tzu* (子) of the Yin royal clan ... [These officers] were direct subordinates of the king who enjoyed his trust and favor.[10]

Shima Kunio's belief that appellations such as Hou (侯) X, Tzu (子) X, Fu (帚) X in the oracle bone inscriptions are not individuals' names but hereditary titles is similar to some of my own ideas but by no means entirely the same. In my 1957 publication *Yin-hsu Wen-tzu: Ping-pien*, part I, Section 1, "K'ao-shih," I wrote:

> Evidently, there were people named Ya (亞) in Periods I, III, IV, and V; some were *hou* (侯) and some were diviners. This period of more than 200 years could not possibly have been encompassed in an individual's lifetime. The leader in charge of the Ya territories was probably called Ya or Ya Hou (亞侯). Thus Ya must be a collective name (belonging to a *shih* or *hsing*) rather than a private name exclusively belonging to a certain individual. From this one can speculate that all the proper names from the oracle bones should be explained in this manner. Because these were collective names (of *shih* or *hsing* clans), grandfathers and grandsons, fathers and sons could all use them. Therefore, the use of these proper names as standards for dating must necessarily be severely restricted. For example, to use diviners for dating, we can only hypothesize that the lord of a certain territory once served as a diviner in a certain period, and that after he eventually had left office for reasons such as falling from favor, old age and sickness, or death, a diviner with that name would not appear again. But in another place or at another time, he, his descendants, his ancestors or his lands might still appear in the oracle bone inscriptions under that name. For [other] examples: the names Kao (羔), T'ang (唐), Ho (河), Hsi (喜), Yung (永), Wo (我) etc. all follow the same pattern in this text.[11]

I got this idea from the fact that people and places often share the same name in the divination inscriptions. Although Shima Kunio noticed this point, he explained the character *fu* (帚) in *fu* X as meaning *fu* (服) or *mu* (牧) and denied that it had the sense of *fu* (婦), as in *fu-nü* (婦女), or womankind. Thus his interpretation not only diverges 180° from mine, but also differs from the view of all contemporary scholars. In my recent article on the scope of Shang political space, I wrote:

> What Shima Kunio says of the term *Fu X*, that it is not an individual's name, must refer to the character X in *Fu X*, rather than the entire term *Fu X*, so of course his interpretation is not sound. For example, the Ching (井) in Fu

10. Shima 1958: 455.
11. P. C. Chang 1957: 26.

Ching (婦井) refers to Ching Fang (井方), and when a spouse was taken from Ching she was called Fu Ching. In Period I, Wu Ting might have taken a wife from Ching, and in Period IV Wen Wu Ting might also have married a woman of Ching. Thus the name Fu Ching might appear in more than one period. It is exactly because the consort Fu Ching was taken from Ching Fang that the Ching of Fu Ching is sometimes written with a nü (女) radical, as Ching (姘).[12]

Now, both the discovery of the Fu Hao tomb and the multitude of grave goods in it clearly demonstrate that the grave's occupant was a noble-woman. So Shima Kunio's theory crumbles of its own accord.

I have only recently looked at Chang Cheng-lang's "Ku-tai Chung-kuo shih-chin-chih shih-tsu tsu-chih" (古代中國十進制氏族組織), published in 1952. In this article he writes:

> In the oracle bone texts from Period I to Period IV, there often appear a number of military officers' names such as Wu (吳), Ch'a (甾), Wang Ch'en (望乘), Shih Pan (師般), Chih Huo (沚馘), ... etc. Is it conceivable that these elder statesmen could have spanned seven reigns in one lifetime? No matter how long their lives, this would be impossible. It is evident that these are all military chieftains, whose duties are inherited within their single clan in perpetuity, so that all successively took the original clan name. However, by the time of the Period V oracle bone inscriptions, these names absolutely never appear. It is clear that just as, in late Shang, the system of succession in the royal house was changing, so too the method of inheriting military leadership in each clan had changed. In other words, these matrilineal clans perished together.[13]

This view coincides with my theory explaining the appearance in the oracle bone inscriptions of people and places with the same name. However, in that article he asserts that in Period V oracle bone inscriptions "those clan names absolutely never appear." Actually, they seldom appear. Also, the reason for their sparse occurrence is not that "these matrilineal clans perished together" but that the customs of divination had changed. For instance, the name Ch'a (甾), cited by him, appears in the following text, which is a divination inscription of Period V:

丁卯卜在查貞：甾告曰：眾來敦
王虫今日呈亡災冎？(Ch'ien [前] 2, 11, 1).
Crack-making on day ting-mou: divination at 查: Ch'a has informed the following: (message obscure).

12. P. C. Chang 1969: 194.
13. C. L. Chang 1952: 15–16.

In addition, Period I inscriptions have the names Hsi (喜) and Fu Hsi (婦喜); Period II inscriptions include a diviner named Hsi; and Period VI texts mention a Hou Hsi (侯喜). Apparently the names Ch'a (㞢) and Hsi (喜), among others, can still be found in the Period V oracle bone inscriptions. The reason for the scarcity of these kinds of names in Period V texts is that Ti Yi (帝乙) and Ti Hsin (帝辛) belonged to what Tung Tso-pin has called the New School of Yin dynasty ritual. The various kings of the New School tended to abridge and omit ritual in many matters rather than repeatedly seeking the spirits' advice.[14] Therefore records of these kinds of things in the oracle bone inscriptions were also decreased. As to whether society at the time was, in the final analysis, patrilineal or matrilineal, one can see from the genealogy of the Yin kings (although there is no direct proof) that it must have long since become a patrilineal, patriarchal society. Also, from the fact that in the divination texts the birth of a boy is considered to be *chia* (嘉), or auspicious, while the birth of a girl is described as *pu-chia* (不嘉), or inauspicious, one can see that contemporary society esteemed males and contemned females. How could this attitude arise if it were a matrilineal society? However, as one can see from the power and influence of Fu Hao and Fu Ching the noblewomen of the time had a rather high social position.

Inscriptions other than "Fu Hao" on grave goods in the Fu Hao tomb include the "Hou Mu Hsin (后母辛)" and "Hou Hsin (后辛)" inscriptions, which have attracted much attention. Beyond these, there is also a considerable number of objects with the inscription "Hou T'u Mu (后㠯母)," second only in number to the objects inscribed with Fu Hao. As to the "Hou" character in these inscriptions, some interpret it as "Ssu (司)" and some as "Hou." Neither of these two interpretations is wrong. In the oracle bone texts there is no discernible difference or distinction between the two characters "Hou" and "Ssu," either in meaning or in usage. For example, plate 514 of *Ping-pien* has the following pair of divination inscriptions:

貞：惟羣后耂好？
Divined: Will Fu Hao suffer calamity because of Lung Hou?
不惟羣司耂婦好？
Will Fu Hao not suffer calamity because of Lung Ssu?

The first of these inscriptions, using "Hou," was originally in plate 7143 of the *Yi-pien* (乙編) collection, and the second, using "Ssu," was

---

14. Tung 1945: 4.

originally in plate 2274 of the *Yi-pien*. Now that we have pieced them together in their original form, we know that they were originally paired divinations from a single plastron. This is the best possible evidence that "Hou" and "Ssu" were originally a single character.

The simultaneous appearance of bronze vessels with the inscription "Hou T'u Mu" in Fu Hao's tomb is hard to understand. In that era the likelihood of two royal consorts being buried together in one tomb was insignificant. It is also not likely that the ritual vessels of another consort could have been taken and used as sacrificial burials in Fu Hao's tomb. Thus Hou T'u Mu must, like Hou Mu Hsin, be closely linked to Fu Hao herself. For this reason some believe that "T'u" is Fu Hao's "Ssu ming (personal name)" or "tzu (style name)."[15] This is a possible explanation, but nothing prevents us from examining and sounding the problem out from the point of view of an explanation other than that of personal name or *tzu* name. Some have interpreted the top half of the character "T'u" in "Hou T'u Mu" as "*hu* (虎, tiger)";[16] others, as "*hs'iang* (象, elephant)";[17] other, as "*t'u* (兔, hare)";[18] others as "*chuan* (豖, pig)";[19] and still others, as "*ch'ou* (兜, harelike mythical beast)."[20] I myself have explained this element as "chu (虗, wild boar)."[21] This character looks like a large mouth with pointed teeth, a turned-up tail (or occasionally a dangling tail), and no feet (except in a few instances), so it is hard to determine what kind of beast it represents. In the oracle bone texts, the character "yang" in "Yang Ch'ia (陽甲)" from the Yin royal genealogy is written in this form. So, one asks, why in later generations was it believed to be the character "yang"? I think this belief arose from two circumstances: one, that these characters are confused because their forms are similar; the other, that they are confused because their sounds are similar. The form of this character is very close to that of the character "yang (陽, or 昜)" in the bronze inscriptions, so perhaps the error arose from this similarity in appearance. As to the factor of pronunciation, Ch'iu Hsi-kuei wrote:

> In the main tradition of oracle bone inscriptions, the character before the *chia* (甲) in the name of the former king corresponding to Yang Chia (陽甲) is

---

15. Chung-kuo-she-hui-k'o-hsüeh-yüan K'ao-ku-yen-chiu-so 1980a: 228.
16. Tung 1933: 233.
17. M. J. Kuo 1933: 31.
18. T'ang 1939: 29–30.
19. Ch'en 1956a: 407.
20. H. T. Li 1965: 4565–66.
21. P. C. Chang 1959: 160–62.

written in the form of 吾, 㐱, 吾, etc. The animal element that this character contains, Tung Tso-pin says is "hu (虎)"; Kuo Mo-jo says it is "hsiang (象)"; T'ang Lan says it is "t'u (兔)": and Ch'en Meng-chia says it is "chuan (豢)." From the fact that a special attribute of this beastlike form is a turned-up tail, it is clear that T'ang's opinion is correct. "T'u (兔)" belongs to the *t'ou* (透, or t') family of phonetic initial sounds and the *yü* (魚, or δγ) rhyming category,* while "Yang (陽)" belongs to the *yi* (以 or r[i]) family of initials and the *yang* (陽, or ang) rhyming category. The two rhyming categories *yü* and *yang* are within the same borrowing group. In ancient times, the *yi* initial group and the *ting* (定) initial group were very close, and *ting* and *t'ou*, both being linguals, were very easily interchanged, so that *t'ang* (湯), originally pronounced *yang* (昜) came to be read with a *t'ou* initial. From this we know that the ancient pronunciations of *t'u* and *yang* were very close. This is why P'an Keng's older brother is called Yang Chia (陽甲) in ancient historical documents, while the oracle bones use T'u Chia (吾甲) instead. "T'u" and "Yang" being within the same borrowing group, they were interchangeable.[22]

For these reasons, Ch'iu asserts that T'ang's interpretation of *t'u* is correct. However, *hsiang* (象) and *yang* (昜[陽]) are both in group 10 of Tuan's (段) classification of ancient pronunciation, while *hu* (虎[虍]), *chu* (虡), and *t'u* (兔) all belong to group 5, so that it is not impossible that they too might be interchangeable because of similarity in pronunciation. Therefore all these interpretations, no matter which, are possible, but all also have difficulties. For example, with respect to the interpretation *t'u* (兔, hare), the character in question sometimes resembles a large mouth with pointed teeth, so that it is really very hard to say it is a pictograph of a hare. Among the various interpretations, *chuan* (豢) is phonetically relatively distant and would seem to be harder to interchange.

Apart from this, there are a few other areas which require brief additional exploration. Underneath the beastlike shape in the character equivalent to the *yang* in Yang Chia there is always appended a "ᴗ" shape, whereas at the bottom of the *T'u* of Hou T'u Mu (后吾母) there is a *shih* (示) element. For this reason, some people suspect that these two forms are really not a semantically single character. Actually, in oracle bone texts, particularly in characters which function as special names, sometimes an element is added, sometimes subtracted from the radical position without making any great difference or having any impact on its

---

*The phonetic symbols used herein are based on Chou Fa-kao's (周法高) system as outlined in the introduction to Chou Fa-kao, 1971a.

22. Ch'iu 1980: 164.

basic form or meaning. For example, T'u Chia (吾甲) was also written T'u Chia (兔甲), with the "ㄇ" radical missing at the bottom of the *t'u* (兔). Fu Ning (婦嬶) was also written Fu Ning (婦嫙), with no "示" radical at the bottom of the *ning* (嫙). K'ang Ting (康丁) was also called Keng Ting (庚丁) in later times, the character *k'ang* (康) simply dropping four dots and thus becoming the character *keng* (庚). Therefore, 兔, 吾, and 槑 are really the same character. This kind of phenomenon is a frequent occurrence in the names of people and places in the oracle bone inscriptions. Consequently, it is very possible that the "*T'u* (吾)" in Hou T'u (后槑) and the *T'u* (吾) in T'u Chia (吾甲) refer to a single place. Perhaps that place was Fu Hao's estate, and also, before that, Yang Chia's place of origin before he succeeded to the throne. In my article "Chia-ku-wen chung-so-chien jen ti t'ung ming k'ao," I pointed out:

> Among the distant ancestors who are sacrificed to in the oracle bone texts, those before Shang Chia all lack temple names based on the *Kan-chih* cyclical characters; but there are those who do not seem to be distant ancestors who also lack *Kan-chih* temple names, merely having a [kinship] designating term added before or after the name, as in: Lung Mu (龍母) (also Mu Lung [母龍]; Huan Mu (萑母) (also Mu Huan [母萑]; Tsu Huan (祖萑); Mu Chuan (母專); Pi Tan (妣丹); Mu? (母䊾); Liang Fu (良父); Fu Kung (父㠯); Mu Hu (母虎); Wo Pi (我妣); Hsieh Hou (謝后); Ju Kung Hou (入龔后); Tzu Hsien (子咸); etc. There are also some which have only a *Kan-chih* temple name before or after the personal name and lack the designating term, as in: Lung Chia (龍甲); Fu Chia (夫甲); Hsien Wu (咸戊), Hsüeh Wu (咸戊); Wu Chih (戊陟); etc. Apart from those, there are some even more worthy of attention, which have a personal name, a designation, and on top of that, a *Kan-chih* temple name; these include Ping Fu Jen (㗬父壬), Ya Pi Chi (亞妣己), etc.... Before Shang Chia, it seems that the names of distant ancestors without *Kan-chih* titles are the names of their original fiefs. After Shang Chia, the Shih in Shih Jen (示壬) and Shih Kuei (示癸); the T'ang (唐) and Hsien (咸 (or Ch'eng [成]) in Ta Yi (大乙); the Yung in Yung Chi (雝己, or 雍己); the Ch'iang in Ch'iang Chia (羌甲) (or Wo Chia [沃甲]; the Nan in Nan Keng (南庚); the Hu (or T'u) in Hu Chia (虎甲) (or T'u Chia (兔甲); the Wu in Wu Ting (武丁) and Wu Yi (武乙); the Lin in Lin Hsin (廩辛); the Keng or K'ang in Keng Ting (庚丁) (or K'ang Ting (康丁); etc., seem also to be the names of these individuals' estates before they came to the throne. Thus, before they came to power they were named according to the names of their estates. This realization is extremely important to the study of oracle bone inscriptions and the pursuit of Yin and Shang history.[23]

---

23. P. C. Chang 1967: 773.

That is to say: the Hsin in Hou Mu Hsin is her ritual name; the T'u in Hou T'u Mu is her fief or estate; the Hao in Fu Hao, like the Ching in Fu Ching, is her place of origin. The character Ching (姘) is sometimes written Ching (井), which is the Ching of Ching Fang (井方), so it should also be possible to drop the *nü* (女) radical in Hao (好) to make the character Tzu (子), which is the Tzu of the Tzu clan. Ting Shan long ago presented this theory.[24] Consequently, Fu Hao was a consort married out of the Tzu clan. If the royal house of the Yin dynasty really was, as is traditionally said, the Tzu clan, then the Yin King Wu Ting's marriage to Fu Hao was endogamous. Other examples: among the *fus* there is Liang Fu (良父), and among the consorts is Fu Liang (婦良 or 婦娘); among the male ancestors is Lung Chia (龍甲), and among the female ancestors is Mu Lung (母龍); among the male ancestors is T'u (or Hu) Chia (兔甲 or 虎甲), and among the female ancestors is Mu T'u (or Hu) (母兔 or 虎). All of these could be traces of endogamous marriages. The same logic that explains Fu Hao's possession of the two appellations Hao and T'u explains Ta Yi's possession of the two designations T'ang (唐) and Hsien (咸) or Ch'eng (成).

After the discovery of the Fu Hao tomb, a conference of several dozen historians, archaeologists, and experts in related fields was called to discuss Fu Hao and draw out each person's views and opinions. Some felt that the Fu Hao tomb belonged to the Wu Ting era, others believed that it dated to the Lin Hsin/K'ang Ting period or the Wu Yi/Wen Ting era. Later came Wang Yü-hsin, Chang Yung-shan, and Yang Sheng-nan's "Shih lun Yin-hsü Wu-hao mu ti Fu Hao,"[25] which, in taking the Fu Hao oracle bone inscriptions as its subject, furthered the investigation. They collected 128 oracle bone inscriptions relating to Fu Hao and, starting with her name, proceeded to inquire into all sorts of activities of Fu Hao. They also believed that

> from the oracle bone materials one can see that Fu Hao had already died in the Wu Ting era. Moreover, the grave goods unearthed in Tomb Five also belonged to the early period of Yin-hsü. Therefore, the Fu Hao still living in the era of Wu Yi and Wen Ting absolutely could not be the same person as the Fu Hao in Tomb Five.[26]

24. Ting 1956: 56.
25. Wang, Chang, and Yang 1979.
26. Ibid., p. 21.

Still later Li Po-ch'ien (李伯謙) wrote "An-yang Yin-hsü wu-hao mu ti nien-tai wen-t'i,"[27] which, although aimed chiefly at deducing the date of the grave's occupant from the forms of the excavated objects, still became involved in some questions about oracle bone inscriptions. He wrote:

> Just as has already been noted in "An-yang Yin-hsü wu-hao mu tso t'an chi-yao" . . . the inscriptions from Period I did contain many records of Fu Hao's name and activities. However, the name "Fu Hao" also appeared in inscriptions from Periods III and IV. Among Wu Ting's consorts there was certainly one whose ritual name was Hsin, but there are records that K'ang Ting's consorts also included one with the ritual name Hsin. Therefore, the speculation that the "Ssu Mu Hsin" large square *ting* was made by Wu Yi for K'ang Ting's consort Pi Hsin, who was one of his mother's generation, is not entirely groundless. There is the possibility that Tomb Five is the tomb of K'ang Ting's consort Pi Hsin.[28]
>
> If the above hypothesis is not wrong, then the Fu Hao in the bronze inscriptions of Tomb Five is not the "Fu Hao" of the Period I oracle bone inscriptions but rather the "Fu Hao" of the oracle bone inscriptions from Periods III and IV. If so, she of course could not, as has been suggested, be one of Wu Ting's consorts. Opinions differ as to whether "Fu Hao" is a personal name or a clan name. From the circumstance that bronzes with the inscriptions "Fu Hao" have in the past been unearthed elsewhere, one can at least say that use of the ritual name "Fu Hao" in the Shang dynasty was clearly not limited to one person.[29]

The two essays cited above represent two kinds of incongruent ideas; two groups advocating dissimilar explanations. The excavators of Tomb Five said, in the conclusion of their excavation report, *Yin-hsü Fu Hao mu*:

> As to the date of the grave's occupant, there are chiefly, at present, two categories of opinion: one believes that this grave belonged to Period II of the Yin-hsü culture and that the grave's occupant must be Wu Ting's consort Fu Hao, whose ritual name was Hsin, that is, the person referred to in the Yi-Hsin period cyclical sacrificial calendar as Pi Hsin (妣辛), who died when Wu Ting was still alive, perhaps in the latter part of his era. The other holds that this grave "may belong to the Wu Yi period" and that its occupant may be

27. P. C. Li 1979.
28. Ibid., p. 165.
29. Ibid., p. 170.

the "Fu Hao" referred to in the oracle bone inscriptions of Periods III and IV: "She was K'ang Ting's consort, called Ssu Hsin after her death, and later referred to as Pi Hsin...." We advocate and support the first view.[30]

Afterward, the authors of this report, Cheng Chen-hsiang and Ch'en Chih-ta, again stated, in "Lun Fu Hao mu tui Yin-hsü wen-hua ho p'u-tz'e tuan-tai ti yi-yi":

> Most recently, the Institute of Archaeology Laboratory ran a carbon-14 determination on a fragment of broken plank of the outer coffin from the Fu Hao grave. The result of the determination was BP 3155 ± 140 (1520 ± 140 B.C.), which can be dendrochronologically calibrated as 3350 ± 190 B.C. (1400 ± 190 B.C.). According to Ch'en Meng-chia's theory that P'an Keng moved the capital to Yin in 1400 B.C., the tree-ring calibrated date is a fraction earlier than Wu Ting's era.[31]

Actually, whether dating is by carbon-14 or tree-ring calibration, all either can prove is that this is a Yin dynasty tomb; ultimately they cannot determine that it is a grave from a certain year in the reign of a certain king. This is because both have standard deviations that can be as much as 140 years or 190 years, respectively, and the Yin dynasty itself lasted only 273 years from P'an Keng's moving of the capital to Yin to Ti Hsin's defeat, according to the generally trusted version of the *Chu-shu Chi-nien*. In this short space of 273 years, how can one tolerate an error of one or two hundred years? Therefore, this scientifically determined numerical evidence is really not much help in determining the date of the Fu Hao tomb. In order to fix the tomb's date, we must depend on the materials of stratigraphy, grave goods, oracle bone inscriptions, etc. But according to the excavation report, there is no way to depend on the stratigraphy, and there is presently still no firmly fixed and reliable standard for judging the form of the objects. Therefore, the oracle bone inscriptions themselves—materials which can "speak"—form the most trustworthy evidence.

Yen Yi-p'ing's "Fu Hao lieh-chuan" is the most complete assemblage of divination inscriptions for the discussion of Fu Hao.[32] He compiled 253 oracle bone inscriptions relating to Fu Hao, making a biographical study of her. Yen believed that the attribution of some of these inscriptions to

---

30. Chung-kuo-she-hui-k'o-hsüeh-yüan K'ao-ku-yen-chiu-so 1980a: 221.
31. Cheng and Ch'en 1981: 511.
32. Yen 1981.

A DESCRIPTION OF THE FU HAO ORACLE BONE INSCRIPTIONS 133

Period IV and the era of Wen Wu Ting are not reliable, and that only one inscription refers to the Fu Hao from the era of the true Wen Wu Ting. He wrote:

> Fu Hao was Wu Ting's consort. Fu Hao's name appears only in Period I inscriptions with the exception of one inscription from *Chia-pien* (甲編) 668. Those who believe that the inscriptions from Period III and IV also refer to Fu Hao cite the following texts as proof:
>
> (1). 戊辰貞:婦好亡囚 (*Ning Hu* [寧滬] 1.491). Divination on day *Wu-ch'en*. Will Fu Hao not suffer a disaster?
>
> (2). 丙戌貞:婦好亡囚 (*Ch'o* [掇] 1.444 [verso], *Ning Hu* 1.493). Divination on day *Ping-hsü*. Will Fu Hao not suffer a disaster?
>
> (3). 囚婦好多 (*Ch'o* 1.447 [recto], *Ning Hu*) ... Fu Hao?
>
> (4). 丙戌貞:婦好亡囚 (*Ye* [鄴] 3.43.8). Divination on day *Ping-hsü*. Will Fu Hao not suffer a disaster?
>
> (5). 己亥卜辛丑歠婦好祀 (*Chia* [甲] 668).
> Crack-making on day *Chi-hai*. On day *Hsin-ch'ou*, offer Fu Hao a sacrifice? [fig. 21, left]
>
> (6). □□卜既囚婦好 (*Yi* [佚] 649, *Ts'un* [存] 1.1457). Crack-making on day. ... Already Fu Hao?
>
> This is mistaken. In the character *Hao* (好) on *Ning Hu* plate 1.491, the bottom part of the *nü* (女) element is particularly long. There is no lack of other examples of this; for example, *Ts'ang-kuei Hsin-pien* (藏龜新編) 672, 675; *Yi-pien* (乙編) 2586; and *Lin* (林) 1, 23, 6. All these have a *nü* radical written like "㚔," with an extended bottom portion. *Ch'o* 1.444 (recto) reads "婦好多," a format often seen in Period I inscriptions of Fu Hao. This variation should not be dated to Periods III or IV. *Yeh* 3.43.8 has the divination serial number "ssu (四, or four)," which must mean that it concerned the same charge as that recorded as "san (三, or 3)" on *Ch'o* 1.444 (verso), but using a different plastron. The forms of the characters in *Yi-ts'un* 649 resemble those of the inscription "Hu Fu Hao ming (乎婦好命)" in *Yi-pien* 9551 (Ping 384) and must date to the same period. Only *Chia-pien* 668 is a Period IV inscription (the *Chia Pien k'ao-shih* dates it to Period IV, Hu's transcription dates it to Period I, the latter date is an error), but it relates to a *ssu* (祀) sacrifice to Fu Hao, so she was certainly not living then. Therefore, all the oracle bone inscriptions now available are from Period I, and Fu Hao must have been one of Wu Ting's consorts.[33]

In his footnote 1, Yen said of these inscriptions listed by him:

---

33. Ibid., p. 1.

甲編668　　　人文389

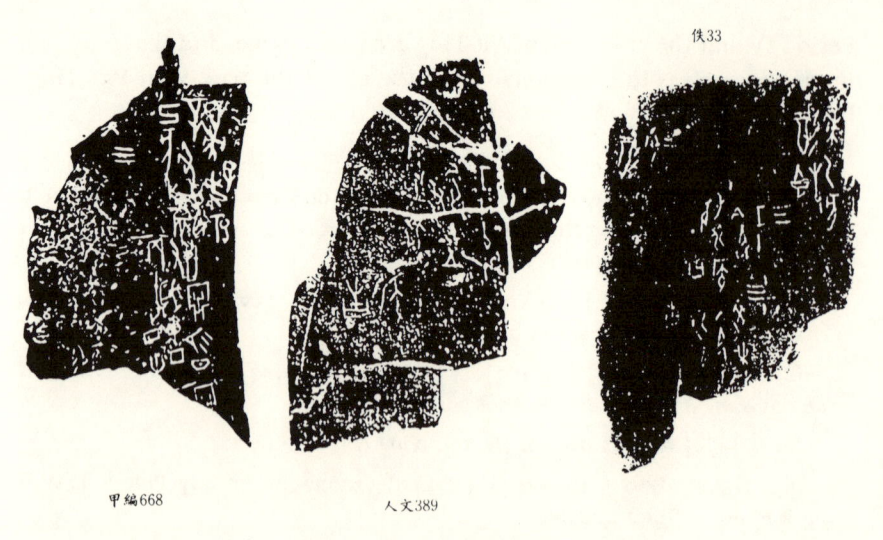

Fig. 21. Rubbings of three Shang oracle bone inscriptions: (*left*) *Chia* 668; (center) *Jinbun* 389; (right) *Yi-tsun* 33.

See Ch'iu Hsi-kui's speech at the conference "An-yang Yin-hsü wu hao mu tso t'an ji-yao" published in *K'ao-ku* 1977 (5). At the same conference, Wang Yü-hsin gave a talk in which he said, "Altogether, the number of [inscriptions] from Period IV concerning Fu Hao does not exceed five or six."[34]

Actually, these Period IV inscriptions cited by them are also listed by Shima Kunio and even lack one such item included by Shima. These inscriptions all lack both diviner's names and generational designations and thus are devoid of effective dating criteria. I do not know what basis Shima Kunio relied on to determine that they belonged to Period IV; nor do I know whose theory Yen sought to refute. Generally speaking, both sides depend for their arguments on the form or style of the characters. But among Tung Tso-pin's ten dating criteria, writing style is one of the weakest. For example, there are some epigraphic styles of *Kan-chih* characters that Tung believed to be Period III or Period IV, but afterward we discovered them in typcial Period I inscriptions. So dating based on epigraphic style is sometimes not entirely reliable; how much less so in this case, since Tung was creating his dating theory at a time when the available materials did not begin to match the abundance now available.

34. Ibid., p. 36.

Another case, as Yen indicated in the above-cited passage, was where the epigraphic style of some of these inscriptions, which had been believed to belong to Period IV, appeared also in Period I inscriptions; for this reason, Yen believed that the inscriptions in question must really belong to Wu Ting's era in Period I. In support of Yen's judgment, I agree that the attribution of these inscriptions to Period IV lacks any substantial basis, and their attribution to Period I is itself not impossible. However, it is hard to explain his statement that "all oracle bone inscriptions now available are from Period I" because he had already pointed out that among the presently available oracle bone inscriptions only *Chia-pien* 668 was Period IV. He understood that there was at least one inscription that did belong to Period IV, so how can one say that "all oracle bone inscriptions now available are from Period I." However, if he did mean to say that, he should have considered the matter more deeply. I think that by these inscriptions he meant all except *Chia-pien* 668. Alternatively, he believed that the Fu Hao in the inscriptions on the Period IV bone had already become an object of sacrifice and was no longer a living person, that in Period IV there was therefore no living Fu Hao, and that all the cases where Fu Hao appears in the inscriptions relate only to one of Wu Ting's consorts. If there is no second Fu Hao in the oracle bone inscriptions, then the identification of the Fu Hao in Tomb Five with Wu Ting's wife should not pose any problem. However, it only needed the existence of that single example of a Period IV inscription to raise the question of the existence of a Fu Hao in that era, whether dead or alive. My reasons for believing this are explained below.

First, let us accept that *Chia-pien* 668 is a Period IV inscription. In that case, the Fu Hao mentioned in the inscription, whether dead or alive, cannot be confused with the Fu Hao of Wu Ting's era. Why? We will analyze this question from the point of view of two different hypotheses: living person and spirit. Because there is in this inscription the character *li* (獻), whose meaning is not very clear, the meaning of the entire inscription is difficult to determine. Some think that the divination inquires about a sacrifice offered by Fu Hao; others think that it inquires about a sacrifice offered to Fu Hao. Now we will first suppose that the Fu Hao mentioned in the divination text was alive at the time and actually presiding over a sacrifice. In that case, this Fu Hao must have been a wife of Wu Yi or Wen Ting and not the Fu Hao of Wu Ting's era because the likelihood of their being the same person is small, almost impossible. A single person's life has its limits. According to Tung Tso-pin's *Chung-kuo Nien-li Chien-p'u* (Part I),[35] the length of time from the last year of Wu Ting, the fifty-ninth of his reign (1281 B.C.), to the first year of Wu Yi's reign (1226 B.C.) was fifty-five years; to the first year of Wen Ting (1222 B.C.), it was fifty-nine years. Although these dates are only an inference of Tung's, the space of time between kings should be accurate.

In addition, the Fu Hao who appears in the Period I inscriptions is an active woman, a person of many parts. Looking at the calendar of divinations about her childbearing, from the oracle bone inscriptions, we find the first, second, fourth, fifth, and tenth months, and so on. It is obvious that she did not give birth only once. Again, examining the evidence of the verification inscriptions, some say she bore a girl on the day *chia-yin*,[36] some say she bore a girl on the day *Kuei-ssu*;[37] and some say she bore a son on the day *Ting-ch'ou*.[38] Evidently she had at least three children. Now 280 days, more or less, are required from conception to childbirth, thus consuming the better part of a year; if the mother breastfeeds, another year will be required. Thus bearing children must have consumed about six years of Fu Hao's life and probably more, as in actuality her children probably numbered more than three.

The Fu Hao of Wu Ting's era was a hero among women; her many capabilities included both civil and military talents. Her civil virtue sufficed to pacify the tribal allies, her military virtue served to solidify the state; within, she presided over sacrifices, while without, she led military troops to attack the four border regions. Her military might reached as far as the T'u Fang (土方), Kung Fang (舌方), Pa Fang (巴方), Jen Fang (人方), and Ch'iang Fang (羌方). She participated in almost all of the famous and important wars of the Wu Ting period. These many enterprises could not have been accomplished by a child. So the Fu Hao of that era, although she may have married early, could not have been too young. Therefore, we calculate that she was twenty years old, more or less. According to Tung's *Yin-li-p'u Wu-ting Jih-p'u*, the Yin king Wu Ting's wars with the northwestern tribes of T'u (土), Kung (舌), and Chih (旨) began in the spring of the twenty-ninth year of his reign and ended in the winter of his thirty-second year, which is still only in the middle

---

35. Tung 1960: 47–57.
36. P. C. Chang 1957–72, part 2, section 1, p. 247.
37. Tung 1948–53, #4729.
38. P. C. Chang 1957–72, part 2, section 1, p. 245.

portion of his reign. Thus at the end of Wu Ting's life, Fu Hao, if not already deceased, must at least have reached the age of about fifty. If she lived into Wu Yi's or Wen Ting's reigns, she would have been over a hundred years of age. Therefore this possibility is really very small. Even if the Fu Hao of that earlier era enjoyed a long life and lived into that period, she must have been the generation of Wu Yi and Wen Ting's great- or great great-grandmother. Examples from the oracle bone inscriptions of female ancestors before the mother and grandmother show that some are called Mu (母); some, Hou Mu (后母); some, Pi (妣); some, Kao Pi (高妣); some, X X Ch'ou Pi X (某某奭妣某); some, X X Ch'ieh X (某某妾某); and some, X X Ch'i X (某某妻某). "Fu (婦)" is the *fu* (or wife) from *fu fu* (夫婦), husband and wife. In the oracle bone inscriptions of Wu Ting's era, she could be called Fu because she was Wu Ting's wife, but in the age of Wu Yi and Wen Ting, how could the generation of her great-grand-children and great great-grandchildren call her "Fu"? Therefore the Fu Hao of the inscriptions of Period IV, if a living person, could not possibly have been the Fu Hao of Wu Ting's era, nor could she have been the Fu Hao of Tomb Number Five because none of the consorts of Wu Yi and Wen Ting bore the appellation Pi Hsin.

Next, we will look at the problem from another angle, supposing that the Fu Hao in the later inscription was a dead person who was the recipient of a sacrifice. In that case, was she or was she not the Fu Hao who was one of the consorts of Wu Ting in Period I? My answer must again be no. Above, we said that neither Wu Yi or Wen Ting could have called Wu Ting's consort Fu Hao. So the Fu Hao in the divination inscription on that single Period IV bone, that is, *Chia* 668, even if she had already joined the category of ancestors and was enjoying the sacrifice, still could not be the Fu Hao of Period I, nor could she be the same person as the Fu Hao in Tomb Five. Again, as Wu Yi and Wen Ting lacked consorts named Pi Hsin (妣辛) and K'ang Ting (康丁) of Period III did have a consort Pi Hsin, therefore some say that the Fu Hao on that oracle bone was K'ang Ting's wife and that the Fu Hao from Yin-hsü Tomb Five was also K'ang Ting's wife. They particularly emphasize that the epigraphic styles of Period III and Period IV were close and at times hard to distinguish. This, although a reasonable and logical explanation, is problematic. If the Period IV inscriptions can be believed to be from period III, then why could they not be taken for Period I inscriptions, since neither has absolutely reliable standards and clues but instead are assigned only on the basis of epigraphic style? One further matter must be discussed, that is, that K'ang Ting's reign lasted just eight years; Wu Yi reigned for four years and Wen Wu Ting for thirteen years (according to the *Yin-li p'u*). In the "wu-yi"chapter of the *Shang Shu* it says:

> Thus it was that Tsu Chia enjoyed the throne for thirty and three years. The emperors which arose after these all their lifetimes enjoyed ease. From their birth enjoying ease, they did not understand the painful toil sowing and reaping, nor hear of the hard labours of the inferior people. They only sought after excessive pleasures, and so not one of them enjoyed the throne for a long period. They continued for ten years, for seven or eight, for five or six, or perhaps only for three or four.[39]

So Lin Hsin, K'ang Ting, Wu Yi, and Wen Wu Ting all lived short lives and did not hold the throne for long. If the Fu Hao of Tomb Number Five was K'ang Ting's consort, then all the bronzes bearing the inscription Fu Hao must have been cast before the reign of Wu Yi because neither Wu Yi nor Wen Ting could call her Fu Hao, but should have called her Mu Hsin. According to the excavation report for Tomb Five, at least three kinds of dissimilar styles and chronological differences between early and late are discernible in the several dozens of vessels inscribed with "Fu Hao."[40] Consider: within that brief period of eight years, how could that many bronzes have been cast and how could there have been adequate time to allow so many stylistic evolutions? Moreover, those evolutions all would have required a relatively long period to develop. Therefore, the possibility is not great that the Fu Hao who was the occupant of Tomb Five was K'ang Ting's consort. Besides, that single oracle bone inscription is not necessarily an inscription of K'ang Ting's era in Period III.

According to the above analysis, the Fu Hao of the so-called Period IV divination inscription cannot be a consort of either K'ang Ting or Wu Ting. If she was a wife of Wu Yi or Wen Ting, then she could not have been the same person as the Fu Hao who as a consort of Wu Ting in the Period I divination inscriptions. Similarly, she could not have been the same person as the Fu Hao from Tomb Five. In this case, the two Periods, I and IV, would each have had a Fu Hao.

Apart from this, we may still examine the problem from another angle. The so-called Period IV divination inscriptions cited by Shima Kunio and

39. James Legge, trans., 1865: 467–68.
40. K'ao-ku-hsüeh-pao 1977a: 91.

others were all, except for *Chia-pien* 668, challenged by Yen and held by him to be creatures of Period I. Yen's argument is convincing. In addition there is *Hsü Ts'un* 1443, which, although not discussed by Yen, must without doubt belong to Period I. As for *Chia-pien* 668, however, Yen also believed that it was a Period IV divination inscription from the era of Wen Wu Ting. He did not clearly state his reasons, but the basis for his theory was probably calligraphic style, the possession of special characteristics of Period IV. For example, in the wu (午) character in another inscription from the plastron in question, the central twisted-silk elements are solid, like dots, and lack empty spaces in the middle. Actually, this kind of writing style is not entirely lacking in the divination inscriptions of the early period, but it is rare. For example:

壬午卜：令般從侯告? (*Jen wen* 389). [fig. 21, center]
Divination on day *Jen-wu*, should we order P'an to accompany Hou Kao?

壬午卜，令般從侯告? (*Yi* 33) [fig. 21, right]
Divination on day *Jen-wu*, should we order P'an to accompany Hou Kao?

One of the above-cited two inscriptions is on the scapula of a bovid and the other is on the shell of a turtle; but the day of divination, the matters divined about, and the divination inscription itself are all the same. The character *wu* (午) in the first inscription has empty spaces inside the twisted-silk element, as is standard for the epigraphy of *kan-chih* characters in Period I and II. The character *wu* in the second inscription has almost become a simple vertical line; not only does it lack empty spaces in the middle of the twisted-silk element, but even the solid round dots have disappeared. This is a writing style often seen in divination inscriptions of the later periods. But these two inscriptions both belong to Period I, so that the style of writing the character *wu* in the later period had also previously appeared in the inscriptions of the early periods. There are more than a few examples of this kind of circumstance in the divination inscriptions. Again, the *kan-chih* character *ssu* (巳) was written in the form "𠂔" in the early period, having the two armlike strokes forming a horizontal lines; in later periods, this character was written "𠃬," with its two arms stretching up to the right and left, making an open, expanding diagonal form. However, these two forms of the character *ssu* have both appeared also in the divination inscription of the Wu Ting era, in particular, on *Ping-pien* (plate 1). Other characters, like *chen* (貞) and *hui* (宙), have epigraphic styles peculiar to the late period, which can also be seen occasionally in divination inscriptions of the early period. Therefore, it is sometimes hard to avoid the possibility of distortion when one depends upon only one or two *kan-chih* characters, or other characters, to determine the date of an inscription. As for epigraphic style, certainly one era will have the custom of that era, but if one depends only on epigraphic style as the criterion for determining date, it is sometimes hard to avoid being subjective. Ultimately, epigraphic style cannot compare with the solid reliability derived from the objective standards of diviners and epithets. For this reason, we are not foreclosed from considering the possibility that the single Period IV Fu Hao inscription, that is, *Chia-pien* 668, does not belong to the era of Wen Wu Ting in Period IV but instead to that of Wu Ting in Period I. Hu Hou-hsüan was in fact of the opinion that it belonged to Period I.[41] If this is so, then the Fu Hao divination inscriptions all belong without question to Period I, and, of course, the Fu Hao who was the occupant of Yin-hsü Tomb Five also belonged to Period I. All that is required is to move these few divination inscriptions from the Wen Wu Ting era of Period IV to the Wu Ting era. This is why Hu Hou-hsüan, Ch'en Meng-chia, and Kaizuka Shigeki all wish to move the oracle bone inscriptions of the so-called "*shih* (𠂤)" and "*wu* (午)" groups back to the Wu Ting period. As for the divination inscriptions of the Wen Wu Ting era, they are still the subject of controversy; I think we must again raise and investigate the question of their dating. But that is a matter that must await specialized research.

41. Yen 1981: 1.

8

A New Approach to the Study of Clan-sign Inscriptions of Shang

Noel Barnard

At the Fourth Chinese Palaeography Symposium, held in T'ai-yüan 太原, Shansi (15–21 September 1981), a brief preview of the present paper was presented.[1] Here, the subject will be further elaborated and special reference will be made to a major undisturbed burial, the Fu Hao tomb, but there is a considerable amount of research required yet to illustrate the full potential of this approach to the study of Shang (and Early Western Chou) clan-sign graphs. The approach is one that may, of course, be usefully applied to inscribed objects from individual burials or groups of burials in cemetery areas of later periods.

INTERRELATED BURIALS IN THE SAME CEMETERY AREA

In principle the research technique to be demonstrated shortly is simple; it is merely a comparative study of the inscribed artifacts recovered from individual burials in the same cemetery area as illustrated and described in the available reports. Investigations along these lines have been attempted in the past but prior to the publication of the long report covering the excavations in the Hsiao-min-t'un 孝民屯 cemetery area in the western sector of Yin-hsü (殷墟西區墓葬; see *KKHP* 1979.1.27–118, pls. 1–20) the full potential of such inscription evidence seems to have

---

1. For a short report and appraisal of the T'ai-yüan symposium together with a list of the 126 papers presented, see Barnard and Cheung 1983, pp. 207–15, 225–38; see also the report by Shaughnessy 1981/82.

Publisher's note: The volume editor and the publisher have taken the responsibility for preparing and proofreading the final artwork (including the archaic characters in the text) in this essay.

141

missed the attention of most researchers in our field. Even in this long report, the concluding observations show a remarkable unawareness of certain of the really significant and interesting features in the inscriptions from this find. It was actually during my writing of the English commentary in our *Chin-wu-shih-nien hsin-huo ch'ing-t'ung-ch'i ming-wen hui-chi* 近五十年新獲青銅銘文彙輯 (hereafter referred to as *Five Decades*) covering the inscribed *ting*, M 907 : 3, from the Hsiao-min-t'un excavations (Entry No. 0022 in our list) and its inscription which bears the identification, or reference, number ins. A/1 : C-7 [V-54] (v.a.), that the additional information available from the Hsiao-min-t'un group of inscriptions suddenly caught my attention.[2]

Ins. A/1 : C-7 [V-54] (v.a.) is not complete, as may be noted in the rubbing (fig. 22, M 907). Before casting commenced—or during the process of casting—the rilievo strokes of part of the graph were dislodged and so did not register; mishaps of this kind occur from time to time in the cast-in inscriptions of Shang and Chou.[3] While checking the several examples of this graph among the twenty-one inscription rubbings in figure 58 (p. 81) of the report it soon became evident to me that a rearrangement of the inscriptions into tomb groups would be rewarding. This has been effected in figure 22 (extracted from *Five Decades*) and further discussion regarding the significance of the grouping will be offered shortly. However, let us look briefly at some minor details attending individual graphs, in particular, the clan-sign graph C-7 [V-54], wherein the following variations in execution may be noted:

2. The first volume of *Five Decades*, which comprises the full list of 2,650 inscriptions excavated for the most part under conditions of control since the early 1930s and reported in the various archaeological journals, is now in press. A second volume comprising the bibliography is planned to follow shortly thereafter. In the present paper several illustrations have been extracted from the camera-ready copy of the main volumes in order to demonstrate aspects of the research approach as effectively as possible. As to the reference numbers applied to individual inscriptions the reader is directed to the introductory volume of Barnard and Cheung 1978, wherein a full exposition is given. For the immediate convenience of the reader a brief outline is incorporated in appendix B at the conclusion of this paper.

3. Several examples are conveniently assembled in Hayashi 1976, figs. 47–54. (Figure 55, however, is erroneously claimed to represent the feature when in fact the apparently missing sections of characters are due to folds in the rubbing paper! Note a similar misunderstanding by Cheng Te-k'un in T. K. Cheng 1971.) In some cases break-away sections of the rilievo graphs may result in an imprint, when cast, far removed from their original locations (Hayashi 1976: figs. 53 and 54). Whether this has happened in the case of A/1 : C-7[V-54] (v.a.) or not is not entirely certain; the description in Honan Province Institute of Cultural Relics 1981 (pl. 240; p. 40) seems to imply that there is no imprint elsewhere on the inside *ting* wall.

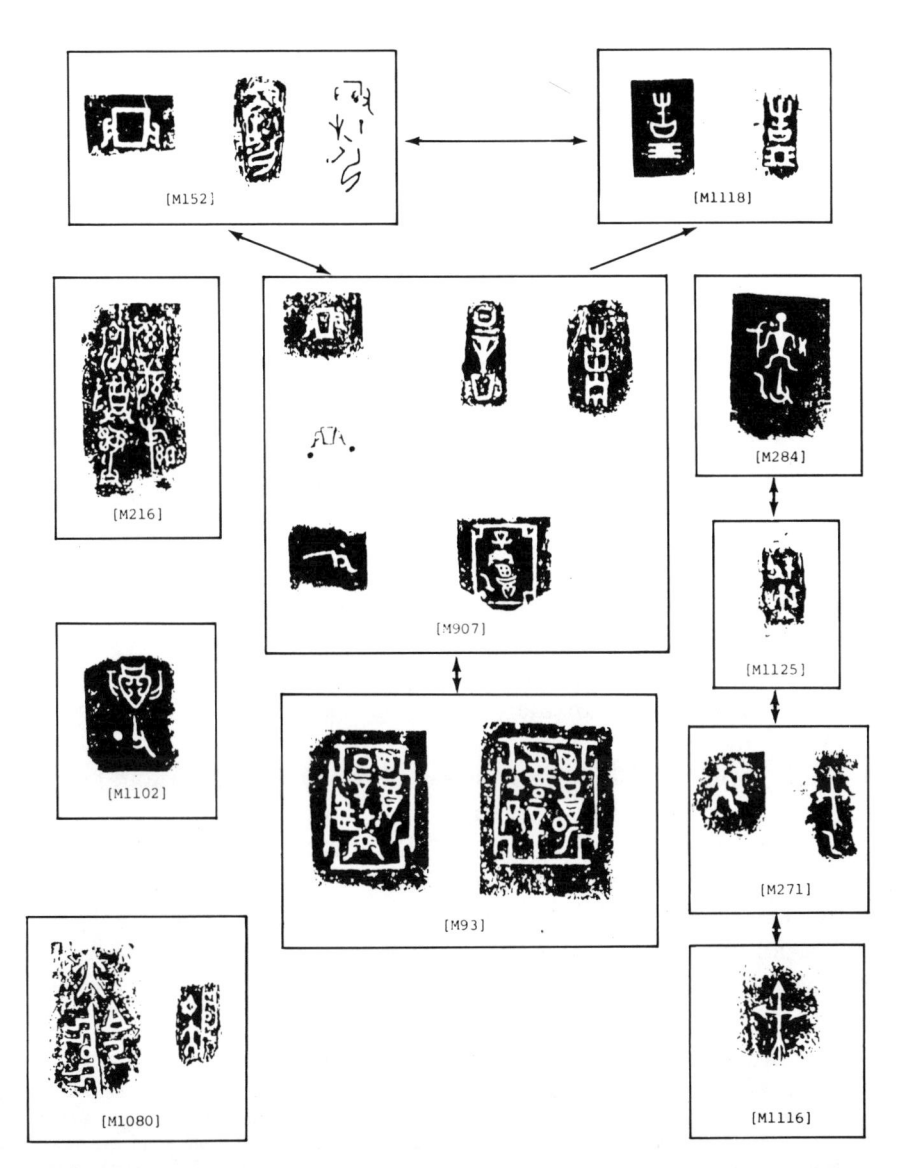

Fig. 22. Inscribed bronzes from Cemetery Areas 4 and 7 (M152, M1118, M907, and M93), and Areas 6 and 8 nearby (M284, M1125, M271, M1116; and M216, M1102, and M1080). Interrelationships are strikingly evident and especially significant features may be observed among the details in the more complex combinations. (Extracted from *Five Decades*, item 0022).

A   B C   D E F G H   I
(M 152)   (M 93)   (M 907)   (M 152)

Graphs A–F each comprise a pair of three fingered hands (*C-7*) holding between them (*C-7* [ ]) a bucket-shaped object (*V-54*). In graph F this center element appears solid; as it is drawn very small the outline form could not, apparently, be maintained when incised in the mold/core assembly. Other such filled-in examples may be noted: 〓 (〓), ● (○=⊖), 苹 (苹; 苹). It is clear, thus, that outline forms and filled-in forms are essentially variants of the same graphs, and the filling-in is due often to technical reasons. Graphs G and H each have two-fingered hands—this is to be regarded as an abbreviated version of the three-fingered hand. Other such attenuated forms are noted below. Graph I is not fully clear in the available rubbings but direct examination (Cheung, 26 April 1983) has resulted in the hand-copy placed alongside.[4] Tentatively this inscription is given the identification, or reference, number A/1: *C-7* [*V-54*], B-11 + *V-18*—it would appear that the object held by the kneeling woman (*B-11*) is identifiable with the graph 甚:告 *kao* (in clan-signs the code *V-18* is employed).

Now, graph *C-7* [*V-54*] occurs singly in an inscribed bronze in M 152 and again singly in M 907 (three cases); it is associated with the combination 旱:日辛 *jih-hsin* in a *chüeh* from M 907; it is also associated with the graph 敚: 敚 in the *chüeh* in M 152, as we have just noted, and accordingly demonstrates a close connection between the burials M 152, M 118, and M 907 in terms of the graph *V-18*.

Three other occurrences of the combination *C-7* [*V-54*] may be noted

---

4. Direct examination of the inscription areas in just over a score of the 259 inscribed artifacts from properly provenanced sites reproduced in the pages of the present survey (or cited from reports wherein rubbings are not reproduced) has been conducted by Cheung Kwong-yue and/or the author in the course of research trips in Mainland China during the last twelve months. These are indicated by asterisks placed before the A/l: section of reference numbers in figure 24b and in tables 3 and 4 in appendix C. As a result some revision of the original hand-out version of this survey has been found necessary; it would not be unexpected to find other instances where valuable clarification may later result following access to some of the remaining 240 inscribed vessels whose published rubbings lack definition of the level required for investigations of this kind.

Original rubbings can be most helpful, too, especially if unmounted and not heavily pressed flat; study of indentations of the rubbing paper from the rear is often rewarding (see Barnard 1959: 231, note 13). Later studies of the same inscriptions may, on occasions, incorporate new and better prepared rubbings. The recently published C. H. Cheng 1983 and Honan Province Institute of Cultural Relics 1981 have been found particularly helpful.

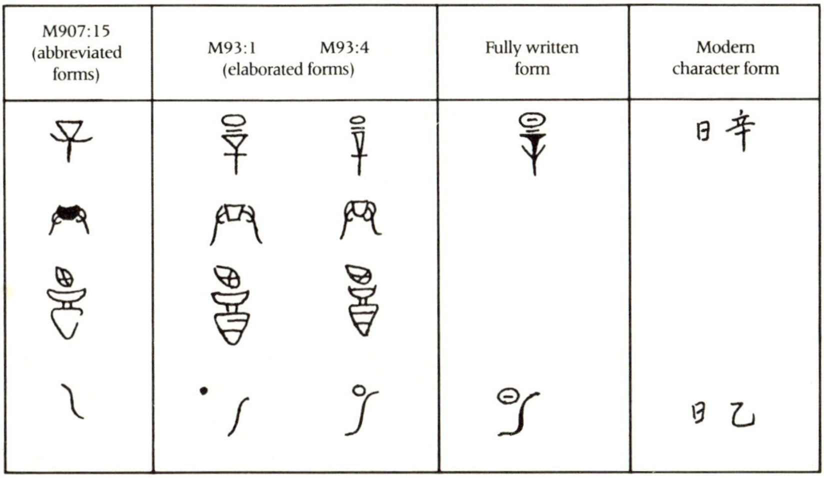

THE STUDY OF CLAN-SIGN INSCRIPTIONS OF SHANG 145

M907:15 (abbreviated forms)	M93:1 M93:4 (elaborated forms)	Fully written form	Modern character form
			日辛
			日乙

Fig. 23. Graphs extracted from the interrelated inscriptions in M907 and M93 which demonstrate the nature and degree of abbreviation present.

within *ya-hsing* and in further combination therein with various other elements; it is here that the investigation becomes rather intriguing, and a not entirely unexpected understanding of the nature of clan-sign construction results. The *ya-hsing* version on a bronze fragment from M 907 contains the following components: ￼, ￼, ￼, and ∫. These are repeated somewhat more elaborately in the *ya-hsing* inscriptions in two large *tsun*-beakers from M 93; when viewed systematically as in figure 23 it will be observed that the graphs ￼ and ∫ in the M 907 *ya-hsing* are essentially attenuated equivalents of the M 93 combinations—each comprising two components: o and ￼, and o and ∫. Upon comparison with the M 907 *chüeh* inscription it would be evident that the graph o (or ●) is an abbreviation of ⊖: 日 *jih*. All three renderings: ￼, ￼, and ￼ are, accordingly, to be read as *jih-hsin*! Similarly, +: *chia* and ∫ *yi* in the smaller of the two M 93 *ya-hsing* inscriptions are to be read as: *jih-chia* and *jih-yi*; interestingly, both *chia* and *yi* in this smaller version share a single o (= ●: ⊖: 日)! In the larger version of M 93 *jih-chia* has a filled-in *jih* and the *jih-hsin* and *jih-yi* combinations have an outline *jih*.

In addition to the *jih-chia* combination the two M 93 *ya-hsing* include also the graph ￼: 受 *shou* (but coded for clan-signs as: C-7 [V-14]). These two components do not appear in the M 907 *ya-hsing* at all, yet there exists ample space to incorporate them if the scribe had intended that

1 Kōsai 17.18 (?)	2 Tsun-ku-chai 1.48 (kuei)	5, a Hsü-chia 5.19 (tsun)	5, b Chi-ku 1.17b (tsun)	5, c Yung-shou 1.6a (tsun)
3 Chi-ku 1.18a (tsun)	4 Hsiao-chiao 2.30b (ting)	6 Hsiao-chiao 6.85b (chia)	7, a Hui-pien 1067 (chio, 1)	7, b Hui-pien 1067 (chio, v)
8 Wu-ying 56 (kuei)	9 Hsi-Ch'ing 23.1 (chio)	10, a Hsiao-chiao 5.8b (tsun, v)	10, b Hsiao-chiao 5.8b (tsun, 1)	
11, a Po-ku 1.32 (ting)	11, b Hsiao-t'ang 2a (ting)	11, c Li-tai 26b (ting)	12 Hsi-Ch'ing 23.26 (ku)	13 Hui-pien 1026 (fang-yi v, 1)

Fig. 24a. A selection of *ya-hsing* combinations relevant to the interrelated clan-sign graphs from M93, 907, and 152 from Cemetery Areas 4 and 7, Hsiao-min-t'un, recorded in repositories dating from Southern Sung times. Note: items 5a and 5b are different reproductions of the same original; 5c, however, is probably a *fan-pen* based on 5b; items

14, a *Hsi-Ch'ing* 13.4 (fang-yi, v) 
14, b *Hsi-Ch'ing* 13.4 (fang-yi, l) 
15, a *Hsiao-chiao* 5.29b (tsun, v) 
15, b *Hsiao-chiao* 5.29b (tsun, l) 
16 *Kōsai* 25.10 (ku)

17 *Hsiao-chiao* 5.29a (tsun) 
18 *Hsi-Ch'ing* 1.25 (ting) 
19 *Hsiao-chiao* 2.49b (ting) 
20 *Hsü-yi* 11.15 (ku) 
21 *Kōsai* 25.12 (ku)

22, a *Hsiao-chiao* 9.95a (an) 
22, b *Hsiao-chiao* 7.72b (kuei) 
23 *Hsi-Ch'ing* 1.18 (ting) 
24 *Pao-yün* 113 (ku)

25 *Hsi-Ch'ing* 1.27 (ting)
26, a *Hsiao-chiao* 2.49b (ting) 
26, b *Hsi-Ch'ing* 1.28 (ting) 
27 *Hui-pien* 1028 (fang-yi) 

11a–c demonstrate variations between three different Sung period catalogues of the same inscriptions; items 22a and b are different rubbings from the same original but mistakenly taken to derive from two different inscribed vessels.

they should appear. Possibly thus the M 907 *ya-hsing* may be regarded as being complete insofar as individual components are concerned. If this interpretation is correct, the two M 93 *ya-hsing* may then be considered to be a later development of the M 907 version. Possibly, it might be speculated, the additional *C-7* [*V-14*] and *jih-chia* indicate inter-clan associations (marriage ?). The former new component functions as the clan-sign while the latter may denote an ancestral figure revered by the *C-7* [*V-14*] clan—a member of which clan had apparently effected a marital alliance with a member of the M 907 *ya-hsing* clan-sign complex. This clan-sign complex, it will be evident, comprises the *C-7* [*V-54*] clan with its ancestral figure *jih-hsin* and the *V-9* clan with its revered forebear, *jih-yi*; both are enclosed in the *ya-hsing*.

Comparable clan-sign combinations may be seen in unprovenanced inscriptions (see fig. 24a), but lacking background information we can make only limited use of this material. To illustrate some aspects of the research potential, however, I have tabulated the relevant inscriptions from figure 22 (six items) along with the twenty-seven unprovenanced inscriptions in figure 24a in accordance with the reference numbers of each, and with the coded elements forming the reference numbers arranged in vertical columns (see fig. 24b). This procedure results in a rather effective analysis of the inscription components and demonstrates at a glance the presence or absence of particular elements as well as the incorporation of additional elements. Shape variations and varying degrees of structural elaboration such as those already noted in figure 23 are not represented by the code system—such finer details attending the calligraphy should be subject to direct examination of rubbings (or their published reproductions) and where necessary direct study of the original inscribed vessel.

Among the provenanced inscriptions two main groups appear: the *C-7* [*V-54*] group and the A-[*C-7* [*V-54*]] group; the latter in two cases contains the graph *C-7* [*V-14*]. Upon comparison with the unprovenanced items it will be observed that there are no instances of *C-7* [*V-54*] without a *ya-hsing*, and no examples of both *C-7* [*V-54*] and *C-7* [*V-14*] within the same *ya-hsing*. There are, however, elements such as *B-5* [*H-10*], *B-8*, *B-14*, *C-3*, and *V-23* which do not appear among the provenanced inscriptions. Lacking provenance information, we cannot at present assess the significance of such variations in component combinations between the provenanced and unprovenanced inscriptions.

A: Properly provenanced group from figure 22.
a. A/1:   C-7[V-54]   (v.a), (v.b), (v.c)
b. *A/1:   C-7[V-54],   Q-8
c. *A/1:   C-7[V-54],   B-11 + V-18
d. A/1: A-[C-7[V-54], V-9, L-8, L-2]
e. A/1: A-[C-7[V-54], V-9, Q-8, L-2, L-1, C-7[V-14]]
f. A/1: A-[C-7[V-54], V-9, Q-8, Q-2, Q-1, C-7[V-14]]

Asterisks placed immediately before the A/1: component of the coded reference numbers indicate here and in later tables that the original inscribed vessel has been personally examined by either Cheung Kwong-yue or me.

B: Unprovenanced examples: A-[C-7[V-54]] group.
1.   A-[C-7[V-54],   J-4]
2.   A-[C-7[V-54],   J-10]
3. T. A-[C-7[V-54], V-9,   J-1]   (v.a.)
4. T. A-[C-7[V-54], V-9,   J-1]   (v.b.)
5. T. A-[C-7[V-54],   J-4, B-8]   (v.a.)
6.   A-[C-7[V-54],   J-4, B-8]   (v.b.)
7.   A-[C-7[V-54],   J-4, B-8]   (v.c.), (l.c.)
8. T. A-[C-7[V-54]   B-8] + J-2
9. T. A-[J-4, B-8]
10.   A-[J-2,   B-8]

C: Unprovenanced examples: A-[C-7[V-14]] group.
11. S. A-[C-7[V-14], B-5[H-10]?,   L-2, Q-1, L-4,   Q-10, B-14]
12. T. A-[C-7[V-14], B-5[H-10], Q-2, L-2,   C-3, L-10, B-14, V-23] (v.l)
13.   A-[C-7[V-14], B-5[H-10], Q-2, L-2,   C-3, L-10, B-14, V-23] (v.j)
14. T. A-[C-7[V-14], B-5[H-10], Q-2?, L-2,   C-3, L-10, B-14, V-23] (v.a)
                                              (l.a)
15.   A-[C-7[V-14], B-5[H-10], Q-2, L-2,   C-3, L-10, B-14, V-23] (v.d),
                                              (l.d)
16.   A-[C-7[V-14], B-5[H-10], Q-2, L-2,   C-3, L-10, B-14, V-23] (v.e)
17.   A-[C-7[V-14], B-5[H-10], Q-2?, ? ,   ? , L-10, B-14, V-23] (v.f)
18.   A-[C-7[V-14], B-5[H-10],   ? , L-2,   ? , L-10, B-14, V-23] (v.g)
19.   A-[C-7[V-14], B-5[H-10], Q-2, L-2,   C-3, L-10, B-14, V-23] (v.h)
20. T. A-[C-7[V-14], B-5[H-10]?, ? , ? ,   ? , ? , B-14, V-23] (v.i)
21.   A-[C-7[V-14]?,   ?   ,   ? , L-2,   ? , L-10, B-14, ?] —
22.   A-[C-7[V-14], B-5[H-10], Q-2, L-2,   C-3, L-10, B-11, V-23] (v.b)
23. T. A-[?   ,   ?   ,   ? , L-2,   ? , L-10, B-14?, ?] —
24.   A-[?   ,   ?   ,   ? , ? ,   ? , L-10, ? , ?]
25. T. A-[C-7[V-14?],   ?   ,   ? , L-2,   ? , L-10, B-14, ?] —
26. T. A-[C-7[V-14], B-5[H-10], Q-2, L-2,   C-3, L-10, B-14, V-23] (v.k)
27. T. A-[C-7[V-14], B-5[H-10], Q-2, L-2,   C-3, L-10, B-14, V-23] (v.c)

Fig. 24b. Coded reference numbers for the properly provenanced inscriptions from figure 22, and the unprovenanced items in figure 24a. The reference number components are extended where necessary to allow common elements to fall in the same columns thus facilitating intercomparisons.

The codification of clan-sign component graphs may be studied in detail in Barnard and Cheung Kwong-yue *Chung, Jih, Ou, Mi, Ao, Niu, so-chien so-t'o so-mo chin-wen hui-pien*, I: 50–7–, (see also appendix B, below).

The unprovenanced inscriptions may be divided into two general groups based respectively upon the *A-[C-7 [V-54]]* and the *A-[C-7 [V-14]]* clan-sign graphs which appear together in the "complete" *ya-hsing* versions of M 93 (items e and f in Group A). Upon perusal of the materials so arranged it will be noted that useful though limited avenues of research exist in the case of unprovenanced inscriptions. Take, for instance, the graph ᕁ to the right of the element ⊢ in the Sung Catalogue renderings (item 11a-c); in view of the inscription contents as a whole, the possibility that the Sung copyists have incorrectly read an original 阝 as two graphs seems certain. Obvious errors in the Imperial Ch'ing Catalogues, as in items 18, 20, and 25, may be certified, while the spurious nature of item 21—obviously copied from item 25—may be recognized. Throughout the unprovenanced inscriptions the reading of certain of the graphs ○ as ● = ⊖ = ᱐ may now be proposed with good support—note especially the rubbing version in item 26a, where the *Hsi-Ch'ing* wood-block rendering (26b) is ● but the rubbing shows it is ○! Furthermore, the possibility that this graph, *jih*, is associated not only with the cyclical graph, *yi*, but also *kuei*, should be kept in mind. As this approach is more extensively applied, and with more extensive "cross-reference" to other related clan-sign combinations, numerous other such minor details may be better appreciated.

Other graphs denoting inter-associations of the tomb occupants are: 𣆶: 告 *kao* (M 1118, M 907, and M 152 [?]); 伐: *B-2* (M 284, M 1152, and M 271); 中: *V-11* (M 271 and M 1116). These are illustrated in figure 22, where the inscriptions are grouped according to the burials from which they were recovered; in figure 25 the locations of these tombs in the western sector cemetery area are indicated on the site map.

Several observations of some significance result from this avenue of research:

1. A better appreciation is obtained of some finer details attending the writing of the archaic graphs, in particular, the nature of abbreviation of writing and the technical mishaps that occasionally occur during the incising of small elements (filling-in).

2. An understanding of certain attenuated phrases results, for example, *hsin = jih-hsin*. Without knowledge of the complete version, of course, the attenuated form (a cyclical character only) might never be properly reconstructed. Knowing this propensity now, however, we are in a more

THE STUDY OF CLAN-SIGN INSCRIPTIONS OF SHANG

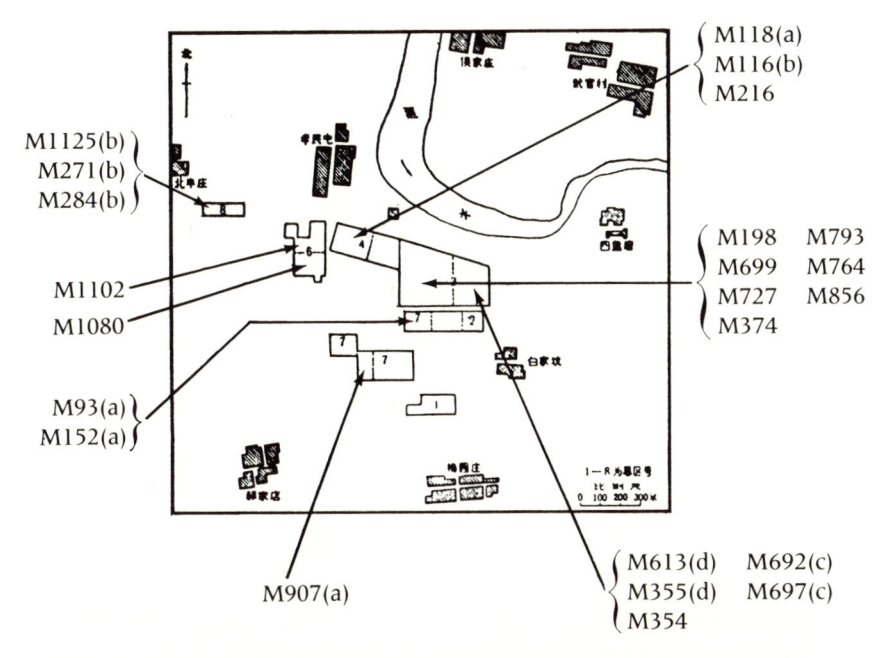

Fig. 25. Site map of the Hsiao-min-t'un area, Western Sector, showing cemetery areas and groups of burials in each furnished with the inscribed bronzes whose inscriptions are illustrated in figure 22. The four interrelated groups are indicated by the letters a, b, c, and d placed in parentheses after the tomb numbers concerned. Maps covering the individual cemetery areas with the burials all depicted may be consulted in the original report.

secure position to review the original significance of many comparable unprovenanced inscriptions in the repositories.[5]

3. Possible interrelationships of tomb occupants in a common cemetery area may now be seen as a fruitful line of investigation.

4. Paired associations of some clan-signs with particular forebears among such complex combinations as those in figures 22 and 24 seem evident.

---

5. It will be appreciated, of course, that while the relevant M907 and M93 graphs indicate quite clearly that the posthumous title *jih* is to be understood before the cyclical characters *chia, yi,* and *hsin* where it has been omitted, other posthumous titles such as *fu, mu, hsiung,* etc. may likewise be unexpressed in inscriptions where abbreviation has been affected. Unless we have a clear-cut situation as in the case of M907 and M93, it would be difficult to decide what posthumous title may have been left out. In the case of the M284, M1125, M271, and M1116 inscriptions the posthumous title omitted before *yi* in M271 would probably be *fu*; with reference to M284 and M1125 a reasonable though not necessarily decisive argument to this effect might be advanced.

5. Possible chronological relationships between simple combinations and more complex combinations involving a common clan-sign may be determined as more data accrue.

In Cemetery Area No. 3 inscribed bronzes from twelve tombs were recovered; two of the burials only exhibit an interconnection: M 613 and M 355 (see fig. 26a). The twelve tombs are concentrated in a smaller area than is the more scattered group of eleven burials (with inscribed bronzes) just discussed, and there are no clan-sign connections evident between the two groups of inscriptions; the variation may suggest that certain burial areas tended to be used mainly by interrelated clans while other areas were less restricted.

A similar corpus of clan-sign inscriptions has long been available for assessments along the present lines—those deriving from the excavations conducted at Hsiao-t'un by Academia Sinica (Nan-kang 南港) under the direction of the late Li Chi 李濟. To demonstrate the interconnections between the several tombs in terms of clan-signs, I extract here figures 0001:2 and 0001:3 from Entry No. 0001 in our forthcoming survey referred to above (note 2). These (figs. 26b and 26c) serve to demonstrate also the way in which this new approach is being applied on a large scale to the entire corpus of inscribed bronzes deriving from controlled excavations and acceptably provenanced finds. Entry No. 0001 is centered on the inscribed *fang-ting*-cauldron, R 1750, from Tomb No. HPKM 1004 excavated during the Third Season (September 1934–December 1936) at Hsi-pei-kang 西北岡. The inscription comprises the drawing of a bovid; along with it were excavated no fewer than ninety-three inscribed artifacts, and among these may be noted inscriptions which are repeated in several of the other tombs. Further instances of interrelationships between the ten tombs with inscribed bronzes excavated by Li Chi are indicated in figure 26b. Reference to figure 26c and its caption will show without recourse to detailed discussion here that in the study of calligraphic details, much the same results as noted above may be observed in this group of inscription data. The clan-signs 舟, 舟, 夳, 弋, and 𠆢 comprise those repeated from one tomb to another: M 1001, M 1769, M 1768, M 1133, and M 1004, and would seem thus to indicate a close affinity between the six tombs. M 1885 and M 1795 may be associated on the basis of the graph 貞: 冀: 共 *kung* while the graph 丁 would appear to connect YM 066 and M 1550.

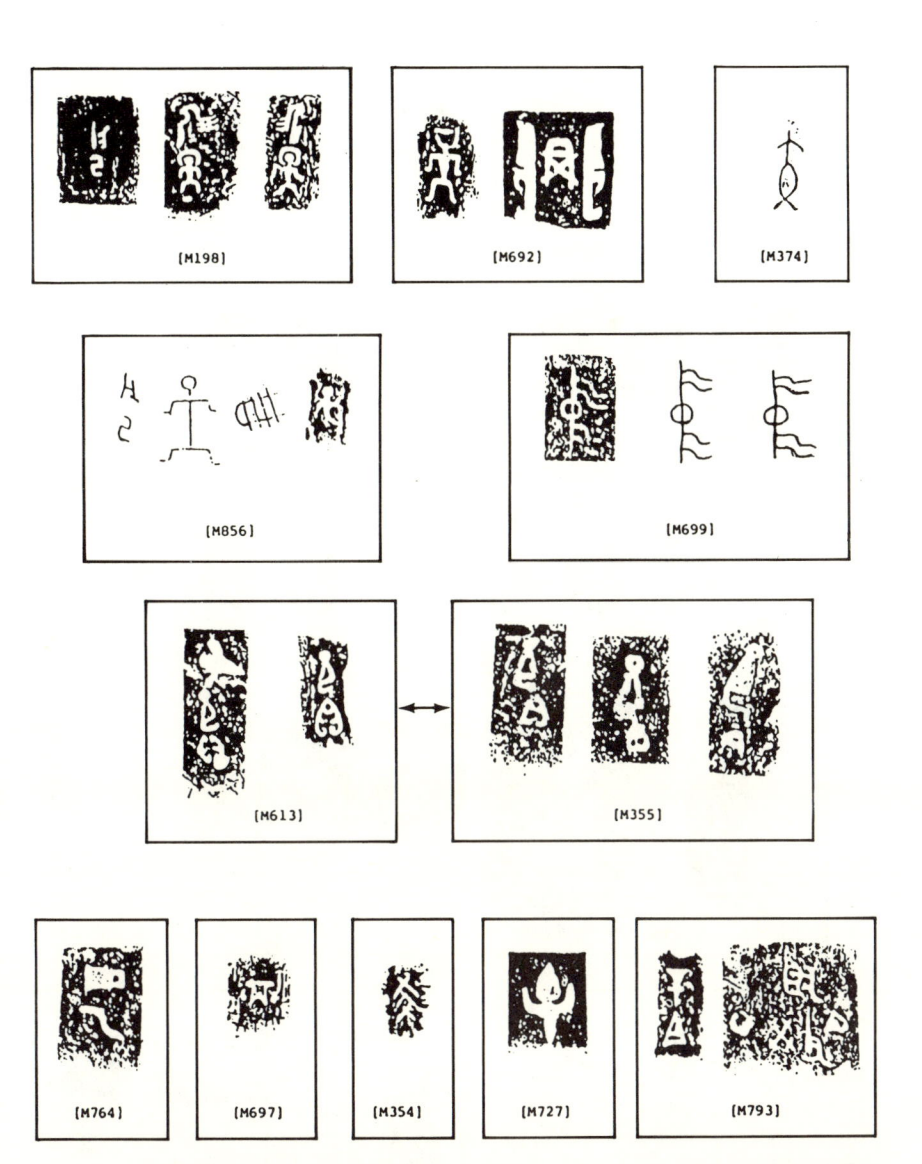

Fig. 26a. Inscribed bronzes from Cemetery Area No. 3, Hsiao-min-t'un. Interrélationship between M355 and M613 is demonstrated in the clan-sign combination: *B-5 + F-7* common to each, a "Kneeling man" (*B-5*) and a "cowrie shell" (*F-7*). M355 is Period III and M613 is Period II, thus illustrating a horizontal association in time. The remaining inscriptions do not show assessable interrelationships between tombs. (Extracted from *Five Decades*, item 0038).

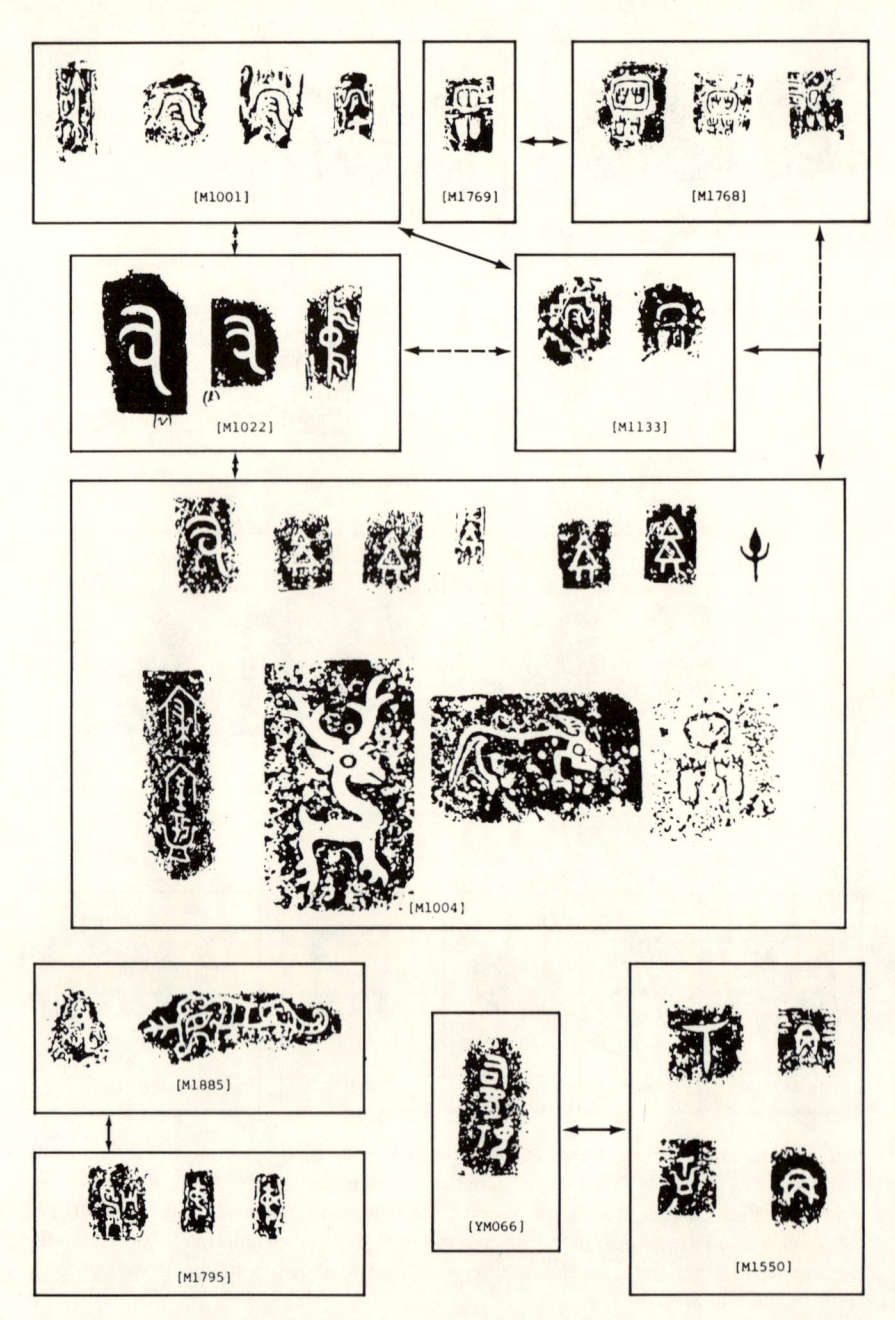

Fig. 26b. Interrelations of clan-signs among burials in the Hsiao-t'un site. (After fig. 0001:2, loc, cit.).

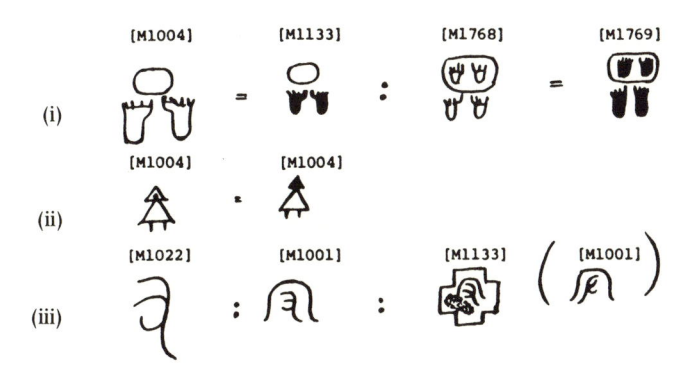

Fig. 26c. Variant versions of clan-sign combinations to be noted in figure 26b. Outline and filled-in elements are obviously of identical significance. However, combinations as in (i) left-hand group and right-hand group cannot be claimed to be identical without more evidence than is presently available. In (ii) the two versions of the "building" may, of course, be equated. In (iii) the hand element on its own, with a "cover" (and in reverse), and enclosed in a *ya-hsing* may be regarded as interrelated combinations because of other clan-sign associations among the same tombs. But they are not to be equated upon the basis of presently available evidence. (After fig. 0001:3, loc. cit.)

SOME DIFFICULTIES CONFRONTING THE RESEARCHER

In investigations of this kind problems soon come to the researcher's attention. A typical example is to be noted in connection with the excavations conducted at Hou-li 后李 in Lo-shan-hsien 羅山縣, Ho-nan (*KK* 1981.2:111–18; *CYWW* 1981.4:4–13). During the first season of digs (27 August to 23 September 1979) six Shang burials were excavated, among which M 1 and M 6 were found in good condition while M 2 and M 5 were badly disturbed; eleven Shang burials were excavated during the second season (29 July to 28 November 1980: M 8, M 9, M 11, M 12, M 15, M 18, M 23, M 27, M 28, M 40, and M 41), and also twenty-four Chou burials. Among the bronzes recovered from M 1, M 5, and M 6 in the first season, ten items bear inscriptions (fig. 27a), and in the second season the total ranges from eighteen inscribed items (see summary *CYWW* 1981.4:13) to as many as twenty-four inscribed items (according to the body of the report: pp. 5–11). The *CYWW* summary also states that in the first season twenty-three inscribed bronzes with the graph "息" were found;[6] these include the first five accidentally discovered

---

6. The archaic forms of 息 or 息 cited here are written in exactly the same structural forms as they appear in the reports under discussion. As the renderings in the reports are incorrect I place quotation marks around each instance cited; the correct structures of the graphs are demonstrated below.

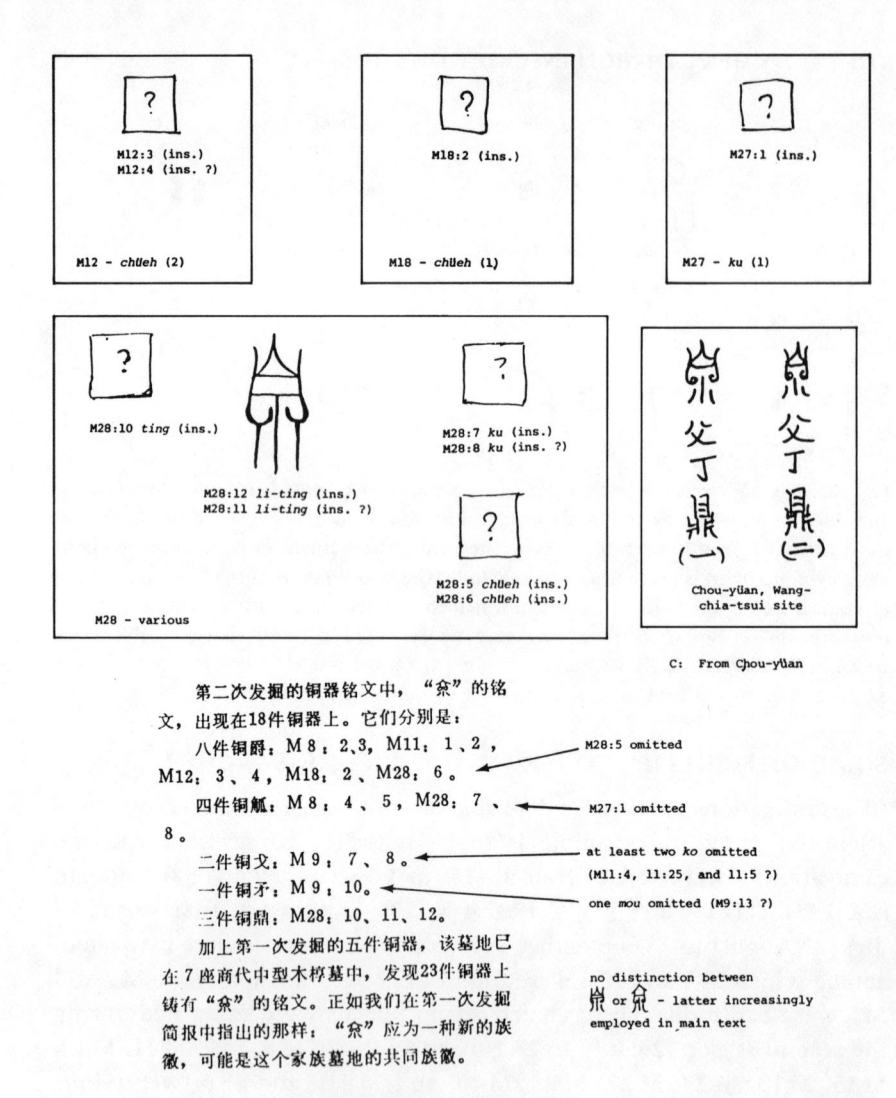

Fig. 27. Inscriptions on bronzes excavated from burials in the Lo-shan-hsien cemetery area. A: Those from Tombs Nos. 1, 5, and 6 (after *KK* 1981.2:111–18)—First Season. B: Second Season: M7, 8, 9, 11, 12, 18, 27, and 28. Question marks following certain items indicate uncertainty as to whether the item is inscribed, and if so, is the inscription identical to the preceding one? C: Two inscribed *Ting*-cauldrons with the same clan-sign from Chou-yüan (pers. comm.). Section of *CYWW* summary of Second Season excavations with author's notes of items omitted in the summary.

M1 - yu, tou

yu (ins. v. only)

tou

M7 - ?

M5 - ting, chüeh

ting

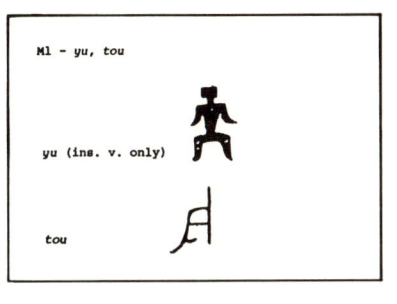

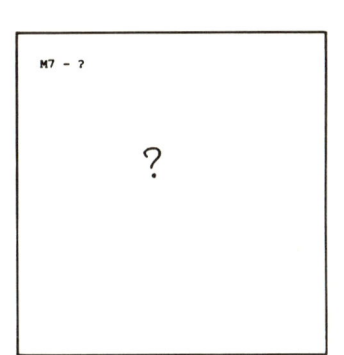

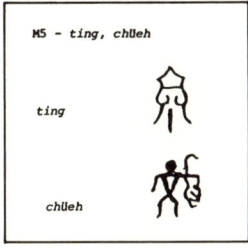

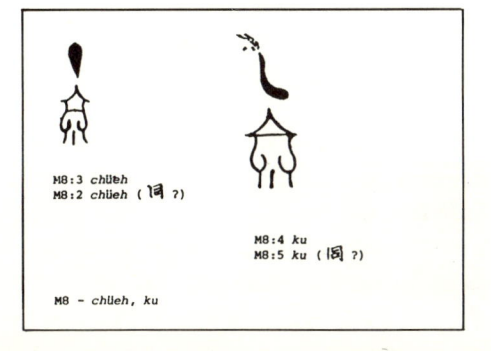

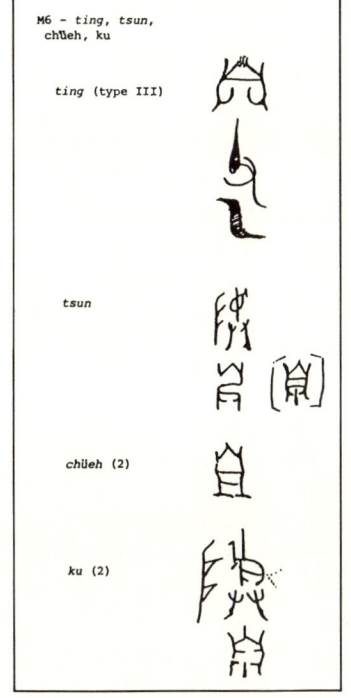

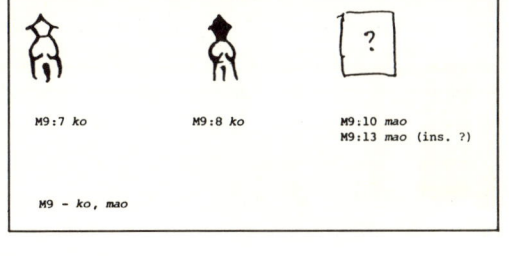

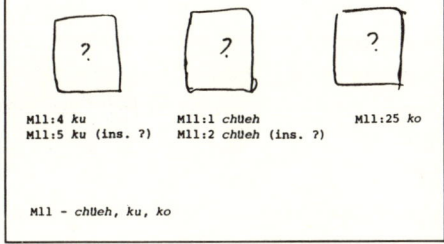

chüeh

M8:3 chüeh
M8:2 chüeh (?)

M8:4 ku
M8:5 ku (?)

M8 - chüeh, ku

M6 - ting, tsun, chüeh, ku

ting (type III)

tsun

chüeh (2)

ku (2)

M9:7 ko

M9:8 ko

M9:10 mao
M9:13 mao (ins. ?)

M9 - ko, mao

M11:4 ku
M11:5 ku (ins. ?)

M11:1 chüeh
M11:2 chüeh (ins. ?)

M11:25 ko

M11 - chüeh, ku, ko

A: First Season

B: Second Season

bronzes (*KK* 1981.2:111) and those from the seven Shang wooden chamber burials. If the statement is correct, this would mean that the five accidentally discovered bronzes were each inscribed with the above graph (but no precise indication that they were so inscribed appears in the first report), while the seventh tomb (not mentioned either in the first report or elsewhere in the second report) must have contained eight further inscribed items with the same graph repeated to give the total of twenty-three. There is no reason to doubt the reliability of the statements—obviously there could be a burial numbered M 7; and doubtless the first five vessels that came to light during work on the canal may each be inscribed. But there is every reason to deplore the lackadaisical aspects of the reporting procedures.

The student of the archaic script and the historian of antiquity who might seek to employ the data effectively have available in reproduction only the inscriptions as presented in figures 27a and b; the squares with a "?" inside represent inscriptions reported but not illustrated; their exact nature is uncertain as the wording in the report is simply: 腹內有銘文, 鋬內有銘文. etc.—we cannot even know how many characters are incorporated in each. Not only the foreign student is at a loss, but also his counterpart in China; in their study of the character "異", Li Po-ch'ien 李伯謙 and Cheng Chieh-hsiang 鄭傑祥 (*CYWW* 1981.4:33–35, 46) seem to have had access only to the same two reports and obviously have not seen the additional inscriptions as totalled in the summary of the *CYWW* report—they merely cite the relevant statement (giving the archaic graph "異" (*viz.* 異) erroneously for the "異" (*viz.* 異) of the original), then they proceed to observe: "eighteen bronzes were unearthed from M 6; among these six had cast-in the clan-sign "異" [but compare exact details in our figure 27b], while among the twelve bronzes recovered from M 28, eight items were cast the clan-sign "異" [according to the body of the report there were seven items and the summary states six items only]. "As may be observed in our figure 27b a rubbing of only one inscription has been reproduced from those in M 28.

Upon due study of the available rubbings of the inscriptions from Season One and Season Two excavations it is immediately evident that there are three slightly different clan-sign graphs, A, B, and C (or possibly three versions of one clan-sign graph), involved:

A 〔graph〕 B¹ 〔graph〕 B² 〔graph〕 C 〔graph〕

↖ accidentally omitted?

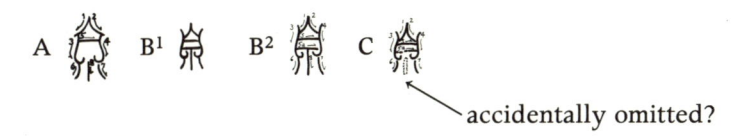

Without going into detail, at this stage of our study it would seem reasonable to conclude that the three variants represent the one clan-sign graph which, if written in full, would appear as in B¹. Abbreviated forms may lack a horizontal stroke as in B² or two strokes as in C. Interestingly, the alternative form 〔graph〕 (note filled-in example M 9:8) is constant in structure in all five examples available to us. How far the aforegoing observations will hold when the nineteen inscriptions not yet reproduced for study are eventually made available remains to be seen.

Meantime, not only minor calligraphic details of this kind must remain unsolved, but also there is the equally obvious problem of the exact nature of the "character text" of each inscription to be clarified before a reliable study of these inscriptions can be attempted. As may be observed in figure 27 the graphs 〔graph〕 (or 〔graph〕) occur in combinations with cyclical characters or with other graphs:

1 〔graph〕 2 〔graph〕 3 〔graph〕 4 〔graph〕 5 〔graph〕

How many such combinations are present among the nineteen inscriptions not yet reproduced? If such combinations are present (and we can well expect this to be the case) what are the additional components? Once armed with this knowledge we would be in a position to apply the approaches proposed in this paper more effectively; and we might reasonably expect to arrive at an understanding of the interassociations among the clan-signs in this remarkable cemetery area comparable to that obtained from the Hsiao-min-t'un inscriptions surveyed above.

INTERRELATED INSCRIPTIONS IN AN UNDISTURBED TOMB—THE FU HAO MU

When it comes to an undisturbed tomb containing inscribed artifacts in such a large number as in the well-known Fu Hao Mu (76AXTM 5, *viz.* M 5, excavated at Hsiao-t'un in the winter of 1975/76), some aspects of

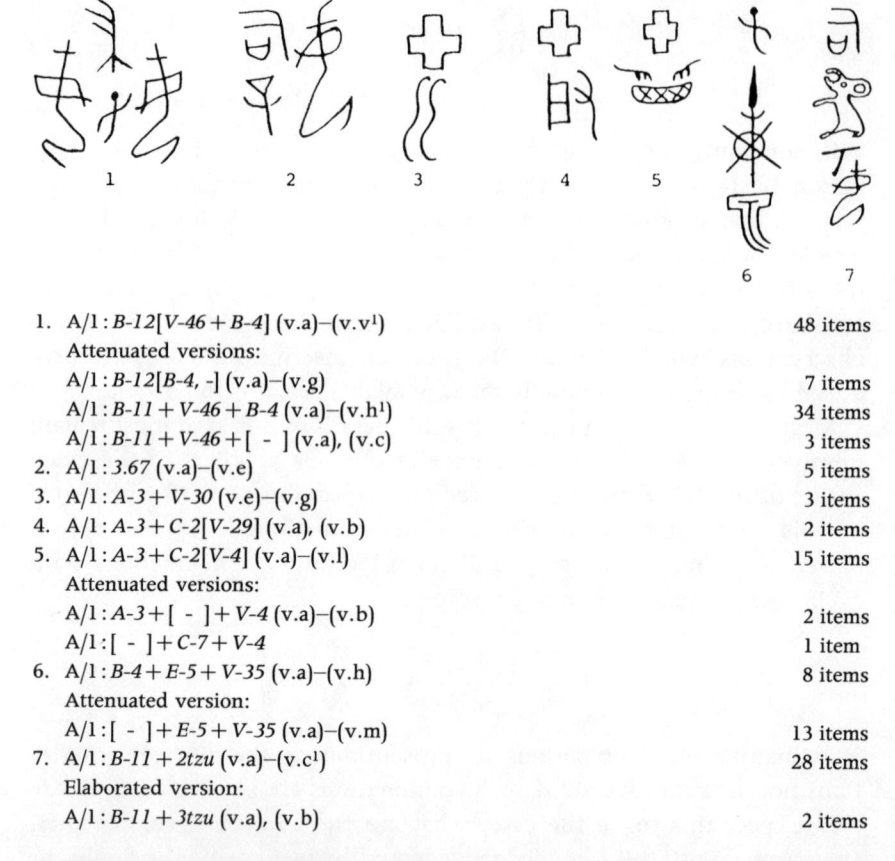

1. A/1 : B-12[V-46 + B-4] (v.a)–(v.v¹)   48 items
   Attenuated versions:
   A/1 : B-12[B-4, -] (v.a)–(v.g)   7 items
   A/1 : B-11 + V-46 + B-4 (v.a)–(v.h¹)   34 items
   A/1 : B-11 + V-46 +[-] (v.a), (v.c)   3 items
2. A/1 : 3.67 (v.a)–(v.e)   5 items
3. A/1 : A-3 + V-30 (v.e)–(v.g)   3 items
4. A/1 : A-3 + C-2[V-29] (v.a), (v.b)   2 items
5. A/1 : A-3 + C-2[V-4] (v.a)–(v.l)   15 items
   Attenuated versions:
   A/1 : A-3 +[-]+ V-4 (v.a)–(v.b)   2 items
   A/1 :[-]+ C-7 + V-4   1 item
6. A/1 : B-4 + E-5 + V-35 (v.a)–(v.h)   8 items
   Attenuated version:
   A/1 :[-]+ E-5 + V-35 (v.a)–(v.m)   13 items
7. A/1 : B-11 + 2tzu (v.a)–(v.c¹)   28 items
   Elaborated version:
   A/1 : B-11 + 3tzu (v.a), (v.b)   2 items

In addition to these 169 items there are 5 miscellaneous inscriptions: two on bronze vessels and three incised in jade artifacts.

Fig. 28. The seven basic clan-signs among inscribed bronzes in the Fu Hao tomb and their attenuated (and elaborated) versions.

the potential attending tomb-by-tomb investigations when further such rich finds are unearthed may be appreciated. Among the inscriptions in the Fu Hao tomb are seven basic clan-sign combinations (see fig. 28). By far the largest group comprises item 1, codified as A/1 : B-12 [V-46 + B-4], of which there are fifty-four examples (counting vessel + lid sets as single items) and forty-one attenuated versions (two varieties; see fig. 29a). Of the latter the combination B-11 + V-46 + B-4 (thirty-three

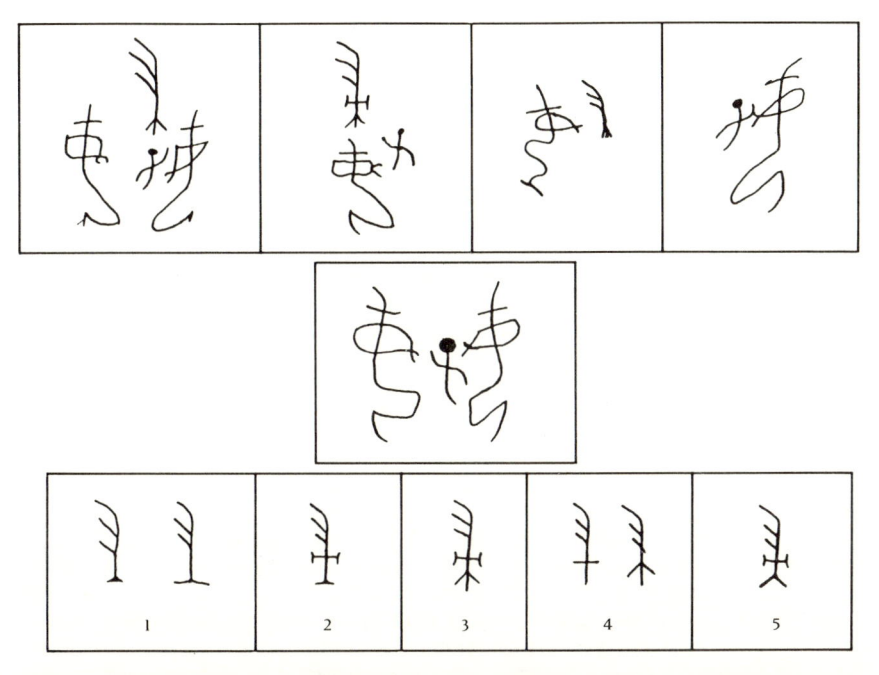

THE STUDY OF CLAN-SIGN INSCRIPTIONS OF SHANG   161

Fig. 29a. (1) The title/name combination Fu Hao, when written in full, comprises two face-to-face women (B-12) with the graphs V-46 (fu) and B-4 (tzu) in between; thus the codification: B-12[V-46 + B-4]. (2) This may be abbreviated to one woman only (b-11); thus the codification: B-11 + V-46 + B-4. (3, 4) Further attenuation results in the versions B-11 + V-16 + [-] and B-11 + [-] + B-4. However, there are only three examples of the former (items 26, 27, and 51), and only one of the latter—the lid text of item 24—thus both combinations may be regarded as a form of "mishap" rather than a degree of abbreviation. (5) There are seven instances where the graph fu is omitted: B-12[- ,B-4].

Several variant forms of the graph fu may be observed. In figures 29b, c, and d, the Fu Hao inscriptions are arranged in accordance with the variations in writing fu (V-46) and the variations of component elements. The two fu versions in 1, above, are covered in figures 29b and c. That in 2, above, in figure 29c. In figure 29d the remaining variants of fu are listed.

In figure 29e Fu Hao inscriptions which are too indistinct are grouped for record purposes.

items) parallels the oracle bone equivalent forms: 帚, 帚, 帚, etc. which likewise have the graphs: 帚, 帚, 帚, etc. in combination. The identification of the tomb occupant as Fu Hao, one of sixty-four consorts of Wu Ting (1334–1275 B.C.), is thus well appreciated (*KKHP* 1977.2:

21).[7] The general dating of the tomb and its inscribed contents toward the end of Wu Ting's reign (Fu Hao predeceasing the king) throws useful light on aspects of characters and calligraphy in both bronze and oracle bone versions in the latter half of Period I.[8]

7. For reasons which I have presented in considerable detail in an early study incorporated in a review article (Barnard 1960) I favor use of the orthodox chronology for Shang and Western Chou dates and have continued to employ this chronology throughout all my writings despite its generally recognized imperfections (and in full awareness of the recent appearances of further chronologies and of new chronological studies). Naturally, I have followed with interest the various investigations by Lai Tung-fang (1102 B.C.), Shirakawa Shizuka (1087 B.C.), Lao Kan (1025 B.C.), Liu Ch'i-yi (1075 B.C.), David S. Nivison (1045 B.C.), David W. Pankenier (1046 B.C.) and since the prepublication distribution of these two Western studies, Chou Fa-kao's resultant sudden change from a cherished 1018 B.C. to 1045 B.C., which are among those that have appeared since the publication of my early study and the follow-up comparative table of chronologies in Barnard 1972. The possible significance of and the variant interpretations possible for apparent key chronological recordings in such recently excavated inscribed vessels as the Li *kuei* (利殷: ins. A/l:*33.20*) and the Ho *tsun* (何尊: ins. A/o:*122:1*) and such others that may seem to have relevance to the problem have been explored. Very pertinent studies such as David N. Keightley's critical appraisal of the *Chu-shu chi-nien* (Keightley 1978b), H. H. Hu (1982), and Fang and Wang 1981 (with special attention to the phrase 以至幽王, which they revise upon good authority to 以至于幽王) should be thoroughly read and digested by all would-be Chou (and Shang) chronology revisionist! The first demonstrates the highly questionable value of the *Bamboo Annals* as a source for Shang–Chou chronology as well as for other aspects of Shang and Chou history; the second shows the curious lack of understanding of the so-called eclipse records in the oracle bones by the numerous scholars who have taken them to be actual records (*yen-tz'u* 驗辭, as Hu phrases it) of eclipses when in fact they are merely prognostications (David Nivison 1982 is closely concerned with this aspect of the oracular texts); while the first has significant bearing on the interpretation of the 275 years' statement: "From Wu Wang's extinguishing the Yin to Yu Wang (inclusive), there were altogether 257 years"—the basis upon which the 1027 B.C. chronology of Ch'en Meng-chia and B. Karlgren rests. This chronological system, slavishly followed in Mainland China as well as in the West, is self-evidently lacking in reliability (see my 1960 review article for details); now with the revision of the 以至幽王 to 以至于幽王, the 1027 B.C. date for the Chou conquest of Shang would have to go back eleven years to 1038 B.C.—a point foreshadowed in my early paper (pp. 492–93). I am still of the opinion offered then that "attempts to compile an acceptable pre-Ch'in chronology will remain merely academic exercises and hopes of prevision illusory.... The best solution is to accept the 'orthodox' chronology until such time as archaeological evidence allows modifications.... With standardisation of chronology, however, a lot of people will be saved a lot of extremely complicated work in later years" (pp. 497–99).

8. Although a number of scholars have opted to date the Fu Hao tomb upon the basis of their identification of the graphs *fu-hao* as the title-name of a consort of the Wu Ting, there is perhaps good reason to reconsider the validity of this early date. In a thought-provoking paper presented at the present conference Virginia C. Kane (1982) has critically examined the problem, devoting due attention to the "excavator's" methodology in dating the find and then concentrating on art historical considerations among other matters. To her appraisals might also be added assessments based upon technical aspects of the casting methodology. Space is not sufficient to allow a digression here, unfortunately, and in any case I have examined to date directly only a dozen items. Nevertheless, some useful detail relating to a score or so items may be gleaned from descriptive data in C. M. Hua et al. 1981 (but note assessments of this article in Barnard and Cheung 1983). There is,

In figure 29a I present an analytical grouping of the Fu Hao clan-sign combinations along with a selection of variant forms of the graph *fu*; it may be noted that the latter appears with several grades of attenuation:

    1 2 3 4a 4b 5   cf.   CKWP   7.27

Some are reversed as in oracle bone texts (examples in most versions); items 3 and 4a closely approach the main varieties in oracle bone script. Each variety is repeated throughout a series of vessels, thus suggesting group calligraphic connections. The possibility that we may have here the calligraphy of different artisan/scribes, and possibly thus a means of dividing the inscribed bronzes into "calligraphic groups," is worth investigating.[9] Specialists in the study of the decor and the typography of the vessels may find that a more thorough calligraphic analysis than I have attempted here may tie up to some extent with the results of their approach to the vessels; it would, of course, be merely wishful thinking to remark upon the role that metal analyses might play in this same exercise.[10]

---

accordingly, an appreciable amount of data presently available; some of this indicates the probability of a late rather than an early date within the Hsiao-t'un Shang context in regard to casting techniques among several items within the somewhat extensive chronological range of bronzes in the Fu Hao tomb. It is, of course, these later datable items—so dated upon stylistic, decorative, and technical grounds—which will indicate the *earliest* possible date of the burial.

9. I have especially coined the term "artisan/scribe" for use in discussions relating to calligraphic matters in bronze inscriptions (it may also have value in regard to oracle bone inscriptions, where one might assume that the incising of the originally brush-written records into the bone or shell surfaces was executed by artisans other than scribes, who were experienced in such work). We have no definite evidence to the effect that an inscription as it is preserved in bronze is the handwriting of a scribe sent to the foundry for copying which has been precisely incised in all its detail in clay; we cannot be sure, either, that the copy sent to the foundry was rewritten there without regard to calligraphic idiosyncracies in the original! And there are other possibilities. To cover all this, the above term is employed. It is simply assumed that common series of calligraphic nuances extant among groups of related inscribed bronzes—especially those with identical texts repeated from one bronze vessel to another—reflect the work either of particular individuals or of groups of two or more individuals.

10. The possibility that inscriptions deriving from the same artisan/scribes may derive also from the same foundries may be further confirmed by similarity of alloys in the parent vessels. When I was writing the above remarks there were no analyses of Fu Hao tomb bronzes available. In her paper presented at the present conference Cheng Chen-hsiang presented several analyses of the bronzes; following the conference I went to Peking and there received from Hua Chüeh-ming a mimeographed paper by Hua et al. 1982. Among the several hundred analyses of Chinese bronzes assembled in this paper are eighteen Fu Hao analyses. In Hua et al. 1981 a few further items are available; it is also noted in this article that sixty-odd Fu Hao bronzes have been analyzed (p. 252).

164   NOEL BARNARD

1. M5:768 (Fig. 32, 2) *tseng* (1)   2. M5:768 (Fig. 32, 3) *tseng* (1)   3. M5:768 (no illus.) *tseng* (1)
   ins. A/1:B-12[V-46+B-4] (v.e-a)   ins. A/1:B-12[V-46+B-4] (v.e-b)   ins. A/1:B-12[V-46+B-4] (v.e-c)

4. M5:769 (Fig. 32, 4) *tseng* (2)   5. M5:769 (Fig. 32, 5) *tseng* (2)   6. M5:769 (no illus.) *tseng* (2)
   ins. A/1:B-12[V-46+B-4] (v.f-a)   ins. A/1:B-12[V-46+B-4] (v.f-b)   ins. A/1:B-12[V-46+B-4] (v.f-c)

Fig. 29b. Rubbings of the inscriptions on the three *tseng* steamer-bowls (M5: 768, 769, and 770) and the inscription on the stand (M5: 790). Four items have not been reproduced—these are indicated by "?," and a reference number is allocated to each. Throughout this set of inscribed vessels, the graph *fu* is written only as 〱; the sole example in the stand, however, is too corroded to allow definition. In the next figure (29c) further examples of this form of *fu* are listed.

Tseng-steamer-bowl (1)
 1. A/1:*B-12*[*V-46*+*B-4*] (v.e-a)   M5:768
 2. A/1:*B-12*[*V-46*+*B-4*] (v.e-b)   M5:768
 3. A/1:*B-12*[*V-46*+*B-4*] (v.e-c)   M5:768 (no rubbing)

In the case of a calligrapher (or calligraphers) writing the full form of the graph: 〱, there would naturally be uncertainty as to whether the calligraphy is the work of one or more persons unless several series of fairly obvious calligraphic idiosyncracies should be present and of a kind that might indicate the handwriting of different scribes. However, in the cases of the variant forms repeated frequently throughout a number of vessels (for example, 〱 or 〱 [ten cases], 〱 or 〱 [twelve cases]) one may be on firmer ground to propose that these calligraphic groupings

---

On the basis of the aforegoing sources I have been able to assemble analyses of twenty-five Fu Hao bronzes (table 1, appendix A) and have arranged the data according to the inscriptions as well as to vessel types. As observed in the appendix there is a distinct tendency toward uniformity of alloy according to certain vessel types and sets, and a tie-up with the inscriptions in them and the calligraphy. Publication of the full set of analyses would assist greatly our ability to check the overall validity of the impressions arising from the restricted data now available.

THE STUDY OF CLAN-SIGN INSCRIPTIONS OF SHANG

7. M5:770 (Fig. 32, 1) *tseng* (3) ins. A/1:*B-12*[*V-46+B-4*] (v.d-a)

8. M5:770 (no illus.) *tseng* (3) ins. A/1:*B-12*[*V-46+B-4*] (v.d-b)

9. M5:770 (no illus.) *tseng* (3) ins. A/1:*B-12*[*V-46+B-4*] (v.d-c)

10. M5:790 (Fig. 32, 6) *chia* ins. A/1:*B-12*[*V-46+B-4*] (v.g)

Tseng-steamer-bowl (2)
4. A/1: *B-12*[*V-46 + B-4*] (v.f-a)   M5:769
5. A/1: *B-12*[*V-46 + B-4*] (v.f-b)   M5:769
6. A/1: *B-12*[*V-46 + B-4*] (v.f-c)   M5:769 (no rubbing)

Tseng-steamer-bowl (3)
7. A/1: *B-12*[*V-46 + B-4*] (v.d-a)   M5:770
8. A/1: *B-12*[*V-46 + B-4*] (v.d-b)   M5:770 (no rubbing)
9. A/1: *B-12*[*V-46 + B-4*] (v.d-c)   M5:770 (no rubbing)

Stand (for the three *tseng*-steamer-bowls)
10. A/1: *B-12*[*V-46 + B-4*] (v.g)   M5:790 (indistinct)

have some significance. Of course, it will be understood, I trust, that I have put the approach rather simply. But if the reader should turn his attention to the various versions of *fu* in *Chin-wen-pien* 金文編, *Ku-chou-pien* 古籀編, etc., he will observe that it is generally the complete form that appears, namely, 𣅀—rarely do we find instances of the other variations noted in figure 29A. Accordingly, it may be expected that the Fu Hao tomb materials should provide an ideal opportunity to explore calligraphic propensities to a greater extent than has been possible before.

Let us then proceed further into the evidence, such as it is: the *san-lien-hsien* 三聯甗 "Triple *Hsien*-steamer," which comprises a set of three *tseng*-steamer-bowls 甑 fitted into perforations in a rectangular stand, contains ten separate inscriptions (see fig. 29b): three in each of the *tseng*

Fig. 29c. Other examples of the Fu Hao inscriptions with the *V-46* element (*fu*) written as 彐 or, in reverse, as 彐; the bottom stroke varies from a small blob: 彐 to a distinct line: 彐.

1. A/1: *B-12*[*V-46* + *B-4*] (v.m)   M5:770
2. A/1: *B-12*[*V-46* + *B-4*] (v.o)   M5:762
3. A/1: *B-12*[*V-46* + *B-4*] (v.w)   M5:763
4. A/1: *B-12*[*V-46* + *B-4*] (v.k)   M5:746
5. A/1: *B-12*[*V-46* + *B-4*] (v.a)   M5:821
6. A/1: *B-11*[*V-46* + *B-4*] (v.e[1])   M5:682
7. A/1: *B-12*[*V-46* + *B-4*] (v.a[1])   M5:827
8. A/1: *B-12*[*V-46* + *B-4*] (v.d)   M5:747
9. A/1: *B-12*[*V-46* + *B-4*] (v.x)   M5:791
10. A/1: *B-11* + *V-46* + *B-4*] (v.c[1]) M5:680
11. A/1: *B-11* + *V-46* + *B-4*] (v.d[1]) M5:664
12. A/1: *B-11* + *V-46* + *B-4*] (v.j)   M5:865

There are two instances where the preceding version is executed with a horizontal cross-stroke 彐:

13. A/1: *B-12*[*V-46* + *B-4*] (v.n[1]) M5:854
14. A/1: *B-12*[*V-46* + *B-4*] (v.o[1]) M5:752

Several indistinct examples now follow: these are inscribed in the same vessel type (Type II *chüeh* as items 6, 10, 11, and 12, above; *V-46* in items 15 and 18 seem to be written 彐 and 彐, respectively, and thus possibly not classifiable as 彐).

15. A/1: *B-11* + *V-46* + *B-4* (v.f[1]) M5:685
16. A/1: *B-11* + *V-46* + *B-4* (v.y)   M5:662

17.	A/1: B-11 + V-46 + B-4 (v.x)	M5:675
18.	A/1: B-11 + V-46 + B-4 (v.z)	M5:653
19.	A/1: B-11 + V-46 + B-4 (v.b¹)	M5:656
20.	A/1: B-11 + V-46 + B-4 (v.a¹)	M5:657
21	A/1: B-11 + V-46 + B-4 (v.i)	M5:650
22.	A/1: B-11 + V-46 + B-4 (v.g)	M5:835

Item 23 which follows is an aberrant form; items 24 and 25 are elaborated as 〄; items 26 and 27 are not entirely distinct.

23.	A/1: B-11 + V-46 + B-4 (v.l)	M5:863
24.	A/1: B-11 + V-46 + B-4 (v.v), (l.v)	M5:866
25.	A/1: B-11 + V-46 + B-4 (v.c) (l.c)	M5:856
26.	A/1: B-11 + V-46 + [-] (v.a)	M5:618
27.	A/1: B-11 + V-46 + [-] (v.b)	M5:633

The following group is appended here as a further example of abbreviation of the title/name Fu Hao; each lacks the graph *fu*:

28.	A/1: B-12[- , B-4] (v.f)	M5:832
29.	A/1: B-12[- , B-4] (v.a)	M5:870
30.	A/1: B-12[- , B-4] (v.g)	M5:811
31.	A/1: B-12[- , B-4] (v.e)	M5:819
32.	A/1: B-12[- , B-4] (v.d)	M5:764
33.	A/1: B-12[- , B-4] (v.c)	M5:767
34.	A/1: B-12[- , B-4] (v.b)	M5:864

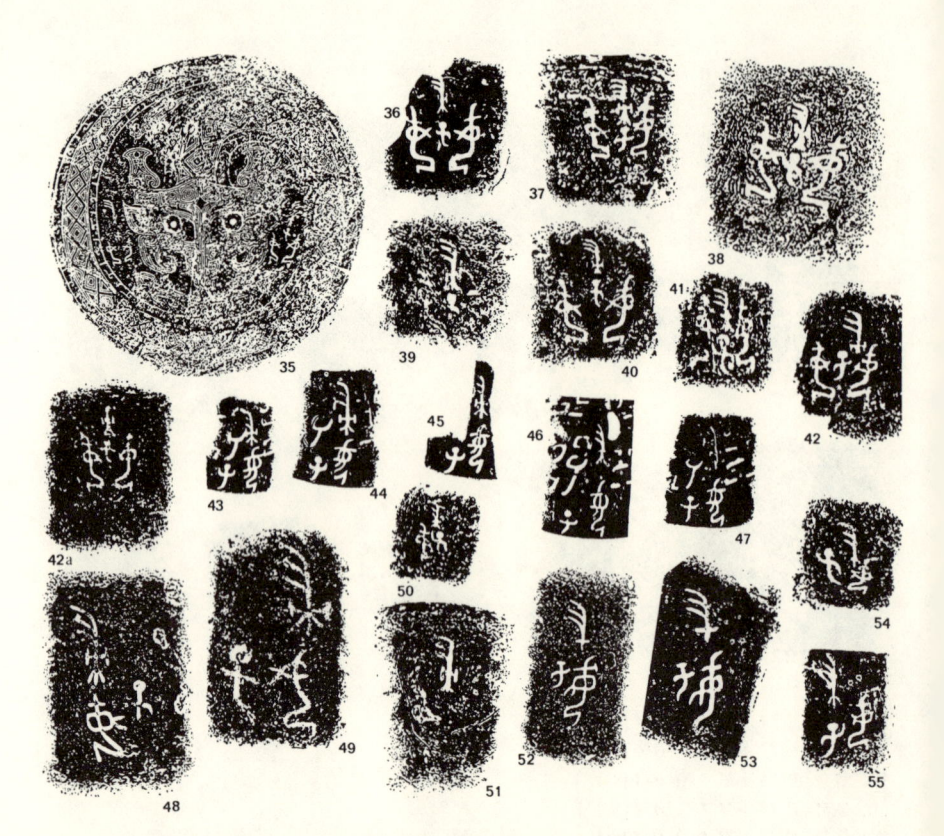

Fig. 29d. More elaborate examples of *fu* (*V-46*) now follow; first are those written as ▩:

35.	A/1 : *B-12*[*V-46* + *B-4*] (v.l¹)	M5 : 777
36.	A/1 : *B-12*[*V-46* + *B-4*] (v.r)	M5 : 760
37.	A/1 : *B-12*[*V-46* + *B-4*] (v.l)	M5 : 799
38.	A/1 : *B-12*[*V-46* + *B-4*] (v.i)	M5 : 798
39.	A/1 : *B-12*[*V-46* + *B-4*] (v.b)	M5 : 785
40.	A/1 : *B-12*[*V-46* + *B-4*] (v.s)	M5 : 761
41.	A/1 : *B-12*[*V-46* + *B-4*] (v.f)	M5 : 639
42.	A/1 : *B-12*[*V-46* + *B-4*] (v.q¹)	M5 : 810
42a.	A/1 : *B-12*[*V-46* + *B-4*] (v.t¹)	M5 : 825
43.	A/1 : *B-11* + *V-46* + *B-4* (v.q)	M5 : 605
44.	A/1 : *B-11* + *V-46* + *B-4* (v.o)	M5 : 604
45.	A/1 : *B-11* + *V-46* + *B-4* (v.e)	M5 : 601
46.	A/1 : *B-11* + *V-46* + *B-4* (v.f)	M5 : 603
47.	A/1 : *B-11* + *V-46* + *B-4* (v.m)	M5 : 602
48.	A/1 : *B-11* + *V-46* + *B-4* (v.a)	M5 : 849
49.	A/1 : *B-11* + *V-46* + *B-4* (v.t)	M5 : 792
50.	A/1 : *B-11* + *V-46* + *B-4* (v.s)	M5 : 1150
51.	A/1 : *B-11* + *V-46* + [-] (v.c)	M5 : 784

Examples of *fu* written as ▩ and ▩ follow; first all *B-11* combinations, then in *B-12* combinations.

| 52. | A/1 : *B-11* + *V-46* + *B-4* (v.d) | M5 : 796 |

Lu-yi 199 *Lu-yi* 256.1.2 *Ning-shou* 3.34 *Shuang-chien-ch'i* 1.21 *Po-ku* 15.25 *Shih-erh-chia* 10.6a

53.	A/1 : B-11 + V-46 + B-4 (v.u)	M5 : 830
54.	A/1 : B-11 + V-46 + B-4 (v.r)	M5 : 817
55.	A/1 : B-11 + V-46 + B-4 (v.k)	M5 : 768
56.	A/1 : B-12[V-46 + B-4] (v.z)	M5 : 648
57.	A/1 : B-12[V-46 + B-4] (v.d^1)	M5 : 621
58.	A/1 : B-12[V-46 + B-4] (v.j)	M5 : 744
59.	A/1 : B-12[V-46 + B-4] (v.j^1)	M5 : 869
60.	A/1 : B-12[V-46 + B-4] (v.i^1)	M5 : 852
61.	A/1 : B-12[V-46 + B-4] (v.c)	M5 : 813
61a.	A/1 : B-12[V-46 + B-4] (?)	M5 : 812

Examples of *fu* written as 〈graph〉 follow:

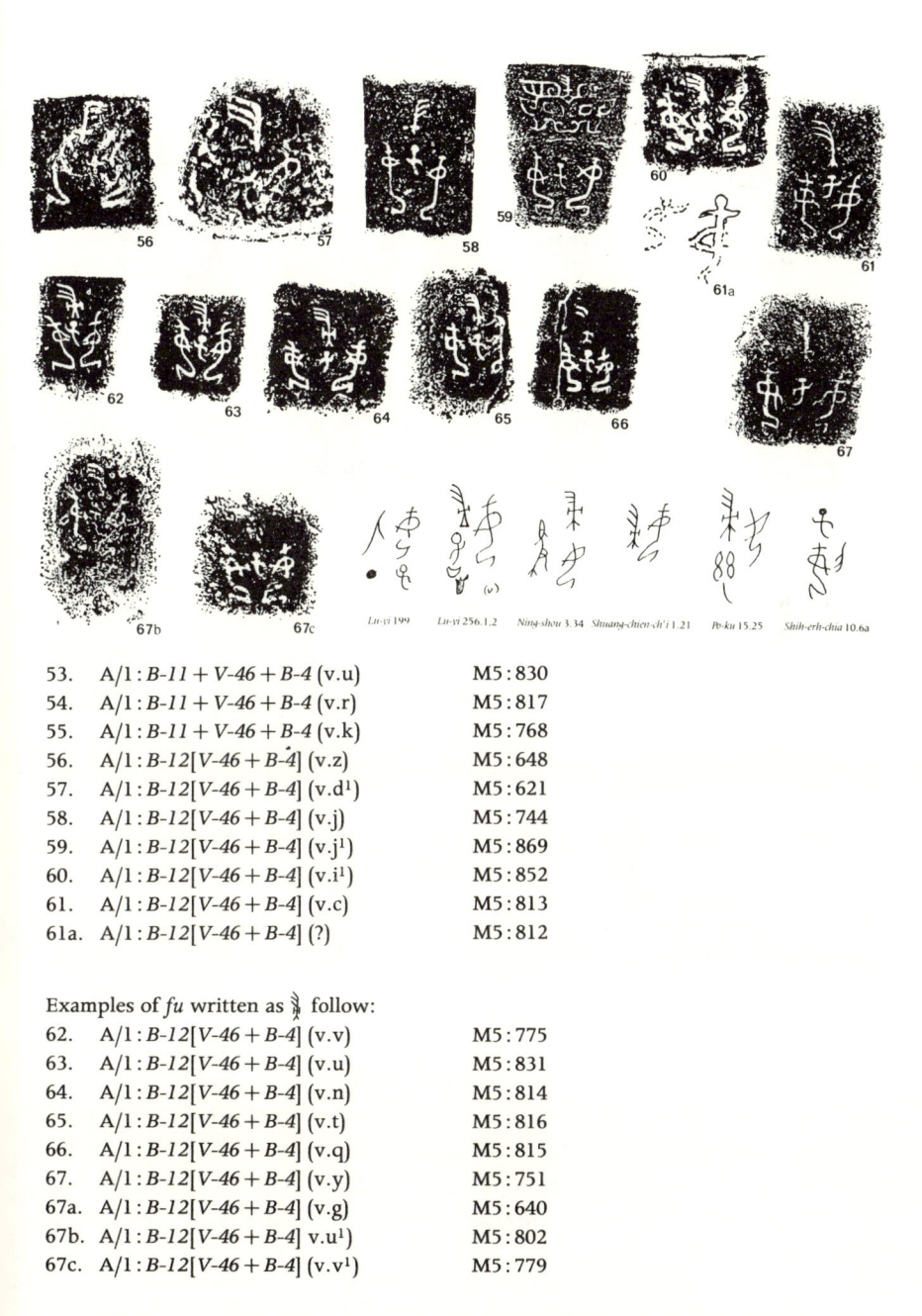

62.	A/1 : B-12[V-46 + B-4] (v.v)	M5 : 775
63.	A/1 : B-12[V-46 + B-4] (v.u)	M5 : 831
64.	A/1 : B-12[V-46 + B-4] (v.n)	M5 : 814
65.	A/1 : B-12[V-46 + B-4] (v.t)	M5 : 816
66.	A/1 : B-12[V-46 + B-4] (v.q)	M5 : 815
67.	A/1 : B-12[V-46 + B-4] (v.y)	M5 : 751
67a.	A/1 : B-12[V-46 + B-4] (v.g)	M5 : 640
67b.	A/1 : B-12[V-46 + B-4] v.u^1)	M5 : 802
67c.	A/1 : B-12[V-46 + B-4] (v.v^1)	M5 : 779

In the body of text only this last group is discussed in detail. However, other possible calligraphic groupings exist among the inscriptions assembled in the present figure, e.g., items 43–47, a series of *ku*-beakers (Type I; note that parts of the open-work decor in the vessel bases sometimes appear as character strokes in the rubbings)—the calligraphy in this series is very clearly the work of one person (note especially the woman graph); items 52 and 53 are close in calligraphic nuances.

68. M5:834 (Fig. 60, 3) *tou* ins. A/1:B-12[V-46+B-4] (v.c¹)
69. M5:745 (Fig. 60, 2) *tou* ins. A/1:B-12[V-46+B-4] (v.b¹)
70. M5:834 (Fig. 27, 2) *ting* ins. A/1:B-12[V-46+B-4] (v.p)
71. M5:742 (Fig. 60, 7) *tou'* ins. A/1:B-12[V-46+B-4] (v.g¹)
72. M5:748 (Fig. 60, 6) *tou* ins. A/1:B-12[V-46+B-4] (v.f¹)
73. M5:749 (Fig. 60, 5) *tou* ins. A/1:B-12[V-46+B-4] (v.e¹)
74. M5:855 (Fig. 47, 3) *chia* ins. A/1:B-12[V-46+B-4] (v.m¹)
75. M5:776 (Fig. 29, 5) *ting* ins. A/1:B-11+V-46+B-4 (v.h)

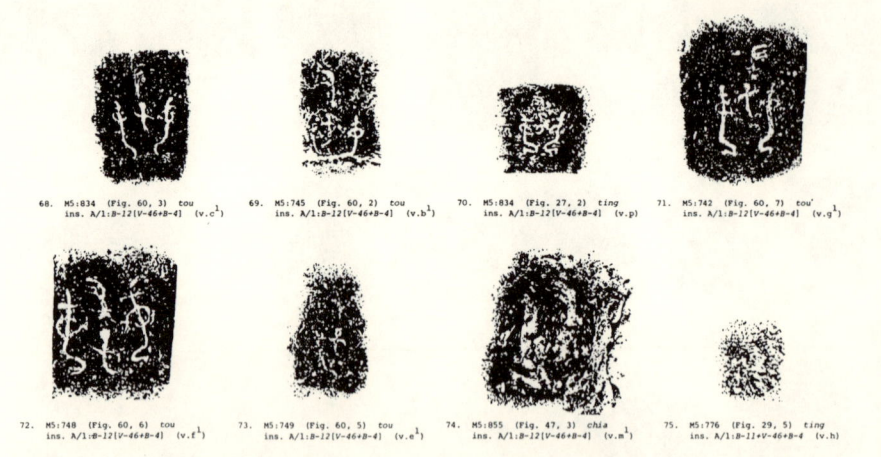

Fig. 29e. Indistinct inscriptions—in whole or in part—which cannot be effectively employed in the present study are grouped together.

68. A/1:B-$12[V$-$46 + B$-$4]$ (v.c¹)	M5:743	?
69. A/1:B-$12[V$-$46 + B$-$4]$ (v.b¹)	M5:745	?
70. A/1:B-$12[V$-$46 + B$-$4]$ (v.p)	M5:834	?
71. A/1:B-$12[V$-$46 + B$-$4]$ (v.g¹)	M5:742	?
72. A/1:B-$12[V$-$46 + B$-$4]$ (v.f¹)	M5:748	?
73. A/1:B-$12[V$-$46 + B$-$4]$ (v.e¹)	M5:749	?
74. A/1:B-$12[V$-$46 + B$-$4]$ (v.m¹)	M5:855	?
75. A/1:B-$12[V$-$46 + B$-$4]$ (v.h)	M5:776	?
76. A/1:B-$12[V$-$46 + B$-$4]$ (v.h¹)	M5:800	?
77. A/1:B-$12[V$-$46 + B$-$4]$ (v.r¹)	M5:859	?
78. A/1:B-$12[V$-$46 + B$-$4]$ (v.p¹)	M5:837	?
79. A/1:B-$12[V$-$46 + B$-$4]$ (v.k¹)	M5:629	?

and one in the central opening in the stand. Four of the inscriptions among the three *tseng* are not clear (and are not reproduced in the report), while that in the stand is not clear but is reproduced. Throughout the three *tseng* inscriptions (five only reproduced) the calligraphic nuances are practically identical; however, closer inspection results in an interesting observation: the writing of the "woman" components in *tseng* Nos. 769 and 770 are practically identical but differ in a particular detail in No. 768:

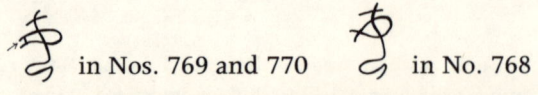

in Nos. 769 and 770   in No. 768

Unfortunately, the sole inscription in the stand (M 5:790) does not allow a reliable assessment of the relevant details. The manner in which the arms of the "woman" graphs are "crossed" in No. 768—and this is the

THE STUDY OF CLAN-SIGN INSCRIPTIONS OF SHANG

76. M5:800 (Fig. 62, 1) yüeh
ins. A/1:B-12[V-46+B-4] (v.h[1])

77. M5:859 (Fig. 47, 7) ho
ins. A/1:B-12[V-46+B-4] (v.r[1])

78. M5:837 (Fig. 47, 4) ho
ins. A/1:B-12[V-46+B-4] (v.p[1])

79. M5:629 (Fig. 52, 11) ku
ins. A/1:B-12[V-46+B-4] (v.k[1])

80. M5:642 (Fig. 52, 7) ku
ins. A/1:B-12[V-46+B-4] (v.e)

81. M5:611 (Fig. 52, 4) ku
ins. A/1:B-11+V-46+B-4 (v.n)

82. M5:1579 (Fig. 58, 10) chüeh
ins. A/1:B-11+V-46+B-4 (v.w)

83. M5:795 (Fig. 34, 6) ku
ins. A/1:B-11+V-46+B-4 (v.h[1])

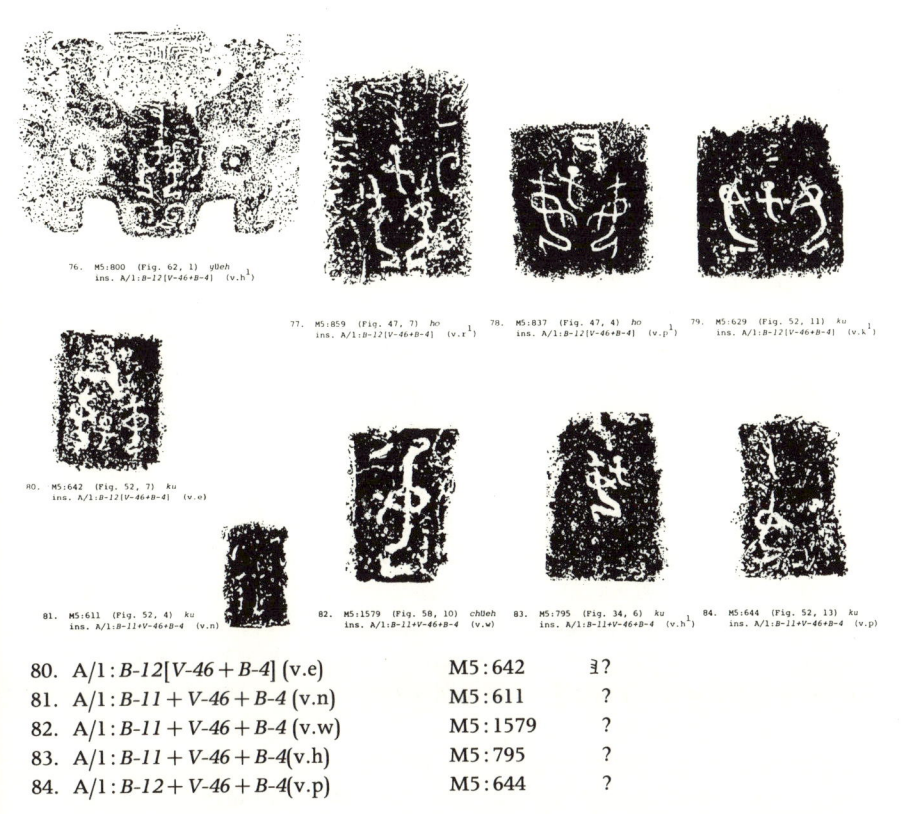

84. M5:644 (Fig. 52, 13) ku
ins. A/1:B-11+V-46+B-4 (v.p)

80. $A/1:B\text{-}12[V\text{-}46+B\text{-}4]$ (v.e)	M5:642	?
81. $A/1:B\text{-}11+V\text{-}46+B\text{-}4$ (v.n)	M5:611	?
82. $A/1:B\text{-}11+V\text{-}46+B\text{-}4$ (v.w)	M5:1579	?
83. $A/1:B\text{-}11+V\text{-}46+B\text{-}4$(v.h)	M5:795	?
84. $A/1:B\text{-}12+V\text{-}46+B\text{-}4$(v.p)	M5:644	?

The reference numbers allocated to items 79–82 may need modification—direct inspection of the inscription areas is required. Many of the *fu* in this group are apparently written either as 🔣 or 🔣 —direct examination of the inscription areas of each artifact would probably resolve the matter.

normal method of executing the feature—contrasts with that involving a small "connecting" stroke in Nos. 769 and 770. Several other Fu Hao inscriptions have this connecting stroke: items 1, 3, 5, 62, and 64 (see figs. 29c, and d). In the case of the *san-lien-hsien* inscriptions—if we may assume that the same propensities hold for the unpublished inscription rubbings in each *tseng*—it would seem reasonable to suggest that two different artisan/scribes were involved.[11] Both favored the 🔣 version for

---

11. A couple of weeks after the present conference while in Peking I included the *san-lien-hsien* in my list of twelve items I wished to examine directly in the National Museum of History. Unfortunately the museum officers were not able to include it among the six bronzes selected from my list. According to them, the inscriptions in question were too badly corroded to allow definition of the calligraphic details in which I was interested. However, this does not preclude the need for direct inspection by those of us experienced in such work.

fu, and the one favoring the connecting stroke in the "woman" component may also have executed the inscriptions in items 1, 5, and 62.

In figure 29d (items 62–67) are assembled all six inscriptions containing the *fu* version: 𩰤. Are these the writing of the same artisan/scribe? If so, why the two versions of the "woman" component in items 62 and 64? Obviously there are problems to contend with should one try to push the theme too assiduously. The main point of value is the fact that there should be distinctive calligraphic nuances which are repeated throughout series of inscribed vessels recovered from an undisturbed tomb. This is unlikely to be mere chance; we may be sure that the feature is sufficiently significant to be subject to explanation other than simplistic assertions of calligraphic caprice. How one or other of us may interpret the evidence may, naturally enough, become a case of "neck-stretching." Until we are furnished with more examples—particularly from undisturbed tombs such as the present—and augment thus our experience in working with such materials there will be some danger of our attempting to read into the evidence more than may be warranted. Over and above the difficulties of attaining direct access to the original inscriptions or to original unmounted rubbings taken from the inscriptions,[12] there is the basic problem observed in note 8: how do we differentiate between the calligraphic nuances of the scribe who presumably wrote out the inscription text with brush and ink and the artisan in the foundry who incised the text into the clay medium—or was all this invested in the hand of a single artisen/scribe in the foundry?

In the final section of figure 29d is a hurriedly compiled series of unprovenanced inscriptions containing the graph *fu*: a *fu-hao*, a couple of *hao*, and some other pertinent examples—one from the Sung Catalogues and one from the Early Ch'ing Catalogues. These examples are entered here mainly as a matter of interest. Similarly in figure 30 the three Fu Hao tomb renderings of the clan-sign *A-3 + V-30* are accompanied by examples selected from unprovenanced sources. Generally *V-30* is transcribed as 弜 *pi* "lath" (for strengthening a bow); usually it appears in combination with a *ya-hsing* (*A-3* form) and in a few instances it is placed inside a *ya-hsing* (both *A-1* [ ] and *A-3* [ ] forms) and accompanied by a posthumous title.

---

12. It is unfortunate that original rubbings cannot be easily obtained from Mainland Chinese archaeological institutes and museums in exchange for scholarly publications or even for comparable research materials from our archives. The full value of the original rubbing (if unmounted) has been discussed elsewhere (see Barnard 1959).

1. M5:808 (Fig. 37, 5) *ting*
   ins. A/1:*A-3+V-30* (v.e)

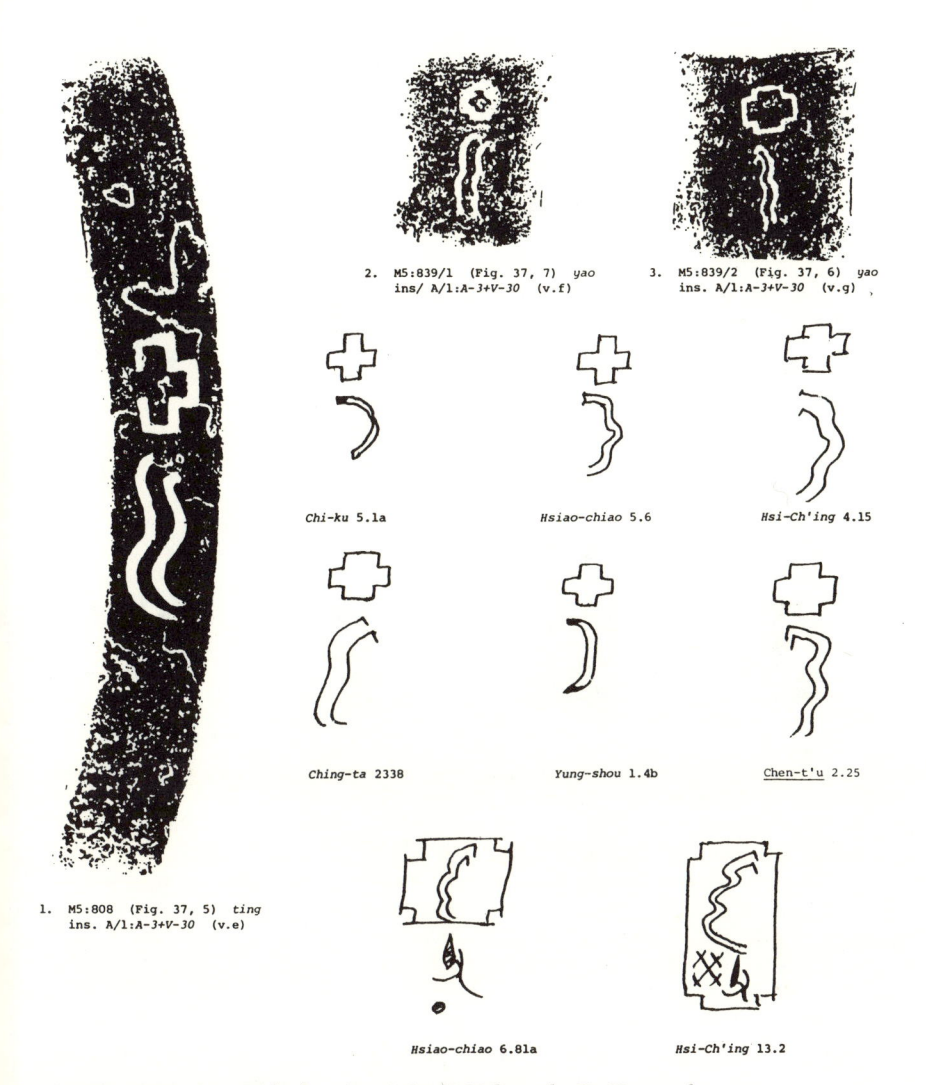

2. M5:839/1 (Fig. 37, 7) *yao*
   ins/ A/1:*A-3+V-30* (v.f)

3. M5:839/2 (Fig. 37, 6) *yao*
   ins. A/1:*A-3+V-30* (v.g)

Chi-ku 5.1a

Hsiao-chiao 5.6

Hsi-Ch'ing 4.15

Ching-ta 2338

Yung-shou 1.4b

Chen-t'u 2.25

Hsiao-chiao 6.81a

Hsi-Ch'ing 13.2

Fig. 30. Inscriptions with clan-sign *A-3 + V-30* from the Fu Hao tomb:
1. A/1 : *A-3 + V-30* (v.e)   M5 : 808
2. A/1 : *A-3 + V-30* (v.f)   M5 : 839/1
3. A/1 : *A-3 + V-30* (v.g)   M5 : 839/2

A selection of unprovenanced examples is added; it will be noted that records of this clan-sign extend back to the Early Ch'ing Catalogues.

174   NOEL BARNARD

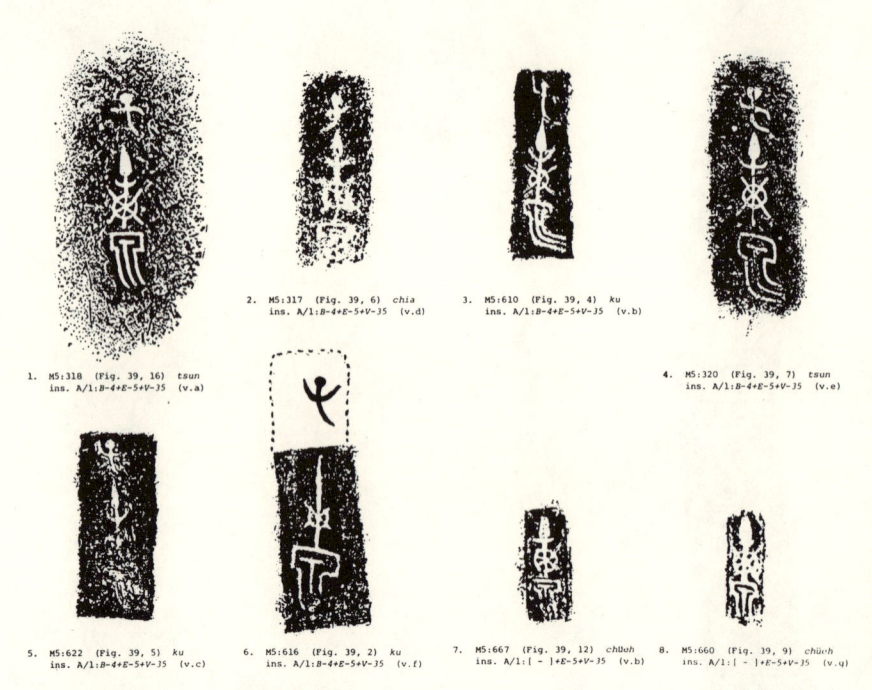

1. M5:318 (Fig. 39, 16) tsun
   ins. A/1:B-4+E-5+V-35 (v.a)
2. M5:317 (Fig. 39, 6) chia
   ins. A/1:B-4+E-5+V-35 (v.d)
3. M5:610 (Fig. 39, 4) ku
   ins. A/1:B-4+E-5+V-35 (v.b)
4. M5:320 (Fig. 39, 7) tsun
   ins. A/1:B-4+E-5+V-35 (v.e)
5. M5:622 (Fig. 39, 5) ku
   ins. A/1:B-4+E-5+V-35 (v.c)
6. M5:616 (Fig. 39, 2) ku
   ins. A/1:B-4+E-5+V-35 (v.f)
7. M5:667 (Fig. 39, 12) chüeh
   ins. A/1:[-]+E-5+V-35 (v.b)
8. M5:660 (Fig. 39, 9) chüeh
   ins. A/1:[-]+E-5+V-35 (v.g)

Fig. 31. Clan-signs incorporating the $E\text{-}5 + V\text{-}35$ combination from the Fu Hao tomb:

1. A/1: $B\text{-}4 + E\text{-}5 + V\text{-}35$ (v.a)   M5:318
2. A/1: $B\text{-}4 + E\text{-}5 + V\text{-}35$ (v.d)   M5:317
3. A/1: $B\text{-}4 + E\text{-}5 + V\text{-}35$ (v.b)   M5:610
4. A/1: $B\text{-}4 + E\text{-}5 + V\text{-}35$ (v.e)   M5:320
5. A/1: $B\text{-}4 + E\text{-}5 + V\text{-}35$ (v.c)   M5:622
6. A/1: $B\text{-}4 + E\text{-}5 + V\text{-}35$ (v.f)   M5:616

Groupings of the remaining inscriptions result in some points of significance. In the case of clan-signs $B\text{-}4 + E\text{-}5 + V\text{-}35$ (five items) and $E\text{-}5 + V\text{-}35$ (eleven items; see fig. 31) the component 束 *shu* (in clan-signs coded as $E\text{-}5$) is written constantly in structure and shape throughout the two series, while the component 原 *yüan* (in clan-signs coded as $V\text{-}35$) is constant in structure but shapewise the "tail" veers markedly toward the right in three of the five clan-signs $B\text{-}4 + E\text{-}5 + V\text{-}35$ (two are heavily corroded but one of these, No. 622, seems definitely to veer to the right). Among the $E\text{-}5 + V\text{-}35$ clan-signs, however, the tendency for the tail of the $V\text{-}35$ graph to adopt a vertical stance and at times only a slight degree of curvature to the right may be observed (in one case, No. 665, it curves slightly to the left). Possibly these shape variations

THE STUDY OF CLAN-SIGN INSCRIPTIONS OF SHANG

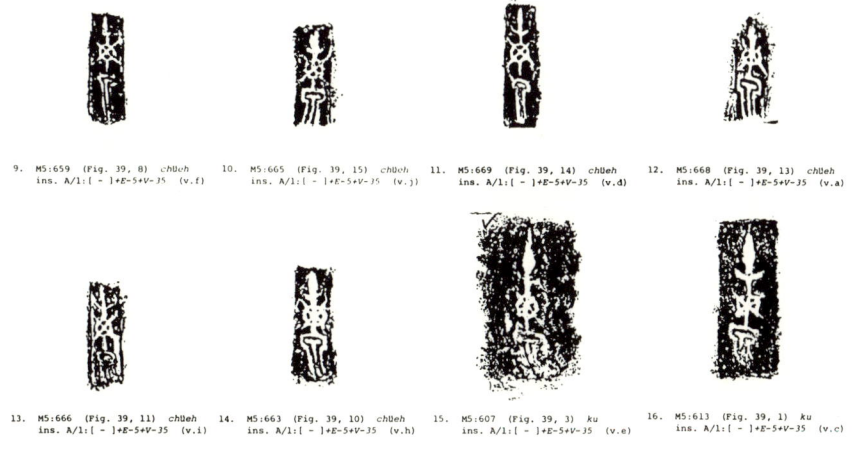

9. M5:659 (Fig. 39, 8) chüeh
   ins. A/1:[-]+E-5+V-35 (v.f)
10. M5:665 (Fig. 39, 15) chüeh
    ins. A/1:[-]+E-5+V-35 (v.j)
11. M5:669 (Fig. 39, 14) chüeh
    ins. A/1:[-]+E-5+V-35 (v.d)
12. M5:668 (Fig. 39, 13) chüeh
    ins. A/1:[-]+E-5+V-35 (v.a)

13. M5:666 (Fig. 39, 11) chüeh
    ins. A/1:[-]+E-5+V-35 (v.i)
14. M5:663 (Fig. 39, 10) chüeh
    ins. A/1:[-]+E-5+V-35 (v.h)
15. M5:607 (Fig. 39, 3) ku
    ins. A/1:[-]+E-5+V-35 (v.e)
16. M5:613 (Fig. 39, 1) ku
    ins. A/1:[-]+E-5+V-35 (v.c)

The remainder lack the *B-4* component:

7. A/1:[-]+*E-5*+*V-35* (v.b)   M5:667
8. A/1:[-]+*E-5*+*V-35* (v.g)   M5:660
9. A/1:[-]+*E-5*+*V-35* (v.f)   M5:659
10. A/1:[-]+*E-5*+*V-35* (v.j) M5:665
11. A/1:[-]+*E-5*+*V-35* (v.d) M5:669
12. A/1:[-]+*E-5*+*V-35* (v.a) M5:668
13. A/1:[-]+*E-5*+*V-35* (v.i) M5:666
14. A/1:[-]+*E-5*+*V-35* (v.h) M5:663
15. A/1:[-]+*E-5*+*V-35* (v.e) M5:607
16. A/1:[-]+*E-5*+*V-35* (v.c) M5:613

Five items are recorded in the Fu Hao Mu Report but not illustrated: M5:609, 624, 635, 608, and 620. See table 3 in appendix C, Tzu-shu-yüan Group.

may indicate the calligraphic nuances of two artisan/scribes in the foundry, or foundries, which produced the vessels; possibly, too, we may have to think in terms of the original handwriting of the "customer" (or the calligrapher in the customer's employ) and then the manner of its copying and transfer into the clay mold assemblies prior to casting; further, it may simply be a technical effect—the narrow space under the *chüeh* handles forced the artisan/scribe to maintain a noncurving tail. So much for the problems that arise in a study of the calligraphy in these two groups. More important, perhaps, is the association of the component *B-4*, 子 or 子 (usually transcribe as 子 *tzu*), with the clan-sign *E-5*+*V-35*. The problem confronting us is to ascertain whether the addition of the *B-4* graph reflects a later stage development (compare the relevant inscriptions in the M 907 and M 93 burials in the Hsiao-min-t'un

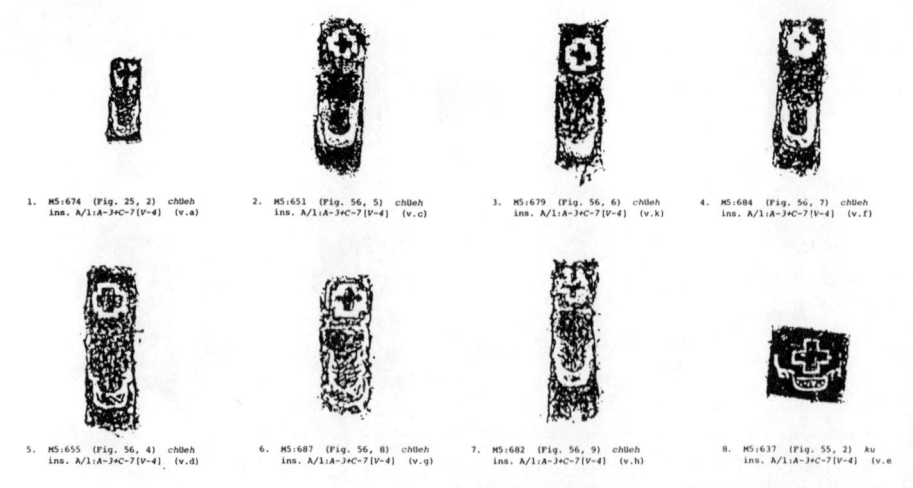

Fig. 32. Clan-signs A-3+C-7[V-4] among inscribed bronze vessels from the Fu Hao tomb:

1. A/1: A-3+C-7[V-4] (v.a)   M5:674
2. A/1: A-3+C-7[V-4] (v.e)   M5:651
3. A/1: A-3+C-7[V-4] (v.k)   M5:679
4. A/1: A-3+C-7[V-4] (v.f)   M5:684
5. A/1: A-3+C-7[V-4] (v.d)   M5:655
6. A/1: A-3+C-7[V-4] (v.g)   M5:687
7. A/1: A-3+C-7[V-4] (v.h)   M5:682

The "pairs of hands," C-7 throughout this series are drawn in vertical stance. This may indicate the calligraphy of the one artisan/scribe as suggested in the body of text, but the limitation of width in the inscription area in each of the *chüeh* has also to be considered. The graph V-4 where definable in details seems to be constantly written as which structure varies from the "X"-shape fillings in items 10, 11, 12, and 14 below.

8. A/1: A-3+C-7[V-4] (v.c)   M5:657
9. A/1: A-3+$[$ - $]$V$-$4$ (v.a)   M5:643

cemetery area discussed at the beginning of the paper); if a later stage development, what interval of time might be involved?

The necessity for direct examination of the inscription areas in the original vessels whenever an opportunity arises is well demonstrated in the case of the *ku*, M 5:616 (Type VI): see item 6, figure 31. The vessel was among several of the Fu Hao tomb vessels examined by Cheung Kwong-yue during his recent visit to the Mainland (April 1983). It was immediately evident that the published rubbing was incomplete; the B-4 graph had been omitted. Mishaps of this kind may occur only too easily. One may wonder if the two other Type VI *ku* similarly have the B-4 graph omitted in the published rubbings? If such were the case, the lack of a B-4 graph throughout the eight *chüeh* inscriptions—where space

THE STUDY OF CLAN-SIGN INSCRIPTIONS OF SHANG 177

9. M5:643 (Fig. 55, 1) *ku*
ins. A/1:A-3+[-]V-4 (v.a)

10. M5:630 (Fig. 56, 2) *ku*
ins. A/1:A-3+C-7[V-4] (v.b)

11. M5:1197 (Fig. 56, 11) *chia*
ins. A/1:A-3+C-7[V-4] (v.i)

12. M5:627 (Fig. 56, 3) *ku*
ins. A/1:A-3+[-]V-4 (v.b)

13. M5:626 (Fig. 56, 1) *ku*
ins. A/1:A-3+C-7[V-4] (v.j)

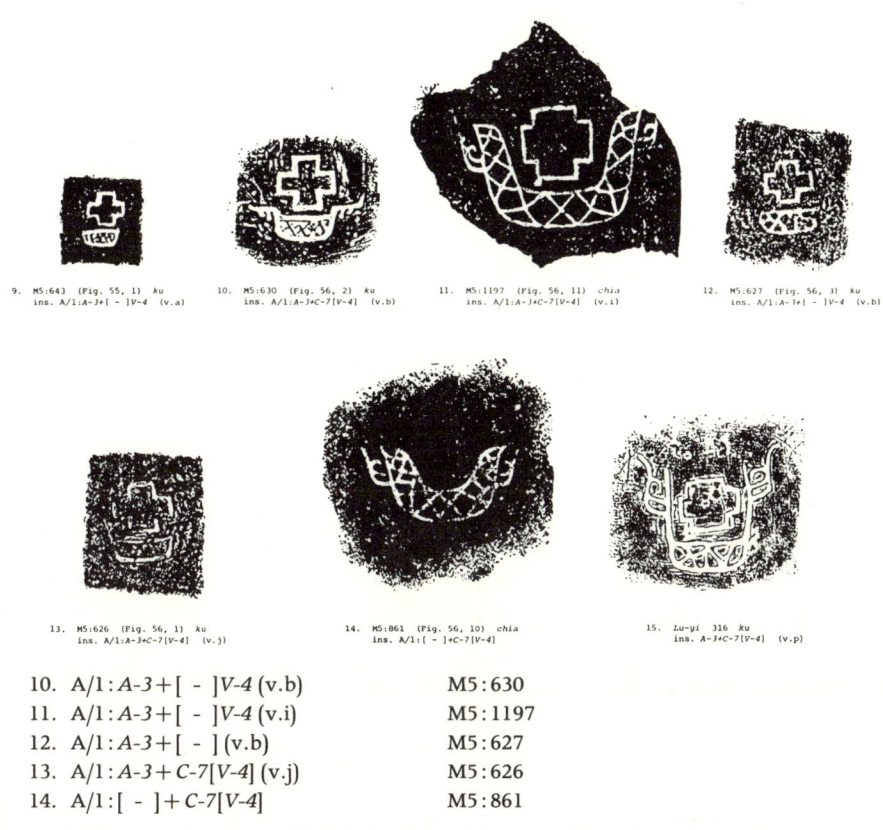

14. M5:861 (Fig. 56, 10) *chia*
ins. A/1:[-]+C-7[V-4]

15. *Lu-yi* 316 *ku*
ins. A-3+C-7[V-4] (v.p)

10. A/1: *A-3*+[-]*V-4* (v.b)   M5:630
11. A/1: *A-3*+[-]*V-4* (v.i)   M5:1197
12. A/1: *A-3*+[-] (v.b)   M5:627
13. A/1: *A-3*+ *C-7*[*V-4*] (v.j)   M5:626
14. A/1:[-]+ *C-7*[*V-4*]   M5:861

In item 13 one of the pair of hands (on the right) is just discernible; direct inspection of item 14 would be required to check if the *ya-hsing* is present or not. Similarly, items 9 and 12 may later have to be reviewed. A comparable inscription in a *ku*-beaker (*Lu-yi* 316) is added here (item 15).

limitation may well have precluded record of the title—may also have to be regarded as a form of textual attenuation. This is a further possible interpretation of the evidence; one which has come to the fore following the above noted mishap.

Reference to figure 32 brings us back to some minor features attending calligraphy, shape variations, and structural variations as they appear among the clan-signs *A-3*+ *C-7* [*V-4*] and *A-3*+ *V-4*. First, observe the series of Type IV *chüeh* (fig. 32, items 1–7); each is inscribed with the "pair of hands holding object" (*C-7* [ ]) in vertical downward stance and the fingers turned inward: , and the object, *V-4*, is held by the furthermost finger of each hand at its uppermost extremity: . In each example the *ya-hsing* (*A-3*) is placed appreciably above the lower unit.

Next, note the five inscriptions from a series of ten Type V *ku* (three are not reproduced because of loss of clarity by damage or severe corrosion; one of the remaining seven is described but the rubbing is not reproduced (M 5:820), and one other is not entered at all [p. 82]). Three of the inscriptions (items 8, 10, and 13) are complete, and the pair of hands (*C-7* [ ]) in each case is in horizontal stance: ⌐⌐. Two, however, are attenuated versions and lack the pair of hands (items 9 and 12). Finally, it will be observed that the two large circular *chia* (item 11 and 14) have the pair of hands in vertical stance but grasping the object well below its "rim"; item 14 is apparently an attenuated form—it seems to lack the *ya-hsing*. The general correspondence here between the three groups of inscriptions—not only in regard to the placement of the hands but also the distinctive variation in the drawing of the object, *V-4*, from one group to another—and between the three groups of vessel types, can hardly be coincidental (the discerning reader may have noted a few further examples among the inscriptions in fig. 29 to 31). Again the urge to engage in more forceful speculation along the lines already attempted is difficult to resist: first of all, it would seem evident that the attenuated versions are merely abbreviations of the complete *A-3 + C-7* [*V-4*] complex, and attenuation may take place by the exclusion of one component or another—the presence or absence of the components in question has no special significance. Second, the three groups of calligraphic (and character-structural) nuances may imply three different artisan/scribes in one foundry (at one time or different times), three different foundries each with its own artisan/scribe, a tie up between vessel types and artisan/scribes (or even the foundries may have specialized in one vessel type or another), and so on. To some extent space limitations in the inscription area may affect the calligraphy (see caption, fig. 32). Among unprovenanced inscriptions there appears to be only the one example which is included in figure 32 (*Lu-yi*, 316). It differs appreciably in certain shape/structural aspects from the provenanced versions of this graph.[13]

In figure 33 the calligraphic groupings again coincide remarkably well

---

13. A reproduction of a rubbing of this inscription appears in P. C. Li 1979: 167; the vessel is in the Display Room of Archaeological Materials, Peking University. In this survey of the problems of dating the Fu Hao tomb, Li opts for a later date than Wu Ting and concludes realistically that "Fu Hao" is not necessarily the name of a single person, nor is it confined to the one period. He, Tsou Heng, and Ch'iu Hsi-kuei are in agreement for a later date (see K'ao-ku 1977b for these and various other assessments).

Fig. 33. Clan-signs $B-11+2tzu$ among the inscribed bronze vessels from the Fu Hao tomb:

(legend continued on p. 180)

1. A/1: *B-11* + *2tzu* (v.f)   M5:661
2. A/1: *B-11* + *2tzu* (v.g)   M5:686
3. A/1: *B-11* + *2tzu* (v.h)   M5:654
4. A/1: *B-11* + *2tzu* (v.i)   M5:677
5. A/1: *B-11* + *2tzu* (v.j)   M5:658
6. A/1: *B-11* + *2tzu* (v.k)   M5:689
7. A/1: *B-11* + *2tzu* (v.l)   M5:678
8. A/1: *B-11* + *2tzu* (v.m)   M5:681
8a A/1: *B-11* + *2tzu* (v.e)   M5:672

The aforegoing are incorporated in Type III *chüeh*. Although the width of the inscription area is limited, the placement of the 'T'-shaped component is either alongside or above the graph, B-11; thus some scope for calligraphic expression exists. Most important, however, is the constant structure of the rodent drawing.

9. A/1: *B-11* + *2tzu* (v.c)   M5:794
10. A/1: *B-11* + *2tzu* (v.d)   M5:807
11. A/1: *B-11* + *2tzu* (v.a)   M5:793
12. A/1: *B-11* + *2tzu* (v.b)   M5:867
13. A/1: *B-11* + *2tzu* (v.x)   M5:857
14. A/1: *B-11* + *2tzu* (v.y)   M5:860
15. A/1: *B-11* + *2tzu* (1.a^1)   M066
16. A/1: *B-11* + *3tzu* (v.a)   M5:868
17. A/1: *B-11* + *3tzu* (v.b)   M5:806
18. A/1: *B-11* + *3tzu* (v.n)   M5:612
19. A/1: *B-11* + *2tzu* (v.p)   M5:615
20. A/1: *B-11* + *2tzu* (v.o)   M5:617
21. A/1: *B-11* + *2tzu* (v.q)   M5:631
22. A/1: *B-11* + *2tzu* (v.r)   M5:614
23. A/1: *B-11* + *2tzu* (v.s)   M5:628
24. A/1: *B-11* + *2tzu* v.t)   M5:625
25. A/1: *B-11* + *2tzu* (v.v)   M5:606
26. A/1: *B-11* + *2tzu* (v.u)   M5:649
27. A/1: *B-11* + *2tzu* (v.w)   M5:632
28. S.*B-11* + *2tzu* (v.b^1), (l.b^1)   *Fu-chai*
29. *B-11* + *2tzu* (v.c^1)   *Shodō*

Pairs of calligraphic nuances, each pair varying from the other, are associated with pairs of vessel types, e.g. items 9 and 10, 11 and 12, 13 and 14, and 16 and 17; while the seven Type IV *ku* all have the "woman" component placed alongside the *2tzu*.

N.B. Codification is sometimes simplified, as above, by the use of *2tzu 3tzu*, etc. More precisely the present clan-sign combination can be rendered as: *B-11* + *P-3* + *D-11*[*V-16*] for the *2tzu* combination and *B-11* + *P-3* + *D-11*[*V-16*] + *L-10* for the *3tzu* with its additional *kuei*.

THE STUDY OF CLAN-SIGN INSCRIPTIONS OF SHANG 181

Illustration Number	Inventory Number		Ears	Mouth	Body
(18)	612	⼂	open(?)	closed	closed
(19)	615	⼂	closed(?)	closed(?)	closed
(23)	628	⼂	open(?)	open(?)	closed(?)
(27)	632	⼂	open(?)	closed(?)	closed(?)
(25)	606	⼂	open(?)	open	closed(?)
(26)	649	⼃	open	open	open
(24)	625	⼃	open	open	open
(20)	617	⼃	open	open	open
(21)	631	⼃	open	open	open
(22)	[614		?	?	?]

Fig. 34. Slope directions of the element ⼂ or ⼃ in relation to the execution of the "rabbit" element in the character *t'u*(?).

with specific vessel types: Type III *chüeh* (items 1–8a), for example, have the small rodent drawn structurally identical in each inscription as 𝆢; the rodents in the two large round *chia* (items 13 and 14) are also practically identical and so, too, that in the inscribed lid (item 15) excavated long ago by Li Chi et al. from M 066 at Hsiao-t'un (*KKHP* 1948.(3):pl.1)—such an association is, of course, interesting but in this case the yield of the highly disturbed M 066 does not allow much scope for comment. Open-mouth rodents with body and ears "filled-in" are characteristic of the two *fang-hu* (items 9 and 10); in the two large round *tsun* (items 11 and 12), however, the latter vary in terms of outline ears. Unfortunately, the inscriptions in the ten Type IV *ku* are highly corroded in two cases (items 22 and 23); nevertheless, a somewhat pronounced pattern of calligraphic variation seems evident and may be analyzed as demonstrated in figure 34.

Where the graph ⼃ is written with the "vertical" line veering to the left the rodents are drawn quite definitely in outline form (ears and body) and with mouths open; where the vertical line veers to the right these features are often filled in, particularly the body. Such variant features may reflect the hands of two artisan/scribes. The two large square *tsun* (items 16 and 17) seem to differ only slightly in minor details (the rodent's ears, for instance), but the addition of the graph *kuei* in each brings to mind the earlier examples of abbreviated *jih-x* combinations —should *kuei* here read as *jih-kuei* or were other posthumous titles as *fu* (父), *tsu* (且), *hsiung* (兄), *tzu* (𣎆:子), etc., also subject to abbreviation?

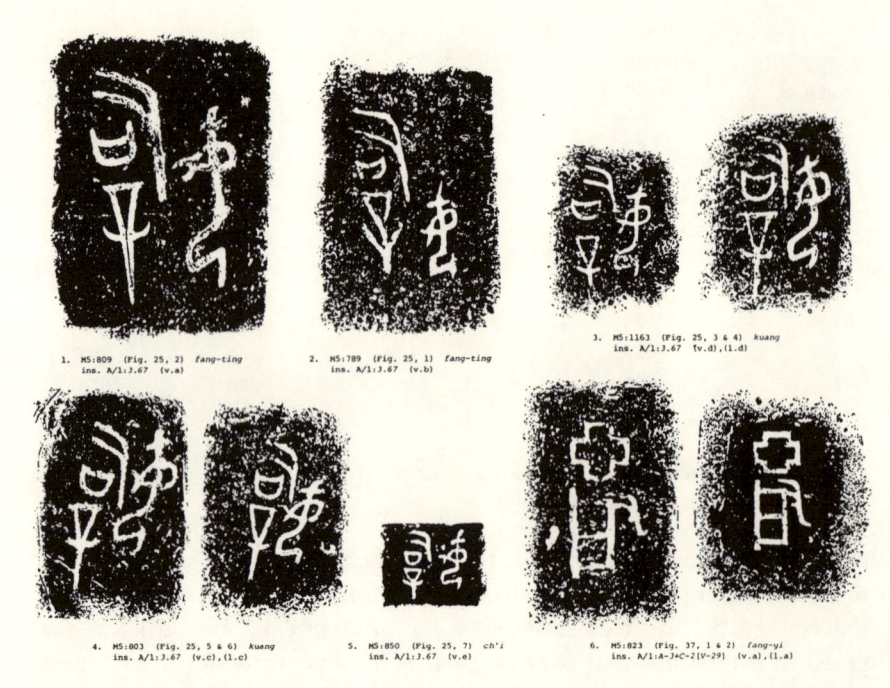

Fig. 35. In this paper practically all the Fu Hao tomb inscriptions have been incorporated in figures 27 to 32; the remaining inscriptions are assembled here so as to form a complete record:

1. A/1 : 3.67 (v.a)   M5 : 809
2. A/1 : 3.67 (v.b)   M5 : 789
3. A/1 : 3.67 (v.d), (l.d)   M5 : 1163
4. A/1 : 3.67 (v.c) (l.c)   M5 : 803
5. A/1 : 3.67 (v.e)   M5 : 850

The small element 丅 may have affinity with the comparable graph in the M 1550 burial (see fig. 26b above). Here, however, it would seem evident from the two general positions it occupies that the "rodent" + 丅 is to be read as a single graph which has been rendered in modern character form as 鼡 *t'u* (?).

As stated in the opening paragraph of this paper, there remains much yet to be researched among currently available inscriptions in order to develop the full potential of the approaches attempted here (fig. 35). This paper is not intended to be a polished scholarly survey; it is simply a form of pilot study. To do the job properly with full reference to extant materials would be almost impossible. Access to the original inscribed

THE STUDY OF CLAN-SIGN INSCRIPTIONS OF SHANG

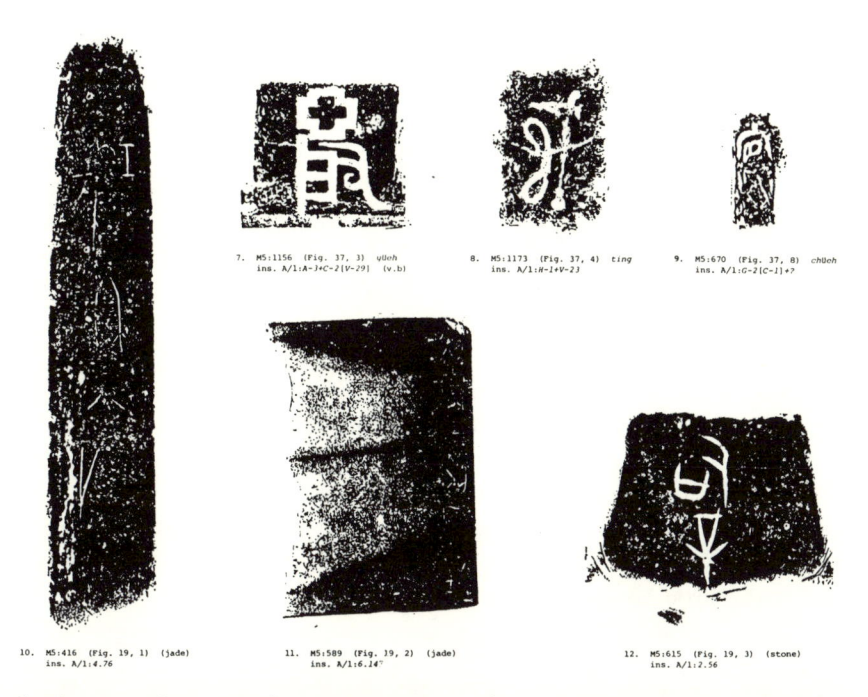

7. M5:1156 (Fig. 37, 3) *yüeh*
   ins. A/1:A-3+C-2[V-29] (v.b)

8. M5:1173 (Fig. 37, 4) *ting*
   ins. A/1:H-1+V-23

9. M5:670 (Fig. 37, 8) *chüeh*
   ins. A/1:G-2[C-1]+?

10. M5:416 (Fig. 19, 1) (jade)
    ins. A/1:4.76

11. M5:589 (Fig. 19, 2) (jade)
    ins. A/1:6.147

12. M5:615 (Fig. 19, 3) (stone)
    ins. A/1:2.56

The distinction between a clan-sign inscription and a *text* inscription is sometimes rather tenuous: should we not perhaps read the *B-11 + 2tzu* inscriptions in figure 33 as Ssu-mu T'u(?)—arguing on the basis of the "two columns" arrangement of the components in items 18–24? Here, however, the combination, Ssu-mu Hsin, is one that is clearly classifiable as a text inscription (i.e., the components are "characters proper").

6. A/1: *A-3+C-2[V-29]* (v.a) (l.a)   M5:823
7. A/1: *A-3+C-2[V-29]* (v.b)   M5:1156
8. A/1: *H-1[V-23]*   M5:1173
9. A/1: *G-2[C-1]+ ?*   M5:670
10. A/1: *6.147*   M5:580 (jade)
11. A/1: *2.56*   M5:315 (stone)
12. A/1: *4.76*   M5:316 (stone)

bronzes would be absolutely essential in order to determine the exact nature of such crucial details as filled-in or outline ears, closed or open mouth of rodents, whether certain elements in a complex clan-sign are actually missing or the rubbing has been too heavily inked (see item 13 in fig. 32, where one of the pairs of hands—the right-hand side—is only just discernible), the nature of inscription preparation in the mold/core assembly prior to casting—at least three technical approaches appear among the Fu Hao inscriptions, and so on.[14] Study of original rubbings of the inscriptions would help advance such investigations, but direct access to the inscribed vessels would be needed to solve such problems as those enumerated above and also to allow the researcher to explore the potential of evidence relating to aspects of casting technology. Study of decor, typology, and iconography is equally necessary but if adequate description and illustration is available in publication, reasonable progress can be made.

The basic problem facing the researcher—whether he is a Chinese scholar domiciled in Mainland China or a Western Sinologist or a Japanese Kangakusha—is that of obtaining reasonable access to the original bronzes. As several of us have learned from scholarly visits to China in recent years there are difficulties of a local kind that affect all three parties—not just the visiting specialist. Original rubbings are practically impossible to obtain, too. However, with the exercise of patience, a sympathetic appreciation of the general situation, and regular research trips, some progress can be expected.

APPENDIX A. ANALYSES OF THE FU HAO TOMB BRONZES

Table 1 below lists twenty-five vessel analyses presently available in the published sources detailed in note 10, above. I have grouped the analyses partly by vessel types and partly by the inscriptions they contain so far as the limitations of the published details allow. Some interesting correlations appear if we allow for margins of "error" in the analyses (that is, the confidence interval [see R. J. Gettens, *The Freer Chinese Bronzes—Technical Studies* (Washington, 1969), pp. 236–38]) and permit the assumption that the bronze founders may have used "rule of thumb" measurements—they would hardly have sought accuracy as much as, let alone greater than, 1 percent. Accordingly, when preparing a melt to cast a series of vessels of 20 kilogram weight each—we may assume that

---

14. The majority of the Fu Hao tomb inscriptions appear to be Group 5 type, i.e., "inscriptions prepared in the form of a 'master-pattern' (see Barnard and Wan 1976: 54–55, fig. 5). Some are clearly Group 4 type, i.e., "inscriptions directly incised in rilievo form" (ibid., p. 52, fig. 3), and a few incorporate rilievo guidelines in the bottoms of stroke grooves; the latter are a technically more elaborate method of executing Group 4 type. These observations require the confirmation of direct study of the inscription areas. It is not certain yet as to the possible chronological significance of the various methods used in the preparation of cores and molds for cast-in inscriptions; it may be expected, however, that an intensive study of the 179 Fu Hao tomb inscriptions would result in useful progress on this point because of the undisturbed nature of the burial.

at least two of such size would be poured from the one melt if crucibles of the capacity of, say, the Cheng-chou Middle Shang item (see Barnard and Satō Tamotsu, *Metallurgical Remains of Ancient China* [Tokyo, 1975], fig. 26, A and B) were employed—the founders would have approached the problem of alloy proportions in much the same way as a Chinese cook intuitively apportions ingredients to obtain a desired flavor. Ingots of copper, tin, and lead would have been selected according to their sizes or weights to add up to the approximate amounts of each required for each batch of alloy melted in the one crucible. Vessels and other artifacts deriving from each crucible melt should thus exhibit a fairly close identity in constituent percentages when analyzed. The same types of vessels issuing from other crucible melts in the same foundry might vary to some extent, however.

Among the twenty-five vessels analyzed in table 1 there are five sets of two vessels each; as a matter of interest I have expressed the data in terms of weight in table 2, where the five sets have been extracted from table 1. The close correspondence of alloy constituent weights between the vessels in each set (and, of course, the percentages as give in table 1) may be taken to indicate that each pair came from the same melt of bronze. But as several of the pairs are "short" sets (for example, *Ku* Type IV with ins. A/1 : *B-11 + 2tzu* comprises ten items and *Ku* type IIA with ins. A/1 : *B-12* [*V-46 + B-4*] comprises at least five items [see *Fu Hao Mu Report*, pp. 235–36]), analyses of the remaining vessels would be required to verify the impression we presently obtain.

An undisturbed tomb with so great a number of bronzes and so high a proportion of them inscribed does offer useful avenues of research in the laboratory which if conducted with a full understanding of the problems involved may help answer questions that might not otherwise be acceptably resolved. It is a matter of luck that of the sixty or so analyses made on the Fu Hao tomb bronzes so many as twenty-five items have been made available, and it is particularly fortunate that among these, analyses of sets of vessels should be present. Despite this good fortune, however, the observations offered above based on these data must be regarded as tentative pending the publication not only of the complete set of analyses but also of full details of the sampling and analytical procedures, of the names of the analysis, and with record alongside each component analyzed of the confidence limits applicable. Without this minimum standard of presentation of data neither Mainland Chinese scholars nor those of us outside China can hope to make effective use of the laboratory derived information and so attempt to write with reasonably well-supported authority on the issues which the properly presented data may clarify or resolve.

Of equal importance, too, is the provision of trace element analyses (estimated by emission spectrometry) along with those of the main alloy components (determined hopefully by wet chemical analysis). Without this supplementary data

Table 1. Analyses of Fu Hao Mu Bronzes

			Cu	Sn	Pb	Zn	Fe	Total Published	Total Author's	Inscription Reference number	Notes
1.	M5:861	Chia	77.42	16.39	6.09	0.14			[100.04]	( )? $A/1:[-]+C-7[v-4]$ (v.i)	
2.	M5:857	Chia	78.10	14.99	5.32	0.07		98.49	[98.48]	$A/1:B-11+2tzu$ (v.x)	} set
3.	M5:860	Chia	81.03	13.79	4.19	0.14		99.15		$A/1:B-11+2tzu$ (v.y)	
4.	M5:806	Ta Fang Tsun	82.53	14.45	0.60	0.08		97.66		$A/1:B-11+3tzu$ (v.b)	} set
5.	M5:868	Ta Fang Tsun	79.17	17.11	0.66	0.14		97.08		$A/1:B-11+3tzu$ (v.a)	
6.	M5:625	Ku (IV)	77.94	20.30	1.31	0.15		99.70		$A/1:B-11+2tzu$ (v.t.)	} set
7.	M5:631	Ku (IV)	82.28	15.13	0.82	0.11		98.34		$A/1:B-11+2tzu$ (v.q)	sample from base area (heavily corroded)
8.	M5:855	Chia	81.57	17.15	1.13	0.15			[100.00]	$A/1:B-12[V-46+B-4]$ (v.m¹)	} set
9.	M5:854	Chia	79.90	16.87	0.79	0.10			[97.66]	$A/1:B-12[V-46+B-4]$ (v.n¹)	
10.	M5:751	Chia	79.45	18.70	0.66	0.07		97.08	[98.88]	$A/1:B-12[V-46+B-4]$ (v.s¹)	
11.	M5:639	Ku (IIA)	80.78	19.01	0.16	—			[99.95]	$A/1:B-12[V-46+B-4]$ (v.x¹)	} set
12.	M5:640	Ku (IIA)	81.44	16.53	0.14	0.10			[98.21]	$A/1:B-12[V-46+B-4]$ (v.y¹)	heavily corroded (rubbing not published)
13.	M5:791	Fang-Yi	80.20	14.16	1.69	0.33		96.83		$A/1:B-12[V-46+B-4]$ (v.x)	
14.	M5:790	Triple hsien Stand	84.61	13.33	1.16	0.22		99.32		$A/1:B-12[V-46+B-4]$ (v.g)	
15.	M5:870	Lien-t'i-hsien	84.71	11.85	1.80	0.23		98.59		$A/1:B-12[-,B-4]$ (v.a.)	
16.	M5:811	Yü	82.02	11.93	4.42	0.47		98.84		$A/1:B-12[-,B-4]$ (v.g)	

17a.	M5:764	Ch'i-chu Tseng	85.82	13.47	—	—	[99.29]	A/1:B-12[-, B-4] (v.d)	vessel and handle (handles precast)
17b.	('')	('' '' handle)	87.44	12.55	—	—	[99.99]	(?) A/1:B-12[- , B-4] (v.d-a)	
18.	M5:808	Ting	80.87	14.95	1.20	0.27		A/1:A-3+V-30 (v.e)	
19.	M5:809	Fang-Ting	84.82	11.96	0.72	0.16	[97.66]	A/1:3.67 (v.a)	
19a.	M5:809	mouth area	85.91	11.60	1.19	0.13	97.29		
19b.	M5:809	body	84.96	11.65	1.28	0.16	96.88		
19c.	M5:809	leg	83.60	12.62	0.50	0.16	98.83		
20.	M5:781	Chia (leg)	75.24	18.32	trace		98.05	(no inscription? see Report, p. 70)	heavily corroded
21.	M5:no no.	Chia	79.51	15.79	1.50	0.07	96.88	—	
22.	M5:619	Ku (IIA)	81.62	16.42	1.85	0.25	[93.56]	(no inscription? see Report, p. 75)	sample from mouth area (heavily corroded)
							[96.87]		
							[100.14]		
23.	M5:?	Ku	81.08	18.53	1.31		[100.92]	—	
24.	M5:?	Ku (?)	80.03	17.9	1.28		[99.21]	—	
25.	M5:765	Yu	92.70	3.82		0.54	[100.06]	(no inscription? see Report, p. 66)	(Si 3%)

SOURCE: Data assembled from various published sources (see note 10 for details).

Table 2. Clan-Sign Inscriptions of Shang

	Actual Weight	Adjusted Weight	Cu	Sn	Pb	Zn	Total	Cu	Sn	Pb	Zn	Total
857	20 kg	19.69(98.49%)	15.62	2.99	1.06	0.01	19.68	16(78.10%)	3(14.99%)	1(5.32%)	t(0.07%)	20
860	20.5 kg	20.32(99.15%)	16.61	2.82	0.85	0.02	20.30	17(81.03%)	3(13.79%)	1(4.19%)	t(0.14%)	21
806	31 kg	30.27(97.66%)	25.58	4.47	0.18	0.02	30.25	26(82.53%)	4(14.45%)	.2(0.60%)	t(0.08%)	30.2
868	32 kg	31.06(97.08%)	25.33	5.47	0.21	0.04	31.05	25(79.17%)	5(17.11%)	.2(0.66%)	t(0.14%)	30.2
855	18.3 kg	18.3(100%)	14.92	3.14	0.20	0.02	18.28	15(81.57%)	3(17.15%)	.2(1.13%)	t(0.15%)	18
854	21.5 kg	20.99(97.66%)	17.17	3.62	0.16	0.02	20.97	17(79.90%)	4(16.87%)	.2(0.79%)	t(0.10%)	21.1
639	1.3 kg	1.29(99.95%)	1.05	0.24	0.002	—	1.29	1(80.78%)	.2(19.01%)	t(0.16%)	t(-)	1.2
640	1.4 kg	1.37(98.21%)	1.14	0.23	0.001	0.001	1.37	1(81.44%)	.2(16.53%)	t(0.14%)	t(0.10%)	1.2
625	1.5 kg	1.49(99.7%)	1.17	0.30	0.001	0.002	1.47	1(77.94%)	.3(20.30%)	t(1.31%)	t(0.15%)	1.3
631	1.7 kg	1.67(98.34%)	1.40	0.25	0.013	0.001	1.65	1(82.28%)	.3(15.13%)	t(0.82%)	t(0.11%)	1.2
809a	117.5 kg	113.83(96.88%)	99.66	14.05	0.84	0.18	114.13	100(84.84%)	14(11.96%)	1(0.72%)	0.1(0.16%)	115.1
809b mouth		116.12(98.83%)	100.94	13.63	1.39	0.15	116.11	101(85.91%)	14(11.60%)	1(1.19%)	0.1(0.13%)	116.1
809c body		115.20(98.05%)	99.82	13.68	1.50	0.18	115.18	100(84.96%)	14(11.65%)	1(1.28%)	0.1(0.16%)	115.1
809d leg		113.81(96.86%)	98.23	14.82	0.58	0.18	113.81	98(83.60%)	15(12.62%)	1(0.50%)	0.1(0.16%)	114.1

Analyses from sets of vessels with weights of alloy components calculated upon basis of the individual vessel weight and the percentage total of the analyses of each. These data are processed into round figures in the right-hand section of the table; percentages are noted in parentheses alongside each for convenient reference.

hypotheses advanced upon the basis of the main alloy components may well remain open to question.

Postscript Shortly before the dispatch of the manuscript to the editor, the first of a projected series of "group authored" reports on analyses of the bronzes from the Fu Hao Mu came to my attention: "Yin-hsü chin-shu ch'i-wu ch'eng-fen ti ts'e-ting pao-kai (yi)" 殷墟金屬器物成分的測定報告 (一), *K'ao-ku hsüeh chi-k'an* 考古學集刊, 1982.2:181–93. Observations somewhat critical in tone offered in the last two paragraphs above are, it is heartening to record here, largely negated by the valuable data—and supplementary information on analytical procedures—presented therein. Neither space nor time allows an adequate review of the analyses and the reporters' conclusions based upon them; this must await a later avenue of publication wherein I plan to survey the thousand or more analyses I have compiled in my files from published (and some unpublished) sources with reference to the ninety-one items analyzed in the above report (and also, hopefully, succeeding reports). At long last we have a viable basis upon which the value of analyses in our field of research may be better demonstrated than hitherto. Suffice it to note here that the overall discussion in the first two paragraphs above is well supported and further verified (in regard to the second paragraph). Other significant information comes to the fore, too; I draw attention to the role of lead and the use of ternary alloy (Cu+Su+Pb) in Shang China long before its appearance in any other metallurgical culture—a feature not hitherto indicated in analyses from properly provenanced artifacts. (Compare my views in *Bronze Casting and Bronze Alloys of Ancient China*, Monumenta Serica Monograph 14, 1961:197–98; and *Metallurgical Remains of Ancient China*, 1975:19–22). The point is naturally noted in the above report. However, the importance of this, the earliest appearance of the ternary alloy, and the understanding of the ancient Chinese founder of the properties of lead in the ternary alloy—points also discussed in the report—have not been considered in relation to the independent nature of the discovery of metallurgy in China. This understanding of the property of lead (and ipso facto the properties of copper and tin) at so early a stage in the world history of metallurgy may be regarded as an additional illustration of the variant (hence independent) discovery and development of metallurgy in China.

APPENDIX B. INSCRIPTION IDENTIFICATION, OR REFERENCE, NUMBERS

In all my publications on the inscriptions, individual inscriptions are allocated an identification, or reference, number. Where a relatively small group of inscriptions is surveyed in an article (such as the present one), the use of identification numbers has definite advantages. Where large numbers of inscriptions are involved, disadvantages may sometimes outweigh the convenient aspects of the identification numbers. However, with an eye to the future and with the expectation that the computer may be brought into inscription studies before long, it is essential that some means of codifying the inscriptions—and even the characters therin, and where necessary the component elements of the characters—be established. It is essential that the system be applicable not only to extant bronze (and other archaeological) documents, but also it should be one fairly easily applicable to newly discovered documents. The system I use seems to meet these and other such requirements reasonably well: basically the identification number is the number of *character-spaces* for separately written graphs in the inscription—this obviates problems inherent in orthodox counting, especially where characters, repetition signs, etc., are obscure. In combination with the character-space count is a second number which merely denotes the order of record of each inscription in my files—there is, of course, an obvious disadvantage here: others must wait the appearance of the allocated number for each new inscription before it becomes generally known. The advantage, however, is that each new inscription that comes to light will fit into the system without causing any disruption. Extant inscriptions are further divided into three major groups: those in the Sung Catalogues denoted by the letter "S" preceding the identification number; those in the Imperial Ch'ing Catalogues and Early Ch'ing Catalogues which are denoted by the letter "T"; inscriptions which first appear since circa 1890–1900 are generally classed as "Recent" and, at present, lack a letter denoting the point.

In a series of inscriptions embodying the same text in different vessels, or in vessel-lid sets, the individual inscriptions are codified as: (v.a), (v.b), (v.c), etc. for vessels, and (l.a), (l.b), (l.c), etc, for the lids.

Clan-sign type inscriptions have a special means of codification which is elaborated upon in the preliminary pages of the introductory volume of *Hui-pien*. It should be noted that in "text" inscriptions where clan-signs may appear, I count the clan-sign (no matter how many component graphs it may comprise) as a single character. Even in the orthodox totals the clan-sign counts as one character; thus variations between our totals and those of others will be found due to this convention in certain cases.

With the tremendous progress in archaeological discoveries over the last few decades the need for a clear distinction between properly provenanced materials and those deriving from unknown sources has become increasingly clear to systematic researchers in our field. In our forthcoming survey of these truly archaeological materials, *Five Decades*, Cheung Kwong-yue and I have applied a distinctive code to indicate the archaeological status of each of the inscribed bronzes that have come to light:

A/1: = Scientifically excavated—full provenanced details published. Precise supplementary background data from the site available.

A/2: = Excavation background information is sparce but of acceptable reliability and is of some degree of value in assessing further understanding of the historical significance of the inscribed artifacts.

THE STUDY OF CLAN-SIGN INSCRIPTIONS OF SHANG 191

A/3: = Excavation background is vague and of little value in allowing assessments of the kind possible in the cases of A/1: and A/2: inscritpions.

A/4: = Strong tradition of the inscribed artifact having been excavated by chance at a particular locality but practically no other details. In applying this classification we may be swayed by the nature of the vessel and its inscription.

It will be appreciated that some degree of subjectiveness will influence the application of codes A/3: and A/4: while occasionally some difference of opinion may arise as to the distinction between A/1: and A/2:. But generally there should be little argument as to the possible value of historical data available between these two more general groups. Such is the basic aim of this system of codification: to indicate at a glance to the user both the nature of the inscription and the extent of relevant supplementary archaeological data available.

NOTE

In a series of inscriptions comprising the same clan-sign combination, missing elements due to corrosion, damage, or scribal mishaps are indicated as follow:

A/1: B-12 [V-46 + B-4]	complete
A/1: B-12 [- + B-4]	V-46 is missing within the B-12 [ ] element
A/1: B-4 + E-5 + V-35	complete
A/1: [-] + E-5 + V-35	B-4 element is missing
A/1: A-3 + C-7 [V-14]	complete
A/1: A-3 + [-] V-14	C-7 [ ] enclosing element is missing

Among unprovenanced inscriptions instances of such "apparent" missing elements are usually difficult to determine.

APPENDIX C. A LISTING OF THE FU HAO TOMB INSCRIBED BRONZES

Tables 3 and 4 are presented here with the Fu Hao tomb inscriptions arranged in order of reference numbers (within the distinctive groups of inscription texts) and in order of the excavators' reference numbers. In both tables the serial numbers allocated to individual inscriptions in *Five Decades* are incorporated so as to facilitate reference to the relevant volumes when published; terms denoting the parent vessel types are given in Chinese and follow the terminology as used in the report. Figure numbers in the present survey also appear; beneath the rubbings reproduced in each figure are noted, among other data, the original figure number of each in the report, thus allowing fairly efficient reference to the report through the tables which follow here.

Table 3. Fu Hao Inscriptions

Reference Code Number	Excavator's Reference Number	Rubbing Available?	*Five Decades* Serial No.	Figure No.	Vessel Type
A/1:*B-12*[*V-46* + *B-4*] (v.a)	M5:821		0048	29C,5	II A 式中型鼎
A/1:*B-12*[*V-46* + *B-4*] (v.b)	M5:785		1152	29D,39	鴞尊
A/1:*B-12*[*V-46* + *B-4*] (v.c)	M5:813		0064	29D,61	長方扁足鼎
A/1:*B-12*[*V-46* + *B-4*] (v.d)	M5:747		1834	29C,8	I 式斗
A/1:*B-12*[*V-46* + *B-4*] (v.d-a)	M5:770		0684	29B,7	三聯甗, 甑
A/1:*B-12*[*V-46* + *B-4*] (v.d-b)	M5:770 M5:769 M5:790	nil	0684	29B,8	三聯甗, 甑
A/1:*B-12*[*V-46* + *B-4*] (v.d-c)	M5:770	nil	0684	29B,9	三聯甗, 甑
A/1:*B-12*[*V-46* + *B-4*] (v.e)	M5:642		1374	29E,80	II A 式甗
A/1:*B-12*[*V-46* + *B-4*] (v.e-a)	M5:768(a)		0684	29B,1	三聯甗, 甑
A/1:*B-12*[*V-46* + *B-4*] (v.e-b)	M5:768(a) M5:70 M5:769 M5:790		0684	29B,2	三聯甗, 甑
A/1:*B-12*[*V-46* + *B-4*] (v.e-c)	M5:768(a)	nil	0684	29B,3	三聯甗, 甑
A/1:*B-12*[*V-46* + *B-4*] (v.f)	M5:639		1375	29D,41	II A 式甗
A/1:*B-12*[*V-46* + *B-4*] (v.f-a)	M5:769		0684	29B,4	三聯甗, 甑
A/1:*B-12*[*V-46* + *B-4*] (v.f-b)	M5:769 M5:768(a) M5:770 M5:790		0684	29B,5	三聯甗, 甑
A/1:*B-12*[*V-46* + *B-4*] (v.f-c)	M5:769	nil	0684	29B,6	三聯甗, 甑
A/1:*B-12*[*V-46* + *B-4*] (v.g)	M5:640	nil	1373	—	II A 式甗
A/1:*B-12*[*V-46* + *B-4*] (v.g-a)	M5:790 M5:768(a) M5:769 M5:770	nil	0684	29B,10	三聯甗, 架

IX式小型鳥足鼎	29E,75	1061	M5:776	A/1:B-12[V-46+B-4] (v.h)
III式盂	29D,38	1043	M5:798	A/1:B-12[V-46+B-4] (v.i)
I式斗	29D,58	1831	M5:744	A/1:B-12[V-46+B-4] (v.j)
II式斗	29C,4	1830	M5:746	A/1:B-12[V-46+B-4] (v.k)
大型鋮	29D,37	2079	M5:799	A/1:B-12[V-46+B-4] (v.l)
II A式中型鼎	29C,1	0049	M5:756	A/1:B-12[V-46+B-4] (v.m)
IX式小型鳥足鼎	29D,54	0050	M5:814	A/1:B-12[V-46+B-4] (v.n)
II A式中型鼎	29C,2	0051	M5:762	A/1:B-12[V-46+B-4] (v.o)
小方鼎	29E,70	0060	M5:834	A/1:B-12[V-46+B-4] (v.p)
II B式中型圓鼎	29D,66	0052	M5:815	A/1:B-12[V-46+B-4] (v.q)
II B式中型圓鼎	29D,36	0053	M5:760	A/1:B-12[V-46+B-4] (v.r)
II B式中型圓鼎	29D,40	0054	M5:761	A/1:B-12[V-46+B-4] (v.s)
II式小型圓鼎	29D,65	0055	M5:816	A/1:B-12[V-46+B-4] (v.t)
V式小型柱足鼎	29D,63	0056	M5:831	A/1:B-12[V-46+B-4] (v.u)
VI式小型柱足鼎	29D,62	0057	M5:775	A/1:B-12[V-46+B-4] (v.v)
帶流袋足鼎形器	29C,3	0059	M5:763	A/1:B-12[V-46+B-4] (v.w)
偶方彝	29C,9	1210	M5:791	A/1:B-12[V-46+B-4] (v.x)
大圓罍	29D,67	1028	M5:751	*A/1:B-12[V-46+B-4] (v.y)
III A式瓿	29D,56	1384	M5:648	A/1:B-12[V-46+B-4] (v.z)
III A式瓿	29C,7	1383	M5:827	A/1:B-12[V-46+B-4] (v.a¹)
I式斗	29E,69	1832	M5:745	A/1:B-12[V-46+B-4] (v.b¹)
I式斗	29E,68	1833	M5:743	A/1:B-12[V-46+B-4] (v.c¹)
II A式瓿	29D,57	1372	M5:621	A/1:B-12[V-46+B-4] (v.d¹)
I式斗	29E,73	1835	M5:749	A/1:B-12[V-46+B-4] (v.e¹)
II式斗	29E,72	1836	M5:748	A/1:B-12[V-46+B-4] (v.f¹)
II式斗	29E,71	1837	M5:742	A/1:B-12[V-46+B-4] (v.g¹)
大型鋮	29E,76	2080	M5:800	A/1:B-12[V-46+B-4] (v.h¹)
雙耳罐	29D,60	2143	M5:852	A/1:B-12[V-46+B-4] (v.i¹)
分體甗(上小甑)	29D,59	2144	M5:869	A/1:B-12[V-46+B-4] (v.j¹)
III A式瓿	29E,79	1382	M5:629	A/1:B-12[V-46+B-4] (v.k¹)

Table 3. (continued)

Reference Code Number	Excavator's Reference Number	Rubbing Available?	Five Decades Serial No.	Figure No.	Vessel Type
A/1:B-12[V-46+B-4] (v.l¹)	M5:777		1468	29D,35	盤
A/1:B-12[V-46+B-4] (v.m¹)	M5:855			29E,74	大方罍
*A/1:B-12[V-46+B-4] (v.n¹)	M5:854		1026	29C,13	大方罍
*A/1:B-12[V-46+B-4] (v.o¹)	M5:752		1027	29C,14	大方罍
A/1:B-12[V-46+B-4] (v.p¹)	M5:837		1044	29E,78	IV 式盂
A/1:B-12[V-46+B-4] (v.q¹)	M5:810		1043	29D,42	I 式瓿
A/1:B-12[V-46+B-4] (v.r¹)	M5:859		1045	29E,77	I 式盂
A/1:B-12[V-46+B-4] (v.s¹)	M5:832	revised see Ho-nan 1:142	(0418) [=0397]	29C,28	I 式小型盨
A/1:B-12[V-46+B-4] (v.t¹)	M5:825		1209	29D,42a	I 式瓿
A/1:B-12[V-46+B-4] (v.u¹)	M5:802		1455	29D,67b	圜足甗
A/1:B-12[V-46+B-4] (v.v¹)	M5:779		1456	29D,67c	圜足甗
A/1:B-12[V-46+B-4] (v.w¹)	M5:812		2189	29D,61a	長方鬲足鼎
A/1:B-12[- , B-4] (v.a)	M5:870		0676	29C,29	大型連體甗
A/1:B-12[- , B-4] (v.b)	M5:864		0677	29C,34	分體甗（下體）
A/1:B-12[- , B-4] (v.c)	M5:767		0678	29C,33	分體甗（上）獻
A/1:B-12[- , B-4] (v.d)	M5:764		0716	29C,32	凍柱敵型器
A/1:B-12[- , B-4] (v.e)	M5:819		0020	29C,31	V 式鋦高柱足鼎
A/1:B-12[- , B-4] (v.f)	M5:832	cf. Ho-nan 1:142	0.397 [=0418]	29C,28	I 式小型盨
A/1:B-12[- , B-4] (v.g)	M5:811		1548	29C,30	大型盂
A/1:B-11+V-46+B-4 (v.a)	M5:849		1208	29D,48	無蓋方彝
A/1:B-11+V-46+B-4 (v.c), (1.c)	M5:856		1221	29C,25	方罍
A/1:B-11+V-46+B-4 (v.d)	M5:796		1294	29D,52	甗
A/1:B-11+V-46+B-4 (v.e)	M5:601		1376	29D,45	I 式瓿
A/1:B-11+V-46+B-4 (v.f)	M5:603		1377	29D,46	I 式瓿

A/1:B-11+V-46+B-4 (v.g)	M5:835	0058	29C,22	VII式小型斂腹鼎
A/1:B-11+V-46+B-4 (v.h)	M5:795	1243	29E,83	扁圓壺
*A/1:B-11+V-46+B-4 (v.i)	M5:650	1385	29C,21	III式瓿
A/1:B-11+V-46+B-4 (v.j)	M5:865	0685	29C,12	小型連體甗
A/1:B-11+V-46+B-4 (v.k)	M5:768(b)	0686	29D,55	分體甗（上小甑）
*A/1:B-11+V-46+B-4 (v.l)	M5:863	1242	29C,23	扁圓壺
A/1:B-11+V-46+B-4 (v.m)	M5:602	1379	29D,47	I式瓿
A/1:B-11+V-46+B-4 (v.n)	M5:611	1380	29E,81	I式瓿
A/1:B-11+V-46+B-4 (v.o)	M5:604	1381	29C,44	I式瓿
*A/1:B-11+V-46+B-4 (v.p)	M5:644	1386	29E,84	III式瓿
*A/1:B-11+V-46+B-4 (v.q)	M5:605	1378	29D,43	I式瓿
A/1:B-11+V-46+B-4 (v.r)	M5:817	0062	29D,54	IX式小型鳥足鼎
A/1:B-11+V-46+B-4 (v.s)	M5:1150	0063	29D,50	IX式小型鳥足鼎
A/1:B-11+V-46+B-4 (v.t)	M5:792	1150	29D,49	方尊
*A/1:B-11+V-46+B-4 (v.u)	M5:830	1295	29D,53	瓴
A/1:B-11+V-46+B-4 (v.v), (l.v)	M5:866	1220	29C,24	方彝
A/1:B-11+V-46+B-4 (v.w)	M5:1579	0921	29E,82	I式爵
A/1:B-11+V-46+B-4 (v.x)	M5:675	0918	29C,17	II式爵
A/1:B-11+V-46+B-4 (v.y)	M5:662	0914	29C,16	II式爵
A/1:B-11+V-46+B-4 (v.z)	M5:653	0911	29C,18	II式爵
A/1:B-11+V-46+B-4 (v.a^1)	M5:657	0917	29C,20	II式爵
A/1:B-11+V-46+B-4 (v.b^1)	M5:656	0913	29C,19	II式爵
A/1:B-11+V-46+B-4 (v.c^1)	M5:680	0916	29C,10	II式爵
*A/1:B-11+V-46+B-4 (v.d^1)	M5:664	0912	29C,11	II式爵
A/1:B-11+V-46+B-4 (v.e^1)	M5:652	0915	29C,6	II式爵
A/1:B-11+V-46+B-4 (v.f^1)	M5:685	0919	29C,15	II式爵
A/1:B-11+V-46+B-4 (v.g^1)	M5:676	0920	nil	—
A/1:B-11+V-46+B-4 (v.h^1)	M5:1579	0922	nil	—
A/1:B-11+V-46+[-] (v.a)	M5:618	1387	29C,26	II B 式瓿
A/1:B-11+V-46+[-] (v.b)	M5:633	1388	29C,27	II B 式瓿
*A/1:B-11+V-46+[-] (v.c)	M5:784	1151	29D,51	鶚尊

Table 3. (continued)

Reference Code Number	Excavator's Reference Number	Rubbing Available?	*Five Decades* Serial No.	Figure No.	Vessel Type
Ya-hsing-pi Group (A-3+V-30)					
A/1:A-3+V-30 (v.e)	M5:808		0065	30,1	大圓鼎
A/1:A-3+V-30 (v.f)	M5:839/1		1812	30,2	鋠
A/1:A-3+V-30 (v.g)	M5:839/2		1813	30,3	鋠
Tzu-shu-yüan Group (B-4+E-5+V-35)					
A/1:B-4+E-5+V-35 (v.a)	M5:318		1153	31,1	圓尊
A/1:B-4+E-5+V-35 (v.b)	M5:610		1358	31,3	VI 式觚
A/1:B-4+E-5+V-35 (v.c)	M5:622		1359	31,5	VI 式觚
A/1:B-4+E-5+V-35 (v.d)	M5:317		1029	31,2	殘琴
A/1:B-4+E-5+V-35 (v.e)	M5:320		1154	31,4	圓尊
*A/1:B-4+E-5+V-35 (v.f)	M5:616		1348	31,6	VI 式觚
A/1:B-4+E-5+V-35 (v.g)	M5:608	nil	1360	—	VI 式觚
A/1:B-4+E-5+V-35 (v.h)	M5:620	nil	1361	—	VI 式觚
A/1:[-]+E-5+V-35 (v.a)	M5:668		0923	31,12	V 式爵
*A/1:[-]+E-5+V-35 (v.b)	M5:667		0929	31,7	V 式爵
A/1:[-]+E-5+V-35 (v.c)	M5:613		1347	31,16	VI 式爵
A/1:[-]+E-5+V-35 (v.d)	M5:669		0930	31,11	V 式爵
A/1:[-]+E-5+V-35 (v.e)	M5:607		1345	31,15	VI 式爵
A/1:[-]+E-5+V-35 (v.f)	M5:659		0925	31,9	V 式爵
A/1:[-]+E-5+V-35 (v.g)	M5:660		0926	31,8	V 式爵
A/1:[-]+E-5+V-35 (v.h)	M5:663		0927	31,14	V 式爵

A/1:[-]+E-5+V-35 (v.i)	M5:666	0928	31,13	V 式爵
A/1:[-]+E-5+V-35 (v.j)	M5:665	0924	31,10	V 式爵
A/1:[-]+E-5+V-35 (v.k)	M5:609	1346	—	VI 式瓿
A/1:[-]+E-5+V-35 (v.l)	M5:624	1349	—	VI 式瓿
A/1:[-]+E-5+V-35 (v.m)	M5:635	1350	—	VI 式瓿

Ya-hsing-ch'i Group (A-3+C-7[V-4])

A/1:A-3+C-7[V-4] (v.a)	M5:674	0938	32,1	IV 式爵
A/1:A-3+C-7[V-4] (v.b)	M5:630	1362	32,10	V 式爵
A/1:A-3+C-7[V-4] (v.c)	M5:651	0933	32,8	IV 式爵
A/1:A-3+C-7[V-4] (v.d)	M5:655	0932	32,5	IV 式爵
A/1:A-3+C-7[V-4] (v.e)	M5:637	1364	32,2	IV 式爵
A/1:A-3+C-7[V-4] (v.f)	M5:684	0935	32,4	IV 式爵
A/1:A-3+C-7[V-4] (v.g)	M5:687	0936	32,6	IV 式爵
*A/1:A-3+C-7[V-4] (v.h)	M5:682	0937	32,7	IV 式爵
*A/1:A-3+C-7[V-4] (v.i)	M5:1197	1021a	32,11	大圓罕
A/1:A-3+C-7[V-4] (v.j)	M5:626	1365	32,13	V 式瓿
A/1:A-3+C-7[V-4] (v.k)	M5:679	0934	—	IV 式瓿
A/1:A-3+C-7[V-4] (v.m)	M5:820	1368 nil	—	V 式瓿
A/1:A-3+C-7[V-4] (v.n)	M5:646	1368a nil	—	V 式瓿
A/1:A-3+C-7[V-4] (v.o)	M5:671	0939 nil	—	IV 式爵
A/1:A-3+C-7[V-4] (v.l)	M5:673	0940 nil	—	IV 式爵
A/1:A-3+[-]+V-4 (v.a)	M5:643	1363	32,9	V 式瓿
*A/1:A-3+[-]+V-4 (v.b)	M5:627	1366	32,12	V 式瓿
A/1:[-]+C-7[V-4]	M5:861	1021b	32,14	大圓罕

Table 3. (continued)

Reference Code Number	Excavator's Reference Number	Rubbing Available?	Five Decades Serial No.	Figure No.	Vessel Type
		Ssu-t'u-mu Group (*B-11 + 2tzu*)			
A/1: *B-11 + 2tzu* (v.a)	M5:793		1164	33,11	大圓尊
A/1: *B-11 + 2tzu* (v.b)	M5:867		1163	33,17	大圓尊
A/1: *B-11 + 2tzu* (v.c)	M5:794		1246	33,9	方壺
A/1: *B-11 + 2tzu* (v.d)	M5:807		1247	33,10	方壺
A/1: *B-11 + 2tzu* (v.e)	M5:672		0990a	33,8a	III 式爵
A/1: *B-11 + 2tzu* (v.f)	M5:661		0983	33,1	III 式爵
A/1: *B-11 + 2tzu* (v.g)	M5:686		0987	33,2	III 式爵
A/1: *B-11 + 2tzu* (v.h)	M5:654		0984	33,3	III 式爵
A/1: *B-11 + 2tzu* (v.i)	M5:677		0985	33,4	III 式爵
*A/1: *B-11 + 2tzu* (v.j)	M5:658		0986	33,5	III 式爵
A/1: *B-11 + 2tzu* (v.k)	M5:689		0988	33,6	III 式爵
A/1: *B-11 + 2tzu* (v.l)	M5:678		0989	33,7	III 式爵
A/1: *B-11 + 2tzu* (v.m)	M5:681		0990	33,8	III 式爵
*A/1: *B-11 + 2tzu* (v.n)	M5:612		1399	33,18	IV 式觚
A/1: *B-11 + 2tzu* (v.o)	M5:617		1400	33,20	IV 式觚
A/1: *B-11 + 2tzu* (v.p)	M5:615		1401	33,19	IV 式觚
A/1: *B-11 + 2tzu* (v.q)	M5:631		1402	33,21	IV 式觚
A/1: *B-11 + 2tzu* (v.r)	M5:614		1403	33,22	IV 式觚
A/1: *B-11 + 2tzu* (v.s)	M5:628		1404	33,23	IV 式觚
A/1: *B-11 + 2tzu* (v.t)	M5:625		1398	33,24	IV 式觚
A/1: *B-11 + 2tzu* (v.u)	M5:649		1405	33,26	IV 式觚
A/1: *B-11 + 2tzu* (v.v)	M5:606		1406	33,25	IV 式觚
A/1: *B-11 + 2tzu* (v.w)	M5:632		1406a	33,27	IV 式觚

A/1: B-11 + 2tzu (v.x)	M5: 857	1032	33,13	大方罍
A/1: B-11 + 2tzu (v.y)	M5: 860	1031	33,14	大圓罍
A/1: B-11 + 2tzu (l.a¹)	M066	2100	33,15	蓋甗
S: B-11 + 2tzu (v.b¹), (l.b¹), B-11 + 2tzu (v.c¹)	復齋 書道			鈇
A/1: B-11 + 3tzu (v.a)	M5: 868	1172	33,16	大方尊
A/1: B-11 + 3tzu (v.b)	M5: 806	1173	33,17	大方尊

Ssu-mu-hsin Group (3.67)

A/1: 3.67 (v.a)	M5: 809	0090	35,1	大方鼎
*A/1: 3.67 (v.b)	M5: 789	0091	35,2	大方鼎
*A/1: 3.67 (v.c), (l.c)	M5: 803	1457	35,4	四足甗
A/1: 3.67 (v.d), (l.d)	M5: 1163	1458	35,3	四足甗
A/1: 3.67 (v.e)	M5: 850	2142	35,4	方形高柱足器

Miscellaneous

A/1: A-3 + C-2[V-29] (v.a), (l.a)	M5: 823	1207	35,6	方彝
A/1: A-3 + C-2[V-29] (v.b)	M5: 1156	2081	35,7	小型鈇
A/1: H-1[V-23]	M5: 1173	0021	35,8	X式鼎
A/1: G-2[C-1] + ?	M5: 670	0906	35,9	IV式爵
A/1: 6.147	M5: 580 (jade)	—	35,10	玉戈
A/1: 2.56	M5: 315 (stone)	—	35,11	石牛
A/1: 4.76	M5: 316 (stone)	—	35,12	石磬

Table 4. Fu Hao Inscriptions (Excavators' Reference Numbers)

Excavator's Reference Number	Vessel Type	Reference Code Number	Five Decades Serial No.	Rubbing Available?	Figure No.
M5:1579	I 式爵	A/1:B-11+V-46+B-4 (v.w)	0921		29E,82
M5:1197	大圓罍	*A/1:A-3+C-7[V-4] (v.i)	1021a		32,11
M5:1173	X 式足鼎	A/1:H-1[V-23]	0021		35,8
M5:1163	四足觥	A/1:3.67 (v.d), (l.d)	1458		35,3
M5:1156	小型觚	A/1:A-3+C-2[V-29] (v.b)	2081		35,7
M5:1150	IX 式小型鳥足鼎	A/1:B-11+V-46+B-4 (v.s)	0063		29D,50
M5:870	大型連體甗	A/1:B-12[- , B-4] (v.a)	0676		29C,29
M5:869	分體甗 (上小甑)	A/1:B-12[V-46+B-4] (v.j¹)	2144		29D,59
M5:868	大圓尊	A/1:B-11+3tzu (v.a)	1172		33,16
M5:867	大圓尊	A/1:B-11+2tzu (v.b)	1163		33,17
M5:866	方壺	*A/1:B-11+V-46+B-4 (v.v), (l.v)	1220		29C,24
M5:865	小型連體甗	A/1:B-11+V-46+B-4 (v.j)	0685		29C,12
M5:864	分體甗 (下體)	A/1:B-12[- , B-4] (v.b)	0677		29C,34
M5:863	扁圓壺	*A/1:B-11+V-46+B-4 (v.l)	1242		29C,23
M5:861	大圓尊	A/1:[-]+C-7[V-4]	1021b		32,14
M5:860	大圓尊	A/1:B-11+2tzu (v.y)	1031		33,14
M5:859	I 式盉	A/1:B-12[V-46+B-4] (v.r¹)	1045		29E,77
M5:857	大方壺	A/1:B-11+2tzu (v.x)	1032		33,13
M5:856	方壺	A/1:B-11+V-46+B-4 (v.c), (l.c)	1221		29C,25
M5:855	大方尊	A/1:B-12[V-46+B-4] (v.m¹)			29E,74
M5:854	大方尊	*A/1:B-12[V-46+B-4] (v.n¹)	1026		29C,13
M5:852	雙耳觶	A/1:B-12[V-46+B-4] (v.i¹)	2143		29D,60
M5:850	方形高柱足器	A/1:3.67 (v.e)	2142		35,4
M5:849	無蓋方彝	A/1:B-11+V-46+B-4 (v.a)	1208		29D,48
M5:839/1	鏡	A/1:A-3+V-30 (v.f)	1812		30,2
M5:839/2	鏡	A/1:A-3+V-30 (v.g)	1813		30,3

M5:837	Ⅳ式盉	A/1:B-12[V-46+B-4] (v.p¹)		1044	29E,78
M5:835	Ⅳ式小型鼓腹鼎	A/1:B-11+V-46+B-4] (v.g)		0058	29C,22
M5:834	小方鼎	A/1:B-12[V-46+B-4] (v.p)		0060	29E,70
M5:832	Ⅰ式小型盉	A/1:B-12[- , B-4] (v.f)	cf. Ho-nan 1:142	0397 [=418]	29C,28
M5:832	Ⅰ式小型盉	A/1:B-12[V-46+B-4] (v.s¹)	revised see Ho-nan 1:142	(0418) [=0397]	29C,28
M5:831	Ⅴ式小型柱足鼎	A/1:B-12[V-46+B-4] (v.u)		0056	29D,63
M5:830	甗	A/1:B-11+V-46+B-4] (v.u)		1295	29D,53
M5:827	ⅢA式瓿	A/1:B-12[V-46+B-4] (v.a¹)		1383	29C,7
M5:825	Ⅰ式瓿	A/1:B-12[V-46+B-4] (v.t¹)		1209	29D,42a
M5:823	方彝	A/1:A-3+C[V-29] (v.a), (l.a)		1207	35,6
M5:821	ⅡA式中型鼎	A/1:B-12[V-46+B-4] (v.a)		0048	29C,5
M5:820	Ⅴ式瓿	A/1:A-3+C-7[V-4] (v.m)		1368	—
M5:819	Ⅴ式鮈高柱足鼎	A/1:B-12[- , B-4] (v.e)		0020	29C,31
M5:817	Ⅸ式小型鳥足鼎	A/1:B-11+V-46+B-4] (v.r)		0062	29D,54
M5:816	Ⅱ式小型圓鼎	A/1:B-12[V-46+B-4] (v.t)		0055	29D,65
M5:815	ⅡB式中型圓鼎	A/1:B-12[V-46+B-4] (v.q)		0052	29D,66
M5:814	Ⅸ式小型鳥足鼎	A/1:B-12[V-46+B-4] (v.n)		0050	29D,54
M5:813	長方扁足鼎	A/1:B-12[V-46+B-4] (v.c)		0064	29D,61
M5:812	長方扁足鼎	A/1:B-12[V-46+B-4] (v.)		2189	29D,61a
M5:811	大型盂	A/1:B-12[- , B-4] (v.g)		1548	29C,30
M5:810	Ⅰ式瓿	A/1:B-12[V-46+B-4] (v.q¹)		1043	29D,42
M5:809	大方鼎	A/1:3.67 (v.a)		0090	35,1
M5:808	大圓鼎	A/1:A-3+V-30 (v.e)		0065	30,1
M5:807	方壺尊	A/1:B-11+2tzu (v.d)		1247	33,10
M5:806	大方尊	A/1:B-11+3tzu (v.b)		1173	33,17
M5:803	四足觥	*A/1:3.67 (v.c), (l.c)	nil	1457	35,4
M5:802	圓足觥	A/1:B-12[V-46+B-4] (v.u¹)		1455	29D,67b
M5:800	大型鈸	A/1:B-12[V-46+B-4] (v.h¹)		2080	29E,76
M5:799	大型鈸	A/1:B-12[V-46+B-4] (v.l)		2079	29D,37

Table 4. (continued)

Excavator's Reference Number	Vessel Type	Reference Code Number	Five Decades Serial No.	Rubbing Available?	Figure No.
M5:798	III式盉	A/1: B-12[V-46 + B-4] (v.i)	1043		29D,38
M5:796	甗	A/1: B-11 + B-46 + b-4 (v.d)	1294		29D,52
M5:795	扁圓壺	A/1: B-11 + V-46 + b-4 (v.n)	1243		29E,83
M5:794	方壺	A/1: B-11 + 2tzu (v.c)	1246		33,9
M5:793	大圓尊	A/1: B-11 + 2tzu (v.a)	1164		33,11
M5:792	方尊	A/1: B-11 + V-46 + B-4 (v.t)	1150		29D,49
M5:791	鴞方鼎	A/1: B-12[V-46 + B-4] (v.x)	1210		29C,9
M5:790	三聯甗,架	A/1: B-12[V-46 + B-4] (v.g-a)	0684	nil	29B,10
M5:768(a)					
M5:769					
M5:770					
M5:789	大方鼎	*A/1: 3.67 (v.b)	0091		35,2
M5:785	鷄尊	A/1: B-12[V-46 + B-4] (v.b)	1152		29D,39
M5:784	鷄尊	*A/1: B-11 + B-46 + [-] (v.c)	1151		29D,51
M5:683		A/1: B-11 + V-46 + B-4 (v.h¹)	0922	nil	—
M5:779	圓足鉞	A/1: B-12[V-46 + B-4] (v.v¹)	1456		29D,67c
M5:777	盤	A/1: B-12[V-46 + B-4] (v.l¹)	1468		29D,35
M5:776	IX式小,型鳥足鼎	A/1: B-12[V-46 + B-4] (v.h)	0061		29E,75
M5:775	VI式小,型柱足鼎	A/1: B-12[V-46 + B-4] (v.v)	0057		29D,62
M5:770	三聯甗,甑	A/1: B-12[V-46 + B-4] (v.d-a)	0684	nil	29B,7
M5:770	三聯甗,甑	A/1: B-12[V-46 + B-4] (v.d-b)	0684	nil	29B,8
M5:768(a)					
M5:769					
M5:790					
M5:770	三聯甗,甑	A/1: B-12[V-46 + B-4] (v.d-c)	0684		29B,9
M5:769	三聯甗,甑	A/1: B-12[V-46 + B-4] (v.f-a)	0684		29B,4
M5:769	三聯甗,甑	A/1: B-12[V-46 + B-4] (v.f-b)	0684		29B,5
M5:768(a)					
M5:770					

M5:769		三聯甗,甗	A/1: B-12[V-46 + B-4] (v.f-c)	0684	29B,6
M5:768(a)	M5:70	三聯甗,甗	A/1: B-12[V-46 + B-4] (v.e-a)	0684	29B,1
M5:768(a)	M5:769	三聯甗,甗	A/1: B-12[V-46 + B-4] (v.e-b)	0684	29B,2
	M5:790				
M5:768(a)		三聯甗,甗	A/1: B-12[V-46 + B-4] (v.e-c)	0684	29B,3
M5:768(b)		分體甗(上小)甗	A/1: B-11 + V-46 + B-4] (v.k)	0686	29D,55
M5:767		分體甗(上小)甗	A/1: B-12[- , B-4] (v.c)	0678	29C,33
M5:764		渙柱甗型器	A/1: B-12[- , B-4] (v.d)	0716	29C,32
M5:763		帶形堃鼎形器	A/1: B-12[V-46 + B-4] (v.w)	0059	29C,3
M5:762		II A 式中型鼎	A/1: B-12[V-46 + B-4] (v.o)	0051	29C,2
M5:761		II B 式中型圓鼎	A/1: B-12[V-46 + B-4] (v.s)	0054	29D,40
M5:760		II B 式中型圓鼎	A/1: B-12[V-46 + B-4] (v.r)	0053	29D,36
M5:756		II A 式中型鼎	A/1: B-12[V-46 + B-4] (v.m)	0049	29C,1
M5:752		大方罕	*A/1: B-12[V-46 + B-4] (v.o¹)	1027	29C,14
M5:751		大圓罕	*A/1: B-12[V-46 + B-4] (v.y)	1028	29D,67
M5:749		I 式斗	A/1: B-12[V-46 + B-4] (v.e¹)	1835	29E,73
M5:748		II 式斗	A/1: B-12[V-46 + B-4] (v.f¹)	1836	29E,72
M5:747		I 式斗	A/1: B-12[V-46 + B-4] (v.d)	1834	29C,8
M5:746		II 式斗	A/1: B-12[V-46 + B-4] (v.k)	1830	29C,4
M5:745		I 式斗	A/1: B-12[V-46 + B-4] (v.b¹)	1832	29E,69
M5:744		I 式斗	A/1: B-12[V-46 + B-4] (v.j)	1831	29D,58
M5:743		I 式斗	A/1: B-12[V-46 + B-4] (v.c¹)	1833	29E,68
M5:742		II 式斗	A/1: B-12[V-46 + B-4] (v.g¹)	1837	29E,71
M5:689		III 式爵	A/1: B-11 + 2tzu (v.k)	0988	33,6
M5:687		IV 式爵	A/1: A-3 + C-7[V-4] (v.g)	0936	32,6
M5:686		III 式爵	A/1: B-11 + 2tzu (v.g)	0987	33,2
M5:685		I 式爵	A/1: B-11 + V-46 + B-4 (v.f¹)	0919	29C,15
M5:684		IV 式爵	A/1: A-3 + C-7[V-4] (v.f)	0935	32,4
M5:682		IV 式爵	*A/1: A-3 + C-7[V-4] (v.h)	0937	32,7
M5:681		III 式爵	A/1: B-11 + 2tzu (v.m)	0990	33,8

nil (col 4 row 1)
nil (col 4 row 4)

Table 4. (continued)

Excavator's Reference Number	Vessel Type	Reference Code Number	Five Decades Serial No.	Rubbing Available?	Figure No.
M5:680	II 式爵	A/1: B-11 + V-46 + B-4 (v.c^1)	0916		29C,10
M5:679	IV 式觚	A/1: A-3 + C-7[V-4] (v.k)	0934		—
M5:678	III 式爵	A/1: B-11 + $2tzu$ (v.l)	0989		33,7
M5:677	III 式爵	A/1: B-11 + $2tzu$ (v.i)	0985		33,4
M5:676		A/1: B-11 + B-46 + B-4 (v.g^1)	0920	nil	
M5:675	II 式爵	A/1: B-11 + V-46 + B-4 (v.x)	0918		29C,17
M5:674	IV 式爵	A/1: A-3 + C-7[V-4] (v.a)	0938		32,1
M5:673	IV 式爵	A/1: A-3 + C-7[V-4] (v.l)	0940	nil	
M5:672	III 式爵	A/1: B-11 + $2tzu$ (v.e)	0990a		33,8a
M5:671	IV 式爵	A/1: A-3 + C-7[V-4] (v.o)	0939	nil	
M5:670	IV 式爵	A/1: G-2[C-1] + ?	0906		35,9
M5:669	V 式爵	A/1: [−] + E-5 + V-35 (v.d)	0930		31,11
M5:668	V 式爵	A/1: [−] + E-5 + V-35 (v.a)	0923		31,12
M5:667	V 式爵	*A/1: [−] + E-5 + V-35 (v.b)	0929		31,7
M5:666	V 式爵	A/1: [−] + E-5 + V-35 (v.i)	0928		31,13
M5:665	V 式爵	A/1: [−] + E-5 + V-35 (v.j)	0924		31,10
M5:664	II 式爵	*A/1: B-11 + V-46 + B-4 (v.d^1)	0912		29C,11
M5:663	V 式爵	A/1: [−] + E-5 + V-35 (v.h)	0927		31,14
M5:662	II 式爵	A/1: B-11 + V-46 + B-4 (v.y)	0914		29C,16
M5:661	III 式爵	A/1: B-11 + $2tzu$ (v.f)	0983		33,1
M5:660	V 式爵	A/1: [−] + E-5 + V-35 (v.g)	0926		31,8
M5:659	V 式爵	A/1: [−] + E-5 + V-35 (v.f)	0925		31,9
M5:658	III 式爵	*A/1: B-11 + $2tzu$ (v.j)	0986		33,5
M5:657	II 式爵	A/1: B-11 + V-46 + B-4 (v.a^1)	0917		29C,20
M5:656	II 式爵	A/1: B-11 + V-46 + B-4 (v.b^1)	0913		29C,19
M5:655	IV 式爵	A/1: A-3 + C-7[V-4] (v.d)	0932		32,5

M5:654	III 式爵	A/1: B-11 + 2tzu (v.h)	0984		33,3
M5:653	II 式爵	A/1: B-11 + V-46 + B-4 (v.z)	0911		29C,18
M5:652	II 式爵	A/1: B-11 + V-46 + B-4 (v.e¹)	0915		29C,6
M5:651	IV 式爵	A/1: A-3 + C-7[V-4] (v.c)	0933		32,8
M5:650	III 式爵	*A/1: B-11 + B-46 + B-4 (v.i)	1385		29C,21
M5:649	IV 式觚	A/1: B-11 + 2tzu (v.u)	1405		33,26
M5:648	II A 式觚	A/1: B-12[V-46 + B-4] (v.z)	1384		29D,56
M5:646	V 式觚	A/1: A-3 + C-7[V-4] (v.n)	1368a	nil	—
M5:644	III 式觚	A/1: B-11 + V-46 + B-4 (v.p)	1386		29E,84
M5:643	V 式觚	A/1: A-3 + [-] + V-4 (v.a)	1363		32,9
M5:642	II A 式觚	A/1: B-12[V-46 + B-4] (v.e)	1374		29E,80
M5:640	II A 式觚	A/1: B-12[V-46 + B-4] (v.g)	1373	nil	—
M5:639	II A 式觚	A/1: B-12[V-46 + B-4] (v.f)	1375		29D,41
M5:637	IV 式爵	A/1: A-3 + C-7[V-4] (v.e)	1364		32,2
M5:635	IV 式觚	A/1: [-] + E-5 + V-35 (v.m)	1350	nil	—
M5:633	II B 式觚	A/1: B-11 + V-46 + [-] (v.b)	1388		29C,27
M5:632	IV 式觚	A/1: B-11 + 2tzu (v.w)	1406a		33,27
M5:631	IV 式觚	A/1: B-11 + 2tzu (v.q)	1402		33,21
M5:630	V 式爵	A/1: A-3 + C-7[V-4] (v.b)	1262		32,10
M5:629	III A 式觚	A/1: B-12[V-46 + B-4] (v.k¹)	1382		29E,79
M5:628	IV 式觚	A/1: B-11 + 2tzu (v.s)	1404		33,23
M5:627	V 式觚	*A/1: A-3 + [-] + V-4 (v.b)	1366		32,12
M5:626	V 式觚	A/1: A-3 + C-7[V-4] (v.j)	1365		32,13
M5:625	IV 式觚	A/1: B-11 + 2tzu (v.t)	1398		33,24
M5:624	VI 式觚	A/1: [-] + E-5 + V-35 (v.l)	1349	nil	—
M5:622	VI 式觚	A/1: B-4 + E-5 + V-35 (v.c)	1359		31,5
M5:621	II A 式觚	A/1: B-12[V-46 + B-4] (v.d¹)	1372		29D,57
M5:620	VI 式觚	A/1: B-4 + E-5 + V-35 (v.h)	1361	nil	—
M5:618	II B 式觚	A/1: B-11 + V-46 + [-] (v.a)	1387		29C,26
M5:617	IV 式觚	A/1: B-11 + 2tzu (v.o)	1400		33,20

Table 4. (continued)

Excavator's Reference Number	Vessel Type	Reference Code Number	Five Decades Serial No.	Rubbing Available?	Figure No.
M5:616	VI 式觚	*A/1:B-4+E-5+V-35 (v.f)	1348		31,6
M5:615	IV 式觚	A/1:B-11+2tzu (v.p)	1401		33,19
M5:614	IV 式觚	A/1:B-11+2tzu (v.r)	1403		33,22
M5:613	VI 式爵	A/1:[ ]+E-5+V-35 (v.c)	1347		31,16
M5:612	IV 式觚	*A/1:B-11+2tzu (v.n)	1399		33,18
M5:611	I 式觚	A/1:B-11+V-46+B-4 (v.n)	1380		29E,81
M5:610	VI 式觚	A/1:B-4+E-5+V-35 (v.b)	1358		31,3
M5:609	VI 式觚	A/1:[ ]+E-5+V-35 (v.k)	1346	nil	—
M5:608	VI 式爵	A/1:B-4+E-5+V-35 (v.g)	1360	nil	—
M5:607	VI 式觚	A/1:[ ]+E-5+V-35 (v.e)	1345		31,15
M5:606	IV 式爵	A/1:B-11+2tzu (v.v)	1406		33,25
M5:605	I 式觚	*A/1:B-11+V-46+B-4 (v.q)	1378		29D,43
M5:604	I 式觚	*A/1:B-11+V-46+B-4 (v.o)	1381		29D,44
M5:603	I 式觚	A/1:B-11+V-46+B-4 (v.f)	1377		29D,46
M5:602	I 式觚	A/1:B-11+V-46+B-4 (v.m)	1379		29D,47
M5:601	I 式觚	A/1:B-11+V-46+B-4 (v.e)	1376		29D,45
M5:580 (jade)	玉戈	A/1:6.147	—		35,10
M5:320	圓尊	A/1:B-4+E-5+V-35 (v.e)	1154		31,4
M5:318	圓尊	A/1:B-4+E-5+V-35 (v.a)	1153		31,1
M5:317	殘尊	A/1:B-4+E-5+V-35 (v.d)	1029		31,2
M5:316 (stone)	石磬	A/1:4.76	—		35,12
M5:315 (stone)	石牛	A/1:2.56	—		35,11
M066	蓋	A/1:B-11+2tzu (l.a¹)	2100		33,15
復齋	盉	S:B-11+2tzu (v.b¹), (l.b¹)			
吉逵	鉞	B-11+2tzu (v.c¹)			

9

The Classification, Nomenclature, and Usage of Shang Dynasty Jades

Hsia Nai

In many respects, jade may be regarded as a form of artistic creation unique to China. It has undergone continuous development for over 4,000 years from the Neolithic Age to the present. As early as the An-yang period of the Shang dynasty jade working had already reached a stage of maturity reflecting high levels of both artistry and craft. A large quantity of exquisite jades has been unearthed at the Yin ruins in An-yang. The more than 755 jades of all types excavated in 1976 from the tomb of Fu Hao, in particular, have attracted the attention of scholars of ancient Chinese jade both within and without China.[1]

In this essay I will examine the classification, nomenclature, and usage of Shang dynasty jades from an archaeological perspective, relying primarily on the Fu Hao tomb material as well as referring to jades previously unearthed at Yin-hsü. The essence of this "archaeological methodology" is to treat the excavated artifacts as the basis of research and then seek to relate this material to written records. This is opposite to the old approach, which took unreliable literary documents or collected pieces as its starting point.

According to the types and usage of Shang dynasty jades, I propose to frame my discussion in terms of three major categories: "ritual jades," weapons and implements (including "daily use" items), and ornaments.

1. Chung-kuo-she-hui-k'o-hsüeh-yüan K'ao-ku-yen-chiu-so 1980a.

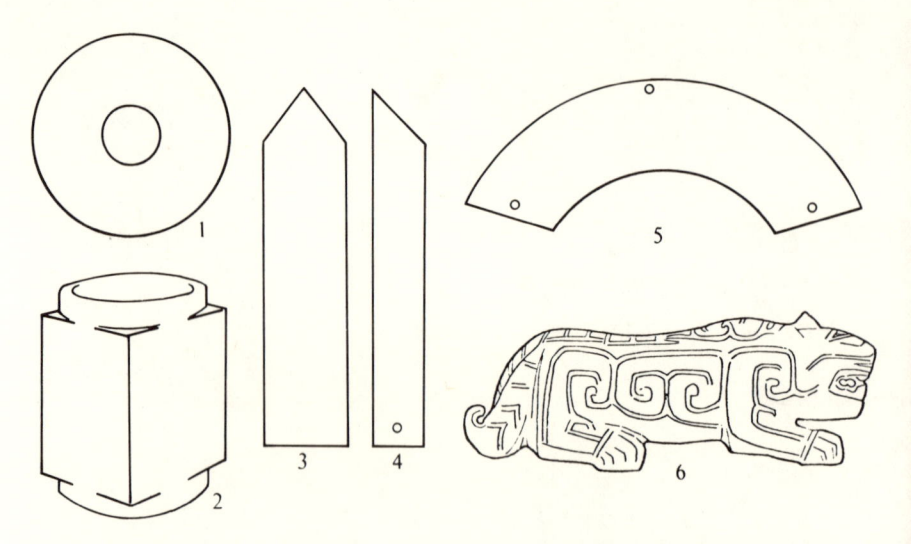

Fig. 36. The six "auspicious jades": (1) *pi*; (2) *tsung*; (3) *kuei*; (4) *chang*; (5) *huang*; (6) *hu*.

"RITUAL JADES"

As used in this essay, "ritual jades" should not be read in the broad sense of referring to all jades that have been used in a ritual context. It specifically denotes the six kinds of jade known as pi 璧, ts'ung 琮, kuei 圭, chang 璋, huang 璜, and hu 琥—collectively termed the "six auspicious" (liu jui 六瑞) or six kinds of "auspicious jade" (jui yü 瑞玉) (fig. 36).

Some people believe that the likes of auspicious jades such as kuei and pi had not only emerged as early as the Shang dynasty, but that their function even then was similar to that of the auspicious jades of later times. So, by the time the *San Li* 三禮 was compiled, the six auspicious had already become an institution of long duration.[2] In actuality, the earliest representation we know of the auspicious jades is the Eastern Han stele *Six Jades Diagram* (*liu yü t'u* 六玉圖)[3] (fig. 37). These drawings were imaginative representations by Han dynasty peoples of descriptions contained in the classic *San Li* and commentaries on the text by Han Confucians. While there may be similar or related objects from the Shang dynasty, it is impossible to know what they were named in those

2. Ling 1965.
3. See Hung Shih 洪适, *Li Hsü* 隸續 (Hung-shih Hui-mu-chai Ts'ung-shu edition, 1872, vol. 5, pp. 3–6).

Fig. 37. The six "auspicious jades" depicted on a Han dynasty stele.

times. And as far as their usage in Shang times is concerned, the excavated archaeological evidence seems to indicate that it was not at all as described in the *San Li*. They have also never been found to occur in groups.

I agree with most historians of ancient China that the *Chou Li* 周禮 is an archaizing work of the late Warring States period. I believe that what this book says about the nomenclature and usage of each jade comprising the six auspicious is the author's synthesis of what was to be found about the names and functions of jades in pre-Ch'in works and popular tradition. Descriptive terms were added to the names of some kinds of jades, which rendered them into proper names. Finally, they were assigned to various ceremonial functions. Certain of these assignments may have had some basis in fact, others may have been forced due to epigraphic considerations or Confucian idealism. In this way the objects and functions were aligned with each other and systematized. When ancient pre-Ch'in texts refer to jades it is usually only by name; rarely is there any description of their appearance. The precise measurements and ranking of auspicious jades frequently set out in *Chou Li* are clearly the result of systematizing and idealizing processes. The commentaries of Han dynasty classicists seem to have an explanation for the shape of each and every kind of jade; however, these explanations are often epigraphically based assumptions and some are entirely fanciful. The drawings of Chou dynasty ritual objects (including auspicious jades) contained in such later works as Nieh Ch'ung-yi's 聶崇義 *San Li T'u* are mostly imaginative reconstructions based on the commentaries of Han and T'ang Confucians. It is not that such objects actually existed in the Chou dynasty.[4]

Wu Ta-ch'eng's 吳大澂 matching of ancient jades newly excavated in his time with those mentioned in such ancient texts as *Chou Li* at least had concrete objects as evidence rather than relying entirely on fantasy. This methodology was a great advance. However, the motive of his study of ancient jades was "to use them as a means of illuminating the *Classics*."[5] Because he insisted on seeking out the names and functions of some "forgotten" ancient jades within the texts of the *Classics*, there were inevitably cases of farfetched comparisons. (fig. 38) His methodology may be termed the *Wu Ta-ch'eng brand* of classicist methodology.

As an archaeological worker, I believe we should now adopt an archaeological methodology that allows full use of the large quantities of material accumulated through excavation work. We begin with jades unearthed by excavation work and subsequently refer to collected pieces and written documents. If a name can be determined, then the ancient name may be used. If the ancient name cannot be found, then a new, easily understandable name may be selected. When function cannot be decided, the issue may be temporarily set aside and judgment reserved. Although little research on ancient jade has yet been undertaken by this methodology, the direction it takes us in is the correct one and the future holds much promise.

First among the six auspicious is the jade *pi*, which is often unearthed in Shang dynasty tombs. Sixteen *pi* were recovered from Fu Hao's tomb, and if these are reckoned along with *huan* and *yüan* there is a total of fifty-seven. I am of the opinion that *huan* and *yüan* are actually identical to *pi*. The *Erh Ya* 爾雅 states: "When the *jou* 肉 is twice the width of the *hao* 好, call it *pi*; when the *hao* is twice the width of the *jou*, call it *yüan*

---

4. Hsia 1983: 128.
5. T. C. Wu 1889: Preface.

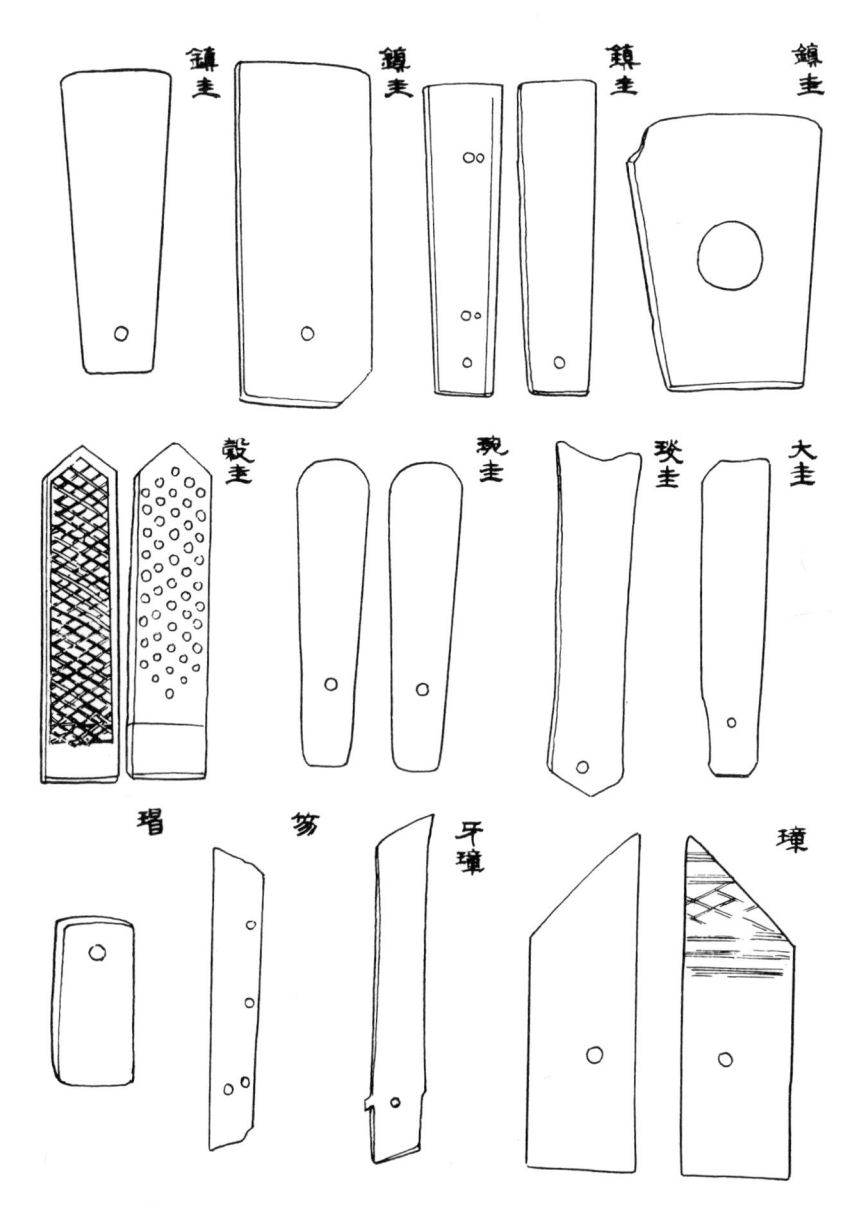

Fig. 38. The "auspicious jades" depicted by Wu Ta-ch'eng in his *Ku Yü T'u*.

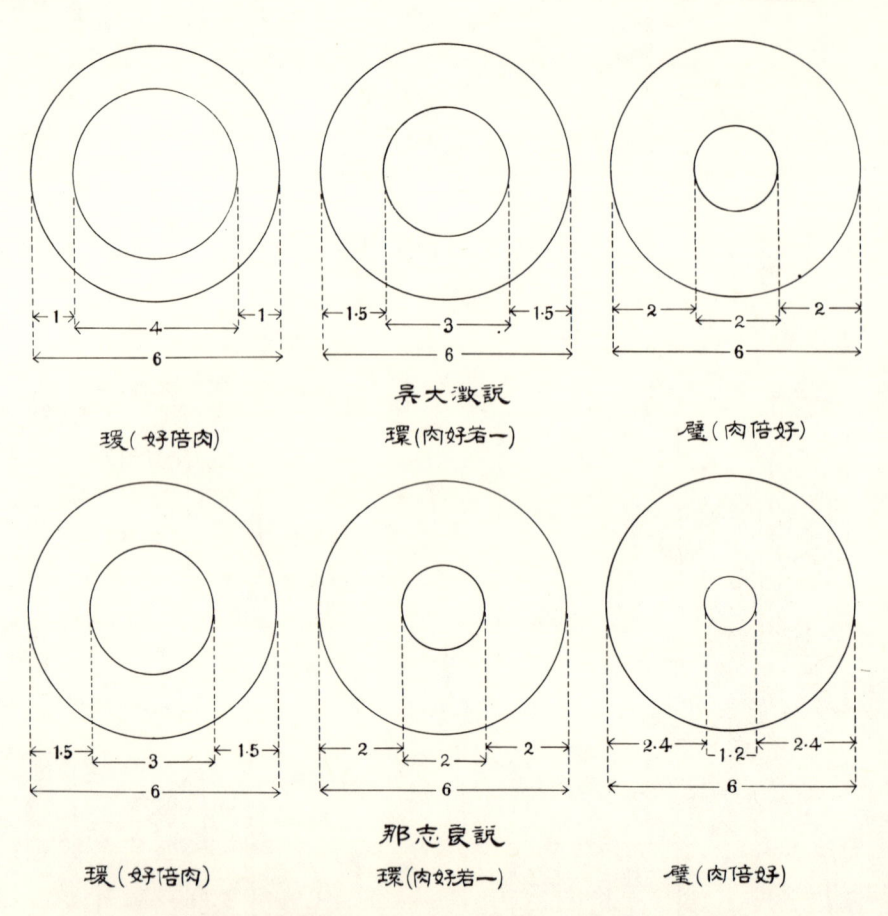

Fig. 39. Two different interpretations of the *pi, huang,* and *yuan* as defined in *Erh Ya*: (*upper row*) according to Wu Ta-ch'eng; (*lower row*) according to Na Chih-liang. (*Left in both rows*), *yüan;* (center) *huan;* (right) *pi.*

瑗; when the *jou* and *hao* are of equal width, call it *huan*" 環. This is a case of hocus-pocus and hairsplitting by early Han classicists. "*Hao*" refers to the central perforation; "*jou*" refers to the encircling ring-body. So there can be two different ways of taking the measurements. This is why Wu Ta-ch'eng and Na Chih-liang's 那志良 explanations differ (fig. 39).[6] No matter which way you interpret the *Erh Ya*, neither conforms to the real situation. Among excavation artifacts the *jou*:*hao* ratios are not uniform. Not only are they not limited to the three classes of

6. Ibid., p. 47; Na 1980: 75.

ratio, the overwhelming majority do not even conform to these three ratios. I suggest that the three kinds of jade be collectively called the *pi-huan* type, or simply *pi*. Those pieces with slender ring-bodies and perforations greater in diameter than one-half that of the whole piece may be especially termed *huan*.

We are not clear as to which jade the character *yüan* originally referred to; however, it certainly was not the jade said by Wu Ta-ch'eng and Lo Chen-yü 羅振玉 to have been used by rulers to grant audiences to high ministers.[7] Although this interpretation can be traced back to Hsu Shen's *Shuo Wen* 說文 in the Eastern Han, this kind of audience-granting jade never existed in ancient times. The explanation is no more than a literary invention, depending on the linking of the homonyms "*yüan*" 瑗 and "*yüan*" 援. From now on the character "*yüan*" 瑗 may be dropped from among the names of ancient jades.

Jades of the *pi-huan* type with large perforations have already been recovered from neolithic burials. Some which encircled the deceased's arm must have been bracelets;[8] some which were placed on the chest or by the waist were perhaps hung as pendants.[9] In Shang dynasty tombs the *pi-huan* type is most often found on the deceased's chest or by the waist, and its usage was likely similar to the neolithic cases. But there is one kind of *pi* whose perforation displays a protruding circumferential collar which would have facilitated sliding it over the arm, so some people believe it might have been used as a bracelet (fig. 40:1).[10] The small jade and stone *pi-huan* found in chariot burials perhaps served to link various parts of the chariot gear.

One special form of *pi* is known by antiquarians as "*ch'i-pi*" 戚璧, or "*pi-ch'i*" 璧戚. Straight chords are cut away on two sides, each displaying a row of teeth, and the cutting edge is ground thin and sharp. The Fu Hao tomb report calls it a Type I *ch'i* 戚 and includes it within the weapon class. This is correct. It cannot be considered an auspicious jade. Two of these were also unearthed at Erh-li-t'ou. Their cutting edges had been partitioned into four facets. The preliminary report terms them "*yüeh*" 鉞 (fig. 40:2).[11] They should be called "*pi-ch'i*" instead.

7. T. C. Wu 1889: 43; see also Lo Chen-yü 羅振玉, "Shih yuan 釋瑗," in his *Yung-feng-hsiang-jen Chia-kao* 永豐鄉人甲稿, 1920 edition, p. 2.
8. At Ta-tun-tzu in P'i-hsien, Kiangsu; see *K'ao-ku-hsüeh-pao* 考古學報, 1964 (2): 21.
9. At tomb No. 2, site at Ching-chih-chen in An-ch'iu, Shantung (Lung-shan culture); see *K'ao-ku-hsüeh-pao* 考古學報, 1959 (4): 21.
10. Chung-kuo-she-hui-k'o-hsüeh-yüan K'ao-ku-yen-chiu-so 1980a: 119, plates 78, 88.
11. *K'ao-ku* 考古, 1976 (4): 262.

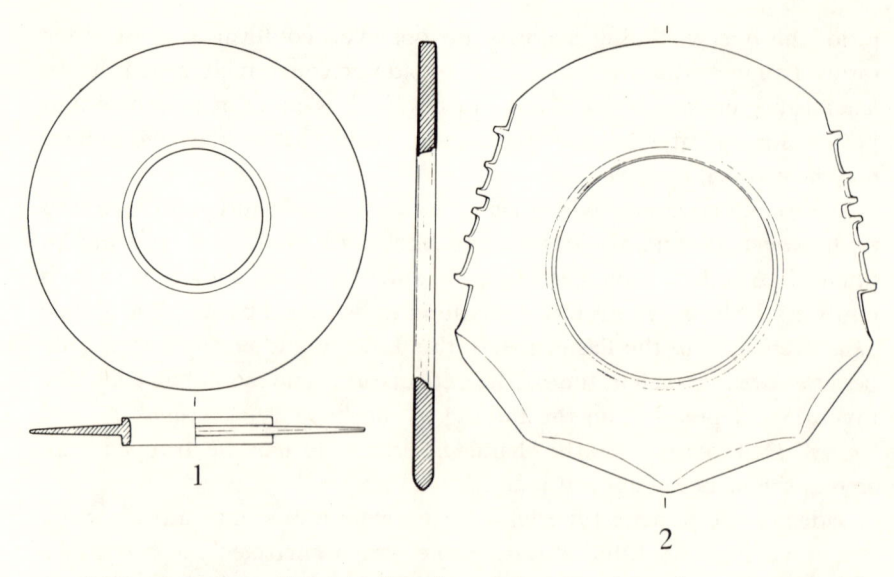

Fig. 40. Two jade types: (1) special-shaped *pi*, #456 in Tomb Number Five at Yin-shü; (2) *pi-ch'i* or *ch'i-pi*, excavated from Erh-li-t'ou.

Another special form of *pi* was called "*hsüan chi*" 璇璣 by Wu Ta-ch'eng. It is said to be a component of an astronomical instrument such as an armillary sphere. On this kind of *pi* there are three groups of toothlike projections on the outer circumference. These are actually *pi* with decorated edges, having nothing to do with astronomical devices. Three groups of toothlike projections grooved out in such fashion that each was of different height and width could not have served as a gear wheel for rotation within an instrument. Even less so could the so-called "*hsüan chi*," such as the one found in Fu Hao's tomb which had only three grooved lines (termed "chi-ya" 機牙) and no fine teeth. One was found in an infant burial at Hsiao-t'un. It was placed on the right side of the chest, and like ordinary *pi-huan* must have been used as an ornament.[12] I believe its origins lie, on the one hand, in the Shang craftsman's propensity for carving toothlike flanges on the profiles of jades, including *ch'i* 戚, *mao* 矛, *ko* 戈, *tao* 刀, and suspended *huang* 璜, *chüeh* 玦, etc., as well as *pi*; and on the other, in the tripartite and quadruple partitioning of *pi* (among the so-called "*hsüan chi*" are also four-toothed examples). The combining of these two sources thus gave rise to the *pi* with circum-

---

12. Chung-kuo-she-hui-k'o-hsüeh-yüan K'ao-ku-yen-chiu-so 1980a: 119, pl. 86:4.

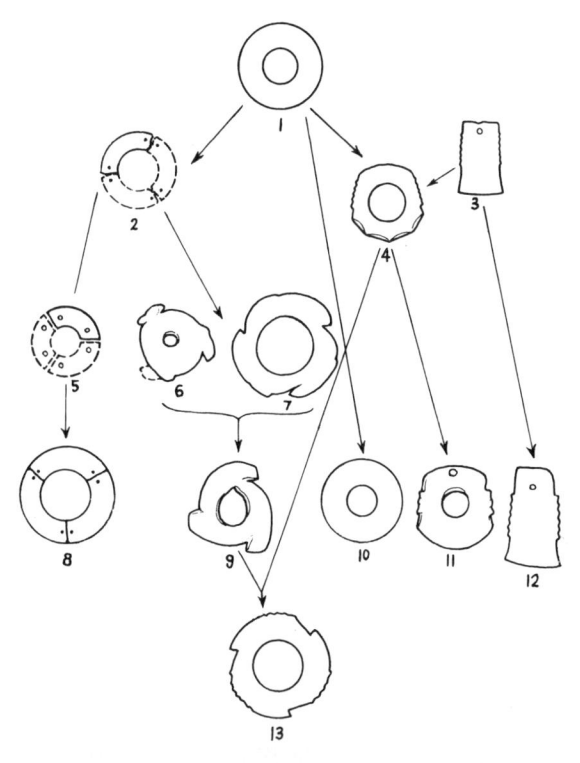

Fig. 41. Hypothesized sequence of the development of the so-called *hsüan chi*. (Explanation: In the past Wu Ta-ch'eng identified a jade in his collection as "*hsüan chi*" (that is, "*yü hsüan chi*"). The reason was that in the pre-Ch'in text *Shang Shu*, ("Shun Tien") there is the phrase "He examined the jade turning sphere, and the jade transverse tube, that he might regulate the seven Directors." Han Confucians explained "*chi* and *heng*" as "astronomical instruments." They believed that *chi* was the *hsüan chi*, an astronomical instrument that could revolve and was used in conjunction with the *heng* (a transverse sighting tube), none other than what has become known as "armillary" since the Han dynasty. Wu Ta-ch'eng said: "The outer circumference of this jade has three sets of gear-teeth, each comprised of six small teeth, apparently capable of meshing with another object and making it revolve. It appears to be a gear wheel used in armillary. Now that knowledge of its use has been lost, we do not know how to employ it" (*Ku Yü T'u K'ao*, p. 51). This illustrative diagram was designed by the author on the basis of recently excavated material, in order to discern the origins and usage of this type of jade. In this fashion the identification of "*hsüan chi*" as an astronomical instrument can be completely rejected. The find-sites and publication information for each piece in the diagram follow: (1) Ta-wen-k'ou stone *pi-huan* (*Ta-wen-k'ou*, pp. 98–99); (2) Pan-p'o stone *huang* (*Sian Pan-p'o*, p. 194, pl. 164:2); (3) Erh-li-t'ou, Yen-shih "jade *yüeh*" (*K'ao-ku* 1978.4:270, fig. 1:2); (4) Erh-li-t'ou "jade *yüeh*" (*K'ao-ku* 1976.4:262, fig. 6:3–4); (5) Cheng-chou Erh-li-kang jade *huang* (*K'ao-ku* 1957.1.72, pl. 4:3); (6) T'ai-hsi-ts'un "jade *hsüan chi*" (*K'ao-ku*

ferential groups of teeth (fig. 41). I propose that from now on the name "*hsüan chi*" be erased from the terminology of ancient jades, and even more strongly that no more grand essays should be written under the mistaken belief that it is an astronomical instrument. Na Chih-liang also believes that it is properly a form of *pi* and has no relation to astronomical instruments.[13]

Due to a misreading of the original text of the *Chou Li*, some people call the ellipsoidal type of *pi*, *hsien pi* 羨璧. The *Chou Li* states "measurement is established by taking the diameter of the *pi*"; and furthermore, "The diameter of the *pi* is one *ch'i*, the perforation three *ts'un*, this makes up a measure." Cheng Chung's 鄭眾 commentary says "*Hsien* 羨 means length." The original text says that the diameter of the *pi* is one *ch'i* long, and that this constitutes the basic unit of linear measurement. In much the same sense, the diameter of the English copper pence coin is set at one inch long. Cheng Hsuan 鄭玄 mistakenly explained that "*Hsien* means not round in appearance." We should discard the term "*hsien pi*." *Chou Li* and other pre-Ch'in texts do not contain the name of a *pi* called "*hsien pi*."

Another kind of jade is called *chüeh* 玦, a *pi* with a slit. Eighteen were found in Fu Hao's tomb—some have plain, polished surfaces, some are incised with dragon or serpent designs.[14] The former is likely an earring; the latter all have a fine perforation so were probably pendants (fig. 46:3).

The second kind of auspicious jade is *kuei* 圭, which are flat and tabular. The proximal end is flat, the distal end forms an equilateral triangle. The *Shuo Wen* states "a sharp point is *kuei*, half of a *kuei* is a *chang* 璋." This, too, is the case in the Han stele *Six Jades Diagram* (see fig. 37). The *Shuo Wen* also states: "*Kuei* are round (*huan* 圜) at the top and square at the bottom." If the character *huan* 圜 is not an incorrect character, this indicates that the end-point was ground off, forming a

13. Na 1980: 225–26.
14. Chung-kuo-she-hui-k'o-hsüeh-yüan K'ao-ku-yen-chiu-so 1980a: 128–30, pls. 104–06.

Fig. 41 legend continued:
1973.5:267, fig. 1:8); (7) Shih-mao, Shen-mu, Shensi, "jade *hsüan chi*" (late Lung-shan culture or early Shang, *K'ao-ku* 1977.3:155, pl. 4:9); (8) Fu Hao tomb "jade *huang*" (#901, see pl. 96:2); (9) Fu Hao tomb "jade *hsüan chi*" (#1029, see pl. 86:4); (10) Fu Hao tomb jade *pi* (#457, see pl. 85:1); (11) Fu Hao tomb "jade *chi*" (#591, see pl. 115:2); (12) Fu Hao tomb "jade *chi*" (#459, see pl. 115:1); (13) *Ku Yü T'u K'ao* (p. 50) mentions "*hsüan chi*" (sometimes written "*hsün chi*"); *Shang Shu* ["Ta Chuan"] has it as "*hsüan chi*").

curve rather than an actual circle. None of the eight *"kuei"* found in Fu Hao's tomb can be considered *kuei*. (fig. 42)[15] One of these is too fragmented to reconstruct its original shape. Another (No. 950) is actually a *ko* weapon whose haft portion is not clearly demarcated. The remaining six are what Wu Ta-ch'eng called *"wan kuei"* 琬圭, *"chen kuei"* 鎮圭, and *"yen kuei"* 琰圭. They all have sharp edges and lack the *"kuei* angle" so cannot be termed *kuei*. They are discussed below with weapons and implements. However, fourteen stone *kuei* and even more stone *chang* were recovered from the over 900 small burials in the western sector cemetery at Yin-hsü.[16] Fu Hao's tomb did not contain any *chang*. From this it is clear that *kuei* and *chang* were not among the ritual objects used by the aristocracy. The two slanted sides of some of these stone *kuei* were ground thin like blades, but they are not sharp and some have no edge at all, so it appears they were not weapons. The majority lack perforations so they do not appear to have been suspended. Their usage is unclear. It is not until the Warring States period that jade and stone *kuei* and *chang* became popular, and in literature *"kuei"* and *"chang"* became general terms for precious jades.

The many different kinds of *kuei* mentioned in *Chou Li* are distinguished by the addition of an adjective before the character *kuei*. For instance, based on size, color, and incised design, there are derived the so-called "large *kuei*," "blue-green *kuei*," "grain *kuei*" and *"chuan kuei"* 瑑圭. Sometimes the meaning is not discernible and one does not know whether the reference is to the type of jade material, its appearance, or its decoration. It may be that even the editors of *Chou Li* had no certain ideas about some of them. The commentaries of Han Confucianists are mostly purely literary exercises. Wu Ta-ch'eng was able to identify as many as six kinds of ancient *kuei* within his personal collection (see fig. 38, upper two rows). In reality, aside from the "grain *kuei*," which is a later piece, the remainder all belong to the category of sharp-edged weapons and lack the *kuei* point, so they cannot be considered *kuei*.

When ancient books such as *Chou Li* and *Shih Ching* refer to *kuei* and *pi* together, as they often do, this should be taken as referring to two different objects. Cheng Hsuan mistakenly explained it as "a *kuei* with a *pi* at its base," thus treating it as a single object—that is, a *pi* with a *kuei*-shaped projection from its circumference. The *Chou Li* also states "four

---

15. Ibid., p. 116, pl. 84.
16. K'ao-ku-hsüeh-pao 1979 (1): 105, fig. 79:1.

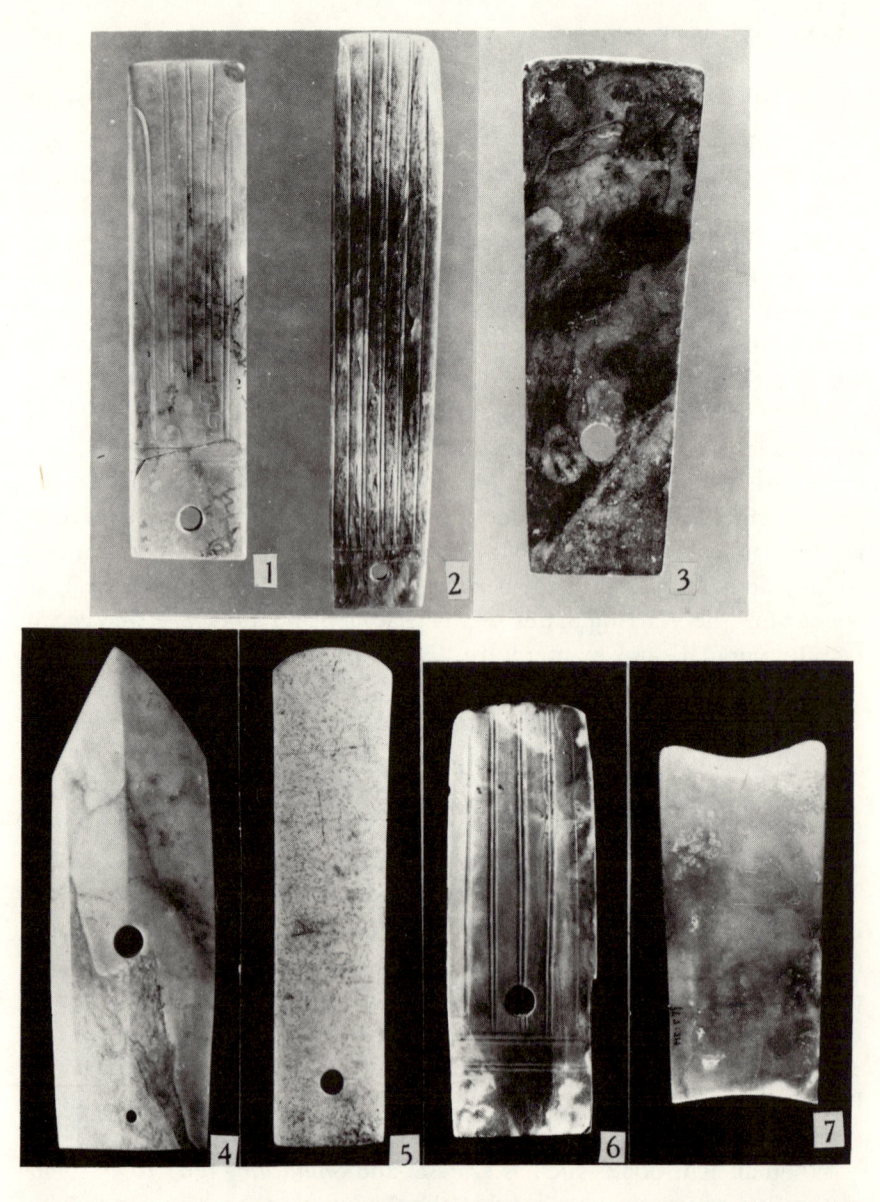

Fig. 42. The so-called jade *kuei* (all from Tomb Number Five at Yin-shü): (1, 2) axes; (3) spade; (4) *ko*-halberd, #950; (5, 6) axes; (7) knife-shaped end-edge implement.

kuei with base" and "two kuei with base" (Tien Jui 典瑞, Yü Jen 玉人). I agree with Na Chih-liang's interpretation of these two objects.[17] "Four kuei with base" should mean four kuei placed flat with their ends facing each other. Cheng Ssu-nung (Chung) 鄭司農 (眾) mistakenly explained this as "a single jade formed by a pi in the center and kuei at each of its four sides." This phrase "two kuei with base" some people believe to be the same as "four kuei with base"—that the base is a pi. Since Nieh Ch'ung-yi followed this explanation for his depiction in San Li T'u, later jade craftsmen reproduced the piece following these depictions either to meet the need in court reenactments of ancient rituals or to satisfy the demands of collectors of ancient jade. However, this kind of "kuei-pi," "two kuei with base," and "four kuei with base" jade is not to be found among pre-Ch'in jades. As for Hayashi Minao's claim that the Yin period handle-shaped jade ornaments are "large kuei"—these kinds of handle-shaped pieces are all small and their upper ends are not sharp like a kuei's, so ancient peoples would not have called them "large kuei." I shall leave this matter for the discussion of jade ornaments.

The third type of auspicious jade is chang 璋, which is like kuei but has a single sloping side at its end. For this reason it is said, "half of a kuei is a chang." Although there were no chang found in Fu Hao's tomb, 183 stone chang were unearthed in 41 of the over 900 small burials in the western sector cemetery of Yin-hsü. The largest number were found in two burials yielding twelve and thirteen, respectively.[18] Many fragmented stone chang were also found in the foundation of house #10 at Hsiao-t'un.[19] Some were ground thin at the smaller edge like a blade but were not sharpened. Some had no edge at all so were probably not weapons; however, neither do they seem to be auspicious jades. The one chang-shaped jade unearthed at Cheng-chou Erh-li-kang, and the two from Yen-shih Erh-li-t'ou, called "jade chang" in the preliminary report, are actually what we describe below as large end-edged tao-like implements. Some are as long as 66 centimeters and should be classed as weapons, but they could not have been weapons for actual use.[20] The ya chang 牙璋 in Ku Yü T'u K'ao 古玉圖考 is 27.7 centimeters long; it is also an end-edged tao-like implement. (fig. 43:1, 2).[21] None of these resemble the chang

17. Na 1980: 89–91, and in Ta-lu-tsa-chih 大陸雜誌, vol. 6, no. 12 (1953), p. 393.
18. K'ao-ku-hsüeh-pao 1979 (1): 105, fig. 79:1 left.
19. K'ao-ku 1976 (4): 266, 271.
20. Wen-wu 1966 (1): 58, with figure; K'ao-ku 1983 (3): 219, pl. 1:4.
21. T. C. Wu 1889: 21.

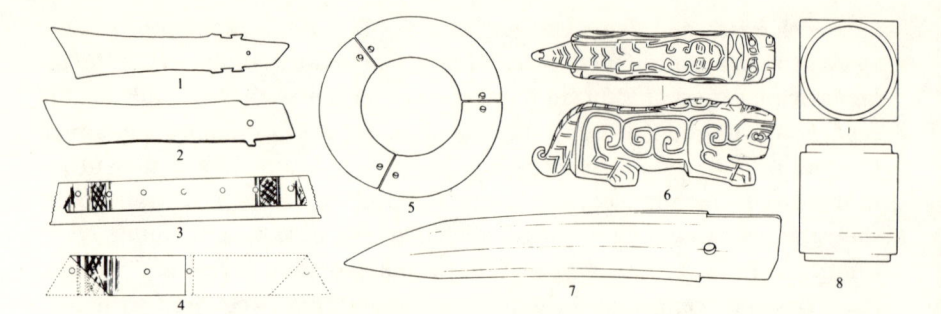

Fig. 43. Several types of jades: (1, 2) knife-shaped end-edge implements misidentified as "ya chang," from Erh-li-kang and *Ku Yü T'u K'ao*; (3, 4) knife-shaped side-edge implements misidentified as "pien chang," from Erh-li-t'ou and *Ku Yü T'u K'ao*; (5) *huang*, #901, 879, 1017 from Tomb Number Five at Yin-hsü; (6) *hu*, #409 from Tomb Number Five; (7) *ko*-halberd, #483 from Tomb Number Five; (8) *ts'ung*, #594 from Tomb Number Five.

described in *San Li*. The so-called "side *chang*" in *Ku Yü T'u K'ao* is actually the fragment of a large, multiperforated *tao*, similar to the whole seven-perforation jade *tao* unearthed at Erh-li-t'ou (fig. 43:3, 4).[22] Kuo Pao-chün 郭寶鈞 believed the two pieces entered in Huang Chün's 黃濬 *Ku Yü T'u Lu* to be the *chang* of Wu,[23] but they are also fragments of this kind of jade *tao*. They still, however, exhibit the sloping end with incised parallel and netted lines of a trapezoidal *tao*.

The fourth type of auspicious jade is the *ts'ung* 琮. *Shuo Wen*: "*Ts'ung*: an auspicious jade, eight *ts'un* large, resembles a chariot axle." Some Han Confucian commentaries believed it to be octagonal in cross-section, some square. On the Han stele *Six Jades Diagram* there are ones with eight, five, and ten angles (octagonal *ts'ung*, see fig. 37). What we find today is a kind of jade with a cylindrical central cavity and four squared sides. This is what *Ku Yü T'u P'u* (a forgery attributed to Lung Ta-yüan 龍大淵 of the Sung dynasty) called "an ancient jade axle nave," and Wu Ta-ch'eng determined to be a *ts'ung*. He also called a kind of shortish, incised jade "*tsu ts'ung*" 組琮. This kind of jade is perhaps a *ts'ung*. The Fu Hao tomb turned up fourteen examples of this type of jade, most relatively short.[24] The height:width ratio of five of these is approxi-

22. Ibid., pp. 19–20; K'ao-ku 1978 (4): 270, fig. 1:3.
23. C. Huang 1935: 11; P. C. Kuo 1949: 9–10.
24. Chung-kuo-she-hui-k'o-hsüeh-yüan K'ao-ku-yen-chiu-so 1980a: 115–16, pls. 81–82.

mately equal and their outer surfaces are smooth and lack incising. Seven are even shorter but all bear incised decorations. Some display the most commonly seen parallel grooved lines and circles carved on the outer edges of the piece, and some have cicada patterns or hemispherical projections (fig. 43:8). The remaining three *"ts'ung*-like jades" are degenerate *ts'ung*. The jade *ts'ung* previously found at Yin-hsü and other Shang sites are also all of the short type. As for the jades reported to be *"ts'ung"* found at the earlier site of Erh-li-t'ou, one is a fragment with incised decoration on adjacent sides of a corner; the other is cylindrical in appearance, round on both inside and outside. It should be regarded as a cylindrical jade bracelet.[25]

Among collected jade *ts'ung* there is a large kind that the *Ku Yü T'u K'ao* calls "large *ts'ung*." The carved decoration is the classic *"ts'ung"* pattern, but there are also undecorated examples and ones with only an abbreviated *"ts'ung"* pattern, lacking the circles and fine parallel lines. In the past it was generally believed that this kind of large *ts'ung* must postdate the Shang dynasty; however, recently quite a few of this large type of jade *ts'ung* have been found in burials of the Liang-chu culture (ca. 2000 B.C.) in southern Kiangsu. Six have been found in the cemetery at Shih-hsia in Ch'ü-chiang, Kwangtung, including both large and short types, which date to a time equivalent to the Liang-chu culture or the late Lung-shan culture period. Short *ts'ung* were also excavated at the late Lung-shan culture cemetery in T'ao-ssu, Hsiang-fen, Shansi.[26] They obviously arose relatively early, persisted throughout the Shang dynasty, and became rarer during the Chou dynasty. Although they have been found in early Western Han tombs, these were only recycled examples of old pieces that had been altered. After the Han they were made only by forgers.

According to *San Li* and the Han Confucian commentaries, *ts'ung* were used in sacrifices to the earth, placed on the belly when laying out the deceased, and presented by the various feudal lords to their ruler's wife at imperial audience. These uses were no more than the fabrications of Confucianists, as no such procedures were followed in the pre-Ch'in era. From their placements in tombs and rate of occurrence, it does not seem

---

25. K'ao-ku 1975 (5): 306, pl. 9:3, fig. 4:8.
26. For southern Kiangsu, see *Wen-wu-tzu-liao-ts'ung-k'an* 3 (1980): 10–12; for Shih-hsia in Ch'ü-chiang, see *Wen-wu* 1978 (7): 7–8, fig. 31–34; for T'ao-ssu in Hsiang-fen, see K'ao-ku 1980 (1): 29, pl. 6:7–8.

that the neolithic and Shang dynasty *ts'ung* were ritual objects used by the emperor in sacrificing to heaven and earth.

The fifth type of auspicious jade is the *huang* 璜, which is an arc-shaped jade. Han Confucians all believed that half of a *pi* was called a *huang*. In general, the *huang* of Yin date are one-third of a *pi*. The definition of Han Confucians is the product of idealization and systematization. Seventy-three jade *huang* were recovered from Fu Hao's tomb. The report states that the overwhelming majority are one-third of the *pi-huan* type, with only a small minority approaching one-half, "so the saying that 'one half of a *pi* is called *huang*' does not accord with the Yin period *huang*."[27] Actually, the *huang* imagined by Han Confucians agrees neither with the Yin system nor the Chou system.

The pendant *huang* began in the neolithic, with the majority having a small perforation drilled at both ends.[28] The Shang period *huang* are mostly made from the *pi-huan* type. Some of the plain *huang* from the Fu Hao tomb come in sets of two or three pieces which can be fitted together to form *pi*; some are equal to one-quarter of the whole circumference (fig. 43:5). These plain *huang* could have been either components of reassembled *pi-huan* or independent pendant ornaments. These latter are generally called pendant *huang*. After the basic shape has been formed, the majority are further carved into dragon or fish forms and then carved with scale or triangulate patterns on their surfaces. Most have fine perforations for suspension. (fig. 46:4) Wu Ta-ch'eng believed that the small and intermediate sized *huang* were pendant *huang*, while the larger ones were ritual objects used to sacrifice to the North. But this kind of large *huang* also bears fine perforations and could also have been used as pendant ornaments.

The sixth kind of auspicious jade is the *hu* 琥. It was the latest addition to the class of auspicious jades, making the "five auspicious" into the "six auspicious." In its manifestation as the White Tiger it was used to worship the West; and in its manifestation as the "tiger tally" it was used to launch military campaigns. Han Confucians all believed the *hu* to denote a tiger pattern or crouching tiger jade. But since this sort of form was not consistent with the geometric forms of the other five auspicious jades, the Han stele *Six Jades Diagram* usually substitutes the *mao* 瑁 for the *hu*, and the *Single Row Six Jades Stele* includes two *huang* to make up

---

27. Chung-kuo-she-hui-k'o-hsüeh-yüan K'ao-ku-yen-chiu-so 1980a: 122–28, pls. 95–103.
28. Hayashi 1969: 224, 225

SHANG DYNASTY JADES

the six pieces. Wu Ta-ch'eng took the *hu* to be a tiger-shaped or tiger pattern jade and even mistook a late Han to Six Dynasties jade pig to be a crouching tiger, calling it a *hu*.[29] I believe that jades decorated with tiger patterns on their surface should be named according to their overall form, adding the modifier "tiger-pattern" before the name. As to tiger-shaped jades, those with perforations may be called tiger-shaped jade pendants, and those lacking perforations ought to be recognized as toys or display pieces and simply be called jade tigers. Fu Hao's tomb yielded four jade tigers carved in the round and four in relief, all with fine perforations. They should be called tiger-shaped jade pendants (fig. 43:6). They belong to the ornament category and certainly were not used to launch troops or ward off drought; neither were they auspicious jades used in ceremony.

Pi, ts'ung, kuei, and *chang,* seemingly the nucleus of the *Chou Li*'s "Six Objects," are sometimes distinguished as the "Four Objects." In places the *Chou Li* only refers to these four, excluding the *huang* and *hu*.[30] Among the four, *pi* and *ts'ung* appeared earliest, existing by the neolithic period. The jade *pi* seems to have had its origin in the stone bracelet or round stone ax. It is still not clear what the origin and function of the *ts'ung* were. *Kuei* and *chang* appeared somewhat later, but were in existence by the Shang period. Most are carved of stone and generally do not have cutting edges so they could not have been weapons. They may, however, be related to the pointed straight-bodied *ko* and side-edged *tao* or slanted end-edged *tao*. As for *huang* and *hu*, during the Shang dynasty they were ornamental pieces used primarily as pendants.

WEAPONS AND IMPLEMENTS

Sharp or pointed implements are akin to weapons in form; a single piece was sometimes able to serve as both weapon and implement. Many weapons were used only for ceremonial purposes, not as functional items; however, they should still be considered weapons.

According to the form, placement, and function of the sharp-edged Shang pieces, we may classify them into five types: (1) pointed end-edge implements, such as *mao* 矛 (spear), and *tsu* 鏃 (arrowhead), which were used for puncturing; *ko* 戈 (halberd), which use both end-edge and two

---

29. T. C. Wu 1889: 73, "*Hu* No. 2."
30. See *Chou Li* 周禮, sections "Tien jui 典瑞" and "Yü jen 玉人."

side-edges, may also be included in this type; (2) flat (or arc) end-edge implements, such as *fu* 斧 (ax), *pen* 錛 (adze), *tsao* 鑿 (chisel), and *ch'an* 鏟 (spade), are used for chopping; (3) slanted end-edge small implements, such as *k'o tao* 刻刀 (engraving knife), are used for carving and incising; (4) tabular side-edge implements, such as the category of *tao* 刀 (knife); (5) *tao*-shaped end-edge implements, frequently occurring in large sizes.

Forty-seven jade *ko* were found in Fu Hao's tomb (originally reported as thirty-nine, but the one so-called "Type IV *kuei*," five so-called "*lien*," and two jade-blade bronze-haft *ko* in the bronze category, are all actually *ko* and should also be included). The *ko* form, like that of the early bronze *ko*, has a blade with nearly straight and opposed upper and lower sides and a triangular point. Overall length is generally from 21 to 40 centimeters. Near the *nei* 內 (stem-blade) there is often a perforation. Short, wide pieces lacking a division between blade and *nei* resemble *kuei*. Those whose lower edge curves slightly inward are termed "*lien*" 鐮 in reports but are actually also *ko*. Late Shang bronze *ko* are also mostly of this kind. There is another *ko* which is long and narrow like a *tao* and has an overall length of 44.2 centimeters (fig. 43:7, 44:3). Jade *ko* are often found in the intermediate and large tombs at Yin-hsü but rarely in the small tombs.[31] One relatively early jade *ko* found in a tomb at Erh-li-t'ou has a number of fine parallel lines incised between the blade and perforation.[32] Three jade *mao* heads were found in the Fu Hao tomb, two shaped like a leaf, and the other being a *mao*-like implement (on two sides of the piece are opposed sawteeth, and near the proximal end are two pairs of extruding railings) (fig. 44:4). One leaf-shaped *mao* head displays the remains of bronze corrosion on its lower end, where there originally must have been a bronze haft (fig. 44:5).[33] No jade *tsu* (arrowheads) were found in the Fu Hao tomb; however, reverse-barbed ones have been unearthed in other large tombs.[34]

Fu 斧, *pen* 錛, *tsao* 鑿, and *ch'an* 鏟 are among the Shang period flat end-edged jades. *Fu* has both a broad and narrow meaning. In the broad sense *fu* refers to all tabular, flat (or slightly arched) end-edged implements. Among these, those with unifacial edges are *pen*. Long and nar-

---

31. Chung-kuo-she-hui-k'o-hsüeh-yüan K'ao-ku-yen-chiu-so 1980a: 130–39, pls. 107–14.
32. K'ao-ku 1976 (4): 261–62, fig. 6:6, pl. 6.
33. Chung-kuo-she-hui-k'o-hsüeh-yüan K'ao-ku-yen-chiu-so 1980a: colorplate 19:2, pl. 117:2, pl. 114:1.
34. K'ao-ku-hsüeh-pao 5 (1951): 33; Liang and Kao 1962–76, esp. vol. 2, p. 118 and pl. 115:1, for R-1578 excavated from M 1001.

SHANG DYNASTY JADES

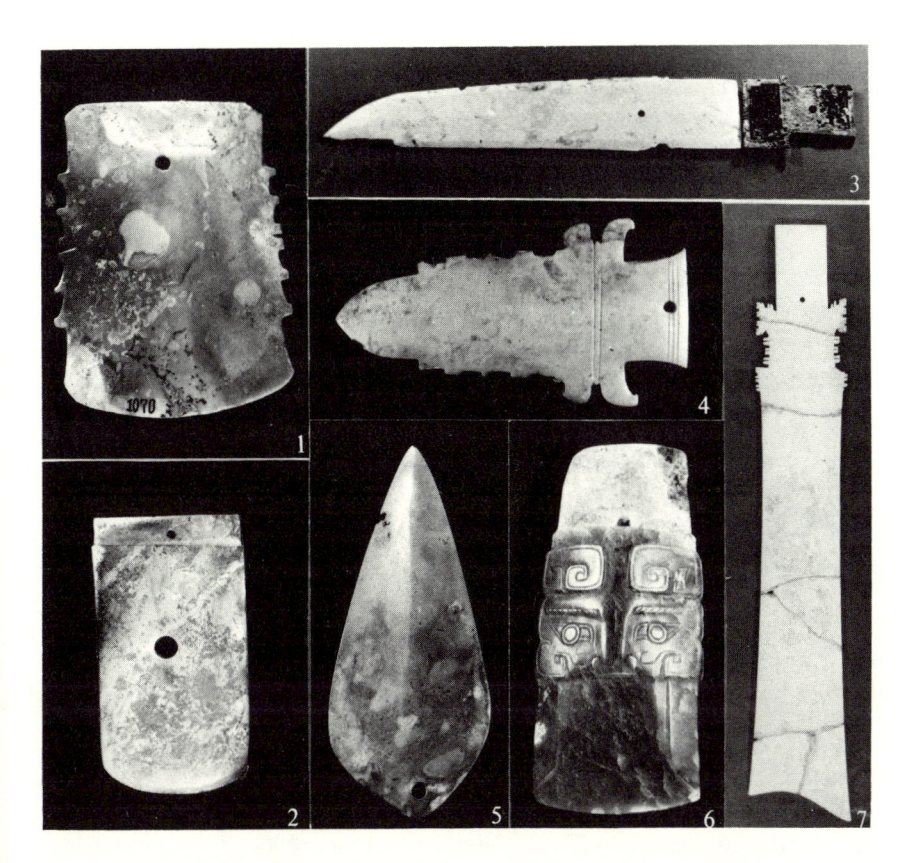

Fig. 44. Several types of jade weapons and implements: (1) *ch'i*, #1070 from Tomb Number Five at Yin-hsü; (2) *yüeh*, #463, from Tomb Number Five; (3) *ko*-halberd, #23 from Tomb Number Five; (4) *mao*, #481 from Tomb Number Five; (5) *mao*, #829 from Tomb Number Five; (6) ax, #920 from Tomb Number Five; (7) end-edge knife, from Erh-li-t'ou.

row *pen* or *fu* are *tsao*. In the narrow sense of the word, *fu* refers to relatively thick and heavy implements, with a thickness:width ratio approximately 2:1 or even thicker. Wide, flattened ones are called *ch'an*. *Ch'an* used as weapons are called flat *fu* or *yüeh*, often having round holes near the hafting end. In the Shang period their thickness was usually only 3 to 5 centimeters, and thickness:breadth ratio usually 1:5 to 1:10. Flat *fu* with serrate projections on two sides are sometimes called *ch'i* 戚. *Ch'i* made from *pi* are sometimes called *pi-ch'i*.

All of the types of *fu* discussed above have been found in the Fu Hao tomb. The expression in the report referring *"fu"* and *"fu liao"* 斧料 [35] uses the narrow sense of *fu* (fig. 44:6). The so-called Type I and Type II *"kuei,"* five altogether, are also *fu*. On one end they have an edge, on the other a perforation for hafting.[36] Among these are three with incised decorations that could not have been functional implements. Among those called *"pen,"* only one with a unifacial edge can be called *pen*; the other four are bifacial blades, three of which should be termed flat *fu*, and one *tsao*. The two *tsao* in addition to the one included among the *"pen"* (No. 919) yield a total of three. They are all relatively long and narrow. There are a total of five *"ch'an"* and *"ch'an*-like implements," all of which are flat *fu*. Among the flat *fu* are also the two called *"yüeh"* and the nine *ch'i* (including one *pi-ch'i*). So Fu Hao's tomb yielded as many as twenty-four flat *fu* of all types. In the *Shang Shu* document *Ku Ming* 顧命, there are the characters *"wan"* 琬 and *"yen"* 琰. The editors of *Chou Li* wrote *"wan kuei"* and *"yen kui."* Cheng Hsuan believed *"wan* is like *huan."* Wu Ta-ch'eng called the flat jade *fu* with arched blades *"wan kuei"* and the large *"wan kuei," "ta kuei"* or *"chen kuei."* In truth, none of them are *kuei*. This issue shall be put aside for discussion along with *"wan kuei"* when *tao*-like end-edge implements are talked about below. *Yüeh* and *ch'i* are also referred to in pre-Ch'in texts. The two are both *fu* types, but it is not clear what the distinguishing characteristics of the two are. *Shuo Wen*: *"yüeh* are large *fu."* If this is the ancient meaning, then *yüeh* should resemble the two large bronze *fu*, with length and width approximately 40 and 38 centimeters, respectively, unearthed from Fu Hao's tomb.[37] Whether or not the small flat jade *fu* (*yüeh*) (fig. 44:2) can also be called *yüeh* still seems to be a question. Wu Ta-ch'eng called the *yüeh* with extruding serrate fins on two sides *ch'i*.[38] Actually, this has no basis in fact. Certainly, we can adopt a popular, easily understood new name, such as flat *fu* and bilateral serrate flat *fu*; however we can also preserve the two names *yüeh* and *ch'i* because according to pre-Ch'in texts we can be sure that they originally belonged to the class of *fu*, unlike *"hsüan-chi"* and similar ancient names which are entirely unrelated to the ancient objects. The perforated flat *fu* (*yüeh*) had already appeared in our neolithic period;[39] however, the flat *fu* (*ch'i*)

---

35. Chung-kuo-she-hui-k'o-hsüeh-yüan K'ao-ku-yen-chiu-so 1980a: 114, pl. 117:3–4.
36. Ibid., pp. 116–18, fig. 69:1–3, pl. 84:1–2.
37. Ibid., pl. 105, pl. 66:1, colorplate 13:1.
38. T. C. Wu 1889: 59.
39. For example, the Lung-shan culture; see *K'ao-ku-hsüeh-pao* 2 (1947): 105, fig. 8:6–7.

SHANG DYNASTY JADES

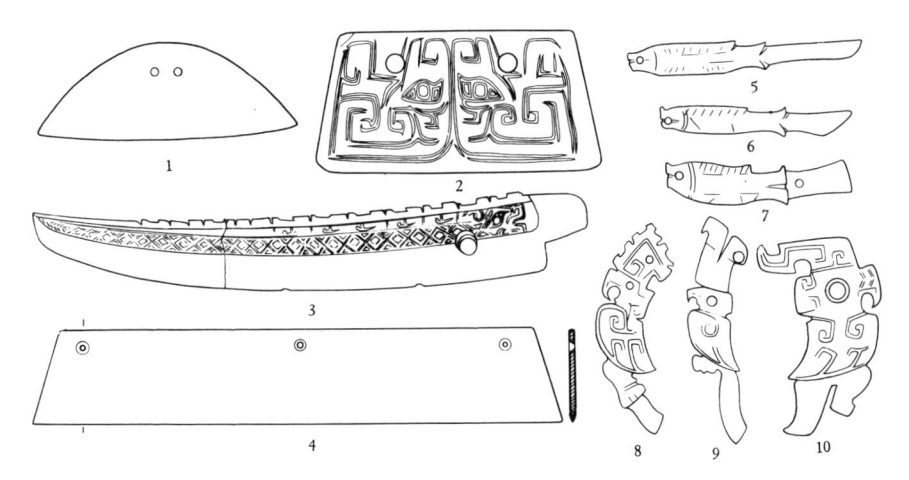

Fig. 45. Several types of jades from Tomb Number Five at Yin-hsü (except for #4): (1) semilunar knife, #559; (2) trapezoidal knife, #918; (3) knife, #501; (4) knife with three holes, from Erh-li-t'ou; (5–7) engraving knives with fish design, #421, 954, 420; (8–10) engraving knives with bird design, #956, 955, 599.

with serrations on two sides began in the Shang period, seen earliest in Yen-shih Erh-li-t'ou tombs.[40] The *pi-ch'i* is also found earliest in Erh-li-t'ou tombs, both examples alike in that their blade portions are partitioned into four sectors.[41] The Fu Hao tomb had seven *ch'i* and one *pi-ch'i* (fig. 44:1).[42]

The third category, jade *k'o tao*, is represented by twenty-three examples in the tomb of Fu Hao.[43] Two of these have awl-shaped handles, and the remaining twenty-one have handles carved into various kinds of animal figures. The greatest number are fish (eleven), next are birds (seven), followed by lizards (two), and *k'uei* dragon (one). The blade projects from the end of the animal's tail, with a ground-out slanted cutting edge. There are small perforations on the handles of most of them, so that they could have been suspended (fig. 45:5–10). Since the carving of the animal figures was accomplished with great artistry, they may also be considered to be pendant ornaments.

The fourth category is the side-edged implements of the *tao* category, which may be divided into two varieties: one is the pointed tabular form

---

40. K'ao-ku 1978 (4): 270, pl. 12:2. Referred to as *"yüeh"* in the original report.
41. K'ao-ku 1976 (4): 262, fig. 6:3–4. Referred to as *"yüeh"* in the original report.
42. Chung-kuo-she-hui-k'o-hsüeh-yüan K'ao-ku-yen-chiu-so 1980a: 140, pls. 115, 116.
43. Ibid., pp. 143–46, pls. 120, 121.

with straight back and convex edge, the other end often having a square (or rectangular) haft portion to which a handle could have been secured. The other variety is rectangular (including trapezoidal) or semilunar, with a perforation or multiperforations near the back. The former variety is primarily an imitation in jade of the bronze curved *tao*. It first appeared in the Shang dynasty. Seven of these were found in the Fu Hao tomb (fig. 45:3).[44] An exquisite example among these displays carved decoration on the blade face and a serrate flange along the back. Among the latter variety one each of the trapezoidal and semilunar scraping *tao* were found in the Fu Hao tomb (fig. 45:1, 2).[45] Near the back they all had an alignment of two perforations similar to the modern-day North Chinese *chao lien* 爪鐮 (claw sickle). This kind of *tao* in stone was already widely used in the Chinese Neolithic; however, in the Shang period jade examples are still rare. A kind of large multiperforation trapezoidal jade *tao* was also in use in the early Shang dynasty. None were unearthed from Fu Hao's tomb, but two were found at Erh-li-t'ou. One had three perforations and the other seven. Overall lengths are 52 and 65 centimeters with the cutting-edge placed on the longer side (fig. 45:4, 43:3).[46] Two *tao* with three and five perforations, respectively, made of black jade, were found at the site of Shih-mao in Shensi, Yü-lin District, Shen-mu County. Their total lengths are 49 and 55 centimeters.[47] Wu Ta-ch'eng called this kind of jade "*hu*" 笏.[48] However, it really belongs to the *tao* category, having its origins in the neolithic multiperforation stone *tao*. It still retained the side-edge and could definitely not have been the *hu* grasped by high ministers at court audiences. What Wu Ta-ch'eng called the "side *chang*" is a fragment of this kind of jade *tao*: We discussed this matter in the preceding section on *chang*.

The fifth category is *tao*-shaped end-edge implements. Their form resembles that of the flat, tabular *tao*; however, the cutting-edge is not on the long side but rather on the relatively broad tail end. It possesses a slanted or flat edge, often slightly concave so as to form an arc. The haft portion is square, frequently with a small perforation. Between the haft and the blade there is a section bearing a projecting guard or serrate fin

---

44. Ibid., pp. 141, 142–43, fig. 74:2, fig. 76:6–7, colorplates 19:3, 20:3.
45. Ibid., p. 143, pl. 118:3 (trapezoidal), pl. 126:1, lower (semilunar).
46. K'ao-ku 1975 (5): 305, fig. 4:10, pl. 8:9; K'ao-ku 1978 (4): 270, fig. 1:3.
47. K'ao-ku 1977 (3): 155, fig. 2:5–6, fig. 3:1–2. Referred to as "shan tao 戔刀" in the brief report.
48. T. C. Wu 1889:17–18.

on the edge of both sides. Between the fins are commonly parallel incised straight lines. The "Type III *kuei*" from Fu Hao's tomb is black-green in color, and what remains of it is 12.5 centimeters long. According to the report "its shape resembles a *'yen kuei.'*"[49] Actually, it is a fragment of this type of *tao*-like end-edge implement. It lacks the haft portion, but retains the body and edge portions. Recently over five of this kind of jade were discovered in "Shang period" tombs in Yü-lin District, Shensi, all made of black jade. The two that have already been published have one perforation in their haft portion. One is 30 centimeters long with both edges straight and smooth; the other is 35 centimeters long, with serrate fins on both sides near the haft.[50] One has also been recovered from an Erh-li-t'ou burial. It is 48 centimeters long (fig. 44:7).[51] This type of jade has been unearthed in the past, and there are a good number existing in collections today as well. Wu Ta-ch'eng called those jades with concave arc end-edge and pointed corners "*yen kuei*," and those with slanted distal ends and guards near the haft "*ya chang*" 牙璋.[52] Ling Shun-sheng 凌純聲 called both of them "*yen kuei.*"[53] The "*wan kuei*" and "*yen kuei*" of the *Chou Li* originated from the phrase "*hung pi wan yen*" 弘璧琬琰 in the *Ku Ming* document of the *Shang Shu*. The latter two characters do not necessarily refer to two different objects, as they are written together, and neither is it possible to determine whether or not they belong to the category of *kuei*. There is no clear explanation in *Chou Li* as to how to distinguish the two. The Han Confucian Cheng Chung took the presence or absence of a sharp edge as the criterion for differentiating the two. This is due to the fact that *wan* was read as its homonym *wan shun* 婉順 (obliging in all directions), and *yen* for *yen shang* 剡上 (sharpen the upper end). This is yet another example of Han Confucian annotation by literary invention. This kind of jade has an end-edge and a haft for securing a handle and could not have been the *kuei* grasped in the hand at court audience. It was already rare by the Yin Period, so the *Chou Li* editors in Warring States times had probably never seen one. They could not have been included in the ritual jades. It is most appropriate if we temporarily call it a *tao*-shaped end-edge implement. We are still not clear about its ancient name and function.

49. Chung-kuo-she-hui-k'o-hsüeh-yüan K'ao-ku-yen-chiu-so 1980a: 118, pl. 84:1.
50. K'ao-ku 1977 (3): 155, fig. 2:2, pl. 4:5. Referred to as "*ch'an* 鏟," or spade, in the brief report.
51. K'ao-ku 1978 (4): 270, fig. 2:1. Referred to as "yü li tao 玉立刀" in the brief report.
52. T. C. Wu 1889: 14, 21, 22.
53. Ling 1965: 200.

ORNAMENTS

Shang period jade ornaments may be divided into two large categories. The first includes functional items which have been embellished with carved decoration or given a polish in order to enhance their aesthetic appearance; the second includes art objects. As yet no large artistic carvings in jade are known from the Shang dynasty (there are several relatively large carvings in the round, but all are of marble). They are all small; those with perforations were most likely pendant ornaments and those without were display objects. Among the latter, some pieces possess mortices, tenons, or grooves that were probably used for attaching the piece to another object. They are ornaments, but we do not rule out the possibility that they also possessed some amuletic or other magic significance.

The *k'o tao* with animal-shaped handles mentioned above belongs to the former category. Relatively numerous at Yin-hsü among this category of decorated functional pieces is a kind of handle-shaped object. As many as thirty-three were found in Fu Hao's tomb alone. They are flat and tabular or square in cross section with varying lengths and thicknesses, but all are small. Several groups of flower petal patterns are commonly carved on the body of the piece. The distal end narrows to form a tenon on which there is a small perforation (fig. 46:4).[54] Some people have identified them as "zither plectrums" and some call them "large *kuei*," but both these views are erroneous. Although its ancient name has not yet been determined, it may simply be termed "handle-shaped object" in the meantime. Two were found in Erh-li-t'ou tombs.[55] In Shang burials they are placed together with other pendant ornaments and personal weapons, by the chest or waist of the deceased.[56] So they appear to have been pendant ornaments. Since the tenon is small and short, there was possibly some object inserted on or bound to the distal end. No large examples of this kind have been found. We do not know its ancient name and function.

Among the decorated functional jades unearthed from the Fu Hao tomb, there are also one pigment-mixing tray (fig. 47:1), two combs, two jade ladles, and one fragmentary handle. There is carved decoration on

---

54. Chung-kuo-she-hui-k'o-hsüeh-yüan K'ao-ku-yen-chiu-so 1980a: 178–80, pls. 156–59.
55. K'ao-ku 1976 (4): 262, fig. 6:1, fig. 6:5, pl. 6:2 (the two items on the right).
56. K'ao-ku-hsüeh-pao 1981 (4): 494–506, 1979 (1): 47.

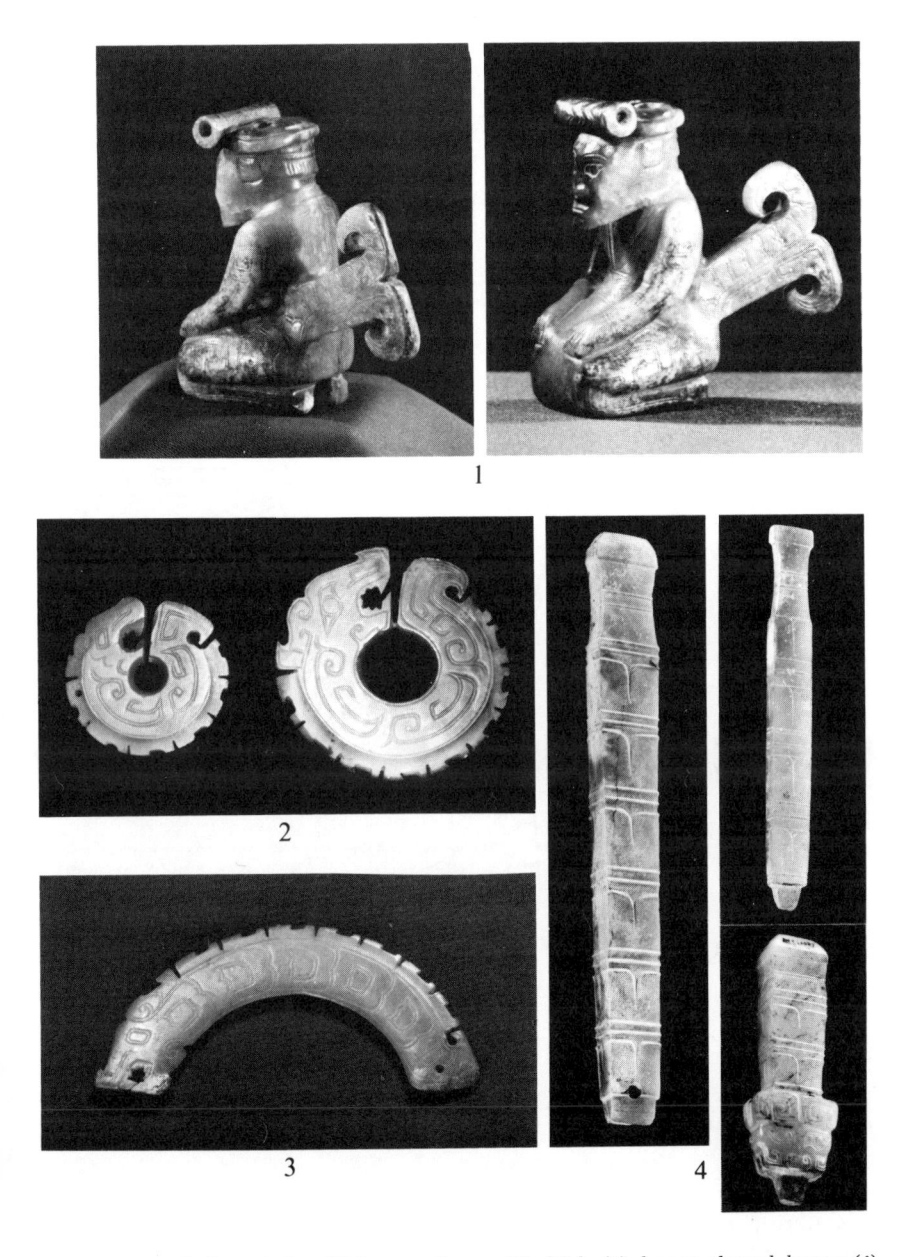

Fig. 46. Several Shang jades: (1) human figure; (2) *chüeh*; (3) dragon-shaped *huang*; (4) handle-shaped objects.

Fig. 47. Several jade objects: (1) pigment-mixing dish; (2, 3) *kuei*-vessels; (4) the use of *pan-chih*; (5) *pan-chih*.

their haft or back portions.⁵⁷ Some other functional items include a *pan-chih* 扳指 (*she* 韘) for drawing a bowstring, decorated with an animal design (fig. 47:4, 5); and two horn-shaped pendant ornaments, perhaps the so-called "*hsi*" 觿 used in ancient times for untying knots. There are

57. For the pigment tray and other containers, see Chung-kuo-she-hui-k'o-hsüeh-yüan K'ao-ku-yen-chiu-so 1980a: 149–50, pls. 127:1–2, 128:1–2.

also twenty-two disk-shaped spindle whorls with central perforations, in varying sizes and thicknesses. They seem to be made from the drill plug that is a by-product of *pi-huan* manufacture. There are also twenty-eight hoop-shaped ornaments which resemble the cylindrical bracelets but on their sides have one or two nail holes, perhaps used to secure them to wooden poles as ornaments.[58]

Aside from suspended ornaments, other personal ornaments of jade found in the Fu Hao tomb include bracelets (eighteen), hairpins (twenty-eight), earrings (four), pendants (thirty-eight), and beads (thirty-three).[59] The jade bracelets are wide-walled circlets similar to the later gold and silver bracelets. The hairpins are the *tsan* 簪 of later times, used to pin swept-up hair into place. The difference is in the head portion: some are flat-topped, some have a round tenon or mortise hole, and some are carved into the shape of a *k'uei* dragon. Earrings have been discussed in the section on *pi-huan*. Pendants are mostly tubular, one end relatively straight, the other with a flared mouth, and the outer surface is often carved with simple designs. Beads include both tubular and round varieties.

The second large category is small art objects, including suspended ornaments, inserted and inlaid ornaments, and display pieces. The Fu Hao tomb produced as many as 188 items of this category.[60] Their realistic and lively representations make them graceful artistic creations; some are exquisite pieces of a sort never before seen. They are among the greatest rewards of this excavation. Carved in the shape of different varieties of animal, some are real animals, some imaginative depictions of mythical creatures, including the dragon and phoenix (fig. 48). Of the *huang* (43), *chüeh* (14), and *k'o tao* (21) discussed before, the majority bear relief carvings of all sorts of animal forms. If all of these are combined, there is a total of 266 pieces, representing 35.5 percent of the total of 755 pieces excavated from the tomb.

Of the 188 small art objects, the suspended ornaments have small perforations for suspension by a cord; the insert and inlay piece lack perforations but bear tenons and mortises. Both carving in the round and relief carving were employed in the carving of the two kinds of orna-

---

58. Ibid., 194, pl. 164:3–4 (鐲); 191, pl. 163:2 (鶴); 146–47, pls. 122–24 (spindle-whorl); 185–88, pl. 154 (cylindrical ornament).

59. Ibid., 176–78, pl. 149 (bracelet); 174–76, pl. 148 (hairpin); 181–83, pl. 151 (pendant); 204, colorplate 36:1 (bead-string).

60. Ibid., 150–74, colorplates 22–34.

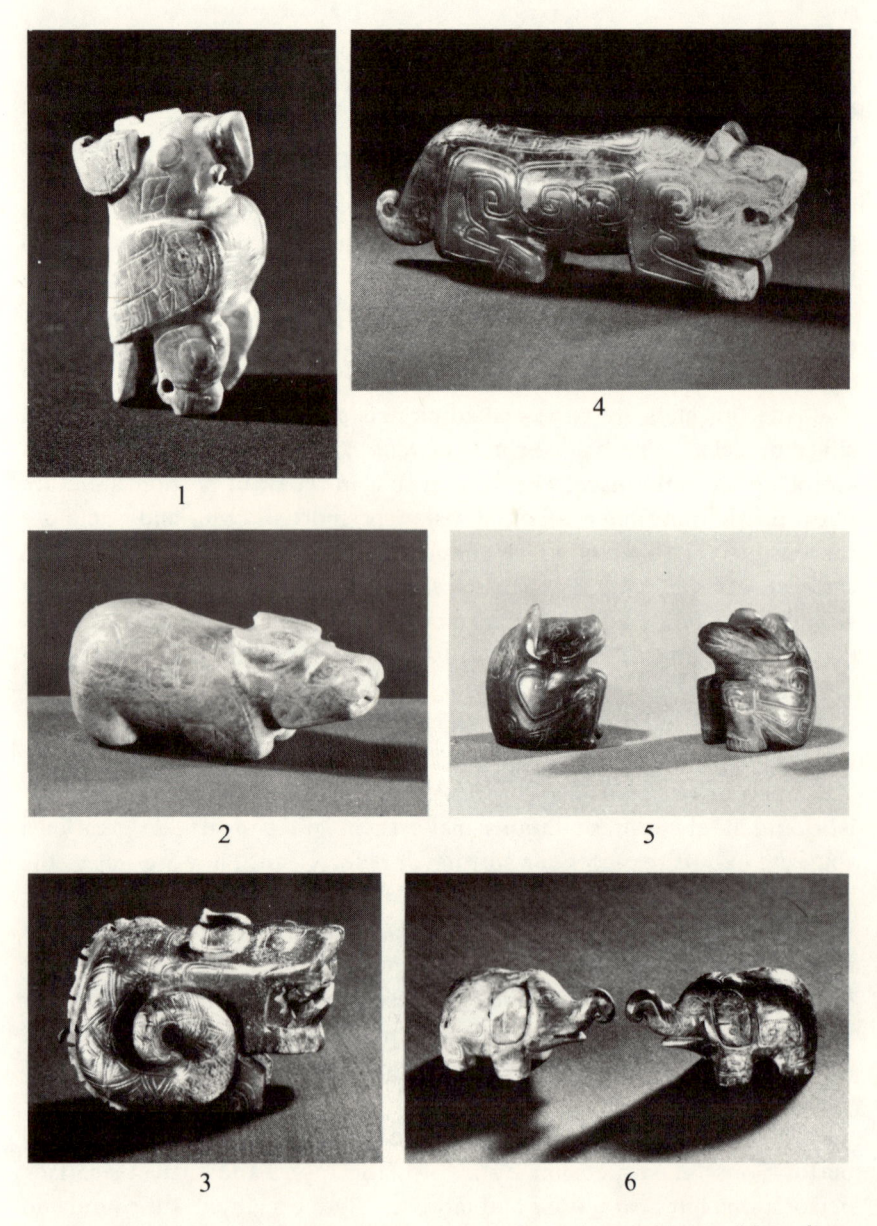

Fig. 48. Shang dynasty jade animals: (1) owl; (2) cattle; (3) dragon; (4) tiger; (5) two bears; (6) two elephants.

ment. The few artistic display pieces are all small carvings in the round which must have been displayed on a table for appreciation. They lack the small perforations as well as mortises and tenons.

As far as subject matter is concerned, in addition to as many as 25 different kinds of animals, there are human figures, mythical creatures, and silkworms. The fish category is the largest (75) and birds next (49; parrots and owls the most common). But it is the human figures (13) that have attracted the greatest interest. (fig. 46:1). The jade figures not only display great artistry, they provide material bearing on our knowledge of the Shang dynasty people's hairstyles, fashion, posture, and racial characteristics, and the appearance of the various classes of people in the contemporary society. However, the expressions of the jade figures are a little wooden and their carriage is overly mannered. For this reason they do not, on the other hand, compare to some of the animal figures in terms of the grace and liveliness that imbues them with the feeling of a beast galloping, a bird flying, or fish darting about. The analysis of their artistic style and design patterns and inquiry into their symbolic meaning are topics beyond the scope of this chapter.

Lastly, I will say something about jade vessels. One blue-green and one white jade *kuei* vessel of exquisite design and decoration were found in the Fu Hao tomb (fig. 47:2, 3).[61] Besides these, there is also a single, undecorated jade *p'an*. Pre-Ch'in literature does refer to jade vessels and there are several among collected pieces. However, since we have rarely encountered them in archaeological excavations, some people believed that the pre-Ch'in craftsmen perhaps did not possess the means with which to carve vessels out of jade. Examples that were known, such as jade *kuei*, may have been executed by Han dynasty jade craftsmen "based on the writings of Warring States authors."[62] Due to the excavations of the Fu Hao tomb, we now know that in addition to the reproductions of latter-day craftsmen, the Shang dynasty craftsmen also produced carved vessels of jade. The two *kuei* vessels were possibly ritual vessels used in sacrifices, but they are not auspicious jades.

My intention in this essay was not to present a comprehensive discussion which touched on each and every Shang dynasty jade, but rather to point out, from an archaeological perspective, a new path for

---

61. Ibid., 130, figs. 71, 72, colorplate 14:1–2.
62. P. C. Kuo 1949: 38.

research into the classification, nomenclature, and function of these jades.[63]

    63. In addition to the scholarly works specifically referenced in the footnotes, I have consulted the following titles in writing this article: Nieh 1935; Hsia 1983; Umehara 1955; C. Huang 1935; C. F. Yang 1982; Hamada 1925; Dohrenwend 1971; Laufer 1912; Loehr 1975; Hansford 1950, 1968; Na 1977; Salmony 1952, 1963; Rawson and Ayers 1975; Willetts 1958.

10

A Reexamination of the Relationship between Bronzes of the Shang Culture and of the Northern Zone

Lin Yün

The relation between bronzes of the Shang Culture and of the Northern Zone is a problem that long ago drew the interest of scholars around the world. The Chinese scholar Kao Ch'ü-hsün wrote a broad introduction to the viewpoints of specialists up to 1950.[1] The Soviet scholar Kiselev, who had done a great deal of archaeological work in southern Siberia and Mongolia, explored the relation between the Chinese Shang culture and bronze cultures within the Soviet Union; his views had a distinct influence on Chinese archaeological circles.

Since the 1960s there has been much progress both in excavation work and in the publication of material for southern Siberia, the Yellow River drainage, and the area in between. This progress is seen especially in the region north of the distribution of Shang culture, namely, the Northern Zone of China, where numerous significant new discoveries have been made. These have increased the potential for advancing the exploration of the relationship between bronzes of the Shang culture and various bronze cultures of northern Asia. The intent of this article is to use the recent accomplishments of Shang archaeology in China as a starting point for addressing this problem.

1. C. H. Kao 1958.

THE NORTHERN FRONTIER OF SHANG CULTURE

The Shang culture that had a history of 496 years, according to the *Bamboo Annals*, was first recognized in modern archaeology through the excavations at Yin-hsü. But the Yin-hsü culture had a history of just 273 years and cannot possibly represent the entire Shang culture. Following the excavations at Erh-li-kang in Cheng-chou, the predecessor of the Yin-hsü culture—the Erh-li-kang culture—has also been identified as Shang culture. Moreover, the characteristics and chronology of the ceramic assemblages of the Erh-li-kang Shang culture and the Yin-hsü Shang culture are now fairly well understood.

The famous site at T'ai-hsi-ts'un in Kao-ch'eng, Hopei, includes separate strata belonging to the late Erh-li-kang culture and the early Yin-hsü culture.[2] But it is by no means the northernmost point in the distribution of the Erh-li-kang culture. Cheng Shao-tsung reports that at Yao-chuang in Man-ch'eng there are "early Shang cultural strata."[3] Tsou Heng also states: "According to what is known from recent excavations, at its farthest north it reaches the Chü-ma River."[4] In fact, pottery of the Erh-li-kang culture has been excavated in the Chang-chia-k'ou region, still farther north.[5] Moreover, bronzes in the Erh-li-kang style have been discovered not only in Yao-chuang in Man-ch'eng[6] and at Liu-chia-ho in P'ing-ku,[7] but even in the Ch'ao-yang district of Liaoning.[8] In the northwest, sites of the Erh-li-kang culture are distributed through southeastern and southwestern Shansi; a grave with typical late Erh-li-kang bronzes was discovered in the northern suburbs of Ch'ang-tzu;[9] a group of structures and a city wall of the Erh-li-kang culture were excavated at Tung-hsia-feng in Hsia-hsien.[10] Most recently, a cultural stratum containing Erh-li-kang pottery in association with local ceramics was discovered at T'ai-ku in the middle of Shansi. In the west the Erh-li-kang culture is distributed westward along the valley of the Wei River; sites of

2. K'ao-ku-hsüeh-pao 1979.
3. Hopei Province Museum 1980: 26.
4. Tsou 1980: 126.
5. K'ao-ku-yü-wen-wu 1982, fig. 5:4, 5.
6. Hopei Province Museum 1980: pl. 45.
7. Wen-wu 1977c.
8. Wen-wu Editorial Committee 1979, p. 39, fig. 4.
9. Y. Kuo 1980.
10. K'ao-ku 1980.

the culture have been found at Nan-sha-ts'un in Hua-hsien[11] and Huai-chen-feng in Lan-t'ien,[12] while a ceramic assemblage very similar to the Erh-li-kang culture was discovered still farther west at the Pai-chia-yao Reservoir in Fu-feng.[13] As for single bronze vessels, not only was an Erh-li-kang style bronze *ting* found in the southern part of the loess plateau at T'ung-ch'uan,[14] but a late Erh-li-kang bronze *ku* was unearthed at Tzu-ch'ang in the northern part of the loess plateau.[15]

In sum, the bearers of the Erh-li-kang Shang culture followed the eastern flank of the Taihang Mountains. They spread up the course of the Yellow River and westward along the Wei River to form a pincerlike encirclement around the southeastern loess plateau. They permeated into the southeastern loess plateau at least as far as central Shansi by means of various valleys.

However, by the Yin-hsü period this northwestern expansion of the Shang culture had lost impetus. Admittedly Yin-hsü style bronzes were distributed deep into the heart of the loess plateau, reaching the region of Hsin-hsien,[16] Pao-te,[17] Sui-te,[18] and Ch'ing-chien;[19] they also reached westward as far as Pao-chi,[20] and north as far as K'o-shih-k'o-t'eng Banner in Inner Mongolia. Nonetheless, these individual bronzes, cut off from the ceramic assemblage of the Yin-hsü culture, should not serve as the basis for discussing the extent of the Yin-hsü culture. The Wei River drainage has already been studied rather completely; it can be established that the predynastic Chou culture here is clearly distinct from the Yin-hsü culture in its basic ceramic assemblage, that it corresponds in time to the second Ta-ssu-k'ung-ts'un phase at Yin-hsü, and that it has already become a distinct culture. Among the bronzes of this culture, some are in Yin-hsü style, but some have their own characteristics.[21] And among the Yin-hsü style vessels found in the Wei River drainage, a certain number were brought as plunder after King Wu overthrew the Shang. For

11. Tsou 1980: 334.
12. Fan and Wu 1980; K'ao-ku-yü-wen-wu 1981.
13. H. C. Lo 1977.
14. K'ao-ku 1982a; Shensi Province Institute of Archaeology 1979: pl. 3.
15. Shensi Province Institute of Archaeology 1979: pl. 4.
16. K'ao-ku 1976a.
17. C. L. Wu 1972.
18. C. Y. Chu 1975; Shensi Province Institute of Archaeology 1979: pls. 79–92.
19. Y. H. Tai 1980; Shensi Province Institute of Archaeology 1979: pls. 61–66, 67–68.
20. K. Y. Wang 1975.
21. Tsou 1980, chap. 7.

example, of the bronzes excavated in the winter of 1973 from grave number M 1 at Ho-chia-ts'un in Ch'i-shan,[22] the *chia* and *p'o* clearly belong to the transitional form from Erh-li-kang to early Yin-hsü, while the *kuei* and *yu* are of the late Yin-hsü style. Inscribed on the *p'o*, *kuei*, and *yu* are three different Shang clan emblems. The association of these bronzes, from different periods and belonging to three Shang patriclans, in one grave in ancient Chou territory, can be explained only by the victor's distribution of war booty.

Given this experience in the Wei River drainage, it is fairly easy to clarify the problem for other regions where Yin-hsü style bronzes are distributed.

A great many bronzes of the Yin-hsü style have been discovered in the part of Shansi around Shih-lou[23] and Yung-ho.[24] Most can be identified as mortuary offerings from graves, but the occupants of the graves, judging by the peculiar gold ear ornaments and bow-shaped finials (?), clearly were not Shang. The associated bronzes have features different from Yin-hsü in their typology, manufacture, and ornamentation (see below). Moreover, no pottery of the Yin-hsü culture has yet been discovered in the southwestern part of Shansi where the Erh-li-kang culture is distributed. The *Tso Chuan* records that when T'ang Shu was enfeoffed in Chin, he was supposed to treat his subjects by *ch'i yi Hsia cheng*, *chiang yi Jung suo* (use the Hsia orthodoxy to lead, use the Jung practices to control); this reflects the fact that this region was not occupied by the Shang in the Late Shang period. A group of late Yin-hsü bronzes unearthed from a grave in Ling-shih in 1976[25] exhibits four altogether different clan emblems. This can be explained by the division of war spoils among those participating in the military alliance that overthrew the Shang and thereby does not constitute proof that the Shang occupied southern Shansi in the late Yin-hsü period.

Yin-hsü style bronzes found in northern Hopei, western Liaoning, and in Ju Ud League likewise were not associated with Yin-hsü pottery. A whole group of bronzes was unearthed from one grave at Liu-chia-ho in P'ing-ku, Peking. These included typical late Erh-li-kang specimens, but most are transitional forms between Erh-li-kang and Yin-hsü. However,

---

22. K'ao-ku 1976a; Shensi Province Institute of Archaeology 1979: pls. 22–40.
23. Wen-wu 1958; S. S. Yang 1959; Hsieh and Yang 1960; Y. Kuo 1962; K'ao-ku 1972b; S. S. Yang 1981b.
24. K'ao-ku 1977c.
25. T. T. Tai 1980.

the date of the grave, by the stylistically latest *chüeh*,[26] may be as late as the second Ta-ssu-k'ung-ts'un phase. The occupant of this grave used funnel-shaped gold earrings and gold bracelets shaped like fan covers at the ends; clearly he, too, was not a Shang. A late Yin-hsü style bronze *ting* and bow-shaped object were found at Tung-yen-ko-chuang, Lu-lung in 1972;[27] similar gold bracelets were found here as well (according to the exhibit in the 1973 "Exhibition of Relics Unearthed in Hopei" in Shih-chia-chuang, a *kuei* decorated with cloud spirals and knobs was found at the same spot). This kind of gold bracelet has been found in so-called Wei-ying-tzu Type graves at Ho-shang-kou in K'a-tso.

Similar bronze earrings have frequently been unearthed from sites and graves of the Lower Hsia-chia-tien culture;[28] the archaeology department of Peking University also excavated some gold ones from a grave at Hsüeh in Ch'ang-p'ing.[29] There was an important change in culture in the broad area of distribution of the Lower Hsia-chia-tien culture during the time of the Yin-hsü culture: this area produced a distinct Wei-ying-tzu Type[30] and similar remains with a fairly broad distribution. The southern boundary of these remains must await further verification. At present, however, it is reliably known that within Hopei sites of the Yin-hsü culture yielding ceramics later than the second phase at Ta-ssu-k'ung-ts'un are concentrated in the area around and south of Hsing-t'ai. Initial Chou bronzes recently found in Yüan-shih bear inscriptions recording battles against the Jung by the Marquis of Hsing in this region in the initial Chou period. The general situation of the region in the late Shang period can be inferred from all of this.

Thus it is apparent that by the Yin-hsü period the area of distribution of the Shang culture came under pressure from the predynastic Chou culture in the west and retreated eastward; its northern border shifted southward. A concurrent phenomenon was the broad dissemination of bronzes of the Northern Complex across the Northern Zone.

CHINESE BRONZES OF THE NORTHERN COMPLEX

A regional analysis of just the bronze artifacts throughout the Shang–Chou period yields two different complexes of bronzes in the area north

26. Wen-wu 1977c, fig. 28.
27. Hopei Province Museum 1980, pls. 79–80.
28. C. M. An 1954: 77; K'ao-ku 1976b, fig. 4:2; Wen-wu-tzu-liao-ts'ung-k'an 1977b: fig. 17:3.
29. Peking University Archaeology Program 1979: 135.
30. K'ao-ku 1982b.

of the distribution of the Shang and Chou bronzes (the Chung-yüan, or Central Plains, Complex). These may be differentiated as the bronzes of the Northern Complex and those of the Northeastern Complex.

Bronzes of the Northeastern Complex appeared during the latter part of the Western Chou period, while Northern Complex bronzes were already well developed during the time of the Yin-hsü culture in the Shang period. Bronzes of the latter complex within China were once called "Sui-yüan bronzes" or "Ordos bronzes." However, their range far exceeds the Ordos region. In addition, their duration was so long that, from what is now known, they can be divided into three major periods. The upper limit of the first period is not yet very clear, while the lower limit can be set in the early Western Chou period. The bronzes of this complex from the early Western Chou grave at Pai-fu-ts'un in Ch'ang-p'ing, Peking municipality, can be seen as late forms of the first period. Three implements—daggers, battle-axes with tubular sockets, and knives—represent bronzes of the Northern Complex in the first period (fig. 49).

Daggers

The Shang culture had no bronze daggers of its own. According to the opinion of Su Pai, the sword with willow-leaf blade and flat stem may have originated on the Iranian plateau. It requires a separate hilt. That of the Northern Complex is characterized by the integral casting of the bronze hilt and hand-guard; moreover, daggers of the first period feature a relatively narrow, straight hand-guard. The examples from Lin-che-yü in Pao-te[31] and Kao-hung in Liu-lin[32] can be dated to the Shang period by the associated bronzes of Yin-hsü style. The six examples from the wood-chambered tomb in Pai-fu-ts'un, Ch'ang-p'ing, can be assigned to the initial Chou by associated items (the wood chamber has a carbon 14 date of 1120 ± 90 B.C.). Those from Pai-fu, except one example without hand-guard, all have a distinct notch on the blade near the point where the hand-guard meets the blade; all six have hollow, perforated hilts; these reflect characteristics of late date. The pommels of hilts in this period come in many forms. Aside from single examples of rattle pommels from Lin-che-yü and Kao-hung, one was collected in Chang-pei, Hopei, in 1967 (exhibited in "Exhibition of Cultural Relics Unearthed in Hopei"), one was unearthed in Ejin Horo League, Inner Mongolia (Museum of

---

31. C. L. Wu 1972: pl. 6:5.
32. S. S. Yang 1981b: pl. 5:1.

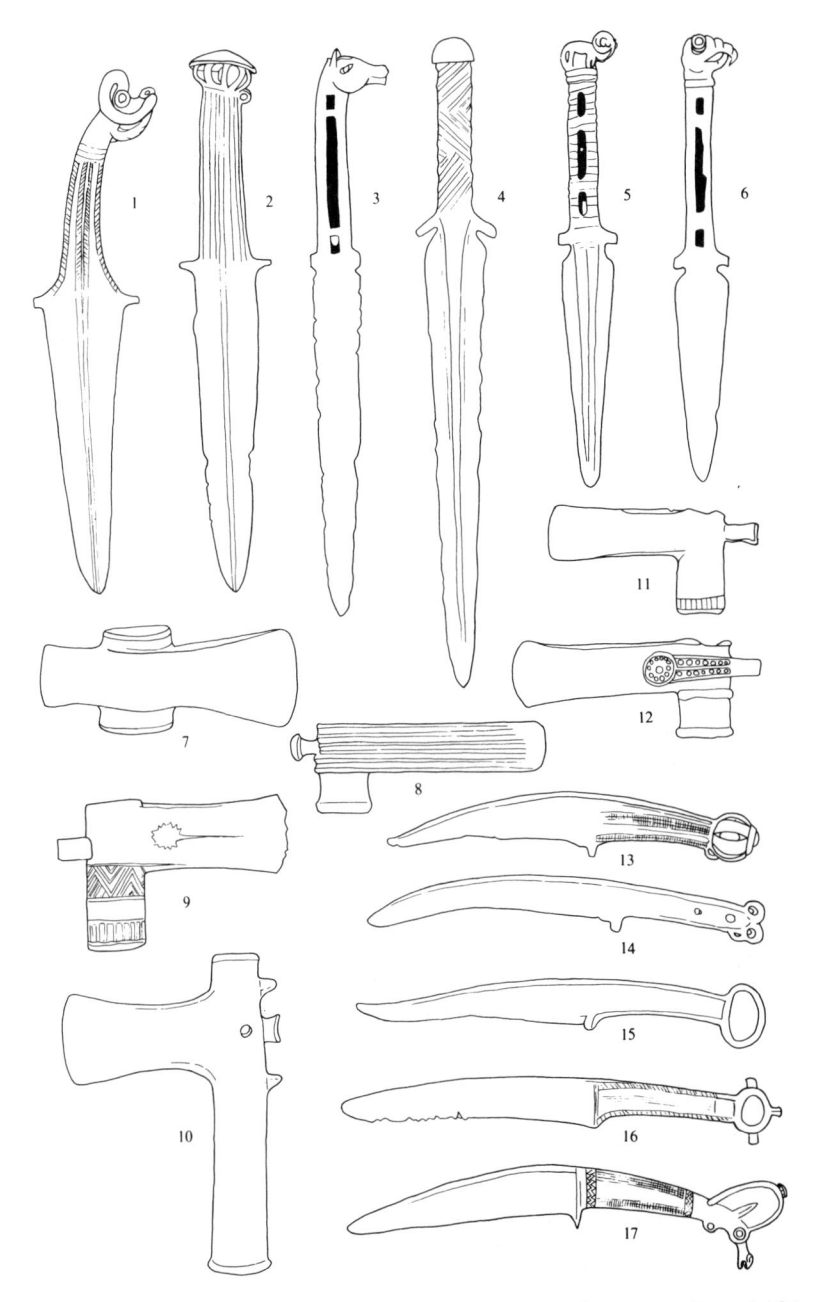

Fig. 49. Three characteristic types of objects of the Northern Complex of Chinese bronzes: (1–6) daggers; (7–12) socketted battle-ax (13–17) knife. (1, 11, 13, 15, 17) from Ch'ao-tao-kuo, Ch'ing-lung, Hopei; (2) Lin-che-yü, Pao-te, Shansi; (3, 4, 6) Pai-fu, Ch'ang-p'ing, Peking; (8, 9) Ta-hung-ch'i, Hsin-min, Liaoning; (10) Ts'ao-chia-yüan, Shih-lou, Shansi; (12) Yang-ho, Hsing-ch'eng, Liaoning; (16) Erh-lang-p'o, Shih-lou, Shansi.

Inner Mongolia exhibit), one bought in Peking is in the collections of the Museum of Far Eastern Antiquities in Sweden,[33] and one published in "Sui-yüan Bronzes" was seen at the Peiping Shan-chung Shang-hui.[34] Pommels in the shape of goats include one example discovered in Chang-chia-k'ou in 1966,[35] one bought in Peking in recent years,[36] and one in the collections of the Swedish Museum of Far Eastern Antiquities said to be from An-yang.[37] An example of a sheep pommel was unearthed at Ch'ao-tao-kou in Ch'ing-lung, Hopei.[38] Ring butts include two of unknown provenance published in "Sui-yüan Bronzes,"[39] while another was discovered in Ih Ju League. Four mushroom pommels were unearthed at Pai-fu;[40] Loehr published two said to be from the Ordos.[41] A single eagle-headed dagger and a single horse-headed dagger were each unearthed at Pai-fu[42] and may have appeared late. Watson has published a dagger of the Northern Complex said to be from Shansi; its style is like those from Pai-fu, but with a pommel in the shape of a standing sheep, and it may also be a late phenomenon.[43]

Battle-axes with Tubular Sockets

The cutting edge of this battle-ax is narrow and the body thick; the body is almost oval in section; it is obviously different from the thin and flat *yüeh*-ax with fan-shaped cutting edge of the Shang culture. In battle-axes of the first period the body is especially narrow and long, while the length of the socket is greater than the width of the body; some are very long. Two were found at Wang-chia-tsui in Ch'i-shan,[44] two at Lin-che-yü,[45] and one at Kao-hung,[46] and these can be dated to the Shang dynasty by associated bronzes of the Yin-hsü style. A group of twelve initial Chou bronzes from northeastern Honan in the collection of the

33. Andersson 1932: pl. 5:3.
34. Egami and Mizuno 1935: pl. 2:1.
35. Hopei Province Museum 1980: pl. 87.
36. Wen-wu-tzu-liao-ts'ung-k'an 1978.
37. Andersson 1932: pl. 32:182
38. K'ao-ku 1962: pl. 5:5.
39. Egami and Mizuno 1935: pl. 2:2, 4.
40. K'ao-ku 1976c: pl. 3:6, 7, 9, 11.
41. Loehr 1949.
42. K'ao-ku 1976c: pl. 3:8, 10.
43. Watson 1971: pl. 82:a.
44. Shensi Province Institute of Archaeology 1979: pls. 12–13.
45. C. L. Wu 1972: pl. inside cover, no. 1.
46. S. S. Yang 1981a.

Freer Gallery of Art in the United States also includes one example.[47] The shape of the one from Pai-fu[48] has clearly been influenced by the *yüeh*-ax and cannot be regarded as typical of Northern Complex battle-axes. Battle-axes with tubular sockets belonging to the first period have also been found at Ts'ao-chia-yüan in Shih-lou, at Ch'ao-tao-kou in Ch'ing-lung,[49] in the Ch'eng-te district (exhibited in the "Exhibition of Cultural Relics Unearthed in Hopei"), and at two sites in Liaoning: Ta-hung-ch'i in Hsin-min[50] and Yang-ho in Hsin-ch'eng; White has published an example said to be from An-yang.[51]

Knives

Among bronze knives of the Shang culture, those in the Erh-li-kang period as a rule had short stems. In the Yin-hsü period there were still many of these knives. The stem was not grasped directly but set into a handle of some other material.[52] Bronze knives of the Northern Complex always have an integrally cast grip in the first period; the grips are either flat or perforated, and some are oval in section, while the later examples include those that are hollow and perforated like the dagger hilts. The backs of the knives show a distinct ridge. The handle part may bear decoration similar in type to the daggers. The posterior part of the blade is clearly wider than the grip. Between the blade and the grip there is often a small point or tongue projecting from the edge of the blade. Northern Complex bronze knives of this type have been found repeatedly in the Yin-hsü excavations.[53] The Fu Hao tomb recently yielded another.[54] In addition, there are several others excavated in association with Yin-hsü bronzes which can be assigned to the Shang period; in Shih-lou one each was unearthed at Erh-lang-p'o,[55] Ch'u-chia-yü,[56] and Hou-lan-chia-kou[57], while another was found at Yen-t'ou-ts'un in Sui-

---

47. Freer Gallery of Art 1946, no. 34.13.
48. K'ao-ku 1976c: pl. 3:4.
49. K'ao-ku 1962: pl. 5:2.
50. Wen-wu 1977a: fig. 8.
51. White 1956.
52. Shih 1970: fig. 1.
53. C. Li 1949: pl. 66:1, pl. 32:1; C. H. Kao 1967: pls. 7:2, 2:2.
54. Chung-kuo-she-hui-k'o-hsüeh-yüan K'ao-ku-yen-chiu-so 1980a: pl. 66:1.
55. Wen-wu 1958: fig. 5.
56. S. S. Yang 1981b: figs. 5, 12.
57. Shansi Cultural Relics Commission 1980: pl. 47.

te.[58] The wood-chambered tomb at Pai-fu yielded one example,[59] which can be assigned to the initial Chou by the associated remains. Northern Complex bronze knives of the first period have also been found in the Beijing district;[60] in Hopei at Ch'ao-tao-kou in Ch'ing-lung,[61] in the Ch'eng-te district (a ram-headed example, specimen in the Ch'eng-te museum), in Chang-chia-k'ou city (a horse-headed example), in Ch'ung-li (ring-pommeled example), and in Ku-yüan (a mushroom-pommel example; the above three were all exhibited in the "Exhibition of Cultural Relics Unearthed in Hopei"); in Inner Mongolia in the Ch'ih-feng district (double-ring pommel, exhibited in the Ch'ih-feng museum) and in Pai-yin-ch'ang, Nai-man League (goat-headed example, exhibited in the Chi-lin Provincial Museum); in Liaoning in Fu-shun city[62] and at Yang-ho in Hsin-ch'eng. Among specimens collected in the Ordos, pommel ornaments include double rings, angle-brace patterns, and single rings with knobs. In sum, the ornamentation on knife pommels was even more varied than for daggers, the single ring pommel with three knobs being the most characteristic.

Examination of these three implements shows that they share the following features: (1) the surface ornamentation is made by combining geometric elements including small squares, triangular sawteeth, wavy lines, circles, dots, and parallel lines or wheat-ear patterns formed by parallel lines enclosing short, angled strokes; (2) animals are depicted in the round in a distinct manner, with the eyes often forming a protruding tube; spherical bells with many segments and projecting knobs are also common; (3) these items generally have rings or small buttons so that they can be suspended.

From the known points of provenance of the three items mentioned above one can discern that the southernmost distribution of bronzes of the Northern Complex in late Shang times already extended southward into the territories of the Yin-hsü culture and the predynastic Chou culture in the Wei River drainage and northern Honan. In the east they spread to the Liao-tung coast. In the north they extended far beyond the northern

58. Shensi Province Institute of Archaeology 1979: pl. 90.
59. K'ao-ku 1976b: fig. 8:5.
60. Wen-wu-tzu-liao-ts'ung-k'an 1978: fig. 15.
61. K'ao-ku 1962: pl. 5:1, 3.
62. K'ao-ku 1981b: fig. 1:1.

border of China, with finds in Mongolia,[63] Transbaikal'ia,[64] Tuva,[65] the Minusinsk Basin,[66] the Krasnoiarsk district,[67] and the Altai.[68] Stray finds have also been made even farther west on the Khirgiz steppe,[69] on the middle course of the Ob' River,[70] and as far as the coast of the Black Sea.[71] Similar specimens also occur among ancient bronzes on the Iranian plateau.[72] I believe that the major area of distribution for bronzes of the Northern Complex, during the initial, developmental period, corresponds with the "Central Asia" defined by the Soviet scholar Chernykh[73] for the late Bronze Age.

Within this broad geographical range, the bronzes associated with the three types of bronze implements mentioned above exhibit regional differences. In China, the snake-handled *pi* (here a spatula) found with these three items[74] has been found in the region of the loess plateau; the handle of the *pi* is straight and triangular in section. The ram-headed *pi* unearthed at T'ai-hsi[75] is a slightly concave *ch'ih*-spoon. There is a bell-pommeled example of exactly the same type housed in the Ch'eng-te museum. This kind of *ch'ih*-spoon has not been found on the loess plateau. Among the bronzes of the Northern Complex found at Ch'ao-tao-kou there is a weapon called a "*pi*-shaped bronze with curved handle" in the original report,[76] rather similar to the socketed *ko*-halberd of the Yin-hsü culture; but it has a heavy cylindrical rib running along the side of the blade; its function was perhaps to pick, and it can be called a socketed pick-*ko*. This type of weapon also exists in the group of Northern Complex bronzes from Yang-ho.[77] Another was discovered in the

63. V. V. Volkov 1961: fig. 1; N. L. Chlenova 1967: pl. 10:23.
64. A. Salmony 1933: pl. 36:1; Iu. C. Grishin 1975: pl. 13:8.
65. L. P. Kyzlasov 1958: pls. 2:25, 4:36.
66. N. L. Chlenova 1967: pls. 8:1, 6:4, 5, 6; S. V. Kiselev 1951: pls. 12:6, 2, 11:2, 5.
67. G. A. Maksimenkov 1961: fig. 1:1–4.
68. M. P. Griaznov 1947.
69. N. L. Chlenova 1967: pl. 10:26.
70. S. V. Kiselev 1960: fig. 20:2.
71. A. I. Terenozhkin 1975: fig. 1:5, 6.
72. N. L. Chlenova 1967: pls. 15, 17; Vanden Berghe 1972.
73. E. N. Chernykh 1978: fig. 9.
74. Shansi Cultural Relics Commission 1980: pl. 47; K'ao-ku 1972b: fig. 6; S. S. Yang 1981b: fig. 14; Shensi Province Institute of Archaeology 1979: pl. 89.
75. Hopei Province Museum 1980: pl. 52.
76. K'ao-ku 1962: pl. 5:6.
77. K'ao-ku 1978: pl. 9:1, bottom.

coastal district of Tung-kou east of the mouth of the Yalu River (exhibited at the Tung-kou Prefecture Palace of Culture), and still another at T'ai-hsi. But none have been discovered on the loess plateau. The long knife[78] with many knobs has frequently been found on the loess plateau;[79] one has been collected in the Peking district[80] but as yet none have been found further east. Furthermore there are ornaments such as the bow-shaped bronzes[81] and gold ornaments;[82] again these are seen only on the loess plateau, while gold and bronze earrings shaped like funnels at one end are seen only in the region east of the loess plateau. Therefore it seems appropriate the take the Taihang Mountains as a boundary and to divide the bronzes of the Northern Complex into distinct eastern and western groups (fig. 50). Bronzes of the Northern Complex of the first period thus far have not been discovered in assemblages in Inner Mongolia. But when so many stray finds have accumulated, as in the Ordos, while not one example of the aforementioned six types has yet been found, one can infer the existence of a northern assemblage. Thus, speaking on the basis of what is presently known, it is already inappropriate to use the term *Ordos*, with its localized connotation, as a general name for bronzes of the Northern Zone in China.

When bronzes of the Northern Zone began within China's borders awaits further exploration. As for the ram-headed *pi*-spatula from T'ai-hsi, the ram's head pommel is identical to that on knives and daggers, and the additional loops with pendants are like the snake-pommeled spoons from Shih-lou.[83] It is a typical bronze of the Northern Complex. Among the Yin-hsü weapons found in the same group with it none was later in date than the first phase at Ta-ssu-k'ung-ts'un.[84] Therefore this ram-pommeled *pi* must be at least as early as the first phase at Ta-ssu-k'ung-ts'un. But judging by the manufacturing technique, it represents rather accomplished casting skill and artistic style. Thus the bronzes of

78. [Lin here uses the traditional name of "*tao*" (knife) for a weapon that William Watson calls a form of "halberd," differentiating it from the more common *ko* by its "long narrow blade set parallel to the shaft and generally curved a little over its end" (*China Before the Han Dynasty* [New York: Praeger, 1961], p. 83).]—ED.

79. Wen-wu 1958: fig. 36; K'ao-ku 1972b: fig. 7; S. S. Yang 1976: fig. 4; Shensi Province Institute of Archaeology 1979: pl. 97.

80. Wen-wu-tzu-liao-ts'ung-k'an 1978: fig. 17.

81. Hsieh and Yang 1960: fig. 4; Y. Kuo 1962: fig. 2; S. S. Yang 1981b: fig. 26.

82. C. L. Wu 1972: fig. 16.

83. S. S. Yang 1976: fig. 3; 1981b: fig. 23.

84. K'ao-ku 1973.

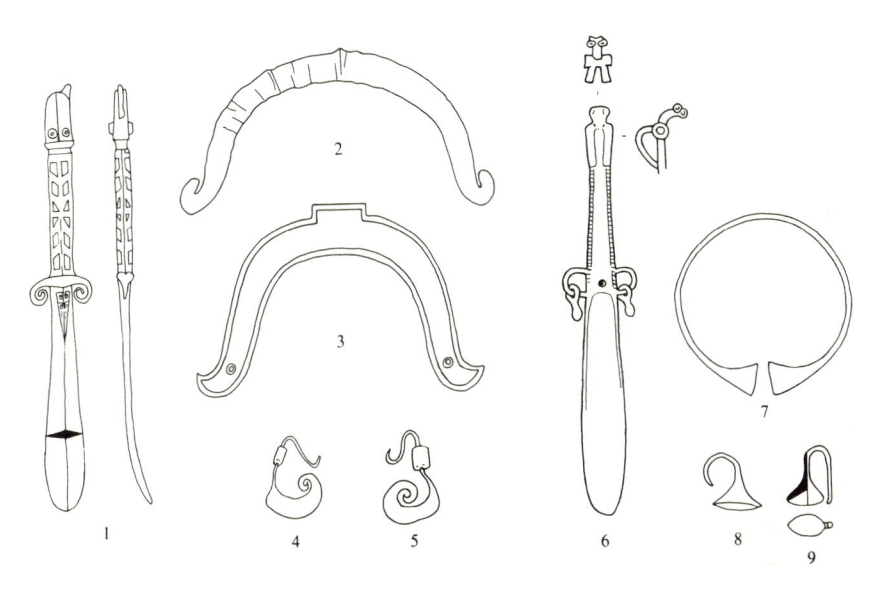

Fig. 50. Examples of regional differences in the bronze of the Northern Complex in China (1, 3, 6. 9, bronze; 2, 4, 5, 7, 8, gold): (1) *pi*-spatula with snake-head-shaped pommel, from Ch'u-chia-yü, Shih-lou, Shansi; (2, 3) head ornaments, from Lin-che-yü, Pao-te, and Ch'u-chia-yü, Shih-lou, in Shansi; (4, 5) ear ornaments, from Hou-lan-chia-kou, Shih-lou, and Hsia-hsin-chiao, Yung-ho, in Shansi; (6) *pi*-spatula with sheep pommel, from T'ai-hsi, Kao-ch'eng, Hopei; (7) armlet, from Liu-chia-ho, P'ing-ku, Hopei; (8, 9) ear ornaments from Liu-chia-ho, P'ing-ku, and Hsiao-kuan-chuang, T'ang-shan, in Hopei.

the Northern Complex had certainly undergone an earlier developmental process of their own. Based on excavations at Wei-hsien in Hopei conducted by the joint archaeological team from the Hopei Cultural Relics Bureau and the Archaeology Program of Chi-lin University it can now be determined that the ceramics of the Lower Hsia-chia-tien culture unearthed from the cemetery at Ta-tien-tzu in Ao-han League are no later than the Erh-li-kang culture.[85] Consequently, the bronzes from this cemetery (already in some cases requiring the use of cored molds) are also no later than the Erh-li-kang culture. In addition, the Inner Mongolian cultural relics team excavated a site at Chu-k'ai-kou in Ejin Horo League with several layers, of which the fifth stratum yielded a radiocarbon date of 3420 ± 70 B.P., while bronzes were discovered in the fourth. One can see that the bronzes in China's Northern Zone not only must have a relationship of parallel development with bronzes of the Erh-li-kang

85. K'ao-ku-yü-wen-wu 1982.

culture, but they can be pushed back even earlier. Therefore, among bronzes of the late Erh-li-t'ou period, there already have been found ring-pommeled knives characteristic of the Northern Complex[86] and a peculiar weapon which resembles the battle-ax of the Northern Complex but has a flat tang in place of the tubular shafthole.[87] These can be explained as showing that bronzes of the Northern Complex already existed in the period of the late Erh-li-t'ou culture and that these bronzes influenced those of the Erh-li-t'ou culture. In the past researchers within and without China frequently were constrained by the preconceived notion that bronzes of the Northern Complex were fairly late. The subjective hypothesis that the bronzes of the Northern Complex are an offshoot of the bronzes of the Chung-yüan Complex is untenable, as is the idea that they originated in the northwest.

THE INFLUENCE OF BRONZES OF THE NORTHERN COMPLEX ON THE YIN-HSÜ CULTURE

Differentiating complexes of bronzes simply on the basis of types and forms is not the same as differentiating archaeological cultures on the basis of ceramic assemblages. One should not put forward some sort of "Ordos Bronze Culture" from "Ordos bronzes," for the bronzes of one complex frequently are prevalent in many archaeological cultures that are sharply distinct. Moreover, one must not believe that every bronze encountered in the Yin-hsü culture is a bronze of the Chung-yüan Complex, for frequently an archaeological culture simultaneously includes bronzes of more than one complex. In this paper the phrase "bronzes of the Yin-hsü style" is not used in a general sense to refer to all bronzes encountered in the Yin-hsü culture but denotes bronzes of the Chung-yuan Complex. Such usage recognizes that there are bronzes of the Northern Complex in the Yin-hsü culture.

The knife of the fourth style unearthed in the Fu Hao grave is an especially typical example of an ibex-pommeled knife of the Northern Complex.[88] But the ram's muzzle has broken off and the ring beneath the jaw lost a half, so that in the original report it was described as "resem-

---

86. K'ao-ku 1983: fig. 10:9.
87. K'ao-ku 1976d: fig. 3:2.
88. Chung-kuo-she-hui-k'o-hsüeh-yüan K'ao-ku-yen-chiu-so 1980a: pl. 66:1.

bling a dragon."[89] The "animal-pommeled knife" previously excavated from grave M 1311 at Hsi-pei-kang originally was another ibex-pommeled knife of the Northern Complex, but the curved horns and long ears apparently were intentionally removed by the user. Li Chi mistakenly interpreted the long, tubular pair of eyes as ears. Above the tube the broken base of the horn can clearly be seen[90] while farther back there are still traces of the broken ear. We now know many complete specimens of this ibex-pommeled knife of the Northern Complex and can determine accurately and without error that as far as the Shang culture is concerned this is an imported element (fig. 51:1).

Speaking only of the Fu Hao tomb, such imported elements also include four bronze mirrors.[91] Besides these four mirrors, only one other was discovered at An-yang, in Hsi-pei-kang grave no. M 1005. Kao Ch'ü-hsün tended to disbelieve that bronze mirrors were an imported element at Yin-hsü, speculating instead from written sources that bronze mirrors originated in the Chung-yüan itself. But if one examines the problem in light of archaeological discoveries, the Erh-li-t'ou and Erh-li-kang cultures, which preceded the Yin-hsü, both lacked mirrors. In the pre-dynastic Chou culture and in the Chou culture of the initial Chou period, bronze mirrors are exceedingly rare.[92] In the final Western Chou and initial Spring and Autumn periods there are only the three examples from the Shang-ts'un-ling cemetery,[93] one example from the cemetery at Hsin-ts'un in Chün-hsien,[94] and one from a cache at the Liu-chia reservoir in Fu-feng.[95] Bronze mirrors did not become commonplace in the Chung-yüan region until after the late Spring and Autumn period. But in the area of distribution for bronzes of the Northern Complex, bronze mirrors of the same, looped type were common rather early. Taking as an example the Minusinsk Basin, fairly well covered by archaeological work, we find that there have been quite a few discoveries of mirrors with loops in the Karasuk culture (before the eighth century B.C.). In the early period of the Tagar culture that developed from the Karasuk, such

89. Ibid., p. 103.
90. C. Li 1949: pl. 34:5a.
91. Chung-kuo-she-hui-k'o-hsüeh-yüan K'ao-ku-yen-chiu-so 1980a: colorplate 12:1, 2; pl. 68: 4, 5.
92. Wang and Ts'ao 1979: figs. 6, 7; Shensi Province Institute of Archaeology 1979: pl. 144.
93. S. C. Lin 1959: pls. 23:1, 2, 40:2.
94. P. C. Kuo 1964: pl. 12.
95. H. C. Lo 1980: pl. 3:2.

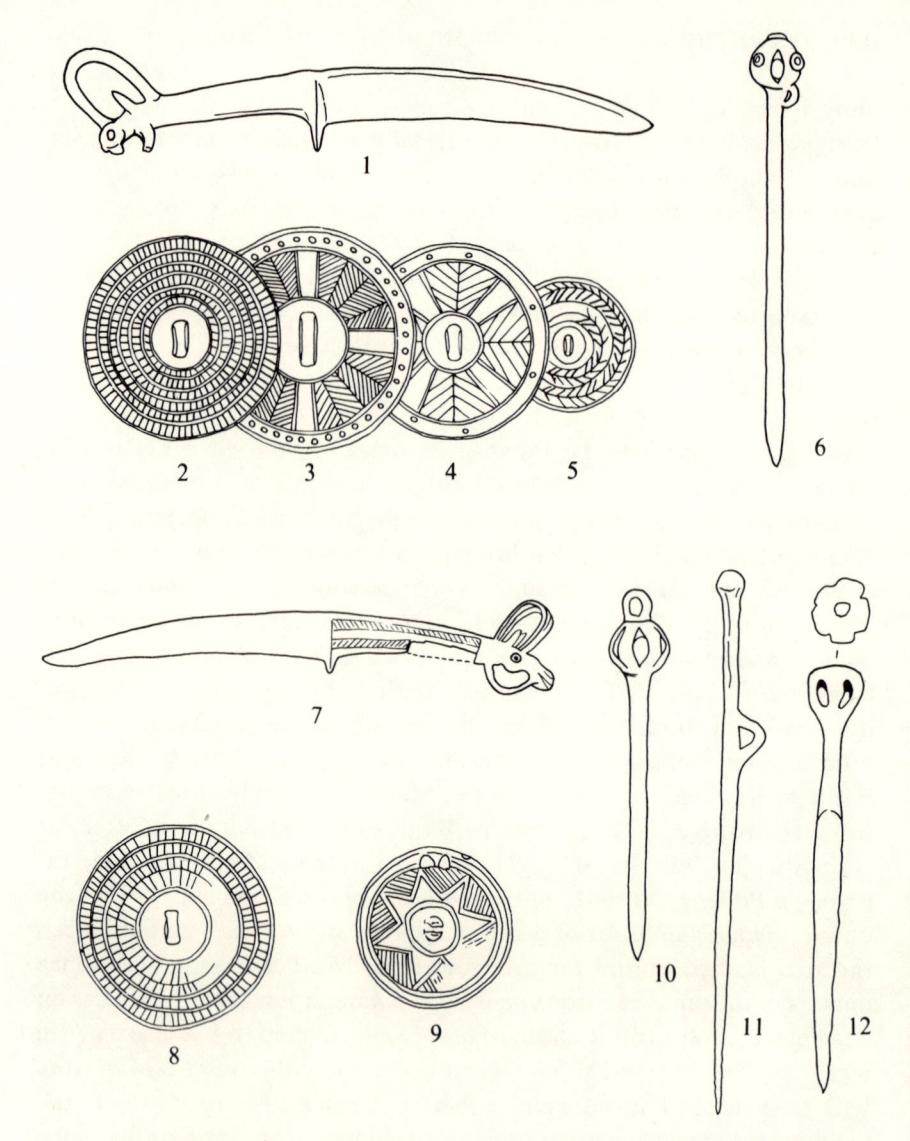

Fig. 51. Bronzes of the Northern Zone type unearthed from the Fu Hao tomb and their Northern counterparts: (1–6) from Fu Hao tomb; (7) from Yen-t'ou-ts'un, Sui-te, Shensi; (8) Inner Mongolia; (9) Nai-ma-t'ai, Kuei-nan-hsien, Chinghai; (10) Lin-che-yü, Pao-te, Shensi; (11) Transbaikal'ia in the Soviet Union; (12) Chirnokovo, Krasnoiarsk, Soviet Union.

mirrors are already very common, totaling 435 by Chlenova's 1967 calculation (of these, 158 were unearthed from graves).[96] Naturally, I by no means believe that the Yin-hsü bronze mirrors were brought from Minusinsk; not only does the upper limit for the period of the Karasuk culture not reach the early period of the Yin-hsü culture, but moreover the bronze mirrors of this type from Minusinsk are plain while the five Yin-hsü examples are all decorated. The pattern on bronze mirror number 44 from the Fu Hao tomb is exactly like that on one discovered in Inner Mongolia long ago;[97] the patterns on the other three belong to the same category as the ornamentation on bronze knives, dagger hilts, and battle-axes of the Northern Complex. A bronze mirror bearing this kind of pattern has also been discovered at the To-ma-t'ai site of the Ch'i-chia culture in Chinghai.[98] The ornamentation on these mirrors is sharply different from patterns traditional in the Chung-yüan, just as ornamentation of the Shang-ts'un-ling mirrors differs sharply from the patterns on the Chung-yüan mirrors dating to the transition from Western to Eastern Chou. However, it is identical to patterns on bronzes of the Northern Complex belonging to the Upper Hsia-chia-tien culture. From this it is apparent that the bronze mirrors unearthed from the Fu Hao grave all spread in from bronzes of the Northern Complex in China (fig. 51:2–5).

The Fu Hao grave also contained a "bronze hairpin with rattle."[99] From the spherical rattle on the end and from the loop just below the rattle, one may say it too is a typical bronze of the Northern Complex. The bronze assemblage from Lin-che-yü in Pao-te included a "nail-shaped object,"[100] which is the same sort of object as the hairpin, differing only in the position of the loop. Such items have also been discovered in the distant Krasnoiarsk district and Transbaikal'ia.[101] Because it has a small loop for suspension, one may infer that it was a tool carried on the person, hung on a belt like a knife or dagger, perhaps an awl (fig. 51:6).

Although the knife, four mirrors, and awl from the Fu Hao grave comprise only a tiny fraction of the bronzes from this tomb, they nonetheless prove that the Shang used a few bronzes of the Northern Com-

---

96. Chlenova 1967.
97. Andersson 1932: pl. 14.
98. C. M. An 1981: fig. 2:10.
99. Chung-kuo-she-hui-k'o-hsüeh-yüan K'ao-ku-yen-chiu-so 1980a: pl. 68:2.
100. C. L. Wu 1972: plate inside back cover, fig. 3:4.
101. Maksimenkov 1961: fig. 1:6.

plex at least by the time of Wu Ting. There is a difference between these and the items carried on the person by foreigners and taken as plunder. Thus it would not be strange if more bronzes of the Northern Complex are found throughout the extent of Yin-hsü culture. I see no need to doubt the ibex-headed dagger published by Andersson and the battle-ax with long socket published by Loehr, both said to come from An-yang. Among the things formally excavated from Hsiao-t'un is a stone copy of a socketed battle-ax;[102] in 1975 a so-called shell pickax was unearthed from structure F 10 north of Hsiao-t'un, and An Chi-min has already indicated that this piece is an imitation of a battle-ax.[103] Both of these discoveries afford food for thought.

The Shang culture did not simply borrow a few complete objects from among the bronzes of the Northern Complex. Some of the bronzes produced by the Shang culture itself also reflect a certain influence from the bronzes of the Northern Complex.

The horse-headed knife from pit H 181 at Hsiao-t'un[104] and the knives with the heads of horse, ox, and ram from grave M 020[105] exemplify imitations by Shang artisans of the animal-headed knives of the Northern Complex. These knives by and large are identical to those of the Northern Complex, differing only in the manner of the portrayal of the animals' heads. The manner of representing the horns of ox and ram are the same as for horns of the "t'ao-t'ieh" on bronzes of the Yin-hsü style. There is a rhombus on the horse's head from pit H 181, just as there is on the forehead in many "t'ao-t'ieh" motifs. The animal heads on all four knives are in a style that rounds off projections, which also differentiates them from animal heads of the Northern Complex. Beneath the jaw there is a long opening and not a small loop, another difference from the customs of the Northern Complex. These clearly are revealing traces left by the Shang artisans who, with their own traditional techniques and aesthetic concepts, copied knives of the Northern Complex.

Even more important than imitation was the introduction of certain elements from the bronzes of the Northern Complex in order to improve the indigenous tools and weapons. The traditional *ko*-halberd and *yüeh*-ax, from the Erh-li-t'ou culture on, was hafted by means of a flat *"nei"*

---

102. C. Li 1952: fig. 2:10a; pl. 32:3.
103. C. M. An 1980.
104. C. Li 1949: item no. 31, pl. 34:1.
105. Ibid., items nos. 32–34, pl. 34:2–4.

[tang]. But by the second Ta-ssu-k'ung-ts'un phase of the Yin-hsü culture, new kinds of socketed *ko* and *yüeh* began to appear. This must have been an attempt to improve hafting following continual contact with socketed weapons of the Northern Complex. But the *ko* is a "hooking weapon," and force is applied to it in a different direction than to a battle-ax. In order to protect the part adjoining the socket from cracking, the Yin-hsü style socketed *ko* adopted the method of reinforcing the attachment of the socket. Another method is to lengthen the part attaching the socket, extending it to form the *hu* "dewlap."[106] However, by extending the dewlap along the wooden shaft and adding to it *ch'uan*-holes, it is very easy to lash the end of the *ko* all the more firmly onto the shaft so that the socket is not necessary.[107] This fashion saves copper and simplifies casting (cored molds are unnecessary). Thus by the Chou dynasty socketed weapons were not common, while forms with long dewlap and *ch'uan* holes continually evolved (fig. 52).

Knives of the Chung-yüan Complex originally were hafted onto handles. During the Chou period the ring-pommeled knives with their own handles became completely dominant. Their time of transformation was during the period of the Yin-hsü culture. At present, aside from the ring-pommeled knife with integral haft from the late Erh-li-t'ou culture, only one such knife of the Erh-li-t'ou culture has been published.[108] During the second Ta-ssu-k'ung-ts'un phase of the Yin-hsü culture they gradually increased, coexisting all along with the traditional short-tanged knife. The ring-pommeled knife is common among Northern Complex bronzes of the first period. The only ring-pommeled knife with integral hilt possibly as early as the period of the Erh-li-kang culture was discovered somewhat to the north, in Hsia-hsien, Shansi. A significant number of these knives of the Yin-hsü culture are very close to the style of the Northern Complex, such as some unearthed from the Fu Hao grave;[109] the shape of the blade and the three paralleled ribs along the hilt are similarities with Northern Complex ring-pommeled knives from Ch'ao-tao-kou in Ch'ing-lung and Yang-ho in Hsing-ch'eng; they differ only in that they lack the protruding point or tongue on the cutting side of the blade where the blade adjoins the hilt. Another group of ring-pommeled knives of the Yin-hsü culture preserves in the shape of the

106. M. J. Kuo 1960: pl. 4:1.
107. Ibid., pl. 4:2.
108. K'ao-ku 1980: fig. 11:1.
109. Chung-kuo-she-hui-k'o-hsüeh-yüan K'ao-ku-yen-chiu-so 1980a: pl. 66:2–6.

Northern Complex

Erh-li-kang, Shang

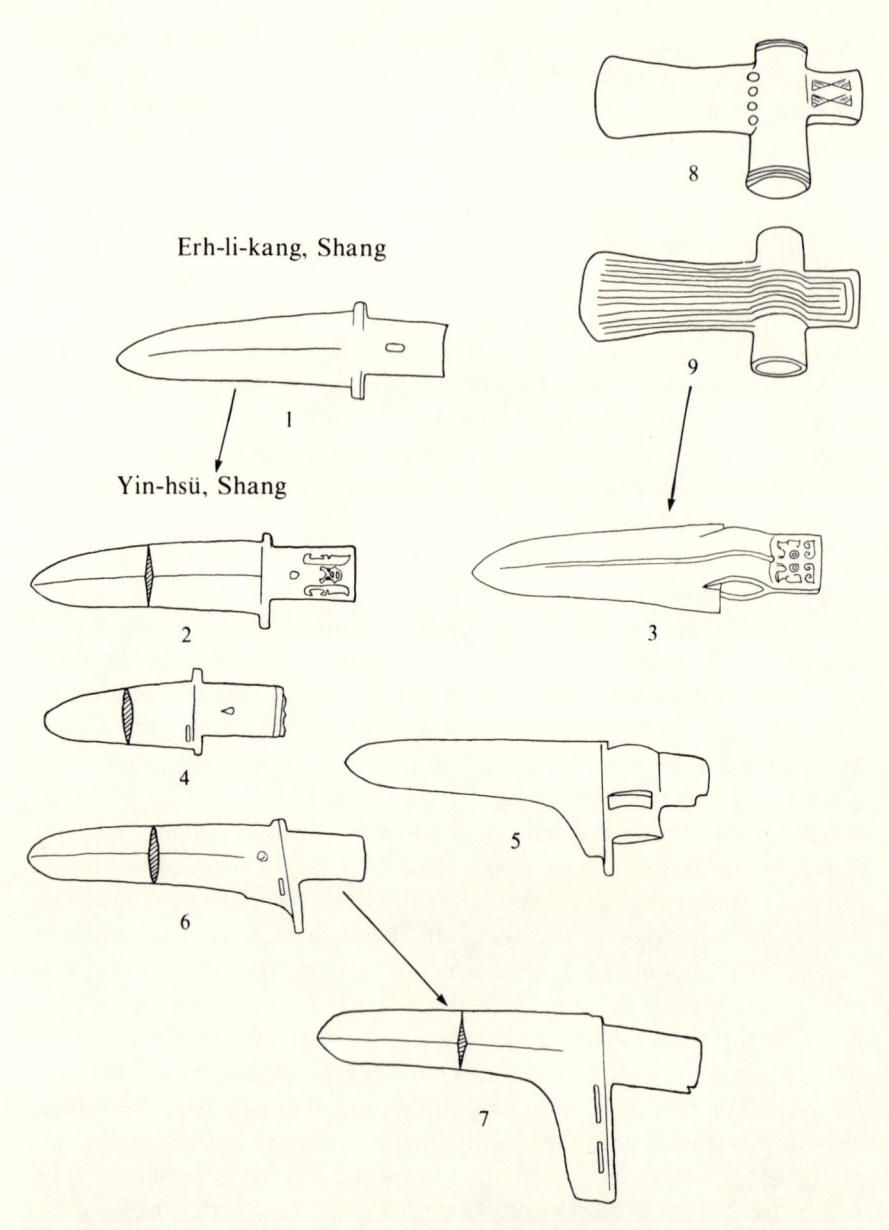

Yin-hsü, Shang

Fig. 52. Influence on *ko*-halberd of Yin-hsü culture from bronzes of the Northern Complex: (1) M123, Liu-li-ko, Hui-hsien; (2) M692, western sector, Yin-hsü; (3) Fu Hao tomb; (4) M626, western sector, Yin-hsü; (5) the round burial pit, Hou-kang, Yin-hsü; (6) M1129, western sector, Yin-hsü; (7) M729, western sector, Yin-hsü; (8, 9) Liu-che-yü, Sui-te, Shensi.

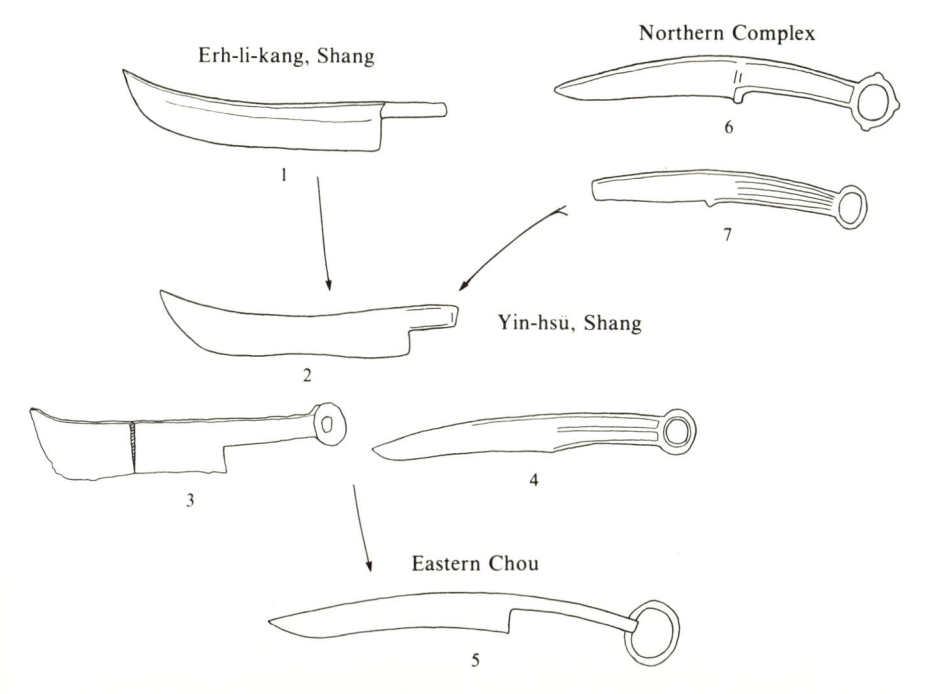

BRONZES OF THE SHANG AND OF THE NORTHERN ZONE   257

Fig. 53. Influence from bronzes of the Northern Complex upon the knife of the Yin-hsü culture: (1) M123, Lui-li-ko, Hui-hsien, Honan; (2, 3) Fu Hao tomb; (4) M166, western sector, Yin-hsü; (5) M1705, Shang-ts'un-ling, Shan-hsien, Honan; (6) Ch'ao-tao-kou, Ch'ing-lung; (7) Yang-ho, Hsing-ch'eng.

blade a feature of the traditional flat-tanged knife: it is broad and upturned toward the pointed tip.[110] Therefore one can surmise that the ring-pommeled knife with integral handle of the Shang culture developed through a process of imitating the ring-pommeled knives of the Northern Complex in an effort to improve and remake the indigenous flat-tanged knife. There are two advantages to ring-pommeled knives: (1) the blade and hilt are firmly joined and easy to make; (2) they are easy to carry on the person. They became in form an indigenous feature of the Chung-yüan Complex because in the end they completely replaced the traditional flat-tanged knife and were commonplace in the Chung-yüan region until the Iron Age (fig. 53).

Some researchers, especially Chinese researchers, often regard all elements of the Chung-yüan as belonging to the region from ancient

110. K'ao-ku-hsüeh-pao 1979: fig. 69:11, 12; K'ao-ku 1979a: fig. 4:5.

times or as being invented there. When Li Chi was researching the Hsiao-t'un bronzes, he supposed that all the knives found at Yin-hsü evolved out of the local stone knives.[111] In reality, the reason any culture can last a long time and constantly advance does not lie in its possessing from the very beginning the embryos of all its good things; rather, an important reason is that the culture can continually adopt new things from other cultures: it can examine and accept or reject on the basis of actual use and fuse the useful elements into itself. The socketed weapons and ring-pommeled knives discussed here are no more than an exploration of this phenomenon.

THE INFLUENCE OF BRONZES OF THE YIN-HSÜ STYLE ON BRONZES OF THE NORTHERN COMPLEX

In the northern area adjacent to the distribution of the Shang culture, bronzes of the typical Yin-hsü style were found fairly commonly together with bronzes of the Northern Complex. The archaeological cultures distinguished in this area are cultures which include bronzes of both the Chung-yüan and Northern Complexes.

The region where Yin-hsü style bronzes and those of the Northern Complex are most clearly associated is the loess plateau along both banks of the Yellow River. The bronzes of the Yin-hsü style discovered here include various ritual vessels and weapons such as *ko*, *yüeh*, and arrowheads, which constitute a fairly large proportion of the find. The local inhabitants not only received bronze products of the Shang culture, but also were able to improve bronzes of the Yin-hsü style on the basis of their own culture. For instance, the bronze *kuei*-vessel unearthed at T'ao-hua-chuang in Shih-lou and Chang-chia-kua[112] represents a peculiar style not seen at Yin-hsü. Some products of this region exhibit a quality of mixing distinctive features of both the Yin-hsü style and the Northern Complex. To give an example, the *tou*-dipper was an important ritual object in the Shang culture, and examples comparable to the Yin-hsü culture in time have been found in the loess plateau. One was unearthed in Yen-t'ou-ts'un in Sui-te[113] and is in pure Yin-hsü style. Another un-

---

111. C. Li 1949.

112. Shansi Cultural Relics Commission 1980: pl. 40; Shensi Province Institute of Archaeology 1979: pl. 4.

113. Shensi Province Institute of Archaeology 1979: pl. 85.

BRONZES OF THE SHANG AND OF THE NORTHERN ZONE 259

Chung-yüan Style

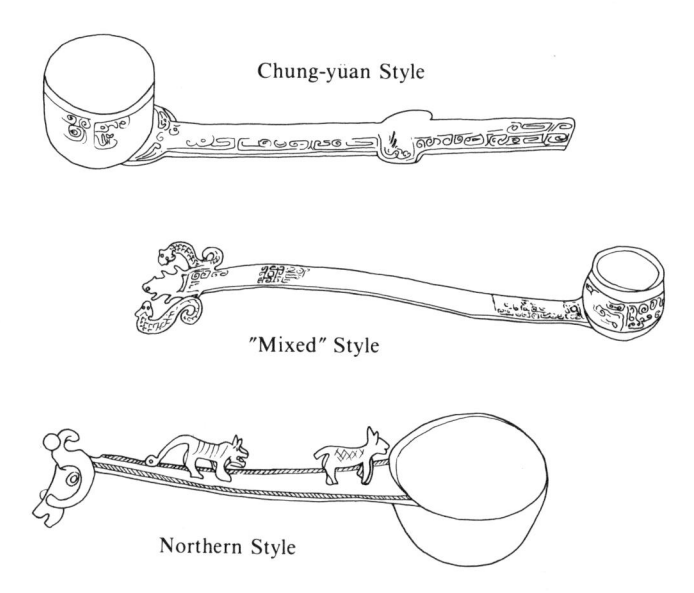

"Mixed" Style

Northern Style

Fig. 54. Bronze *tou*-ladles on the loess plateau of North China.

earthed at Hou-lan-chia-kou in Shih-lou[114] is like those of Yin-hsü style, but the end of the handle is adorned with a frog, flanked by snakes on either side. This kind of frog and snake motif is peculiar to bronzes of China's Northern Complex. On the loess plateau in the Shang period there were *pi* with pommels in the shapes of snakes and frogs,[115] as well as *ch'ih*-spoons[116] and knives[117] with snakes on the handles; the Liu-chia-ho grave in P'ing-ku, Peking, yielded frog-shaped bronze ornaments.[118] Thus this *tou* from Hou-lan-chia-kou includes elements of the Northern Complex (fig. 54, middle). The example unearthed at Hsieh-chia-kou in Ch'ing-chien[119] is almost as long as that from Hou-lan-chia-kou, but the handle is attached to the rim of the *tou*, which is large but shallow. It differs from the Yin-hsü style; aside from the standing tiger on the handle, which somewhat resembles the style of Yin-hsü animals, the ornamentation of the handle and its terminal in the shape of a sheep's

114. Shansi Cultural Relics Commission 1980: pl. 44.
115. C. C. Shen 1972: fig. 6.
116. S. S. Yang 1976: fig. 3; 1981b: fig. 23.
117. Y. Kuo 1962: fig. 4.
118. Wen-wu 1977c: fig. 10.
119. Shansi Cultural Relics Commission 1980: pl. 78.

head are purely in the style of the Northern Complex. Therefore it can be regarded as a *tou* peculiar to the Northern Complex produced under the stylistic influence of Yin-hsü bronzes (fig. 54, bottom).

For bronzes of the Yin-hsü style, this region was just an intermediary zone: their influence spread across a very broad region lacking bronzes of the Yin-hsü style.

The influence of bronzes of the Yin-hsü style on those of the Northern Complex can be divided into two types. The first type consists of those items indigenous to the Northern Complex but improved by the incorporation of elements from the Yin-hsü style. The second consists of those things which had not previously existed in the Northern Complex and later did.

Production of the "pick-*ko*" serves as a good example of the first type. There was a kind of pick with tubular socket which existed in the Northern Complex at the same time as the battle-ax with tubular socket. Its sharp point is for killing and wounding, and it is the predecessor of the "pickax" found in the Northern Complex later on. Weapons of this kind have been assigned to 2300–2100 B.C. on the Iranian plateau,[120] so it is known that the date of its appearance is very early. In China, one was unearthed in 1953 from grave M 24 at Ta-ssu-k'ung-ts'un,[121] and it can be dated to the late Shang period. Another has been found at Pai-ts'ao-p'o in Ling-t'ai, Kansu,[122] and it can be dated to the early Western Chou period. The former is called a "bronze ax" in the original report, and Kao Ch'ü-hsün considered it as "possibly a hybrid between the rectangular socketed axe (namely, the battle-ax with tubular socket) and the *ko*."[123] In fact, it does not have such an edge along the side, and it has nothing to do with the *ko*. Andersson collected one of these weapons made out of stone at T'ang-ch'ih-k'ou in Lung-kuan, Chang-chia-k'ou district, Hopei,[124] which demonstrates that this kind of weapon, very different from the traditional weapons of the Shang, existed in China's Northern Zone. But under the influence of the Yin-hsü style of bronze *ko* there appeared the "pick-*ko*," which really does incorporate elements of the *ko*. One type is the socketed pick-*ko* in the eastern group of bronzes of China's Northern Complex. The device for joining it to the haft is similar

120. Chlenova 1967: pl. 10:18, 19, p. 34.
121. P. C. Kuo 1951: pl. 13:6.
122. K'ao-ku-hsüeh-pao 1977b: fig. 13:2.
123. C. H. Kao 1958: 716.
124. C. Li 1959: fig. 33:9.

to that for the socketed *ko* of the Yin-hsü style, but it is not a long and tubular socket. Nonetheless, this weapon functions mainly as pick. Thus the example unearthed from an early Western Chou grave at Pai-fu was not equipped with a haft and was grasped directly in the hand, perhaps a variant piercing and stabbing weapon similar to a dagger.[125] Apparently this kind of "pick-*ko*" is distributed only in northern Hopei and Liaoning. Another kind preserves the tubular socket: the "pick-*ko* with tubular socket." An example of this was unearthed from the early Western Chou grave at Pai-fu.[126] Although this kind of pick-*ko* is very like a *ko*, it generally has a pronounced central spine which does not afford full play in cutting with the hook and the blade on its side. Its major use was as a pick. This kind of pick-*ko* has been discovered in Shansi, Sui-yüan, Transbaikal'ia, and the Minusinsk Basin.[127] It is a diagnostic weapon among bronzes of the Northern Complex over a vast region in the first period (fig. 55).

An example of the second type—mentioned earlier—is the manufacture, under the influence of the Yin-hsü culture, of a *tou* with Northern Complex features. Generally speaking, an important characteristic of Northern Complex bronzes in the first period is the absence or extreme paucity of containers and ladles. In the region of the loess plateau, however, local ram-handled *tou* and snake-handled *ch'ih*-spoons were produced under the influence of Yin-hsü bronzes such as *tou* and *pi* (there is a *pi* unearthed at T'ao-hua-chuang in Shih-lou[128] which I have seen in the Shansi Provincial Museum and which has a pointed handle typical of *pi* of the Chung-yüan Complex). Moreover, manufacturers produced bronze *kuei*-vessels different from Yin-hsü. Somewhat later, in a group of Late Shang and initial Chou bronzes from Hsia-p'o-t'ai-kou in K'o-tso, Liaoning, there appeared a lid decorated with patterns of triangular sawteeth and millet dots surmounted by a terminal shaped like a ring (exhibited at the Liaoning Museum). Still later, during the transition from Western Chou to Spring and Autumn, a grave of the Upper Hsia-chia-tien culture in the region of Ju Ud Banner yielded a bronze *li*-tripod, a bronze *ting*-tripod, a bronze *tou*-vessel, and a bronze *kuan*-jar cast in the shapes of local ceramics[129] (the Ch'ih-feng Museum still dis-

125. K'ao-ku 1976c: fig. 8:4; pl. 3:2.
126. K'ao-ku 1976c: figs. 6:2, 7:4, pl. 3:1.
127. Chlenova 1967: pl. 10:1–4.
128. Hsieh and Yang 1960: 42.
129. K'ao-ku-hsüeh-pao 1973b: pls. 3:3, 4, 4:2, 2:3.

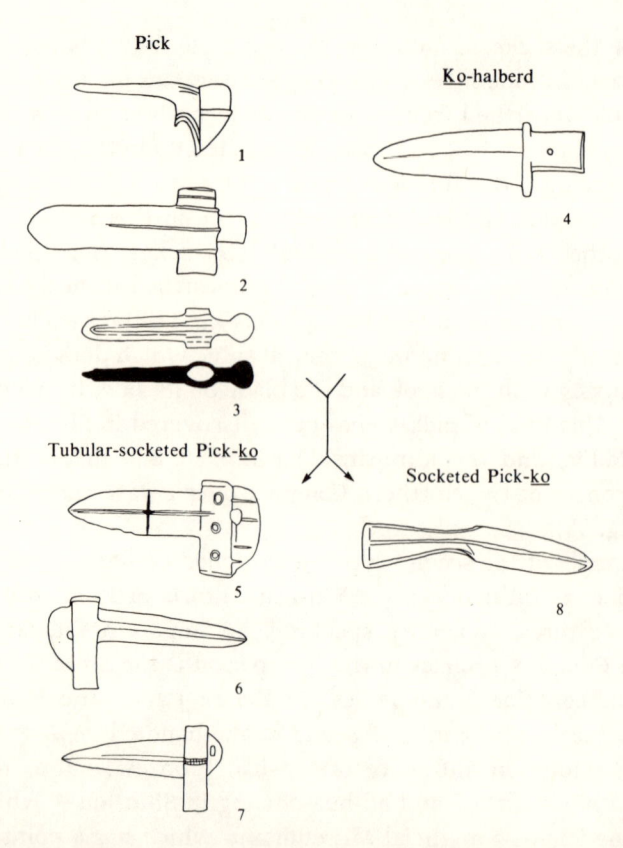

Fig. 55. The convergence of the pick and the *ko*-halberd: (1) Iran; (2, 4) large tomb at Wu-kuan-ts'un, Yin-hsü; (3) Western Chou tomb, Pai-ts'ao-p'o, Ling-t'ai, Kansu; (5) Western Chou tomb, Pai-fu, Ch'ang-p'ing, Peking; (6) Transbaikal'ia; (7) Minusinsk Basin; (8) Ch'ao-tao-kou, Ch'ing-lung.

plays the group from the Hei-shan cemetery at Ning-ch'eng; the cultural exhibition room at Chi-lin University houses a similar *li*). From this it is apparent that starting in the Shang period the Northern Complex, in the southeastern range of its distribution, was influenced by bronzes of the Chung-yüan Complex, and that it produced its own vessels and ladles one after another. Some types were fairly limited in distribution. But *ch'ih*-spoons with handles terminating in snakes, rams, and bells appeared on the loess plateau and in the Yen Shan area during the Shang dynasty. Under their influence bronze *ch'ih*-spoons spread over the region of Inner Mongolia and the Great Wall of China during the second period of the

Northern Complex bronzes, that is, at the time of the transition from the Western Chou to the Spring and Autumn period.[130] They extended as far as Transbaikal'ia,[131] becoming a diagnostic artifact in the eastern region of Northern Complex bronzes.

In the past, the bronze bow-shaped object has attracted widespread interest among those studying the relationship between bronzes of the Yin-hsü style and the Northern Zone. There have been various hypotheses concerning the function of the bow-shaped object. In graves at Yin-hsü and in Siberia these objects were all positioned at the waist of the deceased; in Mongolia on "deer stones" depicting humans this object is always located below the belt around the waist.[132] From these one can determine that this object is a kind of tool used on the belt. I suggest it is a "reins-holder," that is, "a tool [which in antiquity drivers of horse-drawn chariots and horse riders used] for holding the horses' reins, thereby freeing both hands."[133] There have been discoveries throughout the vast area from the Po-hai in the east to the Ob' River in the west.

At present, the earliest bow-shaped objects with known dates are those from the large grave at Wu-kuan-ts'un, dating to the second Ta-ssu-k'ung-ts'un phase[134] and from the Fu Hao grave.[135] The Fu Hao grave can be assigned to the late Wu Ting period by the oracle bone inscriptions, while charcoal from the large grave at Wu-kuan-ts'un has a radiocarbon date of 1255 ± 160 B.C. Thus the earliest date is the thirteenth century B.C. In addition, the example excavated before 1949 in grave YM 238,[136] judging by the evolutionary progression in shape, must be earlier than those from E 9 and the Fu Hao grave. Hayashi Minao dates YM 238 to the first Ta-ssu-k'ung-ts'un phase.[137] Tsou Heng dates it to the "third Yin-hsü period," corresponding to the third phase at Ta-ssu-k'ung-ts'un.[138] I believe that the stratigraphic basis for dating YM 238 to the "third Yin-hsü period" is problematic; the entire bronze assemblage from this grave is like that from the Fu Hao grave and must date to the second phase at Ta-ssu-k'ung-ts'un. This kind of bow-shaped object was

---

130. K'ao-ku 1979d: fig. 2:3.
131. Grishin 1975: pl. 23:11.
132. Chlenova 1962: 32; Y. Lin 1980: figs. 1, 2; Savinov and Chlenova 1978: fig. 1:5.
133. Y. Lin 1980: 163–65.
134. P. C. Kuo 1951: pl. 2:3.
135. Chung-kuo-she-hui-k'o-hsüeh-yüan K'ao-ku-yen-chiu-so 1980a: pl. 75:1–6.
136. Shih 1970: pl. 291:1, 2.
137. Hayashi 1972: appendix 1, pp. 439–41.
138. Tsou 1980: chap. 2, fig. 3.

commonplace in China down to the early Western Chou period, that is, the tenth or early ninth century B.C. Later it disappeared. In the Minusinsk Basin, the bow-shaped object is found in graves of the Karasuk culture and of the early Tagar culture. According to Maksimenkov's analysis of material actually excavated, bow-shaped objects are not seen in graves of the early Karasuk culture (the Karasuk phase) and only began in the later Karasuk (the Kamennyi Log Phase).[139] There are two differing radiocarbon dates for the Kamennyi Log phase, 980 B.C. and 760 B.C., and their upper limit does not reach as far back as the eleventh century B.C. The bronze bow-shaped object unearthed at Tomsk on the middle course of the Ob' River was assigned by Komarova to the seventh to sixth centuries B.C.[140]

Kiselev cited the bronze bow-shaped object as important evidence that the Yin-hsü culture exerted a deep influence on bronze cultures across the broad Northern Zone, including the Karasuk.[141] In the past I also believed that the bronze bow-shaped object was an invention of the Yin-hsü culture. Now, for two reasons this formulation merits reconsideration: (1) When the bronze bow-shaped object first appeared in the Yin-hsü culture, its ornamentation with rattles and horse heads was not from the Shang tradition, reflecting instead features of bronzes from the Northern Complex. T'ang Lan published a bronze bow-shaped object housed in the Palace Museum.[142] It has rattle terminals at either end and is decorated with raised, parallel lines. It is very different from examples in the Yin-hsü style, and T'ang Lan believes "it is from the minority peoples on ancient China's northern frontier."[143] But his statement that this bow-shaped object "may be very late in date" is entirely without foundation. The two rattle terminals on this piece recall the "double spherical bells" found in a group of Shang period bronzes at Lin-che-yü in Pao-te,[144] and this pair of "double spherical bells" closely resembles the arms of the aforementioned bow-shaped object. In other words, not only can the example published by T'ang Lan date as early as the Shang dynasty; one can also raise the reasonable hypothesis that, like a yoke, the bow-shaped object could be made of wood, perhaps with bronze

139. Maksimenkov 1975.
140. Komarova 1952.
141. K'ao-ku 1960; Kiselev 1960, 1962.
142. L. T'ang 1973: fig. 3, right, no. 5.
143. Ibid., p. 183.
144. C. L. Wu 1972: plate inside cover, 3:1, 2.

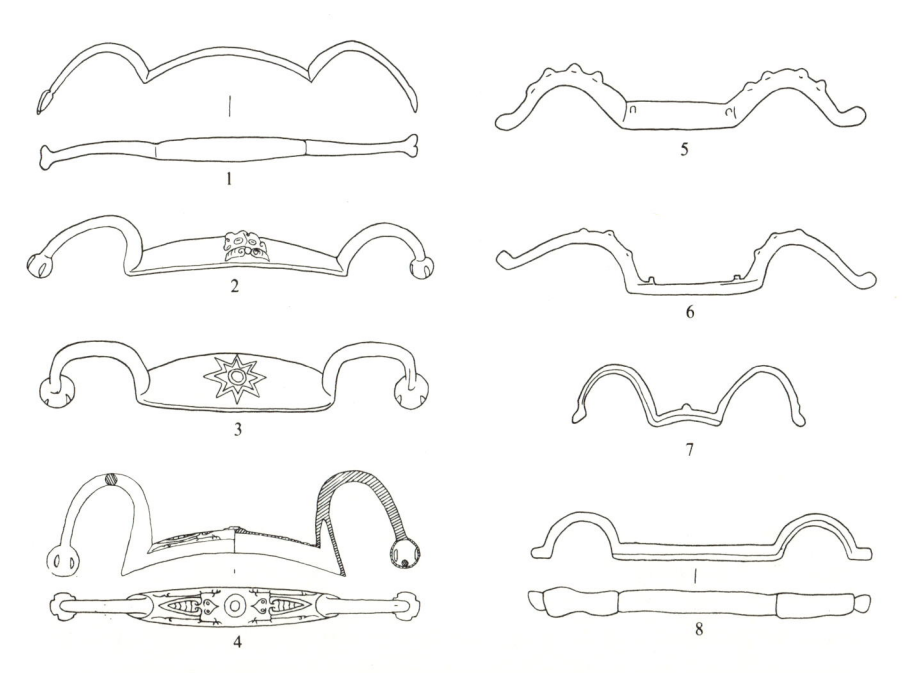

Fig. 56. Examples of bronze bow-shaped objects: (1) YM238, Yin-hsü, early period; (2) large tomb E9, Wu-kuan-ts'un, Yin-hsü, early period; (3) M175, Ta-ssu-k'ung-ts'un, Yin-hsü, late period; (4) M2, Pai-ts'ao-p'o, Ling-t'ai, Kansu, early Western Chou; (5) tomb 3, ASK0Z; (6) tomb 28, Big Cape, Tom River, Tomsk; (7) ancient tomb at Raikov; (8) tomb # 3, Sargov.

ornaments added only to finials over the arms. Therefore, although to date there have been no discoveries of bronze bow-shaped objects in Inner Mongolia and the region around the Great Wall, it cannot be affirmed that the production of these items in this area was later than for the Yin-shü examples. (2) Soon after the bronze bow-shaped object appeared in the Yin-hsü culture it developed its own characteristics: the *t'ao-t'ieh* and cicada were used for decorative patterns, the body generally took on the shape of a shuttle, and small holes were made on the back where the arms join the body. Moreover, from the time of Wu Ting to the early Western Chou period the curvature of the arms gradually increased (fig. 56:1–4). According to what is currently known, the northernmost distribution of bow-shaped objects of the Yin-hsü style reaches only Lu-lung in Hopei.[145] Bronze bow-shaped objects unearthed

145. Hopei Province Museum 1980: pl. 80.

in the Minusinsk Basin are ornamented with the unadulterated small checkerboard patterns and knobs of the Northern Complex, the body forms a rectangular plate, and there are small protrusions on the front where the arms meet the body. Those corresponding to the early Western Chou period show curvature of the arms very like those from the early Yin-hsü culture; this is especially significant in establishing that the bow-shaped objects of the Minusinsk Basin could not have been produced under the direct influence of those from the Yellow River drainage (fig. 56:5—8).

Therefore, given the material currently available, the most reasonable hypotheses are that the bow-shaped object was invented in the Northern Zone adjoining the Yin-hsü culture; that in influencing the Yin-hsü culture, the prototype of the bow-shaped object produced the bronze bow-shaped object of the Yin-hsü style, which developed fairly rapidly in the Yellow River drainage; and that the Northern Zone preserved a fairly primitive form which spread to the Minusinsk Basin and further west at a fairly late date. The influence of the Yin-hsü version of the bow-shaped object on the Northern Zone reached no farther than northern Hopei.

The Soviet scholar Okladnikov has raised an interesting point: the "Angara-Yenisei style" of bronze ax of the southern taiga in eastern Siberia "is a variant of the Yin dynasty prototype from ancient China."[146] The features of this socketed ax are its rectangular cross section, the absence of loops, the slightly splayed shape of the edge on quite a few examples, and geometric designs composed of triangles, parallel lines, and circles.[147] A type of bronze ax with one or two loops and oval or hexagonal in section is distributed over a vast region of the steppe in the Minusinsk Basin, Mongolia, Inner Mongolia, and Soviet Central Asia.[148] Because of this the similar type from the taiga in the Northern Zone has attracted interest as an isolated, regional feature. Okladnikov believes that the "Angara-Yenisei style" of bronze ax is like the Yin-hsü style ax in the shape of its cross section and in its overall proportions. The circles on the upper part and the inverted triangles on the lower part are simplified from motifs on axes of the Yin-hsü style, *t'ao-t'ieh* masks, and inverted triangles. Therefore one can leap over the steppe region and find its prototype in the Yellow River drainage.

146. Okladnikov 1955: 182.
147. Maksimenkov 1960.
148. Chernykh 1978: fig. 11:42, 43, 45, 61; Volkov 1964: fig. 1:10, 12; Egami and Mizuno 1935: pl. 35:1.

While reevaluating this topic, I should point out from the beginning that the socketed ax of the Yin-hsü style inherited a form that already existed in the Erh-li-kang culture. Radiocarbon dates for charcoal from deposits of the late Erh-li-kang culture are as early as 1620 ± 140 B.C.[149] Even if we rely only on written records for the duration of the Shang the socketed axes of Yellow River drainage can be dated no later than the sixteenth century B.C. There are socketed axes datable to the Yin-hsü period by associated artifacts from the northern edge of the distribution of the Shang culture; at present, there are only those from Shih-lou,[150] Sui-te,[151] and Ling-shou.[152] "The Sui-yüan Bronzes" published three similar axes,[153] unfortunately of unknown provenance. These bronze axes certainly have a clear relationship in their shape and ornamentation with those of the Yin-hsü and Erh-li-kang phases; they can be considered derivatives of the Erh-li-kang—Yin-hsü style of socketed axes. Moreover, the ornamentation on these very axes is closest to that on bronze axes of the "Angara-Yenisei style": inverted triangle motifs, vertical parallel strokes, circles like pairs of eyes, and crosses (fig. 57).

Still farther north bronze axes of the Shang period have not yet been found. However, the situation later on in Inner Mongolia is of interest; axes with loops have been discovered, but as determined by their association in graves definitely assigned to the Upper Hsia-chia-tien culture of the middle Chou period, looped axes did not hold a dominant position— loopless axes with square sockets were most common. We know that across a great arc-shaped zone from the Ordos eastward to Ju Ud Banner and then northward to Transbaikal'ia there is a kind of ceramic *li*-tripod with large hollow legs and linear appliqué ornamentation.[154] According to items excavated at Chu-k'ai-kou and Ta-tien-tzu, they could not have appeared later than the period of the Erh-li-kang culture. The loopless axe with square socket that originated in the Yellow River drainage may have passed through this arc to the area of Transbaikal'ia to become common on the southern fringe of the taiga. This process must have occurred before the broad prevalence of socketed axes across the steppe region. At a time when axes with loops exerted influence southward so

---

149. Wen-wu-tzu-liao-ts'ung-k'an 1981: 61.
150. Y. Kuo 1962: fig. 6; S. S. Yang 1981b: fig. 21 center.
151. C. Y. Chu 1975: fig. 2.
152. Wen-wu-tzu-liao-ts'ung-k'an 1981: fig. 6.
153. Egami and Mizuno 1935: pl. 1:14–16.
154. Grishin 1975: fig. 9.

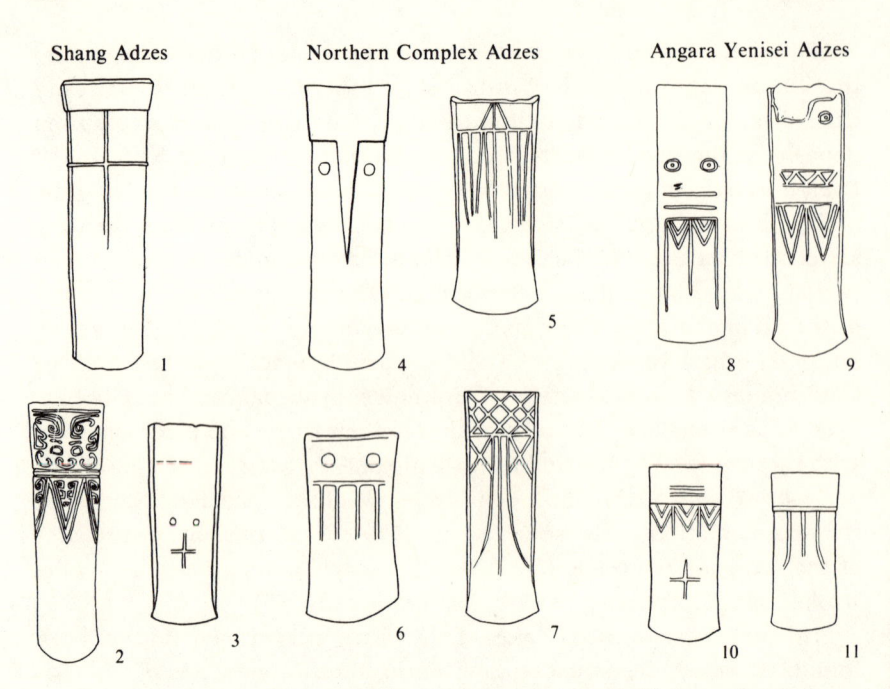

Fig. 57. Influence of Shang bronze adz upon the Northern Zone: (1) Cheng-chou, Henan; (2) An-yang; (3) Ling-pao, Honan; (4) Sui-te, Shensi; (5, 7) Shih-lou, Shansi; (6) unknown provenance; (8) Sokolovo hamlet, Angara River; (9–11) Yenisei River valley.

that some bronze axes of the Yin-hsü culture and the early Chou period also have loops, the bronze axes of the southern taiga in eastern Siberia preserved the ancient form that originated in North China. Therefore Okladnikov's point remains an acceptable hypothesis to this day.

THE PROBLEM OF THE RELATIONSHIP BETWEEN THE KARASUK AND SHANG CULTURES

The middle and lower courses of the Yellow River and the Minusinsk Basin are separated by a considerable distance. Still, archaeologists working in both regions achieved major results early on, and these are used as benchmarks for archaeological discoveries in the surrounding areas. It was inevitable in the growth of our understanding that in the past, when scholars first noticed similar elements between the Shang and Karasuk cultures, they argued who influenced whom.

If we judge them by their ceramic assemblages, the Karasuk and Yin-hsü cultures are distinct and entirely unrelated. The similar elements that have attracted interest are limited to the bronzes. Few bronzes showing similarities with the Yin-hsü culture have been unearthed from graves in the Minusinsk Basin, and most are collected stray pieces. Nonetheless such isolated bronzes were used as the basis for dating the Karasuk culture as a whole. Thus Chlenova, who stresses analysis of the bronzes, insists that the upper limit for the date of the Karasuk culture may be as early as the thirteenth century B.C., although she acknowledges that the greatest number of remains of the Karasuk culture belong to the eighth to eleventh centuries B.C.; she insists that the oldest discoveries may date to the fourteenth century B.C.[155] Admittedly, various bronzes from the Minusinsk Basin may be as early as the period of the Yin-hsü culture on the basis of stylistic analysis. But these pieces are not from Karasuk graves and are not decisive in dating the Karasuk culture. Maksimenkov emphasizes the analysis of material scientifically excavated from graves; continuing the work of Teploukhov and Kiselev on the periodization of ancient cultures in the Minusinsk Basin, he is making an important contribution. Dividing the Karasuk culture into the Karasuk and Kamennyi Log phases, he criticizes Chlenova and others for using bronze not found in the Karasuk phase as the basis for Karasuk periodization. Moreover, he points out that bronze items such as the dagger, the bow-shaped object, and convex knives did not appear in graves of the Karasuk culture until the Kamennyi Log phase.[156] Maksimenkov dates the upper limit of the Kamennyi Log phase to the turn of the first millennium B.C. Consequently this chronology to a great extent eliminates the possibility that bronzes of the Yin-hsü and Karasuk cultures directly influenced each other.

On the other hand, more and more material demonstrates that between the Minusinsk Basin and the Yellow River drainage is a vast area of distribution for bronzes of the Northern Complex. The Minusinsk Basin is only the northernmost outpost of this distribution, while the Yellow River drainage lies on its southern fringe. Moreover, bronzes of the Northern Complex were already well developed in the period of the Yin-hsü culture. From this point of view, the reason why bronzes of the Yin-hsü culture share similarities with those from graves of the Karasuk

155. Chlenova 1972, 1976.
156. Maksimenkov 1975.

culture should be explained as follows: bronzes of the Northern Zone initially passed into the area where the Yin-hsü culture was distributed and influenced some bronzes of the Yin-hsü style; some also passed into the Minusinsk Basin and were adopted by the Karasuk culture somewaht later. The Karasuk culture adopted these bronzes of the Northern Complex mainly in the Western Chou period. Thus, while there are similarities between those bronzes of the Northern Complex adopted by the Karasuk culture and those adopted by the Yin-hsü culture, in fact, there are noticeable changes due to the passage of time. If bronzes of the Karasuk culture are compared with those of Yin-hsü style produced under the influence of the Northern Complex, there are regional as well as chronological differences.

Naturally this raises another question: exactly where in the vast area of distribution for bronzes of the Northern Complex did the common elements originate? On the basis of current progress in research, I believe that the various common elements among bronzes of the Northern Complex all had different origins. For example, there is the knife with a bend in the back of the blade, hunchbacked in shape like a *ch'ing* chime stone. As Novgorodova has determined, this must have originated from the knife with a bronze blade set at an angle in a nonbronze haft, a form shared by the Glazkov culture of Pribaikal'ia and the Okunev culture of the Minusinsk Basin.[157] This "hunchbacked" knife later became a very common form throughout the area where bronzes of the Northern Complex were distributed; thus it is seen in southern Siberia and some were discovered at Yin-hsü. The pick-*ko* with tubular socket may have originated in the earliest pick from the Iranian plateau. But the hybrid form of pick with elements of the *ko*, undoubtedly produced under the influence of the *ko* characteristic of the Shang culture, became common in the vast area of distribution of bronzes of the Northern Complex. Thus, although we cannot yet trace the origin of every element in the bronzes of the Northern Complex, we can sketch the following scenario: the immense steppe of Central Asia was a marvelous historical whirlpool. It gradually blended together elements of differing origins to form a unified and fairly stable composite. In turn, elements of this composite sooner or later sprayed over all the surrounding regions. It is hard to draw sound conclusions when discussing the relationship between the

---

157. Kiselev 1960: 265.

Karasuk and Yin-hsü cultures without considering this historical function of the Central Asian steppe.

Finally, as an aside, when Kiselev came to China in 1959[158] he elaborated on the suggestion made by Loehr in 1949 that bronzes of the Seimo style influenced Yin-hsü bronzes.[159] But after gaining a rather concrete understanding of the bronzes of the Erh-li-kang culture in China, he emended this theory in a subsequent article.[160] But the basis for his argument was that bronzes of the Seimo style date as early as the fifteenth to sixteenth centuries B.C., earlier than the Yin-hsü culture, and he still held this view in a posthumous publication.[161] There are presently some scholars in Soviet archaeological circles who use this deduction for chronology. The bronzes of the Seimo style comprise remains distributed over the forest-steppe and the southern fringe of the taiga from Siberia to eastern Europe, including both eastern elements of the "Karasuk style" (such as crescent-shaped knives with animal figures on the pommels) and western elements of the "Andronovo-Timber Grave style" (such as the dagger). Speaking only of the periodization of cultures in the Minusinsk Basin, one can state that the Andronovo culture is earlier than the Karasuk. But it has long been recognized that when the Andronovo culture had already been replaced by the Karasuk in the Minusinsk Basin, the Andronovo continued to exist in a broad region adjacent to the basin on the west and lasted until the early first millennium B.C. In a synthesizing article entitled "Metallurgical Regions and Periodization of the Early Metal Age on the Territory of the USSR," the Soviet scholar Chernykh recently described bronzes of the Seimo style as representing a contact zone between a "Central Asian region" and a "Eurasian region" where eastern and western elements were blended. In view of the fact that it is chronologically parallel with the Karasuk culture, the fact that it includes Karasuk elements must be seen as "clear proof of influences of Central Asia origin" from the east.[162] This point of view represents a new understanding on the part of a fair portion of Soviet archaeologists achieved through a practical and realistic cognitive process. Therefore, I believe that the so-called influence of the

158. K'ao-ku 1960.
159. Loehr 1949.
160. Kiselev 1960.
161. Kiselev 1965: 51.
162. Chernykh 1978: fig. 2, p. 78.

"Seimo culture" on the Shang culture has already become an outmoded topic.

ADDENDUM

So far as Chinese archaeology is concerned, the Shang and Chou cultures, centered around the middle and lower courses of the Yellow River, were the first to be recognized. Only later did recognition gradually begin of bronzes also existing in the Northern Zone, forming their own complex distinct from bronzes of the Chung-yüan. It is now recognized that these bronzes of the Northern Complex, at least as early as the Late Shang period, were already distributed over a broad area beyond the borders of modern China.

Modern research has also determined that the bronzes of the Shang culture and those of the Northern Complex during the Shang period constitute two mutually independent systems, though each penetrated the other, each enriched the content of the other and each promoted the development of the other. Thus even in examining the Shang culture by itself it is impossible to make concise explanations about the bronzes of the Shang culture without also considering the existence of the Shang period bronzes of the Northern Complex.

However, "bronzes of the Northern Complex" is a concept that has become quite generalized in the process of becoming recognized. The bronzes of the Northern Complex, distributed over a vast geographical range, produced in different regions with different historical traditions and subject to differing external influences, all manifest marked differences in addition to their similarities. According to customary practice, by the basic method of analyzing ceramic assemblages, this complex should be divided into distinct archaeological cultures. One could thereby divide these bronzes and attribute them to "such and such cultures." Seen in this light, it would seem that promoting such a concept as "bronzes of the Northern Complex" is a superfluous effort, detrimental and without advantage.

However, the reality of the current situation is this: while quite a few bronzes of the Northern Complex dating to the Shang period have now been discovered, practically none, except for those few found in sites and graves of the Shang culture, are associated with ceramics. Some sites and graves containing pottery and of the appropriate period have been excavated in the Northern Zone, but as yet no dagger, ax, or knife typical of the Northern Complex has been encountered. On the principle of common range of distribution and appropriate chronology, Tsou Heng assigns all bronzes of the Northern Complex unearthed on the loess plateau to the Kuang-she culture and all those in northern Hopei to the Lower Hsia-chia-tien Culture; but in the final analysis there is no direct proof of this. Naturally, I believe that the cultures of the Northern Zone in the Shang period that possessed developed ceramics must also have had bronzes. Besides adopting bronzes of the Shang style, naturally they could also have adopted those of the Northern Complex. But whether or not this was so, another hypothesis can be postulated: aside from the sedentary, agricultural people utilizing certain kinds of pottery and productive tools similar to those of the Shang culture, there was also active in the Northern Zone a group who utilized the bronzes of the Northern Complex and among whom, because they had adopted a primarily mobile style of life (such as nomadic pastoralism), pottery was not very developed or not used. Precisely because they had increasingly frequent interaction with agricultural peoples among whom settlements were still rather sparse, because of war and trade contacts with the settled people, and because of mixing processes such as subjugation and assimilation the bronzes of the Northern Complex developed a unity across a fairly wide range. Thus the method of relying entirely on ceramic assemblages for distinguishing archaeological cultures has its shortcomings. Moreover, using the principle of commonality of time and place to assign all of the bronzes to a settled culture is by no means absolutely reliable. I believe that if we pay particular attention to collecting and analyzing associated human bones as well as to pottery associated with the bronzes of the Northern Complex, then we may find a new opening for resolving the problem of better defining the Northern Complex.

11

An Introduction to Shang and Chou Bronze *Nao* Excavated in South China*

Kao Chih-hsi

The bronze *nao* 鐃 was one of the earliest metallic musical instruments to appear in China. In its subsequent evolution into the *chung* 鐘, it remained an important ritual and musical instrument throughout the eight-hundred-year period of the Western and Eastern Chou. Shang and Chou bronze *nao* unearthed in south China display pronounced regional characteristics and thus constitute important material for research into both ancient Chinese musical history and the bronze culture south of the Yangtze. This chapter concerns the nomenclature, typology, function, periodization, evolution, and place of manufacture of the Shang and Chou bronze *nao* excavated in south China.

NOMENCLATURE

It would facilitate discussion to deal first with the question of correct terminology. Various scholars have referred to the *nao* differently, Lo Chen-yü termed it *nao*,[1] Jung Keng named it *cheng* 鉦,[2] Kuo Mo-jo pro-

---

*I would like to thank my colleagues in the Chekiang and Fukien provincial museums, the Kwangsi Chuang Autonomous Region Museum, and the Nanking Museum for their assistance in providing photographs of pieces referred to in this essay.

1. Lo Chen-yü 羅振玉, *Chen-sung-t'ang Chi-ku I-wen* 貞松堂集古遺文, vol. 1, p. 24.
2. Jung 1941, vol. 1, pp. 485, 486, 490.

posed *to* 鐸,³ Ch'en Meng-chia called it *chih chung* 執鐘,⁴ and Li Ch'un-yi said it was *chung* 鐘.⁵ Ch'en Meng-chia further differentiated the large *nao* unearthed in the south by naming them *yung* 鏞.⁶ In *Shuo Wen Chieh Tzu* the following appears: "*Nao*, a small *cheng*. In military rules, the commander grasps a *nao*"; also, "*Cheng*, a *nao*, resembles *ling*; the handle is hollow." Hsu Shen, thus, used *cheng* and *nao* to explain each other. The commentary to *Chou Li, Ku Jen* states: "*Nao* is like *ling*, lacks a clapper, possesses a handle; one grasps it for striking." Both *Erh Ya, Shih Yüeh* and *Shuo Wen Chieh Tzu* say, "a large *chung* is called *yung*." From the abovementioned records, we know that the *nao* is small, resembles a *ling*, and has a hollow handle so that one may "grasp it." This description is in exact accord with the small, Shang dynasty bronze *nao* unearthed in sets of three to five at An-yang and Wen-hsien, Honan; but it is at odds with the large *nao* excavated in the south. I believe that the large Shang dynasty *nao* unearthed in the south may be properly termed *yung* 鏞 and that the early Western Chou intermediate-sized *nao* with nipple designs may be called *cheng* 鉦. This would agree with the definitions in *Shuo Wen Chieh Tzu*. In view of the fact that the majority of scholars in archaeological circles still employ the name *nao*, I will await the adoption of a more fitting term and, for the time being, refer to the large Shang dynasty bronze *nao* of the south as "large *nao*."

There are also differences in the terms used by various scholars for the individual components of the *nao*. Since no literary records bear on these points of terminology and the structure of *nao* and *chung* are basically the same, it is now the practice when analyzing the components of the *nao* to borrow the terminology used for the *chung*. There are relatively detailed records of the names of the various parts of the *chung* in the *K'ao Kung Chi* of Spring and Autumn/Warring States times, and these records are relatively reliable, although some differences of interpretation of the text inevitably exist. At present, there is near consensus about which components the terms *luan* 欒, *hsien* 銑, *yü* 于, *cheng* 鉦, *chuan* 篆, *mei* 枚, *yung* 甬, and *heng* 衡 refer to. However, there remains significant dispute over the referents of *hsüan* 旋, *hsüan ch'ung* 旋蟲, (*kan* 幹), *sui* 隧, and *ku* 鼓. *Hsüan* and *kan* are commonly interchanged, as are *ku* and *sui*. On the basis of *K'ao Kung Chi, T'u Shih Wei Chung*, it would appear that Hsia

3. M. J. Kuo 1957b: 322.
4. Ch'en 1956b: 124.
5. S. I. Li 1957: 46.
6. Ch'en 1956b.

Nai's opinion is correct. He believes that the band-shaped piece atop the *yung* is the *hsüan*, and that the knob atop the *hsüan* is the *hsüan ch'ung*, or *kan*. The middle part of the mouth is the *sui*, and the two sides are called *ku*.[7] I would guess that the name *hsüan ch'ung* may have derived from the fact that the knob atop the *hsüan* resembles a *ch'ung* (worm). Some believe that the loop atop the knob on the Ch'i Hou Chung is a *hsüan*, but I am afraid that this is incorrect.[8] The majority of Chou dynasty *yung chung* now recognized lack this loop. In this chapter I adopt Hsia Nai's terminology for describing the various components of the *nao*.

TYPOLOGY

The southern Chinese Shang and Chou dynasty bronze *nao* have been excavated in Hunan, Chekiang, Fukien, Kwangsi, Kiangsi, and Kiangsu provinces. Of the twenty-three pieces with definite archaeological provenience, sixteen are from Hunan, three from Chekiang, and one apiece from Kwangsi, Fukien, Kiangsi, and Kiangsu. Classed by period, fourteen belong to the Shang dynasty and nine to the early Western Chou. They may be grouped into four types:

Type A—Large Nao with Animal Mask (eleven examples) All examples were unearthed in Hunan. The majority are large and heavy, with a short and broad body oblate in form. The *yung* has a *hsüan*. The use of thick relief lines, semicircular (occasionally flattened) in cross section, to make up the principal animal mask motif is a characteristic of this type. Cloud-thunder patterning fills most of the remaining surface. The eleven examples are described individually as follows:

1. Animal Mask Large *Nao* No. 1 Unearthed in 1978, Pei-feng-t'an, Lao-liang-ts'ang, Ning-hsiang County. It was discovered on a slope of the Pei-feng Mountain during the course of road construction, at a depth of 1 meter below the surface. The *nao* is earthen brown in color. Overall height 89 centimeters, inter-*hsien* width 58.5 centimeters, weight 109 kilograms. This large, magnificent *nao* emits a resounding tone when struck. Most noteworthy are the four crouching tigers cast on the rim inside the mouth, which were possibly used to adjust the tonal frequency (fig. 58:1).[9]

---

7. Hsia 1974: 286.
8. Peking University Archaeology Program 1979: 152.
9. Tu et al. 1978: 31, 42, fig. 16.

Fig. 58. Animal mask bronze *nao*-bells from Ning-hsiang, Hunan: (1, 3) Pei-feng-t'an; (2) Shih-ku chai; (4) Ch'en-chia-wan.

2. No. 2 Unearthed on the same occasion as *Nao* No. 1 described above, at a distance of only five meters. The piece is similar in design and decoration but of even larger size and weight. The *yung* portion is broken. Partial height is 84 centimeters, *luan* length 53 centimeters, inter-*hsien* width 63.5 centimeters, weight 154 kilograms. This is the largest of all bronze *nao* (fig. 58:3).[10]

3. No. 3 Discovered in 1971 on a bank of the Fei-chia River, Yüeh-yang County, Huang-hsiu-ch'iao Commune, Pin-hu Brigade. Its mouth was facing upward when it was unearthed, 40 centimeters below the surface. Color is brown intermixed with blue. Overall height 74 centimeters, *luan* length 46 centimeters, inter-*hsien* width 55 centimeters, weight 82 kilograms (fig. 61:1).[11]

4. No. 4 Unearthed in 1974 on a bank of the Ch'u-chiang River in the vicinity of Ch'en-chia-wan, T'ang-shih, Ning-hsiang County. Its mouth was facing upward when it was discovered, only a little over 10 centimeters from the surface. Original surface soil had been previously stripped by agricultural activity. The *nao* is earthen brown. Overall height is 71.8 centimeters, *luan* length 42.8 centimeters, inter-*hsien* width 46.5 centimeters, weight 85.75 kilograms (fig 58:4).[12]

5. No. 5 Unearthed in 1959 atop Mt. Shih-ku-chai, Lao-liang-ts'ang, Ning-hsiang County. Altogether this find consisted of five bronze *nao*, including two elephant pattern and two tiger pattern large *nao*. Four *nao* were arrayed in two rows of two each on the bottom level of the pit, and one above on the upper level. Their mouths were all facing upward, the upper one only 1 meter below the surface. *Nao* No. 5 is earthen brown, with an overall height of 66.7 centimeters, *luan* length 44.7 centimeters, inter-*hsien* width 49.7 centimeters, weight 67 kilograms. Purple-black bodied, black-slipped pottery sherds, some with check marks, thread lines, or appliqué were also found in the pit. There were also red-bodied, plain-surfaced sherds. These ceramic finds display Shang style manufacture (fig. 58:2).[13]

6. No. 6 Unearthed in 1964 at the Shang dynasty culture site at Kou-t'ou-pa, Hsiang-hsiang County. It is relatively small, with a height of 44 centimeters, *luan* length 30 centimeters, inter-*hsien* width 30.5 centimeters, weight 18 kilograms. Coarse, sandy red pottery, fine brown-

---

10. The original piece is in the collection of the Hunan Provincial Museum.
11. Hsiung 1981: 103.
12. The original piece is in the collection of the Hunan Provincial Museum.
13. Wen-wu 1966: 2.

bodied, black-slipped pottery and hard, check-marked, gray-bodied pottery sherds were also found at the site (fig. 60:4).[14]

7. No. 7 Unearthed in 1977 at Wang-ch'eng County, Kao-t'ang-ling Commune, Kao-ch'ung Brigade. Its mouth was facing upward when it was discovered. Overall height 48 centimeters, *luan* length 29 centimeters, inter-*hsien* width 32 centimeters, weight 18.75 kilograms (fig. 60:3).[15]

8. Elephant Pattern Large *Nao* No. 1 Unearthed on the same occasion as Animal Mask Large *Nao* No. 5. Its form and principal motif are similar to those of No. 5; however, this *nao* displays even more elaborate decoration and even finer casting technique. Overall height is 70 centimeters, *luan* length 44 centimeters, inter-*hsien* width 46.2 centimeters, weight 67.25 kilograms. Six tigers, six fish, and eleven nipple bosses adorn the margins of the left, right, and lower sides of the *cheng* portion. An animal mask whose nose-bridge exhibits a cattle head and is flanked by dragon designs occupies the *sui* portion. The *ku* parts each display a standing elephant with curled trunk. Both faces of the *nao* show the same decoration. There are four nipple bosses on the *yung*. Aside from the plain *wu* surface, the entire body, including the surface of the bands composing the animal masks, is filled with cloud-thunder patterning (fig. 59:1, 3, 4).[16]

9. No. 2 Unearthed on the same occasion as No. 1, above. This piece differs in that the bands composing the animal masks are flattened; the left, right, and lower sides of the *cheng* lack the tiger and fish decorations; and there are only nine nipple bosses on one face. The handle is broken off. *Luan* length is 40.3 centimeters, inter-*hsien* width 43 centimeters (fig. 59:2).[17]

10. Tiger Pattern Large *Nao* No. 1 Unearthed on the same occasion as the Elephant Pattern Large *Nao*, above. Somewhat lighter and thinner than the Elephant *Nao*. Open-mouthed, curly-tailed tigers decorate the *ku* portion. Overall height is 70 centimeters, *luan* length 44 centimeters, inter-*hsien* width 47 centimeters, weight 55.25 kilograms (fig. 60:1).[18]

11. No. 2 Unearthed on the same occasion as No. 1, above. Overall

---

14. Wen-wu 1977b: 2. It was an Animal Mask Bronze *Nao* that was unearthed in Kou-t'ou-pa, Hsiang-hsiang County. However, the object pictured in pl. I:1 of Wen-wu 1977b is a Western Chou *yung chung*, unearthed from the Western Chou tomb in Hung-chia-ch'iao, Hua-shih, Hsiang-t'an County. This is a mistaken identification which should be corrected.
15. The original piece is in the collection of the Hunan Provincial Museum.
16. Wen-wu 1966: 2.
17. C. H. Kao 1960: 57–58, figs. 3, 4.
18. Ibid., p. 57, fig. 2.

Fig. 59. Elephant pattern *nao*-bells from Ning-hsiang, Hunan: (1) *Nao* No. 1, from Shih-ku-chai; (2) No. 2 from same site; (3) animal mask pattern on *sui* of *Nao* No. 1; (4) side view of *Nao* No. 1.

Fig. 60. Tiger pattern and animal mask *nao*-bells from Hunan: (1) tiger pattern *nao*-bell No. 1, from Shih-ku-chai, Ning-hsiang; (2) tiger pattern *nao*-bell No. 2, from same site; (3) animal mask *nao*, from Kao-ch'ung, Wang-ch'eng; (4) animal mask *nao*, from Kou-t'ou-pa, Hsiang-hsiang.

Fig. 61. Several types of *nao* from South China: (1) animal mask *Nao*, from Pin-hu, Yüeh-yang, Hunan; (2) *nao* with *mei*, from Pan-ch'iao, Ch'ang-sha; (3) *nao* with *mei*, from Ch'ang-hsing Middle School, Chekiang; (4) *nao* with cloud patterns, from San-mou-ti, Ning-hsiang, Hunan.

height 69.5 centimeters, *luan* length 42.5 centimeters, inter-*hsien* width 47.5 centimeters, weight 71.5 kilograms. The animal mask occupying the *sui* is relatively narrow. "C"-shaped patterning adorns the *hsüan* portion (fig. 60:2).[19]

Type B: Cloud Pattern Nao *(three examples)* Unearthed in Hunan, Chekiang, and Kiangsu. A characteristic of this type is the use of cloud patterning to compose the principal animal mask motif, which has two protruding eyes. Those examples found in Chekiang and Kiangsu are relatively small and lack *hsüan* on their *yung*. They may be classed into two varieties:

B.1. Cloud Pattern Large *Nao* Unearthed in 1973 from an ovoid pit at San-mou-ti, Ning-hsiang County, Hunan Province. It lay 30 centimeters below the surface at the time of discovery. Overall height is 66.3 centimeters, *luan* length 41.8 centimeters, inter-*hsien* width 49.8 centimeters, weight 79 kilograms. Color is jade green. The principal animal mask motif is composed of cloud patterns; its two eyes protrude in the shape of diamonds. Exquisite white jade *huan, chüeh*, tigers, and fish were also found in the vicinity of the *nao* (fig. 61:4).[20]

B.2. Cloud Pattern *Nao* without *Hsüan* No. 1—Unearthed in 1963 at T'ien-chia-pan, Shih-lai, Yu-hang County, Chekiang Province. Relatively small. Overall height is 29 centimeters, *luan* length 17 centimeters, inter-*hsien* width 20.2 centimeters. The principal animal mask motif on the *cheng* is composed of cloud patterns, with circles filling the ground. The *wu* is decorated with cloud patterns. The *yung* lacks *hsüan* and does not pass through to the central cavity inside (fig. 62:4).[21]

No. 2—Unearthed in 1974 from the top portion of an earthen mound in T'ang-tung Village, Chiang-ning County, Kiangsu Province. It lay 40 centimeters below the surface. The *nao* is green. Overall height is 46 centimeters, *luan* length 26 centimeters, inter-*hsien* width 31 centimeters, weight 32 kilograms. The principal animal mask motif on the *cheng* is composed of cloud patterns. The ground is filled with fine circles. Cloud patterns decorate the *wu*. The *yung* lacks a *hsüan* but is open to the central cavity inside (fig. 63:2).[22] The style of this *nao* is similar to that of the Yu-hang piece described above.

19. The Shang section of the exhibits of historical relics from Hunan in the Hunan Provincial Museum.
20. Hunan Province Museum 1981: fig. 29.
21. S. L. Wang 1965: 256, pls. 10, 11, 12.
22. Nan 1975: 87–88.

Fig. 62. Several types of *nao* from South China: (1) *nao* with *mei*, from Chung-shan, Kuan-yang, Kwangsi; (2) *nao* with nipple-bosses, from Huang-ma-sai, Hsiang-hsiang, Hunan; (3) *nao* with *mei* from Hsia-chia-shan, Lei-yang, Hunan; (4) *nao* with cloud pattern, from T'ien-chia-pan, Yü-hang, Chekiang.

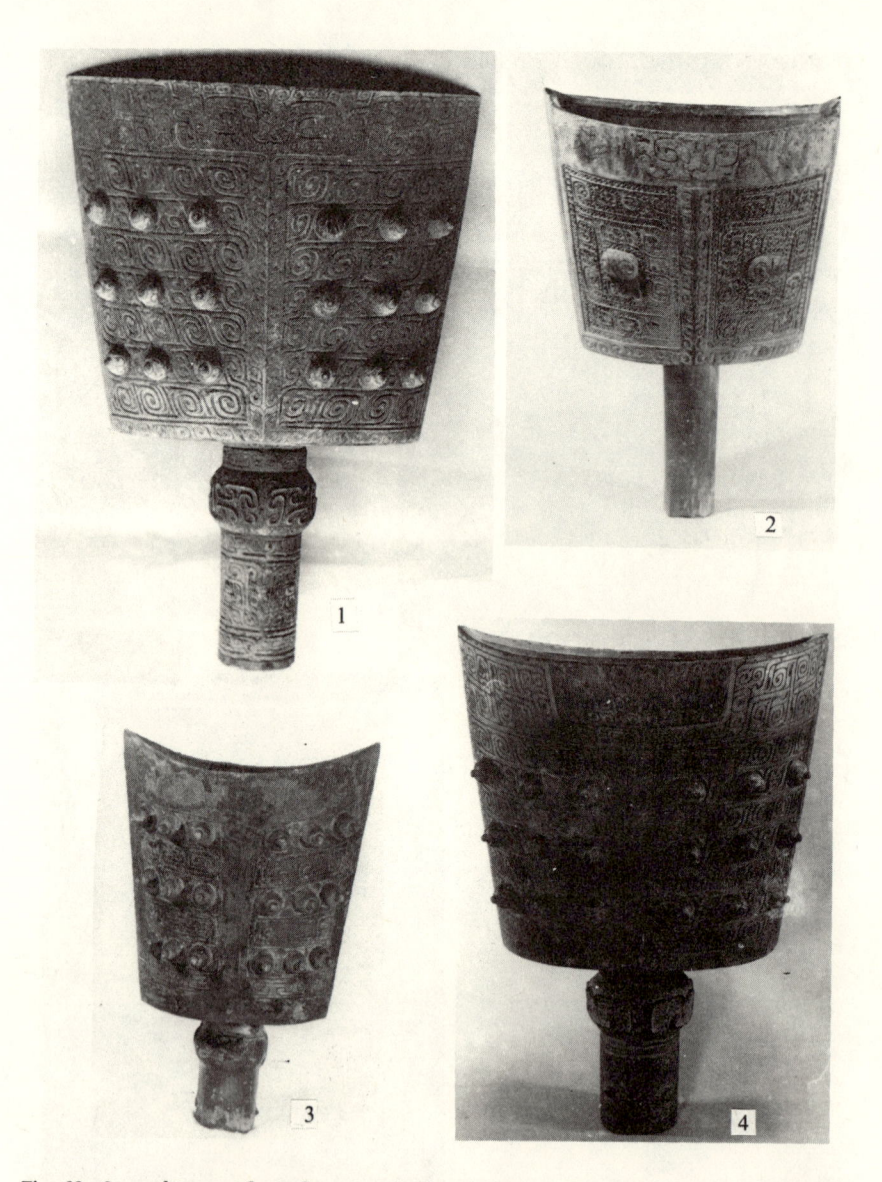

Fig. 63. Several types of *nao* from South China: (1) *nao* with *mei*, from Huang-k'o-shan, Chien-ou, Fukien; (2) *nao* with cloud pattern, from T'ang-tung-ts'un, Chiang-ning, Kiangsu; (3) *nao* with *mei*, from T'ou-pa, Chu-chou, Hunan; (4) *nao* with *mei*, from Ts'ao-lou-ts'un, Ch'ang-hsing, Chekiang.

Type C: Nao with Nipple Bosses (one example) The sole example was unearthed in 1975 at Huang-ma-sai, Chin-shih Commune, Hsiang-hsiang County, in Hunan Province. Overall height is 39 centimeters, *luan* length 25 centimeters, inter-*hsien* width 29 centimeters, weight 14.65 kilograms. Three columns of nipple bosses decorate each face, with a total of thirty-six in all. The bosses are oblate in form and are capped with whorl designs. These are the prototype of the *mei* decorating the later *yung chung*. Triangular cloud patterns decorate the *yung*. There is no *hsüan* (fig. 62:2).[23]

Type D: Nao with Mei (eight examples) Unearthed in Hunan, Fukien, Chekiang, Kwangsi, and Kiangsi. These examples are characterized by principal motifs still composed of cloud patterns but tending toward abbreviation; the gradual heightening of nipple bosses which approach *mei*, transitional to the *yung chung*; and *yung* with *hsüan* but never *hsüan ch'ung*.

1. *Nao* with *Mei* No. 1 Unearthed in 1978 from western slope of Huang-k'o Mountain, in Hsiao-ch'iao Commune, Chien-ou County, Fukien Province. Found with mouth facing downward, 25 centimeters below the surface. Overall height 76.3 centimeters, *luan* length 47 centimeters, inter-*hsien* width 56.6 centimeters, weight 100.35 kilograms. This is the largest example of the Type D *Nao*. The entire body is filled with cloud patterns. Thirty-six *mei* adorn the *cheng* (fig. 63:1).[24]

2. No. 2 Unearthed in 1959 in Ts'ao-lou Village, Ch'ang-hsing County, Chekiang. At the time of discovery it was placed flat on its side, 80 centimeters below the surface. Overall height is 51.4 centimeters. Decoration is similar to the Chien-ou piece; however, it is slightly smaller (fig. 63:4).[25]

3. No. 3 Unearthed in 1969 at the Ch'ang-hsing Middle School, Chekiang Province. With a fragmentary *yung*, partial height is 28.5 centimeters, *luan* length 21 centimeters, inter-*hsien* width 27 centimeters, weight 16 kilograms. Form and decoration resemble the *nao* described above, but it is even smaller (fig. 61:3).[26]

4. No. 4 Unearthed in 1980 from a slope of Mt. Hsia-chia, in Lei-yang County, Hunan Province. At the time of discovery it was placed flat on

---

23. The Western Chou section of the exhibits of historical relics from Hunan in the Hunan Provincial Museum.
24. C. Y. Wang 1980: 95, pl. 8:1, 2.
25. Wen-wu 1960: 48–49.
26. Wen-wu 1973.

its side, 20 centimeters below the surface. Overall height is 32 centimeters, *luan* length 24 centimeters, inter-*hsien* width 25 centimeters, weight 5 kilograms. The incipient form of a *chuan tai* 篆帶 is already visible, as are fine thread thunder patterns. The *mei* take conical form, even more closely resembling the *mei* on *yung chung* (fig. 62:3).[27] There are four *nao* of the same kind in the collection of the Hunan Provincial Museum.

5. No. 5 Unearthed in 1976 on Mt. Chung, Jen-chiang, Kuan-yang County, Kwangsi. The *yung* is fragmentary. Partial height is 36 centimeters, inter-*hsien* width 28 centimeters, weight 10.5 kilograms. The *chuan* is decorated with fine thread thunder patterns, bordered by ringlet designs. The *mei* are conical (fig. 62:1).[28]

6. No. 6 Unearthed in 1962 on Mt. Chu-lung, in Hsin-yu City, Kiangsi Province. Pale green. The *mei* are of a "double-layered disk form." "C" designs decorate the *hsüan*, with cloud patterns on the *chüan* and *sui*. Overall height is 51 centimeters, weight 25 kilograms.[29]

7. No. 7 Unearthed in 1972 from a mountain slope in T'ou-pa, T'ai-hu Commune, Chu-chou County, Hunan Province. Overall height is 34.5 centimeters, *luan* length 24.5 centimeters, inter-*hsien* width 22 centimeters, weight 14.65 kilograms. The *mei* are already relatively high. The *chuan* are decorated with thunder patterns. The *yung* has a *hsüan*, while the *wu* and *ku* are undecorated (fig. 63:3).[30]

8. No. 8 Unearthed in 1979 in Pan-ch'iao, Wang-hsin Commune, Chang-sha County, Hunan Province. Its mouth was facing upward when it was discovered, 60 centimeters below the surface. Overall height is 43.5 centimeters, *luan* length 30.5 centimeters, inter-*hsien* width 25.7 centimeters, weight 10.5 kilograms. "C" shaped designs decorate the *hsüan*, and the *mei* are relatively high (fig. 61:2).[31]

FUNCTION

There have been many theories concerning the usage of the *nao*, *cheng*, and *chung*. It is commonly believed that *cheng* (meaning the large, southern *nao*) were "used solely in the military" and that *kou-t'iao* were "used

27. The material was provided by Ts'ai Te-ch'u of the Lai-yang County Office of Cultural Affairs.
28. C. C. Liang 1978: 93, fig. 1.
29. Hsüeh 1963: 416–17.
30. Hsiung 1981: 103, pl. 8:3.
31. Hsiung 1981: 104.

solely in sacrifices"; "however, *chung* [meaning the small, Shang dynasty *nao* of the Central Plains] could be used for both purposes."[32] I believe that the large, southern *nao* could be used not only in military campaigns, like the bronze drum which when "struck on the mountaintop, was enough to call up the troops, and direct military maneuvers,"[33] but also in sacrifices and feasts.

Of the twenty-three bronze *nao* unearthed in the south, those discovered on the top, slope, or foot of a mountain include five from Shih-ku-chai, two from Pei-feng-t'an, and one from San-mou-ti, in Niang-hsiang, Hunan. In addition, one each has been found in Chin-shih, Hsiang-hsiang; Hsia-chia-shan, Lei-yang; Kao-t'ang-ling, Wang-ch'eng; Chiang-ning, Kiangsu; Chien-ou, Fukien; and Hsin-yu City, Kiangsi. Among those discovered in river banks or lake shores are the two from Hu-pin, Yu-yang, Hunan, and T'ang-shih, Ning-hsiang. For the most part, these *nao* represent single occurrences. Only at the mountaintop find of Shih-ku-chai, Ning-hsiang, were five found together. Almost all of the *nao* were found with their mouths facing upward and *yung* downward. Only a few were placed flat on their sides or with mouth facing downward. They lay within one meter of the surface and were unaccompanied by other goods. These characteristics indicate that the bronze *nao* were very likely relics of contemporary sacrifices to mountains and rivers, lakes and marshes, wind and rain, stars and planets. In Hunan, the finds of a Shang dynasty elephant *tsun* at Shih-hsing-shan, Li-ling; the four-ram square *tsun* at Yüeh-shan-p'u, Ning-hsiang; and the pig *tsun* at Yang-li, Chin-p'en, Hsiang-t'an, are all of a similar nature.

We know that the Shang people were extremely religious and paid great attention to the worship of ancestors and natural spirits, through a great variety of sacrifices. The abundance of records of all kinds of sacrifice contained in the oracle bone inscriptions clearly testifies to this fact. "The subjects of the Yin people's sacrifices included the winds and rain, stars and planets, the river, the mountain, the Earth ... etc."[34] Each occasion of sacrifice required large quantities of sacrificial victims and ritual vessels. This is the reason a large number of bronze ritual vessels and musical instruments were buried after the sacrifice was concluded. The state of Ch'u was an ally of the Shang. It developed in the south

32. S. I. Li 1957: 46.
33. Kwangsi Chuang Autonomous Region Museum 1982: 13.
34. P. C. Kuo 1963: 2.

following the Shang culture, to the extent that by Spring and Autumn/ Warring States times it preserved these kinds of customs. For example, artifacts of Ch'u people's sacrifices to Mt. T'ai or to Heaven have been discovered in T'ai-an, Shantung.[35] This provides supporting evidence for the hypothesis we have advanced above.

PERIODIZATION

Many archaeologists date the bronze *nao* unearthed in south China to the terminal Shang/early Western Chou period. This basically accords with the facts of the matter. However, I believe that the overall time span of the *nao* may be properly pushed back to an earlier period and that an even more concrete periodization can be determined. The Type A *Nao* may be as early as the late period of the Shang dynasty; the Type B *Nao* can be placed at the end of the Shang dynasty; the Type C *Nao* should fall within the first years of the Western Chou; and the Type D *Nao* belongs to the early period of the Western Chou. My reasons for positing such a periodization are as follows:

Of all the types of *nao*, Type A *Nao* are the most finely cast, most elaborately decorated, and largest. These characteristics reflect the prevailing style of their times. In the periodization proposed by Chang Ch'ang-shou for Yin-Shang period bronze vessels, he divided the late period Shang dynasty, or Yin-hsü, bronze vessels into three periods. Period II represents a period of efflorescence. Such representative pieces as the Fu Hao tomb bronze vessels, the cattle *ting*, the deer *ting*, and the Ssu Mu Wu *ting* all belong to this period. He also believes that the bronzes discovered in Huang-ts'ai, Ning-hsiang, Hunan, "for the most part are Yin-hsü Period II or III pieces."[36] I feel his judgment is correct. Most of the bronzes unearthed in Ning-hsiang, Hunan, belong to Period II. The Type A *Nao* should also be placed in this period: they could not possibly be as late as terminal Shang. The characteristics of Yin-hsü Period II bronzes are that their "vessel walls are relatively thick and decoration quite elaborate, with the appearance of three-layer relief and great popularity of animal designs."[37] The Type A *Nao* unearthed in Hunan exhibit precisely all of these characteristics. For example, among

---

35. T. F. Yang 1956: 65.
36. C. S. Chang 1979: 288.
37. Ibid., p. 283.

the decoration of the Elephant Pattern Large *Nao* there is three-layer relief; design patterns include animal mask, elephant, tiger and fish motifs; and the style of the cloud pattern on the *nao* is identical to that on the Yin-hsü Period II animal mask *p'ou* unearthed in Huang-ts'ai, Ninghsiang, and on the cover of the "Ssu T'ien Ch'uan" square *yi* unearthed in Ch'i-chia-ho, T'ao-yüan.[38] So, judging from the period style of the Type A *Nao*, it should belong to Yin-hsü Period II and therefore may be placed in the late period of the Shang dynasty.

Cloud patterns are the principal design of the Type B *Nao*. Examined in detail, they may be seen as the development of the type of cloud pattern decorating both the *ku* portion of Type A *Nao* and the thick bands composing the animal mask designs. Although their design already tends to abbreviation, unlike the elaboration of the elephant and tiger designs, their form and animal mask decoration still display the Shang dynasty style. This accords with the period style of Yin-hsü Period III, when casting was in a state of stagnation. So they may be placed in terminal Shang dynasty times. The *nao* unearthed in Chiangning, Kiangsu, and Yu-hang, Chekiang, were originally dated to early Western Chou.[39] Although they are slightly later than the cloud pattern *nao* from San-mou-ti, Ning-hsiang, their *chuan* still lacked nipple bosses, and they may yet be as early as terminal Shang.

The size of the Type C *Nao* becomes smaller, but cloud patterns remain the principal design. This indicates a closeness in time to the period of the Type B *Nao*. However, the appearance of thirty-six nipple bosses on the *chuan* ought to suggest the very beginning of the *mei* on the Western Chou *yung chung*, thus indicating that its time is somewhat later. The shape of the nipple bosses is oblate and they are topped with whorls like those on the margins of the *cheng* portion of the Elephant Pattern *Nao* of Type A. This suggests that they developed from Type A bosses and that they could not be too far removed in time from the period of the Type A *Nao*. So a dating to the early years of the Western Chou is appropriate.

The *cheng* of Type D *Nao* has gradually lengthened, changing from a short and broad to a squarish or long and narrow form. The nipple bosses have also lengthened to become conical in appearance. The inter-*cheng* space, as well, has gradually emerged. Design is even more ab-

---

38. C. H. Kao 1963: 12, pl. 4:3.
39. Nan 1975.

breviated, almost to the point of carelessness, consisting primarily of fine line thunder patterns. Be it in form or design, they even more closely approach the *yung chung* of the middle Western Chou period. However, the *hsüan ch'ung* (*kan*) has yet to appear, and they were possibly still placed upward on a base for striking, thus remaining within the domain of *nao*. The three *yung chung* excavated from the Ch'ang Fu tomb, P'u-tu Village, Ch'ang-an County, Shensi Province, are at present the earliest reliably dated examples of this type.[40] They belong to the reign of King Mu, in the early middle Western Chou period. The form of *yung chung* of this time are even longer and narrower, with even higher *mei*, and possess *hsuan ch'ung*. The *yung chung* which flourished in later times had already taken form by this date. On the basis of the developmental sequence, the Type D *Nao* are earlier than the Ch'ang Fu tomb *yung chung*. So it may be dated to the early Western Chou period. *Yung chung* unearthed in Hunan of date comparable to those of the Ch'ang Fu tomb include one cloud pattern *yung chung* excavated in the vicinity of Huang-ts'ai, Ning-hsiang County. This piece was originally attributed to the "Spring and Autumn or early Warring States period."[41] However, its appearance and decoration are very much like that of the Ch'ang Fu tomb *yung chung* and indicate that they both are objects of the middle Western Chou period.

EVOLUTION

With the periodization of the *nao* established, it is not a difficult task to investigate its evolutionary process. According to present evidence, the earliest southern bronze *nao* are the Type A *Nao* unearthed in Hunan. The extremely fine casting and mature form of this type of *nao* suggest that there must be an even earlier and more primitive type of *nao* awaiting discovery.

The developmental sequence of the *nao* is: Type A, Type B, Type C, Type D, and *yung chung*. It is instructive to examine the evolutionary process of the *nao* from the aspects of form, decoration, and nipple bosses.

Type A *Nao* are mostly large, becoming smaller among later examples. The majority of Type B *Nao* are small, with Type C even smaller. Aside from isolated large examples, Type D *Nao* are mostly small. The *cheng*

---

40. K'ao-ku-hsüeh-pao 1957: 78, 80, figs. 3, 4, pl. 2:1.
41. Wen-wu 1966: 4, 5, fig. 13.

bodies of Type A to Type C *Nao* are short and broad, that is, the inter-*hsien* width exceeds the length of the *luan*. With the development of the Type D *Nao* it approximates a square or long and narrow form.

Changes in decoration are most obvious. Animal masks composed of thick bands are commonly the principal motifs of Type A *Nao*. This kind of animal mask design disappears by the time of the Type B *Nao*, leaving only the cloud patterns of the Type A *Nao*, which fill the entire piece as principal decoration. Two eyes representing the animal mask are added amidst the cloud patterns. The Type A *Nao* elephant, fish, and tiger designs are nonexistent or rarely seen. Cloud patterns remain the principal decoration of Type C *Nao*; however, they no longer compose an animal mask. By the time of the Type D *Nao* the cloud patterns have become abbreviated, few in number, or have been transformed into fine lines. There are no longer cloud patterns on the *ku* portion.

Nipple bosses already appear on the two Elephant Pattern *Nao* of Type A, adorning the margins of the *cheng* portion. One displays eighteen, the other twenty-six. By the time of the development of Type C, this kind of nipple boss has shifted to the *chuan tai* and increased in number to thirty-six. At first they are oblate in form with whorl patterns on top. By the time of the Type D *Nao* they gradually grow in height, first in the area of the central whorl pattern, later changing to a conical appearance, and finally to the flat-topped, cylindrical form *mei* atop the *yung chung*. The emergence of the nipple *mei* was not only for appearance' sake; they also have a controlling effect on the velocity of high frequency vibrations and exert a definite influence on tonal coloration.[42] Thus, they underwent rapid development. In this respect, the evolutionary sequence of the nipple *mei* is quite evident. Therefore, the hypothesis advanced by Ch'en Meng-chia that the animal mask on the *yung* of the Type B *Nao* "has a protruding pair of eyes, which are the source of the nipple *mei*"[43] should be reconsidered. The two eyes on the animal masks are mostly diamond-shaped and are apparently unrelated to this kind of round nipple boss. The nipple *mei* on the *chuan tai* of the *nao* must have evolved from the nipple bosses on the *cheng* border of the Type A Elephant Pattern *nao* or on other bronzes. Nipple bosses are seen over and over again on Shang dynasty bronzes, so one need not seek the origins of the nipple *mei* in the two eyes of the animal mask.

42. J. Lin 1981: 27.
43. Ch'en 1956b: 126.

There was little change in the *yung* portion. Aside from there being a rare number of Type A, B, and C *nao* whose *yung* portion lacks *hsüan*, the rest all have *hsüan*. The "C"-shaped design atop the *hsüan* changes from elaborate to simple. The appearance of the *hsüan ch'ung* marks the evolution of the *nao* into the *yung chung*.

From the above analysis, we may clearly see that the *yung chung* evolved directly from the large southern *nao*. Therefore, the theory that *yung chung* evolved from the small, Yin period *nao* of the Central Plains[44] is not very convincing. Although there are certain points of similarity between the small, Shang *nao* of the Central Plains and the large southern *nao*, such as their oblate shape and dual tonality, their differences are manifest. For instance, the Central Plains *nao* are very small; they often occur in sets of three (sets of four and five have also been found); they exhibit simple decoration, limited to simple animal masks or banded designs; they lack *hsüan* on their *yung*; they can be attached to a wooden handle, grasped in the hand, and struck; and sometimes they bear inscriptions. The southern *nao*, on the contrary, are large and heavy, often occur singly, are elaborately decorated with a unique animal mask design composed of thick bands, profuse cloud patterns, and animal and nipple boss designs; they often have *hsüan* on their *yung* portions, are set in stands with their mouths upward for striking, and they lack inscriptions. Such contrasts reveal that their lines of development were different. The small, Central Plains *nao* had disappeared by the outset of the Chou dynasty, whereas the large, southern *nao* developed uninterruptedly until its evolution into the *yung chung*.

The evolutionary sequence of the Nao bells is shown in table 1.

PLACE OF MANUFACTURE

Lacking the evidence of any bronze casting sites, we must base our speculation on the place of manufacture of the southern bronze *nao* on the material at hand, examining its characteristics and assessing its points of similarity and thereby seeking a logical hypothesis.

At present some scholars believe that the Shang dynasty bronzes unearthed in Hunan were all brought in from the north.[45] The large bronze *nao* is naturally also included among the bronzes thought to have

---

44. S. I. Li 1957: 46.
45. C. S. Chang: 288.

Table 1. Evolution of the Southern Chinese Bronze *Nao*

Date	Type	Form	Decoration	Mode of Striking	Evolutionary Sequence of Representative Pieces
Late Shang	A	Large and heavy. Short, broad *cheng*. Has *hsüan*.	Principal motif is an Animal Mask composed of broad bands. There are also elephant, tiger, fish, and cloud patterns and nipple bosses. Some decoration in trilevel reliefs.	Struck upward, set on stand.	Large, Animal Mask *Nao*. Tiger, Elephant Pattern Large *Nao*.
Terminal Shang	B	Some become small, some lack *hsüan*.	Principal motif is an Animal Mask composed of cloud patterning, with protruding eyes.	Struck upward, set on stand.	Ning-hsiang San-mou-ti Cloud Pattern Large *Nao*, Kiangsu (Chiang-ning), Chekiang (Yü-hang) Cloud Pattern *Nao*
Initial Western Chou	C	Size becomes small, bodies thin and light, lacks *hsüan*.	Principal motif is cloud patterning; there are thirty-six oblate nipple bosses on the *chuan tai*, the prototypes of *mei*.	Struck upward, set on stand.	Hunan, Hsiang-hsiang *Nao* with Nipple Bosses
Early Western Chou	D	Lengthening of *cheng* body, has *hsüan*.	Principal motif is cloud thunder pattern, tending to abbreviation. Nipple bosses gradually increase in height, becoming conical in form.	Struck upward or suspended for striking.	Fukien, Chekiang, Kiangsi and Hunan, Lei-yang, Chu-chou, Ch'ang-sha, *Nao* with *Mei*.
Middle Western Chou	Yung Chung	Thin, long, *cheng* body, has *hsüan*.	Cloud Thunder pattern remains principal motif, but even more abbreviated. Mostly small, nipple bosses on *cheng* body, *mei* become postlike with flat tops.	Suspended for striking	Hunan, Ning-hsiang Huang-ts'ai, Cloud Pattern *Yung Chung*.

come from the Central Plains. Actually, we only need analyze the characteristics of the large *nao* to discover that they were very likely cast locally.

With respect to aspects of form, the bronze *nao* unearthed in the south are large and heavy. The largest attains 89 centimeters in height, the heaviest 154 kilograms. On the other hand, the bronze *nao* of the same period unearthed at An-yang[46] and Wen-hsien[47] have a maximum height of only 21 centimeters, with the smallest reaching only 7.7 centimeters tall.[48] The majority of southern bronze *nao* have *hsüan* on their *yung*, while all northern *nao* lack *hsüan*.

The decoration displayed by the southern *nao* is elaborate, for a time dominated by animal mask designs composed of thick bands, later developing cloud patterns as the principal motif. Such decoration has not been encountered among northern *nao*. Indeed, this style is rarely seen on bronzes of any other kind. The southern and northern *nao* are clearly differentiated by the fact that the body of the former is filled with decoration, while the latter displays only the most simple decoration.

As far as casting is concerned, some large, southern *nao* are composed of pure copper. For example, the copper content of Elephant Pattern Large Nao No. 2 is as high as 98.22 percent. Such a composition was employed to satisfy the demand for resilience required of a musical instrument that is struck for sounding. Among the *nao* of the Central Plains region, however, there do not appear to be any pieces cast in pure copper.

With regard to archaeological context, all of the large, southern *nao* came out of storage pits, mostly as isolated finds on the top, slope, or foot of mountains, or beside rivers. They were likely the relics of sacrifices to mountains and rivers, lakes and marshes, wind and rain, stars and planets. In contrast, all northern bronze *nao* were found in tombs, mostly in sets of three or five. This indicates that their usage was different. The large, southern *nao* were set upward on stands for striking, while the northern *nao* were attached to a wooden handle and grasped in the hand for sounding. The *yung* portion of the bronze *nao* recovered from the tomb of Fu Hao at An-yang showed traces of wood.[49] The methods of striking the two kinds of *nao* were thus different.

46. K'ao-ku-hsüeh-pao 1979: 98, pl. 14:1; Ch'en 1954: 7, pls. 32, 33; Chung-kuo-she-hui-k'o-hsüeh-yüan K'ao-ku-yen-chiu-so 1980a: 100, pl. 62:1.
47. P. S. Yang 1975: 88, 91, fig. 16.
48. Chung-kuo-she-hui-k'o-hsüeh-yüan K'ao-ku-yen-chiu-so 1980a: 100.
49. Ibid.

The large, southern *nao* clearly underwent a continuous evolution from the bronze *nao* of the late Shang dynasty to the *yung chung* of the middle Western Chou period, as described above. The evolutionary sequence of the small, northern *nao* cannot yet be determined. By the early Western Chou it had already disappeared. After King Wu of Chou had conquered Yin, the Chou people so successfully carried on the bronze casting technique of the Yin people that even now we have difficulty distinguishing terminal Shang bronzes from initial Chou bronzes. Early Western Chou bronzes continue to be unearthed, but as yet no bronze *nao* have appeared.

From the five points reviewed above, it is apparent that the large, southern *nao* possessed extremely marked local characteristics. For this reason, it is very likely that they were cast locally in the south. Among the large *nao* in museum collections, the Elephant Pattern Large *Nao* in the Palace Museum,[50] the Dragon Pattern Large *Nao* in the Shanghai Museum,[51] and the Animal Mask Large *Nao* in the Royal Ontario Museum all exhibit the style of the Type A Bronze *Nao* unearthed in Hunan. The Cloud Pattern *Nao* in the Wacker Collection, New York,[52] seems to have been cast from the same mold as the Cloud Pattern *Nao* from San-mou-ti, Ning-hsiang, Hunan. These pieces must have been the product of southern Chinese manufacture. But where in south China were they manufactured? I believe that the majority were manufactured in Hunan and some possibly in the lower Yangtze River region.

The characteristics of the southern bronze *nao* mentioned above actually derive principally from examination of the bronze *nao* unearthed in Hunan. In my essay "The Debate on Whether or Not Shang Culture Crossed the Yangtze River—An Examination of the Shang Culture of Hunan Based on Archaeological Finds" I discussed the local characteristics of the Shang bronzes unearthed in Hunan,[53] proposing that most of these bronzes were cast locally in Hunan under the strong influence of the Shang culture of the Central Plains. The recent archaeological finds at the Shang site in Tsao-shih, Shih-men, Hunan, support this hypothesis. In the winter of 1981, a Shang tomb was discovered for the first time during archaeological excavations at the Tsao-shih site in Shih-men. Among the remains were double-barbed and square-cross-sectioned arrow points, large quantities of copper slag, and what may very well be

50. *Ku-kung Po-wu-yüan Yüan-k'an* 故宮博物院院刊, no. 1 (1958), cover picture.
51. Wen-wu 1959: 35, 33, fig. 3.
52. Ch'en 1956b: 125, pl. 12, left.
53. C. H. Kao 1981.

the remains of a crucible for melting copper.[54] The gray pottery *li, chia, chüeh,* false belly *tou,* and red-ware, large mouth *kang* found at the site are hard to distinguish from comparable types excavated from the upper Erh-li-kang level at Cheng-chou.[55] (Ceramics displaying regional character are also present in abundance.) From this it appears that at least as early as the Middle Shang period, Shang culture had already spread to Hunan, and that the Hunan region then had a bronze casting industry. Hunan is rich in copper, tin, and lead ores. With the merging of Shang and local Hunan cultures, development of bronze casting technique was rapid, attaining a very high standard as early as the Late Shang period. If such important bronzes as the four-ram square *tsun,* human face square *ting,* elephant *tsun,* and pig *tsun,* which display such a high level of artistry and local character, could be cast, then the casting of this kind of bronze *nao* would naturally present no problem. For this reason, I believe that all Type A *Nao* and the majority of pieces of the other types were likely cast within the borders of Hunan.

As for the Cloud Pattern *Nao* excavated in the Kiangsu region, including the piece said to have been unearthed in Ch'ien-shan, Anhwei,[56] they exhibit features not found on the Hunan *nao.* These include the minute ringlets interspersed within the cloud patterning, the lack of a *hsüan* on the *yung,* and a somewhat different overall style. They may, therefore, have been manufactured locally in the region of the lower Yangtze. Research has revealed that many Western Chou bronzes found in the Chen-chiang region of Kiangsu—all displaying unusual form and decoration identical to that on locally produced hard pottery ware—were cast locally.[57] Therefore, in terminal Shang/initial Chou times the lower Yangtze region possessed the resources and technology necessary for casting this kind of bronze *nao.* Judging from the bronze casting stone molds discovered at the Shang site in Wu-ch'eng, Ch'ing-chiang County, Kiangsi,[58] it is possible that the Kiangsi region could also have cast bronzes locally.

Last, I will examine the question of the origins of the middle Western Chou *yung chung* in the north. The excavated evidence at hand provides

---

54. Material concerning the 1981 excavation at the Shang site in Tsao-shih, Shih-men County, was supplied by Ho Chieh-chün.
55. Hunan Province Museum 1979: 311, 321.
56. Ch'en 1956b: 125, pl. 11, left.
57. H. Liu 1981: 116.
58. Wen-wu 1975b: 53, 67.

no possible local source for the middle Western Chou *yung chung* unearthed in Shensi. The small bronze *nao* of the Yin people seems to have disappeared without being taken over by the Chou people. This is why not a single bronze *nao* dating to the early Western Chou has yet been found. On the other hand, the form and decoration of the northern and southern *yung chung* of the same period are identical, indicating that they enjoyed an intimate relationship. Since the development of the large, southern *yung chung* can be traced through a clear, uninterrupted evolutionary sequence from the large, southern *nao*, I believe that the appearance of the middle Western Chou *yung chung* in the north must have come about due to the influence of the southern bronze *nao* or *yung chung*. Both literary records and archaeological evidence attest to the fact that during the Western Chou period an intimate relationship and cultural interaction existed between north and south. The Chou people could very well have adopted this kind of relatively advanced musical instrument of the south.

References Cited

Akatsuka, Kiyoshi 赤塚忠, et al.
1954   *Shodō Zenshū* 書道全集 vol. 1, *Chūgoku ichi: In Shū Shin* 中國 I：殷, 周, 秦. Tokyo: Heibonsha.

An, Chih-min 安志敏
1952   "Yi-chiu-wu-erh nien ch'iu-chi Cheng-chou Erh-li-kang fa-chüeh chi 一九五二年秋季鄭州二里岡發掘記," *K'ao-ku-hsüeh-pao* 考古學報, 8: 65–108.
1954   "T'ang-shan shih kuan mu chi ch'i hsiang-kuan ti yi-wu 唐山石棺墓及其相關的遺物", *K'ao-ku-hsüeh-pao* 考古學報, 7: 77–86.
1980   "Hsi-Chou ti liang-chien yi-hsing ping-ch'i—Lueh lun wo-kuo Shang Chou pei-fang t'ung wen-ming ti lien-hsi 西周的兩件異形兵器——略論我國商周北方銅文明的聯系," *Wen-wu-chi-k'an* 文物集刊, 2: 151–59.
1981   "Chung-kuo tsao-ch'i t'ung-ch'i ti chi-ko wen-t'i 中國早期銅器的幾個問題," *K'ao-ku-hsüeh-pao* 考古學報, 1981 (3): 269–84.

An, Chin-huai 安金槐
1961   "Shih lun Cheng-chou Shang tai yi-chih—Ao tu 試論鄭州商代遺址——隞都," *Wen-wu* 文物, 1961 (4/5): 73–80.

Andersson, J. G.
1932   "Hunting magic in the animal style," *Bulletin of the Museum of Far Eastern Antiquities, Stockholm*, no. 4.

Averkieva, Yu. P.
1961   "Razlozhenie radovoi obshchiny i formirovanie raunekassovykhotnosheniiv obshchstve indeitsev severozapadnogo poberezh'ya svernoi Ameriki," *Trudy Instituta Etnografii*, tom. LXX (novaya ser'ya).

Bader, O. N., and V. F. Chernikov
1978   "Novyi mogil'nik seiminskogo tipa na Oke," *Sovetskaia Arkheologiia* 1978 (1).

Barnard, Noel
1959   "Some remarks on the authenticity of a Western Chou style inscribed bronze," *Monumenta Serica* 18: 213–44.
1960   "Review of Chou Hung-hsiang, *Shang Yin ti-wang pen-chi*," *Monumenta Serica* 19: 486–515.

1972   *The First Radiocarbon Dates from China.* Monographs on Far Eastern History. Canberra: National Australian University.

Barnard, Noel, and Kwong-yue Cheung

1978   *Chung Jih Ou Mei Ao Niu So-chien So-t'o So-mu Chin-wen Hui-pien* 中日歐美澳紐所見所拓所摹金文匯編. Taipei: Yi-wen.

1983   *Studies in Chinese Archaeology, 1980–82,* Reports on Visits to Mainland China, Taiwan, and the U.S.A.; Participation in Conferences in These Countries; and Some Notes and Impressions. Hong Kong: Wen-hsüeh-she.

Barnard, Noel, and Chia-pao Wan

1976   "The casting of inscriptions in Chinese bronzes—with particular reference to those with relievo guide-lines," *Soochow University Journal of Chinese Art History* 6: 43–134.

Chalfant, Frank H., and R. S. Britton

1935   *K'u Fang Erh-shih Ts'ang Chia-ku P'u-tz'u* 庫方二氏藏甲骨卜辭. Shanghai: Commercial Press.

1939   *Chin-chang So Ts'ang Chia-ku P'u-tz'u* 金璋所藏甲骨卜辭. New York: Chalfant Publication Fund.

Chang, Ch'ang-shou 張長壽

1979   "Yin Shang shih-tai ti ch'ing-t'ung jung-ch'i 殷商時代的青銅容器," *K'ao-ku-hsüeh-pao* 考古學報, 1979 (3): 271–300.

Chang, Cheng-lang 張政烺

1952   "Ku-tai Chung-kuo ti shih-chin-chih shih-tsu tsu-chih hsü 古代中國的十進制氏族組織, 續," *Li-shih-chiao-hsüeh* 歷史教學, 2: 195–96.

1973   "P'u-tz'u p'ou-t'ien chi ch'i hsiang-kuan chu wen-ti 卜辭裒田及其相關諸問題," *K'ao-ku-hsüeh-pao* 考古學報, 1973 (1): 93–118.

Chang, Kwang-chih 張光直

1967   "Yin li chung ti erh fen hsien-hsiang 殷禮中的二分現象," *Essays Presented to Dr. Li Chi On His Seventieth Birthday,* pp. 353–70. Taipei: The Tsinghua Journal.

1980   *Shang Civilization.* New Haven: Yale University Press.

Chang, Ping-ch'üan 張秉權

1957–72   *Yin-hsü Wen-tzu Ping Pien* 殷虛文字丙編. Taipei: Institute of History and Philology, Academia Sinica.

1967   "Chia-ku-wen chung so-chien jen ti t'ung ming k'ao 甲骨文中所見人地同名考," *Essays Presented to Dr. Li Chi on His Seventieth Birthday,* pp. 687–776. Taipei: The Tsinghua Journal.

1969   "P'u-tz'u chung so-chien Yin Shang cheng-chih t'ung-yi ti li-liang chi ch'i ta-tao ti fan-wei 卜辭中所見殷商政治統一的力量及其達到的範圍," *Bulletin of the Institute of History and Philology, Academia Sinica* 50: 175–229.

Chao, Hsin-lai 趙新來

1966   "Cheng-chou Erh-li-kang hsin fa-hsien ti Shang tai yü chang 鄭州二里岡新發現的商代玉璋," *Wen-wu* 文物, 1966 (1): 58.

Ch'en, Meng-chia 陳夢家

1954   "Yin tai t'ung-ch'i 殷代銅器," *K'ao-ku-hsüeh-pao* 考古學報, 7: 15–59.

1956a   *Yin-hsü P'u-tz'u Tsung Shu* 殷墟卜辭綜述. Peking: Science Press.

1956b   "Hsi-Chou t'ung-ch'i tuan-tai (V) 西周銅器斷代(五)," *K'ao-ku-hsüeh-pao*

考古學報, 1956 (3): 105–27.
Cheng, Chen-hsiang 鄭振香
1983 "Fu Hao mu ch'u-t'u Ssu T'u Mu ming-wen t'ung-ch'i ti t'an-t'ao 婦好墓出土司䛅母銘文銅器的探討," K'ao-ku 考古, 1983 (8): 716–25.
Cheng, Chen-hsiang, and Chih-ta Chen 鄭振香, 陳志達
1981 "Lun Fu Hao mu tui Yin-hsü wen-hua ho p'u-tz'u tuan-tai ti yi-yi 記婦好墓對殷墟文化和卜辭斷代的意義," K'ao-ku 考古, 1981 (6): 511–18.
Cheng, Te-k'un 鄭德坤
1971 "Inconstancy of character structures," *Journal of the Institute of Chinese Studies* 4, no. 1: 137–72.
Chernykh, E. N.
1978 "Metallurgicheskie provintsii i periodizatsiia epokhi rannego metalla na territorii SSSR," *Sovetskaia Arkheologiia* 4.
Cheung, Kwong-yue, and Noel Barnard
in prep. *Chin Wu-shih Nien Hsin-huo Ch'ing-t'ung-ch'i Ming-wen Hui Shih* First volume in press.
Ch'iu, Hsi-kuei 裘錫圭
1980 "Chia-ku-wen k'ao-shih: Shih Chia T'u Chia chi Yang Chia shuo 甲骨文考釋: 石甲兔甲即陽甲説" *Ku-wen-tzu-yen-chiu* 古文字研究, 4: 163–64.
Chlenova, N. L.
1961 "Osnovnye voprosy proiskhozhdeniia tagarskoi kulk'tury," in *Voprosy istorii Sibiri i Dal'nego Vostoka.*
1962 "Ob olennykh kamniakh Mongolii i Sibiri," in *Mongol'skii arkheologicheskii sbornik.*
1967 *Proiskhzhdenie i ranniaia istoriia plemen tagarskoi kul'tury.*
1972 *Khronologiia pamiatnikov karasukskoi epokhi.*
1976 *Karasukskie kinzhaly.*
Chou, Fa-kao 周法高
1960–61 "Certain dates of the Shang period," *Harvard Journal of Asiatic Studies* 23: 108–13.
1971a *Han Tzu Ku Chin Yin Hui* 漢字古今音彙. Hong Kong: The Chinese University of Hong Kong Press.
1971b "Chronology of the Western Chou dynasty," *Journal of the Institute of Chinese Studies* 4 (1): 173–205.
1983 "Lun chin-wen yüeh hsiang yü Hsi Chou wang nien 論金文月相與西周王年." *Palaeographic Essays from the International Conference on Chinese Palaeography.* Hong Kong, 1983.
Chu, Chen-yüan 朱振遠, et al.
1975 "Shan-hsi Sui te Yen t'ou ts'un fa hsien yi p'i chiao-ts'ang Shang ti t'ung-ch'i 陝西綏德媽頭村發現一批窖藏商代銅器," *Wen-wu* 文物, 1975 (2): 82–87.
Chu, Feng-han 朱鳳瀚
1981 "Yin-hsü p'u-tz'u chung ti 'chung' ti shen-fen wen-t'i 殷墟卜辭中的'眾'的身份問題," *Nan-k'ai-hsüeh-pao* 南開學報, 1981 (2): 57–74.
Chung-kuo-she-hui-k'o-hsüeh-yüan K'ao-ku-yen-chiu-so 中國社會科學院考古研究所
1980a *Yin-hsü Fu Hao Mu* 殷墟婦好墓. Peking: Wen-wu Press.
1980b *Hsiao-t'un-nan-ti Chia-ku* 小屯南地甲骨. Peking: Chung-hua.

1982   *Yin-hsü Yü Ch'i* 殷墟玉器. Peking: Wen-wu Press.

Chung-yüan-wen-wu 中原文物
1981   "Lo-shan Mang-chang Hou-li Shang Chou mu-ti ti-erh-ts'e fa-chüeh chien pao 羅山蟒張后李商周墓地第二次發掘簡報," *Chung-yüan-wen-wu* 中原文物, 1981 (4): 4–13.

Dohrenwend, D.
1971   *Chinese Jades in the Royal Ontario Museum.* Toronto.

Egami, Namio, and Mizuno, Seiichi 江上波夫, 水野清一
1935   *Nai Mōko Chōjō Chitai* 內蒙古長城地帶. Tokyo and Kyoto: East Asiatic Archaeological Society.

Fan, Wei-yüeh, and Chen-feng Wu 樊維岳, 吳鎮峰
1980   "Shan-hsi Lan-t'ien hsien ch'u-t'u Shang-tai ch'ing-t'ung-ch'i 陝西藍田縣出土商代青銅器," *Wen-wu-tzu-liao ts'ung-k'an* 文物資料叢刊, 3: 25–27.

Fang, Shih-ming, and Hsiu-ling Wang 方詩銘, 王修齡
1981   *Ku-pen Chu-shu-chi-nien Chi Cheng* 古本竹書紀年輯證. Shanghai: Ku-chi Press.

Freer Gallery of Art
1946   *A Description and Illustrated Catalogue of Chinese Bronzes Acquired during the Administration of John Ellerton Lodge.* Washington, D.C.

Griaznov, M. P.
1947   "Pamiatniki maiemirskogo etapa epokhi rannikh kochevnikov," *Kratkie Soobshcheniia Instituta Istorii Material'noi Kul'tury,* 18.

Grishin, Iu. C.
1975   *Bronzovyi i panni zheleznyi vek vostochnogo Zabaikal'ia.*

Hamada, Kōsaku 濱田耕作
1925   *Yūgyokusai zō Kogyokufu* 有玉齋藏古玉譜. Kyoto.

Hansford, S. H.
1950   *Chinese Jade Carving.* London.
1968   *Chinese Carved Jades.* London.

Hayashi, Minao 林巳奈夫
1969   "Chūgoku kodai no saigyoku zuigyoku 中国古代の祭玉瑞玉," *Tōhōgakuhō* (Kyoto) 東方学報(京都), 54: 161–323.
1972   *Chūgoku In Shū Jidai no Buki* 中国殷周時代の武器. Kyoto: Institute of Humanistic Science, Kyoto University.
1976   "In Shō seidōki meibun chūzōhō ni kansuru jakkan no mondai 殷商青銅器銘文鑄造法に関する若干の問題," *Tōhōgakuhō* (Kyoto) 東方学報(京都), 51: 1–57.
1982   "Chūgoku kodai hōchōkei gyokuki to kotsusankei gyokuki 中国古代庖丁形玉器と骨鏟形玉器," *Tōhōgakuhō* (Kyoto) 東方学報(京都), 54.

Honan Province Bureau of Culture 河南省文化局
1959   *Cheng-chou Erh-li-kang* 鄭州二里岡. Peking: Science Press.

Honan Province Institute of Archaeology 河南省考古研究所
ms-a   *Cheng-chou Lo-ta-miao chi Tung-chai Shang tai yi-chih fa-chüeh pao-kao* 鄭州洛達廟及董砦商代遺址發掘報告.
ms-b   *Cheng-chou Shang Tai Chu-t'ung Yi-chih Fa-chüeh Pao-kao* 鄭州商代鑄銅遺址發掘報告.

REFERENCES CITED

Honan Province Institute of Cultural Relics 河南省文物研究所
1981   *Ho-nan Ch'u-t'u Shang Chou Ch'ing-t'ung-ch'i (yi)* 河南出土商周青銅器(一). Peking: Wen-wu Press.

Hopei Province Museum 河北省博物館
1977   *Kao-ch'eng T'ai-hsi Shang-tai Yi-chih* 藁城台西商代遺址. Peking: Wen-wun Press.
1980   *Ho-pei-sheng Ch'u-t'u Wen-wu Hsüan-chi* 河北省出土文物選集. Peking: Wen-wu Press.

Hsia, Nai 夏鼐
1951   "Ho-nan Ch'eng-kao Kuang-wu-ch'ü k'ao-ku chi lüeh 河南成皋廣武區考古紀略," *K'o-hsüeh-t'ung-pao* 科學通報, 1951 (2): 724.
1974   "Shen Kua yü k'ao-ku-hsüeh 沈括與考古學," *K'ao-ku* 考古, 1974 (5): 277–89.
1977   "T'an-14 ts'e-ting nien-tai ho Chung-kuo shih-ch'ien k'ao-ku-hsüeh 碳-14測定年代和中國史前考古學," *K'ao-ku* 考古, 1977 (4): 217–32.
1983   "Han tai ti yü-ch'i 漢代的玉器," *K'ao-ku-hsüeh-pao* 考古學報, 1983 (2): 125–45.

Hsieh, Ch'ing-shan, and Shao-shun Yang 謝青山，楊紹舜
1960   "Shan-hsi Lü-liang-hsien Shih-lou-chen yu fa-hsien t'ung-ch'i 山西呂梁石樓鎮又發現銅器," *Wen-wu* 文物, 1960 (7): 51–52.

Hsiung, Ch'uan-hsin 熊傳新
1981   "Hu-nan hsin fa-hsien ti ch'ing-t'ung-ch'i 湖南新發現的青銅器," *Wen-wu-tzu-liao-ts'ung-k'an* 文物資料叢刊, 5: 103–05.

Hsüeh, Yao 薛堯
1963   "Chiang-hsi ch'u-t'u ti chi-chien ch'ing-t'ung-ch'i 江西出土的幾件青銅器," *K'ao-ku* 考古, 1963 (8): 416–18.

Hu, Hou-hsüan 胡厚宣
1944   "Wu-ting shih-tai wu chung chi-shih k'o-tz'u k'ao 武丁時代五種紀事刻辭考," *Chia-ku-hsüeh Shang-shih Lun-ts'ung Ch'u-chi* 甲骨學商史論叢, 初集. Ch'eng-tu: Ch'i-lu University.
1954   *Chan-hou Ching Chin Hsin-huo Chia-ku Chi* 戰後京津新獲甲骨集. Shanghai: Ch'ün-lien Press.
1955   *Yin-hsü Fa-chüeh* 殷墟發掘. Peking: Hsüeh-hsi-sheng-huo Press.
1982   "P'u-tz'u 'Jih yüeh yu shih' shuo 卜辭'日月又食'說," manuscript.

Hu, P'ing-sheng 胡平生
1982   "An-yang Hsiao-t'un YM-238 ti shih-tai wen-t'i 安陽小屯YM-238的時代問題," *K'ao-ku-yü-wen-wu* 考古與文物, 1982 (3): 51–56.

Hua, Chüeh-ming 華覺明, et al.
1981   "Fu Hao mu ch'ing-t'ung-chi ch'un chu-tsao chi-shu ti yen-chiu 婦好墓青銅器羣鑄造技術的研究," *K'ao-ku-hsüeh-chi-kan* 考古學集刊, 1: 244–72.
1982   "Shang Chou ch'ing-t'ung jung-ch'i ho-chin ch'eng-fen ti k'ao-ch'a chien lun chung ting chih ch'i ti hsing-ch'eng 商周青銅容器合金成份的考察，兼論鐘鼎之齊的形成." Paper presented at the 1982 annual meeting of the Chinese Society of the History of Science.

Huang, Chün 黃濬
1935   *Ku Yü T'u Lu Ch'u-pien* 古玉圖錄初編. Peiping.

Huang, Shih-lin 黃石林
1978 "Kuan-yü t'an-so Hsia wen-hua wen-t'i 關於探索夏文化問題," *Ho-nan-wen-po-t'ung-hsün* 河南文博通訊, 1978 (1): 37–48.

Hunan Province Museum 湖南省博物館
1964 *Hu-nan-sheng Wen-wu T'u-lu* 湖南省文物圖錄. Changsha: Hunan People's Press.
1979 "San-shih-nien-lai Hu-nan wen-wu k'ao-ku kung-tso 三十年來湖南文物考古工作," in *Wen-wu K'ao-ku Kung-tso San-shih-nien* 文物考古工作三十年, pp. 310–24. Peking: Wen-wu Press.
1981 *Hu-nan-sheng Po-wu-kuan* 湖南省博物館. Tokyo: Kodansha–Wen-wu Press.

Hupei Province Museum 湖北省博物館
1976 "I-ch'ang Ch'ien-p'ing Chan-kuo Liang-Han mu 宜昌前坪戰國兩漢墓," *K'ao-ku-hsüeh-pao* 考古學報, 1976 (2): 117–21.

Jung, Keng 容庚
1941 *Shang Chou Yi-ch'i T'ung-k'ao* 商周彝器通考. Peking: Harvard-Yenching Institute.

Kane, Virginia
1973 "The chronological significance of the inscribed ancestor dedication in the bronze vessels," *Artibus Asiae* 35: 335–70.
1975 "A re-examination of An-yang archaeology," *Ars Orientalis* 10: 93–110.
1982 "Art-historical issues arising from the M-5 burial at An-yang," manuscript.

Kao, Chih-hsi 高至喜
1960 "Shang tai jen mien fang ting 商代人面方鼎, *Wen-wu* 文物, 1960 (10): 57–58.
1963 "Hu-nan Ning-hsiang Huang-ts'ai fa-hsien Shang-tai t'ung-ch'i ho yi-chih 湖南寧鄉黃材發現商代銅器和遺址," *K'ao-ku* 考古, 1963 (12): 646–48.
1981 "Shang wen-hua pu-kuo Ch'ang-chiang pein—Ts'un k'ao-ku fa-hsien k'an Hu-nan ti Shang-tai wen-hua 商文化不過長江辨—從考古發現看湖南商代文化," *Ch'iu-so* 求索, 1981 (2): 102–07.

Kao, Ch'ü-hsün 高去尋
1958 "Yin tai ti yi-mien t'ung ching chi ch'i hsiang-kuan ti wen-t'i 殷代的一面銅鏡及其相關的問題," *Bulletin of the Institute of History and Philology, Academia Sinica* 29: 685–719.
1967 "Tao fu tsang chung ti t'ung tao 刀斧葬中的銅刀," *Bulletin of the Institute of History and Philology, Academia Sinica* 37: 355–82.

K'ao-ku 考古
1960 "S. V. Kiselev t'ung-hsun yüan-shih tsang Pei-ching so tso ti hsüeh-shu pao-kao (2) Su-lien ching nei ti ch'ing-t'ung wen-hua yü Chung-kuo Shang wen-hua ti kuan-hsi S. V. 吉謝烈夫通訊院士在北京所作的學術報告 (2) 蘇聯境內的青銅文化與中國商文化的關係," *K'ao-ku* 考古, 1960 (2): 45–53.
1961a "1958–1959 nien Yin-hsu fa-chüeh chien pao 1958·1959年殷墟發掘簡報," *K'ao-ku* 考古, 1961 (2): 63–76.
1961b "1959-nien Ho-nan Yen-shih Erh-li-t'ou shih chüeh chien pao 1959年河南偃師二里頭試掘簡報," *K'ao-ku* 考古, 1961 (2): 82–85.
1962 "Ho-pei Ch'ing-lung hsien Ch'ao-tao-kuo fa-hsien yi-p'i ch'ing-t'ung-ch'i 河北青龍縣抄道溝發現一批青銅器," *Kao-ku* 考古, 1962 (12): 644–45.
1964 "1962-nien An-yang Ta-ssu-k'ung-ts'un fa-chüeh chien pao 1962年安陽大司

REFERENCES CITED

空村發掘簡報,＂*K'ao-ku* 考古, 1964 (8): 380–84.

1965 "Ho-nan Yeh-shih Erh-li-t'ou yi-chih fa-chüeh chien pao 河南偃師二里頭遺址發掘簡報,＂ *K'ao-ku* 考古, 1965 (5): 215–24.

1972a "1971-nien An-yang Hou-kang fa-chüeh chien pao 1971年安陽後岡發掘簡報,＂ *K'ao-ku* 考古, 1972 (3): 18–21.

1972b "Shan-hsi Shih-lou yi-tieh fa-hsien ti Shang-tai t'ung-ch'i 山西石樓義牒發現的商代銅器,＂ *K'ao-ku* 考古, 1972 (4): 29–30.

1973 "Ho-pei Kao-ch'eng T'ai-hsi-ts'un ti Shang-tai yi-chih 河北藁城台西村的商代遺址,＂ *K'ao-ku* 考古, 1973 (5): 266–76.

1974 "Ho-nan Yeh-shih Erh-li-t'ou tsang-Shang kung-tien yi-chih fa-chüeh chien pao 河南偃師二里頭早商宮殿遺址發掘簡報,＂ *K'ao-ku* 考古, 1974 (4): 234–50.

1975 "1973-nien An-yang Hsiao-t'un-nan-ti fa-chüeh chien pao 1973年安陽小屯南地發掘簡報,＂ *K'ao-ku* 考古, 1975 (1): 27–46.

1976a "Shan-hsi Ch'i-shan Ho-chia-ts'un Hsi-Chou mu-tsang 陝西岐山賀家村西周墓葬,＂ *K'ao-ku* 考古, 1976 (1): 31–38.

1976b "Pei-ching Liu-li-ho Hsia-chia-tien hsia-ts'eng wen-hua mu-tsang 北京琉璃河夏家店下層文化墓葬,＂ *K'ao-ku* 考古, 1976 (1): 59–60.

1976c "Pei-ching ti-ch'ü ti yu yi chung-yao k'ao-ku shou-huo 北京地區的又一重要考古收獲,＂ *K'ao-ku* 考古, 1976 (4): 246–58.

1976d "Yen-shih Erh-li-t'ou yi-chih hsin fa-hsien ti t'ung-ch'i ho hü-ch'i 偃師二里頭遺址新發現的銅器和玉器,＂ *K'ao-ku* 考古, 1976 (4): 259–63.

1976e "1975-nien An-yang Yin-hsü ti hsin fa-hsien 1975年安陽殷墟的新發現,＂ *K'ao-ku* 考古, 1976 (4): 264–72.

1977a "Liao-ning K'o-shih-k'o-t'eng-ch'i T'ien-pao-t'ung fa-hsien Shang-tai t'ung hsien 遼寧克什克騰旗天寶同發現商代銅甗,＂ *K'ao-ku* 考古, 1977 (4): 354.

1977b "An-yang Yin-hsü wu-hao mu tso-t'an chi yao 安陽殷墟五號墓座談紀要,＂ *K'ao-ku* 考古, 1977 (5): 341–50.

1977c "Shan-hsi Yung-ho fa-hsien Yin-tai t'ung-ch'i 山西永和發現殷代銅器,＂ *K'ao-ku* 考古, 1977 (5): 355–56.

1978 "Liao-ning Hsing-ch'eng-hsien Yang-ho fa-hsien ch'ing-t'ung-chi 遼寧興城縣楊河發現青銅器,＂ *K'ao-ku* 考古, 1978 (6): 387.

1979a "Ho-nan Ling-pao ch'u-t'u yi-p'i Shang-tai ch'ing-t'ung-ch'i 河南靈寶出土一批商代青銅器,＂ *K'ao-ku* 考古, 1979 (1): 20–22.

1979b "Ho-pei Yüan-shih-hsien Hsi-chang-ts'un ti Hsi-Chou yi-chih ho mu-tsang 河北元氏縣西張村的西周遺址和墓葬,＂ *K'ao-ku* 考古, 1979 (1): 23–26.

1979c "An-yang Wu-kuan-ts'un pei ti yi-tso Yin mu 安陽武官村北的一座殷墓,＂ *K'ao-ku* 考古, 1979 (3): 223–26.

1979d "Pei-ching-shih Yen-ch'ing-hsien Hsi-pa-tzu-ts'un chiao-ts'ang t'ung-ch'i 北京市延慶縣西撥子村窖藏銅器,＂ *K'ao-ku* 考古, 1979 (3): 227–30.

1980 "Shan-hsi Hsia-hsien Tung-hsia-feng yi-chih tung-ch'ü chung-ch'ü fa-chüeh chien pao 山西夏縣東下馮遺址東區中區發掘簡報,＂ *K'ao-ku* 考古, 1980 (2): 97–107.

1981a "Ho-nan Lo-shan-hsien Mang-chang Shang-tai mu-ti ti-yi-tz'u fa-chüeh chien pao 河南羅山縣蟒張商代墓地第一次發掘簡報,＂ *K'ao-ku* 考古, 1981 (2): 111–18.

1981b	"Liao-ning Fu-shun-shih fa-hsien Yin-tai ch'ing-t'ung huan-shou tao 遼寧撫順市發現殷代青銅環首刀," *K'ao-ku* 考古, 1981 (2): 190.
1982a	"Shan-hsi T'ung-ch'uan fa-hsien Shang Chou ch'ing-t'ung-ch'i 陝西銅川發現商周青銅器," *K'ao-ku* 考古, 1982 (1): 107.
1982b	"Chi Liao-ning K'o-tso-hsien Hou-fen-ts'un fa-hsien ti yi-tsu t'ao-ch'i 記遼寧喀左縣後墳村發現的一組陶器," *K'ao-ku* 考古, 1982 (1): 108–09.
1983	"1980-nien ch'iu Ho-nan Yen-shih Erh-li-t'ou yi-chih fa-chüeh chien pao 1980年秋河南偃師二里頭遺址發掘簡報," *K'ao-ku* 考古, 1983 (3): 201–05.

K'ao-ku-hsüeh-pao 考古學報

1957	"Ch'ang-an P'u-tu-ts'un Hsi-Chou mu ti fa-chüeh 長安普渡村西周墓的發掘." *K'ao-ku-hsüeh-pao* 考古學報, 1957 (1): 75–85.
1973a	"Cheng-chou Nan-kuan-wai Shang-tai yi-chih fa-chüeh pao-kao 鄭州南關外商代遺址發掘報告," *K'ao-ku-hsüeh-pao* 考古學報, 1973 (1): 65–92.
1973b	"Ning-ch'eng-hsien Nan-shan-ken ti shih kuo mu 寧城縣南山根的石槨墓," *K'ao-ku-hsüeh-pao* 考古學報, 1973 (2): 27–39.
1977a	"An-yang Yin-hsü wu-hao mu ti fa-chüeh 安陽殷墟五號墓的發掘," *K'ao-ku-hsüeh-pao* 考古學報, 1977 (2): 57–98.
1977b	"Kan-su Ling-t'ai Pai-ts'ao-p'o Hsi-Chou mu 甘肅靈台白草坡西周墓," *K'ao-ku-hsüeh-pao* 考古學報, 1977 (2): 99–130.
1979	"1969–1977-nien Yin-hsü hsi ch'ü mu-tsang fa-chüeh pao-kao 1969·1977年殷墟西區墓葬發掘報告," *K'ao-ku-hsüeh-pao* 考古學報, 1979 (1): 27–147.
1981	"An-yang Hsiao-t'un-ts'un pei ti liang tso Yin-tai mu 安陽小屯村北的兩座殷代墓," *K'ao-ku-hsüeh-pao* 考古學報, 1981 (4): 491–517.

K'ao-ku-yü-wen-wu 考古與文物

1981	"Shan-hsi Lan-t'ien Huai-chen-fang Shang-tai yi-chih shih chüeh chien pao 陝西藍田懷鎮坊商代遺址試掘簡報," *K'ao-ku-yü-wen-wu* 考古與文物, 1981 (3): 48–53.
1982	"Wei hsien k'ao-ku chi lüeh 蔚縣考古記略," *K'ao-ku-yü-wen-wu* 考古與文物, 1982 (4): 10–14.

Karlgren, Bernhard

1950	*The book of Documents*. Stockholm: The Museum of Far Eastern Antiquities.

Keightley, David N.

1978a	*Sources of Shang History*. Berkeley and Los Angeles: University of California Press.
1978b	"The bamboo annals and Shang chronology," *Harvard Journal of Asiatic Studies* 38: 423–38.

Kiselev, S. V.

1951	*Drevniaia istoriia iuzhnoi Sibiri*.
1960	"Neolit i bronzovyi vek Kitaia," *Sovetskaia Arkheologiia* 4.
1962	"K izucheniiu minusinskikh kamennykh izvaianii," in *Istoriko-arkheologicheskii sbornik*.
1965	"Bronzovyi vek SSSR," in *Novoe v Sovetskoi Arkheologii*. Komarova, M. N.
1952	"Tomskii mogil'nik: pamiatnik istorii drevnikh plemen lesnoi polocy zapadnoi Sibiri," *Materialy i issledovaniia po arkheologii SSSR* 24.

Kuo, Mo-jo 郭沫若

1933	*P'u-tz'u T'ung-ts'uan K'ao-shih* 卜辭通纂考釋. Tokyo: Bunrindō Kinzoku.

REFERENCES CITED

1934   *Ku-tai Ming-k'o Hui-k'ao Hsü-pien* 古代銘刻匯考續編 Tokyo: Bunkyūdō.
1937   *Yin ch'i ts'ui pien* 殷契萃編. Tokyo: Bunkyūdō.
1957a   *Liao Chou Chin-wen-tz'u Ta-hsi T'u-lu K'ao-shih*
        Peking: Science Press.
1957b   "Yi-ch'i hsing-hsiang-hsüeh shih t'an 彝器形象學試探," in *Ch'ing-t'ung Shih-tai* 青銅時代. Peking: Science Press.
1960   "An-yang yüan-k'eng-mu chung ting ming k'ao-shih 安陽圓坑墓中鼎銘考釋," *K'ao-ku-hsüeh-pao* 考古學報, 1960 (1): 1–5.

Kuo, Mo-jo 郭沫若, editor
1978–   *Chia-ku-wen Ho-chi* 甲骨文合集. Peking: Chung-hua.

Kuo, Pao-chün 郭寶鈞
1949   "Ku yü hsin ch'üan 古玉新詮," *Bulletin of the Institute of History and Philology, Academia Sinica* 20: 1–46.
1963   *Chung-kuo Ch'ing-t'ung-ch'i Shih-tai* 中國青銅器時代. Peking: San-lien.
1964   *Chün-hsien Hsin-ts'un* 濬縣辛村. Peking: Science Press.

Kuo, Te-wei 郭德維
1982   "Chiang-ling Ch'u mu lun-shu 江陵楚墓論述," *K'ao-ku-hsüeh-pao* 考古學報, 1982 (2): 155–82.

Kuo, Yung 郭勇
1962   "Shih-lou Hou-lan-chia-kou fa-hsien Shang-tai ch'ing-t'ung-ch'i chien pao 石樓后蘭家灣發現商代銅器簡報," *Wen-wu* 文物, 1962 (4/5): 33–35.
1980   "Shan-hsi Ch'ang-tzu-hsien pei-chiao fa-hsien Shang-tai t'ung-ch'i 山西長子縣北郊發現商代銅器," *Wen-wu-tzu-liao-ts'ung-k'an* 文物資料叢刊 3: 198–201.

Kwangsi Chuang Autonomous Region Museum 廣西壯族自治區博物館
1982   "Ku-tai t'ung-ku hsüeh-shu t'ao-lun hui chi yao 古代銅鼓學術討論會記要," in *Ku-tai T'ung-ku Hsüeh-shu T'ao-lun Hui Lun-wen Chi* 古代銅鼓學術討論會論文集. Peking: Wen-wu Press.

Kyzlasov, L. P.
1958   "Etapy drevnei istorii Tuvy," *Vestnik Moskovskovo Gosudarstvennogo Universiteta, seriia istoriko-filosofskaia* 4.

Lai, Tung-fang (Orient Lee) 黎東方
1975   *Chronological Data from Western Chou Bronzes*. Taipei.

Lao, Kan 勞榦
1981   "Shang Chou nien-tai ti hsin ku-chi 商周年代的新估計," in *Kuo-chi Han-hsueh Hui-yi Lun-wen Chi* 國際漢學會議論文集 (Li-shih-k'ao-ku-tsu 歷史考古組, pp. 279–302). Taipei.

Laufer, B.
1912   *Jade: A Study in Chinese Archaeology and Religion*. Chicago: Field Museum of Natural History.

Legge, James
1865   *The Chinese Classics, Vol. III The Shoo King or The Book of Historical Documents*. Hong Kong and London: Oxford University Press.

Li, Chi 李濟
1949   "Chi Hsiao-t'un ch'u-t'u chih ch'ing-t'ung-ch'i 記小屯出土之青銅器," *K'ao-ku-hsüeh-pao* 考古學報, 4: 1–70.

1952 "Yin-hsü yu-jen shih-ch'i t'u-shuo 殷墟有刄石器圖說," *Bulletin of the Institute of History and Philology, Academia Sinica* 23: 523–615.
1956 *Yin-hsü Ch'i-wu Chia pien T'ao-ch'i shang pien* 殷虛器物甲編陶器上編. Taipei: Institute of History and Philology, Academia Sinica.
1959 "Chi hsing pa chung chi ch'i wen-shih chih yen-pien 箕形八種及其文飾之演變," *Bulletin of the Institute of History and Philology, Academia Sinica* 30: 1–69.
1977 *Anyang*. Seattle: University of Washington Press.

Li, Hsiao-ting 李孝定
1965 *Chia-ku Wen-tzu Chi Shih* 甲骨文字集釋. Taipei: Institute of History and Philology, Academia Sinica.

Li, Hsüeh-ch'in 李學勤
1977 "Lun Fu Hao mu ti nien-tai chi yu-kuan wen-t'i 論婦好墓的年代及有關問題," *Wen-wu* 文物, 1977 (11): 32–37.

Li, Po-ch'ien 李伯謙
1979 "An-yang Yin-hsü wu-hao mu ti nien-tai wen-t'i 安陽殷墟五號墓的年代問題," *K'ao-ku* 考古, 1979 (2): 165–70.

Li, Po-ch'ien, and Cheng, Chieh-hsiang 李伯謙, 鄭傑祥
1981 "Hou-li Shang-tai mu-tsang tsu-shu shih hsi 后李商代墓葬族屬試析," *Chung-yüan-wen-wu* 中原文物, 1981 (4): 33–35, 46.

Li, Shun-yi 李純一
1957 "Kuan-yü Yin chung ti yen-chiu 關於殷鐘的研究," *K'ao-ku-hsüeh-pao* 考古學報, 1957 (3): 40–50.

Liang, Ching-chin 梁景津
1978 "Kuang-hsi ch'u-t'u ti ch'ing-t'ung-ch'i 廣西出土的青銅器," *Wen-wu* 文物, 1978 (10): 93–96.

Liang, Ssu-yung 梁思永
1933 "Hou-kang fa-chüeh hsiao chi 後岡發掘小記," *An-yang-fa-chüeh-pao-kao* 安陽發掘報告, 4: 609–26.

Liang, Ssu-yung, and Kao, Ch'ü-hsun 梁思永, 高去尋
1962–76 *Hou-chia-chuang Ta-mu* 侯家莊大墓. Taipei: Institute of History and Philology, Academia Sinica (Tomb No. 1001, 1962; No. 1002, 1965; No. 1003, 1967; No. 1217, 1968; No. 1004, 1970; No. 1500, 1974; No. 1550, 1976).

Liao, Yung-min 廖永民
1957 "Cheng-chou-shih fa-chüeh ti yi-ch'u Shang-tai chü-chu yü chu-tsao t'ung-ch'i yi-chih chien chieh 鄭州市發掘的一處商代居住與鑄造銅器遺址簡介," *Wen-wu-ts'an-k'ao-tzu-liao* 文物參考資料, 1957 (6): 73–74.

Lin, Jui 林瑞, et al.
1981 "Tui Tseng Hou Yi mu pien-chung ti chieh-kuo t'an-t'ao 對鄫侯乙墓編鐘的結構探討," *Chiang-Han-k'ao-ku* 江漢考古, 1981 (1): 25–30.

Lin, Shou-chin 林壽晉
1959 *Shang-ts'un-ling Kuo-kuo Mu-ti* 上村嶺虢國墓地. Peking: Science Press.

Lin, Yün 林澐
1980 "Kuan-yü ch'ing-t'ung kung-hsing-ch'i ti jo-kan wen-t'i 關於青銅弓形器的若干問題," *Chi-lin-ta-hsüeh She-hui-k'o-hsüeh Lun-ts'ung* 吉林大學社會科學論叢, 2.

REFERENCES CITED

Ling, Shun-sheng 凌純聲
1965 "Chung-kuo ku-tai jui kui ti yen-chiu 中國古代瑞圭的研究," *Bulletin of the Institute of Ethnology, Academia Sinica* 20: 163–205.

Liu, Ch'i-yi 劉啟益
1982 "Hsi-Chou chin-wen chung ti yüeh-hsiang yü Kung-ho Hsüan Yu chi-nien t'ung-ch'i 西周金文中的月相與共和宣幽紀年銅器." Paper presented at the Fourth Annual Conference of Chinese Palaeography, T'ai-yüan.

Liu, Hsing 劉興
1981 "T'an Chen-chiang ti-ch'ü ch'u-t'u ch'ing-t'ung-ch'i ti t'e-se 談鎮江地區出土青銅器的特色," *Wen-wu-tzu-liao-ts'ung-k'an* 文物資料叢刊, 5: 112–16.

Liu, Yüan-lin 劉淵臨
1974 "P'u ku ti kung-chih chi-shu yen-chin kuo-ch'eng chih t'an-t'ao 卜骨的攻治技術演進過程之探討," *Bulletin of the Institute of History and Philology, Academia Sinica* 46: 99–130.

Lo, Hsi-chang 羅西章
1977 "Fu-feng Pai-chia-yao shui-k'u ch'u-t'u Shang Chou wen-wu 扶風白家窰水庫出土商周文物," *Wen-wu* 文物, 1977 (12): 84–86.
1980 "Fu-feng ch'u-t'u ti Shang Chou ch'ing-t'ung-ch'i 扶風出土的商周青銅器," *K'ao-ku-yü-wen-wu* 考古與文物, 4: 6–22.

Loehr, Max
1949 "Weapons and tools from Anyang and Siberian analogies," *American Journal of Archaeology* 53: 126–44.
1953 "The bronze styles of the Anyang period (1300–1028 B.C.)," *Archives of the Chinese Art Society of America* 7: 42–53.
1975 *Ancient Chinese Jades.* Cambridge: Fogg Museum.

Lowie, Robert H.
1920 *Primitive Society.* New York: Boni & Liveright.

Maksimenkov, G. A.
1960 "Bronzovye kel'ty krasnoiarsko-angarskikh tipov," *Sovetskaia Arkheologiia* 1.
1961 "Novye dannye po arkheologii raiona Krasnoiarska," in *Voprosy istorii Sibiri i Dal'nego Vostoka.*
1975 "Sovremennoe sostoianie voprosa o periodizatsii epokhi bronzy minusinskoi kotloviny," in *Pervobytnaia arkheologiia Sibiri.*

Na-chih-liang 那志良
1977 *Chinese Jades, Archaic and Modern.* London.
1980 *Ku Yü Chien Ts'ai* 古玉鑑裁. Taipei: Kuo-t'ai Art Gallery.

Nan, Po 南波
1975 "Chieh-shao yi-chien ch'ing-t'ung ching 介紹一件青銅鏡," *Wen-wu* 文物, 1975 (8): 87–88.

Nieh, Ch'ung-yi 聶崇義
1935 *San Li T'u* 三禮圖, Ssu-pu-ts'ung-k'an 四部叢刊 edition.

Nivison, David
1982 "The 'question' question," manuscript.
1983 "The dates of Western Chou," *Harvard Journal of Asiatic Studies* 43: 481–580.

Okladnikov, A. P.
1955 *Istoriia Iakutskoi ASSR*, vol. 1.

Pankenier, David W.
1981/82   "Astronomical dates in Shang and Western Chou," *Early China* 7: 2–37.
Peking University Archaeology Program
1979   *Shang Chou K'ao-ku* 商周考古. Peking: Wen-wu Press.
Rawson, J., and J. Ayers
1975   *Chinese Jades Throughout the Ages*. London.
Salmony, A.
1933   *Sino-Siberian Art in the Collection of C. T. Loo*.
1952   *Archaic Chinese Jades*. Chicago.
1963   *Chinese Jade Through the Han Dynasty*. New York.
Savinov, D. G., and N. L. Chlenova
1978   "Zapadnye predely rasprostraneniia olennykh kamnei i voprosy ikh kul'turno-etnicheskoi prinadlezhnosti," in *Arkheologiia i etnografiia Mongolii*.
Shang, Ch'eng-tso 商承祚
1933   *Yin Ch'i Yi-ts'un* 殷契佚存. Nanking: Nanking University.
Shansi Cultural Relics Commission, ed.
1980   *Shan-hsi Ch'u-t'u Wen-wu* 山西出土文物. Tai-yuan.
Shaughnessy, Edward L.
1981/82   "Fourth Annual Conference of the Chinese Palaeography Association," *Early China* 7: 114–18.
Shen, Cheng-chung 沈振中
1972   "Hsin-hsien Lien-ssu-kou ch'u-t'u ti ch'ing-t'ung-ch'i 忻縣連寺溝出土的青銅器," *Wen-wu* 文物, 1972 (4): 67–68.
Shensi Province Institute of Archaeology
1979   *Shan-hsi-sheng Ch'u-t'u Shang Chou Ch'ing-t'ung-ch'i* 陝西省出土商周青銅器, vol. 1. Peking: Wen-wu Press.
Shih, Chang-ju 石璋如
1933   "Ti ch'i-tz'u Yin-hsü fa-chüeh: E-ch'ü kung-tso pao-kao 第七次殷虛發掘: E 區工作報告," *An-yang-fa-chüeh-pao-kao* 安陽發掘報告, 4: 709–28.
1947   "Yin-hsu tsui-chin chih chung-yao fa-hsien fu chi Hsiao-t'un ti-ts'eng 殷墟最近之重要發現, 附記小屯地層," *Chung-kuo-k'ao-ku-hsüeh-pao* 中國考古學報, 2: 1–81.
1955   "Hsiao-t'un Yin-tai ti chien-chu yi-chi 小屯殷代的建築遺蹟," *Bulletin of the Institute of History and Philology, Academia Sinica* 26: 131–88.
1959   *Yin-hsü Chien-chu Yi-ts'un* 殷墟建築遺存. Taipei: Academia Sinica.
1961   "Yin-tai ti 'chi-pei-tao' 殷代的'脊背刀'," *Tsinghua Journal of Chinese Studies*, n.s. 2 (2): 131–42.
1969   "Yin-tai ti hang-t'u pan-chu yü i-pan chien-chu 殷代的夯土版築與一般建築," *Bulletin of the Institute of History and Philology, Academia Sinica* 41: 127–68.
1970–80   *Hsiao-t'un Mu-tsang* 小屯墓葬. Taipei: Academia Sinica (Pei-tsu mu-tsang 北組墓葬, 1970; chung-tsu mu-tsang 中組墓葬 1971; nan-tsu mu-tsang 南組墓葬, 1973; Yi-ch'ü chi-chih shang-hsia chih mu-tsang 乙區基址上下之墓葬, 1976; Ping-ch'ü mu-tsang 丙區墓葬, 1980).
Shima, Kunio 島邦男
1958   *Inkyō bokuji kenkyū* 殷墟卜辭研究. Hirosaki: Hirosaki Daigaku Bunritsu

gakubu Chūgokugaku Kenkyū kai.
1967 *Inkyō bokuji Sōrui* 殷墟卜辭綜類. Tokyo: Kyuko Shoin.

Shirakawa, Shizuka 白川靜
1975 "Rekihōteki kenkyū no hōhō 曆法的研究の方法," *Kinmon Tsūshaku* 金文通釈, nos. 44–45, Kobe.

Soper, Alexander
1966 "Early, middle, and late Shang: A note," *Artibus Asiae* 28: 5–38.

Sosnovskii, G. P.
1941 "Plitochnie mogily Zabaikal'ia," *Trudy Otdela Istorii Pervobytnoi Kul'tury Gosudarstvennogo Ermitazha* 1.

Sun, Hua 孫華
1980 "Kuan-yü Erh-li-t'ou wen-hua 關于二里頭文化," *K'ao-ku* 考古, 1980 (6): 521–25.

Tai, Tsun-te 戴遵德
1980 "Shan-hsi Ling-shih-hsien Ch'ing-chien-ts'un Shang-tai mu ho ch'ing-t'ung-ch'i 山西靈石縣旌介村古代墓和青銅器," *Wen-wu-tzu-liao-ts'ung-k'an* 文物資料叢刊, 3: 46–49.

Tai, Ying-hsin 戴應新
1980 "Shan-pei Ch'ing-chien Mi-chih Chia-hsien ch'u-t'u ku-tai t'ung-ch'i 陝北清澗米脂佳縣出土古代銅器," *K'ao-ku* 考古, 1980 (1): 95.

T'ang, Lan 唐蘭
1934 *Yin-hsü Wen-tzu Chi* 殷墟文字記
1939 *T'ien-jang-ko Chia-ku Wen-tzu K'ao-shih* 天壤閣甲骨文字考釋. Peiping.
1973 "Kung-hsing-ch'i yung-t'u k'ao 弓形器用途考," *K'ao-ku* 考古, 1973 (3): 178–84.

Terenozhkin, A. I.
1975 "Kimmeriiskie mechi i kinzhaly," in *Skifskii mir*.

Ting, Shan 丁山
1956 *Chia-ku-wen Chung So-chien Shih-tsu chi ch'i Chih-tu* 甲骨文中所見氏族及其制度. Peking: Science Press.

Tsou, Heng 鄒衡
1964 "Shih lun Yin-hsü wen-hua fen ch'i 試論殷墟文化分期," *Pei-ching Ta-hsüeh Jen-wen Hsüeh-pao* 北京大學人文學報, 1964 (4): 37–58; 1964 (5): 63–90.
1978 "Cheng-chou Shang ch'eng chi Shang tu Po shuo 鄭州商城即商都亳說," *Wen-wu* 文物, 1978 (2): 69–71.
1979 "Kuan-yü t'an-t'ao Hsia wen-hua ti chi ko wen-t'i 關于探討夏文化的幾個問題," *Wen-wu* 文物, 1979 (3): 64–67.
1980 *Hsia Shang Chou K'ao-ku Lun-wen Chi* 夏商周考古論文集. Peking: Wen-wu Press.
1981 "Tsai lun Cheng Po shuo 再論鄭亳說," *K'ao-ku* 考古, 1981 (3): 271–76.

Tu, Nai-sung 杜廼松
1980 "Ssu Mu Wu ting nien-tai wen-t'i hsin-t'an 司母戊鼎年代問題新探," *Wen-shih-che* 文史哲, 1980 (1): 63–64.

Tu, Nai-sung 杜廼松, et al.
1978 "Chi ko sheng shih tzu-chih-chü cheng-chi wen-wu hui-chi chan-lan 記各省市自治區徵集文物匯集展覽," *Wen-wu* 文物, 1978 (6): 26–45.

Tung, Tso-pin 董作賓
1933 "Chia-ku-wen tuan-tai yen-chiu li 甲骨文斷代研究例," *Essays Presented to Mr. Ts'ai Yuan P'ei on His 60th Birthday*, pp. 323–424. Nanking: Academia Sinica.
1945 *Yin Li P'u* 殷曆譜. Li-chuang: Academia Sinica.
1948–53 *Yin-hsü Wen-tzu Yi-pien* 殷虛文字, 工編. Nanking: Academia Sinica.
1960 *Chung-kuo Nien-li Chien P'u* 中國年曆簡譜. Taipei: Yi-wen.

Umehara, Sueji 梅原末治
1955 *Chūgoku Kodai Gyoku Zusetsu* 中國古代玉圖説. Kyoto.

Vanden Berghe, L.
1972 *La Chronologie de la Civilisation des Bronzes du Pusht-i Kuh, Luristan*.

Volkov, V. V.
1961 "Bronzovyi kinzhai iz Gobi," *Sovetskaia Arkheologiia* 4.
1964 "Bronzovye kel'ty iz muzeev Mongol'skoi Narodnoi Respubliki," in *Pamiatnik kamennogo i bronzovogo vekov Evrazii*.
1975 "Olennye kamni Ushkiin-Uver," in *Pervobytnaia arkheologiia Sibiri*.

Wang, Chen-yung 王振鏞
1980 "Fu-chien Chien-ou-hsien ch'u-tu Hsi-Chou t'ung chung 福建建甌縣出土西周銅鐘," *Wen-wu* 文物, 1980 (11): 95.

Wang, Hou-chih 王厚之
1802 *Wang Fu-chai Chung Ting K'uan-shih* 王復齋鐘鼎款識 Chi-ku-chai ts'ang Sung t'o mu-k'e-open 積古齋藏宋拓慕刻本.

Wang, Kuang-yung 王光永
1975 "Shan-hsi-sheng Pao-chi-shih Yü-ch'üan sheng-ch'an-tui fa-hsien Hsi-Chou tsao-ch'i mu-tsang 陝西省寶雞市峪泉生產隊發現西周早期墓葬," *Wen-wu* 文物, 1975 (3): 72–73.

Wang, Kuang-yung, and Ming-t'an Ts'ao 王光永, 曹明檀
1979 "Pao-chi-shih chiao-ch'ü ho Feng-hsiang fa-hsien Hsi-Chou tsao-ch'i t'ungching teng wen-wu 寶雞市郊區和鳳翔發現西周早期銅鏡等文物," *Wen-wu* 文物, 1979 (12): 90–91.

Wang, Kuo-wei 王國維
1959 "Nü tzu shuo 女字說," in *Kuan-t'ang Chi Lin* 觀堂集林 Peking: Chung-hua Edition.

Wang, Shih-lun 王士倫
1965 "Chi Che-chiang fa-hsien ti t'ung-nao yu-t'ao chung ho Yüeh wang shih mao 記浙江發現的銅鐃釉陶鐘和越王石矛," *K'ao-ku* 考古, 1965 (5): 256.

Wang, Yü-hsin 王宇信; Yung-shan Chang 張永山; and Sheng-nan Yang 楊升南
1977 "Shih lun Yin-hsü wu-hao mu ti Fu Hao 試論殷墟五號墓的婦好," *K'ao-ku-hsüeh-pao* 考古學報, 1977 (2): 1–22.

Watson, William
1971 *Cultural Frontiers in Ancient East Asia*. Edinburgh: University Press.

Wen-wu 文物
1954 "Cheng-chou-shih Yin Shang ti-ts'eng kuan-hsi chieh-shao 鄭州市殷商地層關係介紹," *Wen-wu-ts'an-k'ao-tzu-liao* 文物參考資料, 1954 (12): 86–93.
1955a "Cheng-chou fa-hsien ti Shang-tai chih-t'ao i-chih 鄭州發現的商代製陶遺址," *Wen-wu-ts'an-k'ao-tzu-liao* 文物參攷資料, 1955 (9): 64–69.

REFERENCES CITED

1955b "Cheng-chou-shih Pai-chia-chuang Shang-tai mu fa-chüeh pao-kao 鄭州市白家莊商代墓發掘報告," *Wen-wu-ts'an-k'ao-tzu-liao* 文物參考資料, 1955 (10): 24–42.

1957 "Cheng-chou Lo-ta-miao Shang-tai yi-chih shih chüeh chien pao 鄭州洛達廟商代遺址試掘簡報," *Wen-wu-ts'an-k'ao-tzu-liao* 文物參考資料, 1957 (10): 48–51.

1958 "Shan-hsi Shih-lou-hsien Erh-lang-p'o ch'u-t'u Shang Chou ch'ing-t'ung-ch'i 山西石樓縣二郎坡出土商周青銅器," *Wen-wu-ts'an-k'ao-tzu-liao* 文物參考資料, 1958 (1): 36.

1959 "Chin nien lai Shang-hai-shih ts'un fei t'ung chung ch'iang-chiu ch'u ti chung-yao wen-wu 近年來上海市從廢銅中搶救出的重要文物," *wen-wu* 文物, 1959 (10): 32–36.

1960 "Che-chiang Ch'ang-hsing-hsien ch'u-t'u liang-chien t'ung-ch'i 浙江長興縣出土兩件銅器," *Wen-wu* 文物, 1960 (7): 48–49.

1966 "Hu-nan-sheng Po-wu-kuan hsin fa-hsien ti chi chien t'ung-ch'i 湖南省博物館新發現的幾件銅器," *Wen-wu* 文物, 1966 (4): 1–6.

1973 "Che-chiang Ch'ang-hsing-hsien ti liang chien ch'ing-t'ung-ch'i 浙江長興縣的兩件青銅器," *Wen-wu* 文物, 1973 (1): 62.

1974 "Cheng-chou Shang ch'eng yi-chih nei fa-chüeh Shang-tai hang-t'u t'ai-chi ho nu-li t'ou ku 鄭州商城遺址內發掘商代夯土台基和奴隸頭骨," *Wen-wu* 文物, 1974 (9): 1–2.

1975a "Cheng-chou hsin ch'u-t'u ti Shang-tai ch'ien-ch'i ta t'ung ting 鄭州新出土的商代前期大銅鼎," *Wen-wu* 文物, 1975 (6): 64–68.

1975b "Chiang-hsi Ch'ing-chiang Wu-ch'eng Shang-tai yi-chih fa-chüeh chien pao 江西清江吳城商代遺址發掘簡報," *Wen-wu* 文物, 1975 (7): 51–71.

1976 "P'an-lung-ch'eng 1974-nien tu t'ien-yeh k'ao-ku chi yao 盤龍城1974年度田野考古紀要," *Wen-wu* 文物, 1976 (2): 5–15.

1977a "Cheng-chou Shang-tai ch'eng-chih shih chüeh chien pao 鄭州商代城址試掘簡報," *Wen-wu* 文物, 1977 (1): 21–31.

1977b "Hua Kuo-feng chu-hsi kuan-huai hsi Shao-shan kuan-ch'ü wen-wu k'ao-ku kung-tso ti chung-ta ch'eng-kuo 華國鋒主席關懷下韶山管區文物考古工作的重大成果," *Wen-wu* 文物, 1977 (2): 1–4.

1977c "Pei-ching-shih P'ing-ku-hsien fa-hsien Shang-tai mu-tsang 北京市平谷縣發現商代墓葬," *Wen-wu* 文物, 1977 (11): 1–8.

1977d "Liao-ning-sheng K'o-tso-hsien Shan-wan-tzu ch'u-t'u Shang Chou ch'ing-t'ung-ch'i 遼寧省喀左縣山灣子出土商周青銅器," *Wen-wu* 文物, 1977 (12): 23–33.

1979 "Ho-pei Kao-ch'eng T'ai-hsi-ts'un Shang-tai i-chih fa-chüeh chien pao 河北藁城台西村商代遺址發掘簡報," *Wen-wu* 文物, 1979 (6): 33–43.

1983a "Teng-feng Wang-ch'eng-kang yi-chih ti fa-chüeh 登封王城崗遺址的發掘," *Wen-wu* 文物, 1983 (3): 8–20.

1983b "Huai-yang P'ing-liang-t'ai yi-chih fa-chüeh chien pao 淮陽平粮台遺址發掘簡報," *Wen-wu* 文物, 1983 (3): 21–36.

1983c "Cheng-chou hsin fa-hsien Shang-tai chiao ts'ang ch'ing-t'ung-ch'i 鄭州新發現商代窖藏青銅器," *Wen-wu* 文物, 1983 (3): 49–59.

1983d "Cheng-chou Shang-tai ch'eng nei kung-tien-ch'ü ti-yi-tz'u fa-chüeh pao-kao

鄭州商代城內宮殿區第一次發掘報告," *Wen-wu* 文物, 1983 (4): 1–14.

Wen-wu Editorial Committee

1979   *Wen-wu K'ao-ku Kung-tso San-shih Nien* 文物考古工作三十年. Peking: Wen-wu Press.

Wen-wu-tzu-liao-ts'ung-k'an 文物資料叢刊

1977a   "Cheng-chou Shang-tai ch'eng yi-chih fa-chüeh pao-kao 鄭州商代城遺址發掘報告," *Wen-wu-tzu-liao-ts'ung-k'an* 文物資料叢刊, 1: 1–47.

1977b   "T'ien-chin Chi-hsien Chang-chia-yüan shih chüeh chien pao 天津薊縣張家園試掘簡報," *Wen-wu-tzu-liao-ts'ung-k'an* 文物資料叢刊, 1: 163–171.

1978   "Pei-ching-shih hsin cheng-chi ti Shang Chou ch'ing-t'ung-ch'i 北京市新徵集的商周青銅器," *Wen-wu-tzu-liao-ts'ung-k'an* 文物資料叢刊, 2: 14–21.

1981   "Ho-pei Ling-shou-hsien Hsi-mu-fo-ts'un ch'u-t'u yi-p'i Shang-tai wen-wu 河北靈壽縣西木佛村出土一批商代文物," *Wen-wu-tzu-liao-ts'ung-k'an* 文物資料叢刊, 5: 117–19.

White, William

1956   *Bronze Culture of Ancient China*. Toronto.

Willetts, W.

1958   *Chinese Art*. Hammondsworth: Penguin Books.

Wu, Chen-lu 吳振彔

1972   "Pao-te-hsien hsin fa-hsien ti Yin-tai ch'ing-t'ung-ch'i 保德縣新發現的殷代青銅器," *Wen-wu* 文物, 1972 (4): 62–64.

Wu, Ta-ch'eng 吳大澂

1889   *Ku Yü T'u K'ao* 古玉圖考.

Yang, Chien-fang 楊建芳

1982   *Chung-kuo Ku Yü Shu-mu* 中國古玉書目. Hong Kong: Chinese University.

Yang, Hsi-chang 楊錫璋

1981   "An-yang Yin-hsü Hsi-pei-kang ta mu ti fen-ch'i chi yu-kuan wen-t'i 安陽殷墟西北岡大墓的分期及有關問題," *Chung-yüan-wen-wu* 中原文物, 1981 (3): 47–52.

Yang, Hsi-chang, and Pao-ch'eng Yang 楊錫璋, 楊寶成

1977   "Ts'ung chi-ssu-k'eng k'an Shang-tai nu-li she-hui ti jen-sheng 從祭祀坑看商代奴隸社會的人牲," *K'ao-ku* 考古, 1977 (1): 13–19.

Yang, Pao-shun 楊寶順

1975   "Wen-hsien ch'u-t'u ti Shang-tai t'ung-ch'i 溫縣出土的商代銅器," *Wen-wu* 文物, 1975 (2): 88–91.

Yang, Shao-shun 楊紹舜

1959   "Shih-lou fa-hsien ku-tai t'ung-ch'i 石樓發現古代銅器," *Wen-wu* 文物, 1959 (3): 71–72.

1976   "Shan-hsi Shih-lou hsin cheng-chi ti chi-chien Shang-tai ch'ing-t'ung-ch'i 山西石樓新徵集的幾件商代青銅器," *Wen-wu* 文物, 1976 (2): 94.

1981a   "Shan-hsi Liu-lin-hsien Kao-hung fa-hsien Shang-tai t'ung-ch'i 山西柳林縣高紅發現商代銅器," *K'ao-ku* 考古, 1981 (3): 211–12.

1981b   "Shan-hsi Shih-lou Ch'u-chia-yü Ts'ao-chia-yüan fa-hsien Shang-tai t'ung-ch'i 山西石樓褚家峪曹家垣發現商代銅器," *Wen-wu* 文物, 1981 (8): 49–53.

Yang, Shu-ta 楊樹達

1954   *Chi-wei-chü Chia-wen Shuo* 積微居甲文説. Peking: Science Press.

REFERENCES CITED

Yang, Tzu-fan 楊子範
1956 "Shan-tung T'ai-an fa-hsien ku-tai t'ung-ch'i 山東泰安發現古代銅器," *Wen-wu-ts'an-k'ao-tzu-liao* 文物參考資料, 1956 (6): 65.

Yao, Hsiao-sui 姚孝遂
1963 "Chi-lin Ta-hsüeh so-ts'ang chia-ku hsüan shih 吉林大學所藏甲骨選釋," *Chi-lin Ta-hsüeh She-hui-k'o-hsüeh Hsüeh-pao* 吉林大學社會科學學報, 1963 (4): 78–92.

Yen, Yi-p'ing 嚴一萍
1978 *Chia-ku Hsüeh* 甲骨學. Taipei: I-wen.
1981 "Fu Hao lieh-chuan 婦好列傳," *Chung-kuo Wen-tzu* 中國文字, n.s. 3: 1–104.

Yin, Wei-chang 殷瑋璋
1978 "Erh-li-t'ou wen-hua t'an-t'ao 二里頭文化探討," *K'ao-ku* 考古, 1978 (1): 1–4.

Index

adze. See *pen*
agriculture, commercial, 45; commune, 59, 62
altar, covered Fu Hao burial, 67
Altai, 247
An-yang, 35; lacks city wall, 37; siting, 38; neolithic, 68; socketed ax, 268; *nao*, 276, 296. See also Hou-kang; Hsi-pei-kang; Hsiao-t'un; Ta-ssu-k'ung-ts'un
Andronovo culture, 271
Angara-Yenisei ax, 266-68
animal-headed knives, 244-54 passim, 271; *illus.*, 243, 252
animal mask, Erh-li-t'ou, 7; *illus.*, 5; *nao*, 277-84, 291, 293, 295, 296; formed by cloud pattern, 284
Ao, capital, 3, 47-48; identified with Cheng-chou, 48
architectural remains: Erh-li-t'ou, 7, 12; *hang-t'u* platforms, 33-36; Erh-li-kang, 34-35; Yin-hsü, 35-36; Cheng-chou, 38-41; Hsiao-t'un, 68-70; ritual bronzes, 70. See also palaces
arrowheads, molds for, 44; jade, 223, 224; bronze, 258
astronomical instruments, misidentification, 214-16
ax, socketed, 266-68. See also *fu*; *yüeh*

Bamboo Annals, 31, 75-77, 162*n*, 238. See also *Chu-shu Chi-nien*
battle-ax, 254-55
bear, jade, *illus.*, 234
bone industry, 34, 41, 43, 44
bow-shaped object, 243, 250, 263-66
bracelets, *pi*-jades used as, 213; neolithic, 221; Erh-li-t'ou jade, 221; Fu Hao jade, 233; gold, 241; Northern Complex, *illus.*, 249
bronze alloy composition, 85, 87-88, 89, 91, 163*n*, 188-89; Fu Hao burial bronzes, 184-87; *nao*, 296; suggests independent metallurgy, 189
bronze casting technology, 7, 92; Fu Hao bronzes, 163*n*; cored molds, 249, 255; Northern Zone, 249

bronze inscriptions, 66, 81-102, 141-206; calligraphic groups, 163, 165; manner of inscribing, 172, 174-75
bronze ritual vessels, Erh-li-t'ou, 6-7, 12; Cheng-chou, 41, 45-46; *illus.*, 39; molds for, 44; in burials, 54-56, 58, 61-62, 70-71; decoration, 66, 71, 72, 82-92 passim; pairs and sets of, 82-90 passim; regional styles of, 261-62, 298
bronze workshops, 34, 43-44, 297-99; *illus.*, 39
burials, Erh-li-kang, 41; slave, 46, 50; with ramps, 50-53, 54, 67, 73-75; coffin types, 55, 57-58; classified, 58; Hsiao-t'un, 70. See also cemeteries

cattle, sacrificed, 100; jade, 234; *ting*, 289
cemeteries, 49-63; Erh-li-kang, 45; lineage, 50, 55-59, 61; aristocratic, 50, 61-62; royal cemetery, xii, 50-54. See also Hsi-pei-kang
Central Asia, 247
ceramics, Erh-li-t'ou, Erh-li-kang compared, 2-13; Erh-li-kang, 19-22, 238; *illus.*, 16, 17; hard pottery, 26, 40, 298; workshops, 34, 39, 43, 44
chariot, 58
chisel. See *tsao*
cicada motif, 265
city, sitings, 37-38; orientation, 38; gates, 42-43; etymology, 45; Cheng-chou industrial areas, 43; commercial center, 45
city walls, Cheng-chou, 22-28; absence at An-yang, 37; purpose, 43. See also *hang-t'u*
clan-signs, 66, 141-206; variant forms allowed, 127-30; geographic components in, 129-30; abbreviation, 150, 159, 163-72; *kao* component, 143-44, 149-50; *kung* component, 152; *shu* component, 174-75; *tzu* component, 174-75; *yüan* component, 174-75; Shang signs in Chou territory, 240
cloud pattern, on Erh-li-t'ou bronzes, 7; *nao*, 284, 287-88, 291; *illus.*, 283, 285, 286, 295
cloud and thunder pattern, 7
comb, jade, 230
consorts, 54-55; Fu Hao, 65, 82-83; other

319

than *fu*, 112; to Wu Ting, 131, 161-62. *See also* Pi Hsin; Pi Kuei; Pi Wu
culture, blending and variety, 9-10; archaeological, 11, 250, 272-73

chang jade, 7-8, 208, 219-20, 223; *illus.*, 5, 208, 220
Chang-chia-k'ou, Hopei, 238, 244, 246, 260
Chang-chia-kua, Shensi, 258
Chang-pei, Hopei, 242
Chen-hsün, 12
cheng bell, 275-76, 288
Cheng-chou, 15-48; archaeological importance, x, 15; stratigraphy, 16-22; city wall, 22-28; layout of Shang city, 38-45; Cheng-chou Yen-ch'ang, 45; as capital, 46-48; socketed ax, 268
Chiang-ning, Kiangsu, *nao*, 289
Chieh, 12
Chih (diviner), 106-07
Chih (tribe), 136
Chin-shih, Hsiang-hsiang, *nao*, 289
Chou (dynasty), predynastic, 239, 246, 251
Chòu (Shang king) 10, 47
Chu-k'ai-kou, Ejin Horo League, 249, 267
Chu-lung, Mt., 288
Chü-ma River, 238
Chu-shu Chi-nien, 123, 132, 162*n*. See also *Bamboo Annals*
chüeh jade, 214, 216, 284; as earring, 216; *illus.*, 231
chung bell, 275-76, 289
Chung-shan, Kuan-yang, *nao*, 288; *illus.*, 285
Chung Ting, 3, 47-48

ch'an spade, 224-26; *illus.*, 218
Ch'ang-hsing Middle School, Chekiang, *nao*, 287; *illus.*, 283
Ch'ang-tzu, Shansi, Erh-li-kang bronzes, 238
Ch'ao-tao-kou, Ch'ing-lung, bronze knives, 244, 246, 255; *illus.*, 243, 255; battle-ax, 245; pick-*ko*, 247; *illus.*, 262
Ch'ao-yang, Liaoning, Erh-li-kang bronzes, 238
ch'en functionary, 109-11
Ch'en-chia-wan, Ning-hsiang, *nao*, 279; *illus.*, 278
Ch'eng T'ang, 34, 47
Ch'eng-te, Hopei, battle-ax, 245; bronze knife, 246
ch'i jade, 213-14, 225-26; *illus.*, 214, 225
Ch'i-chia culture, 253

Ch'i-chia-ho, T'ao-yüan, 291
Ch'iang, sacrificed, 106, 116; Ch'iang Fang, 136
Ch'ien-p'ing, Yi-chang, 11
Ch'ien-shan, Anhwei, *nao*, 298
ch'ih spoon, 247, 248, 259, 261-63
Ch'ih-feng, Liaoning, bronze knife, 246
Ch'in, 10-11
ch'ing chimestone, 7, 270
ch'ing functionary, 107, 111
Ch'ing-chien, Shensi, 259; Yin-hsü remains, 239
Ch'u (diviner), 100, 105; group, 119
Ch'u culture, 11, 289
Ch'u-chia-yü, Shih-lou, bronze knife; *illus.*, 249
ch'üan functionary, 118
Ch'üeh, 104, 118
Ch'ung-li, Hopei, bronze knife, 246

daggers, 242-44
deer, *ting*, 290
"deer stones," 263
ditch, Erh-li-kang, 41; Hsiao-t'un, 68-69
divination, 65; change in practices, 125

earrings: jade, 216, 233; gold, 240; funnel-shaped, 241, 248; *illus.*, 249
Ejin Horo League, dagger, 242
elephant, jade, *illus.*, 234; on *nao*, 278-81, 291, 295, 296; *tsun*, 289, 298
engraving knife. See *k'o-tao*
Erh-lang-p'o, Shih-lou, bronze knife, 245; *illus.*, 243
Erh-li-kang, 1-13, 15-48 passim; site, 16-17; *illus.*, 39; period defined, 18
Erh-li-t'ou culture, 1-13; distribution, ix, 1; periodization, 3-12; as Hsi Po, 12, 34; related to Lo-ta-miao, 18-19; palace, 33-34; siting, 38

feudal lords, 62-63, 111, 221
fish, jade, 235, 284; on *nao*, 280, 291, 293, 295
floors, 40
Freer Gallery of Art, 245
frog, 259
frontier, as interaction zone, xiii; of Shang culture, 238-41; Seimo style represents, 271
fu ax, defined, 224-25; jade, 224-26
Fu (female attendant), meaning, 82, 103-15,

INDEX

123-25; term of address, 137; variant graphs, 163-72
Fu Ching, 102, 105, 124-26, 130
Fu Hao, 54, 65-79; bronze inscriptions, 81-102; *tzu*-name, 96-97, 101, 127; oracle bone inscriptions, 103-19, 121-40; in different periods, 104-05, 113, 123, 131-32, 178*n*; military leader, 136; as K'ang Ting's consort, 138; clan-signs, 159-89; *fu* axes, 225-27. *See also* consorts; Pi Hsin
Fu Hao burial, 54-55, 65-79; archaeological importance, xi; dated around Wu Ting period, 66-79, 82, 99-102; bronze ritual vessels, 81-102 passim; dated to K'ang Ting period, 131-32; dated before Wu Ting period, 162-63*n*; listing of inscribed bronzes, 191-206; jade, 207, 215-20; engraving knives, 227; bronze knife, 245, 250-51, 255-57; *illus.*, 252, 257; Northern Complex, 250; mirrors, 250-53; awl, 253; *illus.*, 252; bronze *ko*, 256; bow-shaped object, 263
Fu Hsüan, 115-19
Fu-shun, Liaoning, bronze knife, 246
Fu Tzu, alternate reading of Fu Hao, ix, 103-19 passim

"ginger rock," 33, 34, 40
Glazkov culture, 272

hairpins: jade, 41, 233; bronze, 41, 253
"handle-shaped objects," 230; *illus.*, 231
hang-t'u tamped earth: Erh-li-t'ou, 7, 32-34; method, 22-26, 30, 32-36; city walls, 22-39, 42-43; Lung-shan, 29-30; foundation platforms, 33-36, 38-41, 68-70; Erh-li-kang, 34-36; Late Shang, 35-36. *See also* palaces
hard pottery, 26, 40, 298
Hei-shan, Ning-ch'eng, 261-62
hereditary offices, 110-11; Fu Hsüan, 119
Ho-chia-ts'un, Ch'i-shan, 240
Ho-shang-kou, K'a-tso, 241
Hopei, Yin-hsü remains, 241
horse burial pits, 58
Hou (honorific), 82, 124-25, 137; "queen," 110; alternate reading of "Ssu," 81-83, 126-27
Hou (feudal lord), 111, 123-24
Hou Hsin, 66
Hou-kang, 49, 55, 58, 59; neolithic, 68; bronze *ko*, 256

Hou-lan-chia-kou, Shih-lou, bronze knife, 245; *tou* dipper, 258-61; ear ornaments, *illus.*, 249
Hou-li, Lou-shan, 49, 50; aristocratic cemetery, 61-62; clan-signs, 155-59
houses, 43-44, 46, 67-70; semisubterranean, 67, 68, 72; with jade, 219
hu jade, 208, 222-23
Hu-pin, Yu-yang, *nao*, 289
Huai-chen-feng, Lan-t'ien, Erh-li-kang culture, 239
huan jade, 284. See *pi*
huang jade, 208, 222, 223; suspended, 214; *illus.*, 231
Huang (diviner), 106-07
Huang-k'o-shan, Chien-ou, *nao*, 287; *illus.*, 286
Huang-ma-sai, Hsiang-hsiang, *nao*, 287; *illus.*, 285
Huang-ts'ai, Ning-hsiang, 290; animal-mask *p'ou*, 291; *yung chung*, 292, 295

hsi marlinspike, 232
Hsi Po, x, 12, 37; as Po, 34
Hsi-pei-kang, 49, 50-54, 67, 73-75; burials identified, 77-78; clan-signs, 152-55; animal-headed knife, 251-52, 254
Hsia, ix-x, 1-13, 31-32
Hsia-chia-shan, Lei-yang, *nao*, 287-89; *illus.*, 285
Hsia-hsien, Shansi, 255
Hsia-hsin-chiao, Yung-ho, 249
Hsia-p'o-t'ai-kou, K'a-tso, 261
Hsiang-hsiang, Hunan, 279-80, 282, 285, 287
Hsiao Hsin, 63-79 passim
Hsiao-kuan-chuang, T'ang-shan, 249
Hsiao-min-t'un, 141-52, 176, 178; *illus.*, 151
Hsiao-t'un, 49, 60, 70-71; burials M 17 and M 18, 65-66, 92, 95; burial M 066, 93-95, 100-01
Hsiao Yi, 63-79 passim
Hsieh, 113
Hsieh-chia-kou, Ch'ing-chien, 259
Hsin-hsien, Shensi, Yin-hsü bronzes, 239
Hsin-ts'un, Chün-hsien, 251
hsing clan name, 57, 113, 124
Hsing, 47; Marquis of, 241
Hsing-t'ai, Hopei, 241
Hsiung (diviner), 100
hsüan-chi (jade), 214-16; location in burial, 214

Hsüeh-shan, Ch'ang-p'ing, gold earrings, 241
hsün musical instrument, 7

Iranian plateau, 247, 260

jade, 207-37; ritual objects, 7-8, 223, 235; *illus.*, 232; offerings, 41; hairpins, 41, 233; funerary, 45, 213, 230; in house foundation, 219; neolithic, 221, 223; tools, 223-29; ladle, 230; personal ornaments, 233; figures, 235; *illus.*, 234; fish, 235, 284; found with *nao*, 284. See also *chang; hu; huang; kuei; pi; ts'ung*
Jen Fang, 107, 136
Jen-min Kung-yuan, 17-18; Late Shang remains, 21
Ju Ud Banner, 261, 267
Jung, 240, 241

Kammenyi Log Phase, 264, 269
Kao-hung, Liu-lin, dagger, 242; battle-ax, 244
Kao-t'ang-lin, Wang-ch'eng, *nao*, 289
Kao-ch'ung, Wang-ch'eng, *nao*, 280-82, 284
Karasuk culture, 251, 268-72; date, 264, 269; influenced by Northern Complex, 270
Khirghiz steppe, 247
king, 53-54, 62-63
knives, engraving, 224, 227; jade, 225, 227-29; bronze, 245-57 passim; animal-headed, 246, 250-51, 254; "long," 248; ring-pommel, 250, 255-57; hafting of, 255. See also *tao*
ko halberd, 7, 71, 258; mold for, 44; jade, 223-34; *illus.*, 218, 225; pick-*ko*, 247-48; Northern Complex, 247, 254-56; hafting of, 254-55
Kou-t'ou-pa, Hsiang-hsiang, *nao*, 279-80, 282
Krasnoiarsk, 247, 252
Ku-yüan, Hopei, bronze knife, 246
kuei jade, 208, 216-19, 223; as *fu* ax, 226
Kung Fang, 136
Kuang-she culture, 272

K'a-tso, Inner Mongolia, 261
K'ang Ting, 51, 73, 77, 103; Pi Hsin as his consort, 131-32, 137-38; Fu Hao as his consort, 137-38
K'o (diviner), 116-19
K'o-shih-k'o-t'eng, Inner Mongolia, Yin-hsü bronzes, 239
k'o-tao engraving knife, 224, 230; *illus.*, 227

K'ou (diviner), 106-07
k'uei dragon, 86, 89, 233
K'uo Ti Chih, 31, 47

Li (diviner group), 119
li, tripod, Erh-li-t'ou, 3-5; Transbaikal'ia, 267. See also bronze ritual vessels; ceramics
lien sickle, 224
Lin-che-yü, Pao-te, 249, 253; dagger, 242; *illus.*, 243; battle-ax, 244; *illus.*, 252, 256; rattle terminals, 264
Lin Hsin, 51, 73, 77, 94, 103
lineage organization, 56-63; house clusters, 69; of diviners, 107; hereditary offices, 107-09; matrilineal clans, 125; clan-signs, 151-52
Ling-pao, Honan, socketed ax, 268
Ling-shih, Shansi, Yin-hsü bronzes, 240
Ling-shou, Hopei, socketed ax, 267
Liu-chia-ho, P'ing-ku, bronzes, 238, 240-41; *illus.*, 249; *pi* spatula, 259
Liu-chia Reservoir, Fu-feng, 251
Liu-li-ko, Hui Hsien, site, 49, 71, 256
Lo-ta-miao, Cheng-chou, 18; Period, 18-19, 27; ceramics, 20-21; as progenitor of Erh-li-kang, 21
loess plateau, 239, 248, 258-59, 273
Lower Hsia-chia-tien culture, 241, 249; bronzes attributed to, 272-73
Lu-lung, Hopei, bow-shaped object, 265
Lung-shan, at Cheng-chou, 27; city walls, 28-30, 32; T'ao-ssu jade, 221

marble, 230
mao spear, 223, 224; *illus.*, 225
Miao-p'u, 49, 55, 59, 60, 71, 94
Minusinsk Basin, 247, 251, 261-62, 264, 266, 268-71
mirrors, Fu Hao, 251-53
Mongolia, 247, 263
Mu (honorific), 83, 88-89, 109, 137
musical instruments, 7; *nao*-bells, 101, 275-99

Nai-ma-t'ai, Chinghai, 252
Nan-kuan-wai, Cheng-chou, 16-21
Nan-sha-ts'un, Hua-hsien, Erh-li-kang culture, 239
nao bell, 101, 275-99; nomenclature, 275-77; distribution, 277; typology, 277-88; function, 288-90; sitings, 289, 296; periodiza-

INDEX

tion, 290-92, 298-99; evolution, 292-95, 297; regionalism, 294-99; method of striking, 296
neolithic, 67-68. *See also* Lung-shan culture
"New School," 76, 116, 126
Ning-hsiang, Hunan, 278-96 passim
nomadic pastoralists, 273
"Northeastern Complex," 242
"Northern Complex," characteristic objects, 241-50; *illus.*, 243, 249; distribution, 246-47, 269-70; east-west division, 248; Erh-li-kang culture and, 249-50; Erh-li-t'ou culture and, 250; influence on Yin-hsü culture, 250-58; influenced by Yin-hsü culture, 258-68
"Northern Zone," 237-73; defined, 246-47; expansion, 239-41
nü woman, 171-72; as term of address, 82, 92, 98-99; as optional part of name, 103-04, 125, 130

Ob' River, 247, 263
Okunev culture, 270
oracle bones, 7, 46, 57, 59, 72; periodization, 65-66, 72-77, 115-19
"Ordos bronzes," 242, 246, 250; inappropriate term, 248
owl, jade, *illus.*, 234

Pa Fang, 136
Pai-chia-chuang Cheng-chou, 17, 45, 71; *illus.*, 39
Pai-chia-yao Reservoir, 241
Pai-fu, Ch'ang-p'ing, Western Chou grave, 242; daggers, 242, 244; *illus.*, 243; ax, 245; bronze knife, 246; pick-*ko*, 261-62
Pai-ts'ao-p'o, Ling-t'ai, 260, 262; bow-shaped object, *illus.*, 265
Pai-yin-ch'ang, Nai-man League, bronze knife, 246
palaces, 12, 33-34; Pan-lung-ch'eng, 35; sacrificial pits, 53-54
pan-chih bowstring-pull, 232
Pan-ch'iao, Ch'ang-sha, *nao*, 288; illus., 283
Pan-p'o, Ch'ang-an, jade, 215
Pao-chi, Shensi, Yin-hsü bronzes, 239
Pao-te, Shansi, Yin-hsü bronzes, 239. *See also* Lin-che-yü
Pei-feng-t'an, Ning-hsiang, *nao*, 277-79, 289
Peking, 248

pen adze, 44, 224-26
Pei-kuan-wai, Cheng-chou, 17
periodization, 65-79; Yang Hsi-chang, 51-52, 73-74; oracle bone, 65-66, 68, 73, 76, 104-07, 134-40; ceramic, 66-67; schemes compared, 73, 75; Ta-ssu-k'ung-ts'un, 82, 239-48 passim
Pi (honorific), 98-99, 137
pi jade, 208, 213-16, 223; Fu Hao burial, 210; nomenclature, 210-13; *pi-huan*, 210-14; *hsüan-chi*, 212-14; placement in burial, 213
pi spatula, 247, 248, 259, 261; *illus.*, 249
Pi Hsin, 83, 98, 102; as Fu Hao, 131; K'ang Ting's consort, 131, 137
Pi Kuei, 83, 98, 101-02
Pi Wu, 54, 83, 98, 102
pick-*ko*, 247-48, 260-62, 270
pig, *tsun*, 289, 298
pigment mixing tray, jade, 230; *illus.*, 232
Pin (diviner group), 105, 114, 119
Pin-hu, Yüeh-yang, *nao*, 279; *illus.*, 283
Po (capital), 3, 34, 47-48. *See also* Hsi Po
proto-porcelain, 26, 40

P'an Keng, 47, 72-79, 131
P'an-lung-ch'eng, Huang-p'i, city wall, 28, 37; palace, 35; siting, 38; bronzes, 71
P'ing-liang-t'ai, Huai-yang, 32
P'u-tu-ts'un, Ch'ang-an, *yung chung*, 292

ram, knives, 246, 248, 250-51, 254; *pi*, 248; *tou*, 259-61; *tsun*, 289, 298
ritual name, 83, 97, 130, 131
ritual objects. *See* bronze ritual vessels; jade; *tou*
roads, Cheng-chou, 43

San-mou-ti, Ning-hsiang, *nao*, 284, 289, 295, 296; *illus.*, 283
sacrifices, 76, 106, 109-15 passim, 106; of humans, 35-36, 41, 53-55, 60, 62, 70-72, 100, 106, 116; of dogs, 41, 70-72; pits, 51-53; of oxen and sheep, 100; to nature, 289
Seimo culture, 271-72
sheep, motif, 261-63; sacrifice, 100
silk, impression of, 88
slaves, burials, 46, 60-61; distinguished from commoners, 59; excluded from lineages, 60; included aristocrats, 60
snake, 247, 248, 259, 261

social structure, 12-13, 36, 41, 43, 44-45, 49-63 passim; agricultural commune, 59, 62; commoners, 59; lineages, 55-59; characterized, 62-63; validation of king, 53-54
spade. See *ch'an*
spindle whorls, jade, 233
"Ssu" inscriptions, 82-83, 97
ssu-ming personal name, 99, 127
Ssu Mu Hsin *ting*, 54, 82; name interpreted, 126, 130; made by Wu Yi, 131
Ssu Mu Wu *ting*, 51, 54, 78, 82, 102, 290; *illus.*, 51
Ssu T'ien Ch'uan *yi*, 291
Ssu T'u Mu, 81-102, 126-30; inscribed only on wine vessels, 95; name interpreted, 130
storage pits, Erh-li-kang, 46; Hsiao-t'un, 68-69
Sui-te, Shensi, 245-46, 253, 258; Yin-hsü bronzes, 239; socketed ax, 267; *illus.*, 268
Sui-yüan, 261; "Sui-yüan bronzes," 242, 244, 267

Shang, distribution, vii-viii, 239-41, 298; material culture summarized, 65-67
Shang-ts'un-ling, 251, 253, 257
she officials, 118
shih generation, 111
shih lineage, 56, 124; tribe, 108
Shih (diviner group), 73, 75, 106-07, 140
Shi-chi, vii, 31, 47, 75-76, 108
Shih-hsia, Ch'ü-chiang, Kwangtung, 219
Shih-hsing-shan, Li-ling, elephant *tsun*, 289
Shih-ku-chai, Ning-hsiang, *nao*, 279, 289; *illus.*, 278, 281, 282
Shih-lou, Shansi, 245, 261; *illus.*, 243, 249; Yin-hsü bronzes, 240; socketed ax, 267; *illus.*, 268
Shih-mao, Yü-lin, Shensi, 216, 229; *illus.*, 215

Ta, Shih-group diviner, 106-07
Ta-hung-ch'i, Hsin-min, battle-axes, 245; *illus.*, 243
Ta-ssu-k'ung-ts'un, An-yang, 49, 55, 60, 262, 265; neolithic, 68; periodization, 82, 239-48 passim
Ta-tien-tzu, Ao-han League, 249, 267
Ta-wen-k'ou, T'ai-an, 215
Tagar Culture, 251
Taihang Mountains, 239, 248

tao knife, 7; mold for, 44; jade, 227; *illus.*, 225, 227
temple name, 129-30
Teng-feng. *See* Wang-ch'eng-kang
thunder pattern, *nao*, 288, 295
Ti Yi, 51-52, 73, 77
Ti Hsin, 51-52, 73, 77; possible tomb, 52
tiger, jade motif, 222-23, 259; *illus.*, 208, 220, 234; on *tou*, 259; on *nao*, 280, 291, 293; *illus.*, 278, 282; jade figure, 284; *illus.*, 232
titles, posthumous, 181
To-ma-t'ai, Chinghai, 253
tou dipper, 258-60
Transbaikal'ia, 247, 252, 261-63; socketed ax, 267
Tu-ling, Cheng-chou, 45; large *ting*, 43, 45
Tung-hsia-feng, Hsia-hsien, 238
Tung-kou, pick-*ko*, 248
Tung Tso-pin, oracle bone periodization, 65, 73, 76
Tung-yen-ke-chuang, Hopei, late Yin-hsü bronzes, 241
Tuva, 247

T'ai-hsi, Kao-ch'eng, 49-50, 72; lineage cemetery, 61, 238; jade, 215; *pi* spatula, 247, 248; *illus.*, 249; pick-*ko*, 248
T'ai-ku, Shansi, Erh-li-kang pottery, 238
T'ang, king, 3, 12-13, 34, 37, 47, 114, 116-19
T'ang-chih-k'ou, Lung-kuan, 260
T'ang-tung-ts'un, Chiang-ning, *nao*, 284; *illus.*, 286
T'ao-hua-chuang, Shih-lou, 258, 261
T'ao-ssu, Hsiang-fen, Shansi, 221
t'ao-t'ieh, 85-90 passim; 254, 265, 266
T'ien-chia-pan, Yu-hang, *nao*, 284; *illus.*, 285
T'ou-pa, Chu-chou, *nao*, 288; *illus.*, 286
T'u Fang, 136
T'ung-chuan, Shensi, *ting*, 239

tsao chisel, 7, 224-25
Tsao-shih, Shih-men, 297-98
Tsou Heng, x; ceramic periodization, 66, 73
tsu lineage, 57-58, 105, 108. *See also* lineage organization
tsu arrowhead, 223, 224
Tsu Chi, 78
Tsu Chia, 54, 77, 78, 118; period, 51, 73, 82, 100

INDEX

Tsu Keng, 77, 78; period, 51, 73, 100
tsung lineage, 55, 112-13

Ts'ao-chia-yüan, Shih-lou, battle-ax, 245; *illus.*, 243
Ts'ao-lou-tsun, Ch'ang-hsing, *nao*, 287; *illus.*, 286
ts'ung jade, 7, 208, 220-22, 223

tzu style name, 96-97, 99, 101, 127
Tzu (term of address), 124-25; derivation, 107-08; component in clan-signs, 174-75
Tzu (Shang royal clan), xii, 57, 113, 130
Tzu-ch'ang, Shensi, *ku*, 239
Tzu Su Ch'üan, 81, 92
Tzu Yü, 55, 66, 92, 104

Upper Hsia-chia-tien Culture, 253; socketed ax, 267
urbanism, 12

waist pit, 71
Wang-ch'eng-kang, Teng-feng, 28-33; city wall, 28, 29, 33; siting, 38
Wang-chia-tsui, Ch'i-shan, battle-axes, 244
weapons, 56, 61; jade, 223-27. *See also* daggers; *ko; yüeh*
Wei River, 240; Erh-li-kang remains, 238; predynastic Chou, 239
Wei-hsien, Hopei, 249
Wei-ying-tzu Type, gold bracelets, 241
wells, 46
Wen-hsien, Honan, *nao*, 276
Wen Ting, 51, 54, 94, 137
Wen Wu Ting, 73, 77
Western Po. *See* Hsi Po
workshops, 34, 43; bronze, 297-98
Wu (king), 10, 239, 297
Wu (diviner group), 140
Wu-ch'eng, Ch'ing-chiang, 298
Wu-kuan-ts'un, large grave, 51, 52, 54, 262; radiocarbon date, 263; smaller graves, 53, 71, 72
Wu Ting, 54, 65, 78-79, 130, 161-62; reign characterized, 74-75
Wu Yi king, 51, 54, 73, 77, 137

Ya cruciform graves, 50; cartouche, 92-94; component in clan-signs, 81, 124, 145-50, 155, 172-73
Yalu River, 248
Yang-chuang, Cheng-chou, 45
Yang-ch'eng, 12, 31-32
Yang-ho, Hsing-ch'eng, battle-ax, 245; *illus.*, 243; bronze knife, 246, 255; *illus.*, 257; pick-*ko*, 247
Yang-li, Hsiang-t'an, pig *tsun*, 289, 298
Yang-shao culture, 68
Yao-chuang, Man-ch'eng, Erh-li-kang bronzes, 238
Yen Shan, 262
Yen-t'ou-ts'un, Sui-te, bronze knife, 245-46; *illus.*, 253; *tou* dipper, 258
Yin-hsü, 49; architectural remains, 35-36; siting, 38; Yin-hsü western sector burials, 49, 55-56, 57, 151, 219, 256, 257; chronology, 51, 65-79; expansion, 71-73; burial YM 238, 263. *See also* Fu Hao burial; Hsi-pei-kang; Hsiao-min-t'un; Hsiao-t'un
Yü-lin District, Shensi, jade knife, 228
yüan jade, 210-13
yüeh-ax, 7, 94, 101, 213, 226, 244-45; as inscription, 71; from Fu Hao burial, 82, 223-24; *illus.*, 223; neolithic, 224; hafting of, 254-55
Yüeh-shan-p'u, Ning-hsiang, square, ram *tsun*, 289
Yung (diviner), 106-07
yung chung bell, 276-77, 291-94; influenced north, 298-99
Yung-ho, Shansi, Yin-hsü bronzes, 240, 249